Elinor Ostrom and the Bloomington School of Political Economy

Also of Interest

DANIEL H. COLE AND MICHAEL D. MCGINNIS, EDS.
Elinor Ostrom and the Bloomington School of Political Economy

Volume 1, Polycentricity in Public Administration and Political Science
Volume 2, Resource Governance
Volume 3, A Framework for Policy Analysis
Volume 4, Policy Applications and Extensions

VINCENT OSTROM
The Political Theory of a Compound Republic: Designing the American Experiment (3rd edition; 2008)

VINCENT OSTROM
The Quest to Understand Human Affairs: Natural Resources Policy and Essays on Community and Collective Choice, volume 1.
Edited by Barbara Allen (2011)

VINCENT OSTROM
The Quest to Understand Human Affairs: Essays on Collective, Constitutional, and Epistemic Choice, volume 2.
Edited by Barbara Allen (2012)

Interior design and typesetting by Patty Lezotte.

Elinor Ostrom and the Bloomington School of Political Economy

Volume 4, Policy Applications and Extensions

Edited by Daniel H. Cole and Michael D. McGinnis

LEXINGTON BOOKS
A division of
ROWMAN & LITTLEFIELD PUBLISHERS, INC.
Lanham • Boulder • New York • Toronto • Plymouth, UK

Published by Lexington Books
An imprint of The Rowman & Littlefield Publishing Group, Inc.
4501 Forbes Boulevard, Suite 200, Lanham, Maryland 20706
www.rowman.com

Unit A, Whitacre Mews, 26-34 Stannary Street, London SE11 4AB

British Library Cataloguing in Publication Information Available

Library of Congress Cataloging-in-Publication Data Available

ISBN 978-0-7391-9113-2 (cloth)
ISBN 978-0-7391-9112-5 (electronic)

Contents

Acknowledgments

When the editors first approached Joseph Parry of Lexington Books, back in 2012, with an idea for a four-volume compendium of readings in honor of our dear colleagues Elinor and Vincent Ostrom, and of the broader Bloomington School of Political Economy, we were heartened by his immediate support. Now, as we complete the fourth and final volume six years later—not exactly on schedule—we are so grateful for his patient and unwavering belief in the project. Our gratitude extends to his Lexington Books colleague, Emily Roderick, who worked so hard to keep the project on track.

Mere words cannot express our gratitude to Patty Lezotte, an extraordinarily talented professional, who has spent her entire career at the Ostrom Workshop. Patty's skills as an editor, proofreader, typesetter, and record-keeper are legendary in the Workshop, as is her good-natured patience with distracted academics. As the keeper of the Ostrom Workshop archives, Patty helped us locate potential readings, including some that are quite obscure. She organized the process of obtaining copyright permissions for previously published works, making it as painless as possible. She is a joy to work with, and we certainly would not have been able to complete the first, let alone the final, volume without her.

We also thank the Ostrom Workshop, currently directed by Lee Alston, for its generosity in allowing Patty the time to work on this legacy project, in addition to all of her other work on current projects in the Workshop. The Indiana University Foundation, which holds copyrights for the published and unpublished papers of Vincent and Elinor Ostrom, generously allowed us permission to reprint their papers in this collection at no charge. Similarly, the editors and publishers of the journals and books in which many of the papers included in our volumes originally appeared have graciously permitted us to republish them, in many cases without fee or at a steep discount. We are especially grateful to the authors of all the works collected in our four volumes, including a few that had never previously been completed for publication.

It has been our experience that anyone who ever worked closely with Elinor and Vincent Ostrom came away from that experience with a deep impression and lasting appreciation of both their intellectual prowess and their basic humanity. They cared deeply about their work, but also about their colleagues and students. Editing these volumes has been a work of love for us, as well as a work of gratitude to the Ostroms for having taught us so much. Personally and professionally, we feel extremely fortunate to have known them. This volume is dedicated to all present and future Workshoppers.

Introduction to Volume 4

Scaling Up and Extending Bloomington-School Analysis

This, the final volume of *Elinor Ostrom and the Bloomington School of Political Economy*, may come as something of a shock to scholars who think of Lin mainly as someone who traveled to remote regions of the world to study local common-pool resource (CPR) problems. In this volume, we explore the later stage of Lin's career, when she turned her attention, and her analytical frameworks, from local CPR problems to large-scale problems of the global commons—climate change and sustainability—and from natural to "artifactual" commons, including information and the "knowledge commons." These extensions were fully consistent with Lin's systematic approach to institutional analysis and polycentric governance, since the analytical frameworks she developed (in collaboration with Workshop colleagues)—the IAD and SES frameworks—were designed to be applicable to all problems of collective choice. As Lin stated in her Nobel Prize address (Ostrom 2010a, 646; original emphasis): "The IAD *framework* is intended to contain the most general set of variables that an institutional analyst may want to use to examine a diversity of institutional settings including human interactions within markets, private firms, families, community organizations, legislatures, and government agencies." Similarly, Vincent Ostrom's conception of polycentric governance was never meant to be limited to local (metropolitan) governments (V. Ostrom, Tiebout, and Warren 1961). Both he and Lin applied this same concept to federal governance systems, and suggested its relevance for global or regional problems requiring international negotiation and cooperation (V. Ostrom 1969; E. Ostrom 2010b).

This volume includes several examples of research topics that Workshoppers have been investigating since the deaths of Vincent and Elinor

Ostrom in 2012. Some are continuations of projects on which Ostrom was working; others take her work as a starting point and advance it. Some are methodologically or theoretically oriented; others carry on Lin's tradition of empirical work, closely examining local common-pool resources. What they all share in common is continued reliance on Bloomington School ideas, methods, techniques, and approaches to institutional analysis. They represent the beginning of the future of the Ostrom Workshop, without the Ostroms, but very much in their spirit and in dedication to empirically informed theory as the touchstone of good social science.

Part I: Climate Change and Sustainability

Before exploring these recent and future directions of research, this book returns to the time when the Bloomington School had not yet been born. Chapter 1 is a paper written by Vincent Ostrom in 1968, but which was not published until 2011. It concerns the use, development, and management of the atmosphere, which he described then as a "common-pool, flow resource." To this day, most social scientists refer to the atmosphere inaccurately as a "public good." Apparently, Vincent already had in mind a distinction between public goods and CPRs that he would elucidate nearly a decade later in a paper with Elinor ("Public Goods and Public Choices," Ostrom and Ostrom 1997), which was reprinted as the first chapter in volume 2 of this series. Vincent also presciently analyzed the atmosphere as a combined social-ecological system, though not in so many words: "Any consideration of the human use of the atmosphere involves an analysis of interaction between two systems—the atmosphere as a resource system and the organization of human endeavor and of human action as a social system concerned with the utilization and exploitation of the resource system" (p. 5). The conclusion of his paper foreshadows arguments explored in subsequent papers in Part I: "In the long run, national arrangements will not suffice. International arrangements will be required to deal with the continental and global dimensions of atmospheric phenomena" (p. 20).

Chapter 2 is a relatively early indication that Lin intended not just to focus on problems of small-scale local commons. Published in *Science* in 1999 with several coauthors, this paper begins to apply lessons learned from studying local and regional CPRs to "challenges of the global commons." It tackles, in brief, all of the major issues involved in scaling-up institutional analysis of CPRs, including homogeneity (e.g., cultural diversity), complications associated with interlinked CPRs, the unanimity rule for collective-choice decisions in international governance, and the lack of multiple planets with which we might experiment and from which we could learn by trial and error. Even before this paper, Lin had sketched out many of the relevant ideas and problems in the introduction of a book she coedited with Robert Keohane, *Local Commons and Global Interdependence: Heterogeneity and Cooperation in Two Domains* (Keohane and Ostrom 1995).

When she began writing about the global commons, Lin's initial topic was not climate change but sustainability, as demonstrated in chapter 3, another coauthored piece. The paper is a "call to action," intended to mobilize the scientific community to focus research on sustainable development in the context of global environmental change. More specifically, the paper lists five "grand challenges" that require global coordination: (1) "Improve the usefulness of forecasts of future environmental conditions and their consequences for people"; (2) "Develop, enhance, and integrate observation systems to manage global and regional environmental change"; (3) "Determine how to anticipate, avoid, and manage disruptive global environmental change"; (4) "Determine institutional, economic, and behavioral changes to enable effective steps toward global sustainability"; and (5) "Encourage innovation (and mechanisms for evaluation) in technological, policy, and social responses to achieve global sustainability." It was a "call to action" Ostrom would reiterate throughout the remainder of her career, particularly as her attention shifted to the uniquely challenging problem of climate change. She believed strongly that Bloomington School approaches to institutional analysis and its normative commitment to polycentricity could be usefully applied to the largest-scale social-ecological dilemma humans have ever confronted.

Chapter 4 reprints Lin's first paper specifically directed to the topic of climate change, which she produced for the World Bank in the same year she received the Nobel Memorial Prize. In it, and in subsequent publications (Ostrom 2010b, 2010d, 2014), she urged a polycentric approach to that immense collective-action problem, explaining that national governments, state governments, local governments, private enterprises, and individuals did not have to wait for a workable global agreement before taking valuable steps to reduce their greenhouse gas emissions. It was a pathbreaking work that spawned a veritable cottage industry among scholars and policymakers seeking alternatives to the uniform, and generally unsuccessful, United Nations-based approach under the Kyoto Protocol. Other scholars began recommending various kinds of polycentric approaches (see Cole 2011, 2015, 311–12), whether labeled as "bottom-up" (Leal-Arcas 2011), "building-blocks" (Stewart, Oppenheimer, and Rudyk 2013a, 2013b), or "regime complexes" (Keohane and Victor 2011) for climate change.

The final chapter in Part I, authored by one of this series' coeditors, reinforces Ostrom's arguments favoring a more polycentric approach to climate governance by explaining how cooperation in the international arena, as in local communities, depends on mutual trust between the parties. Among heterogeneous populations, mutual trust is difficult to generate and takes time to build. It is more easily developed if successful interactions between parties are more numerous and diverse (including activities unrelated to the chief issue of concern). Polycentric approaches to policy provide for more numerous and diverse interaction. This same point was highlighted in Lin's 1994 book with Roy Gardner and James Walker on *Rules, Games, and Common-Pool Resources*—one of her most important but often overlooked works—which combined field studies and laboratory experiments to explore questions of trust and reciprocity in common-pool resource settings. As Cole explains in chapter 5, the bilateral US–China Climate Change Working Group had a pronounced effect on international negotiations leading up to the 2015 Paris Agreement, exemplifying how (quieter) interactions at lower levels—in this case, bilateral negotiations held in private, outside the intense media glare of the global UN meetings—can increase mutual trust between important players, thereby creating positive feedback to global negotiations. By the same token, cessation of such interactions, such as the Trump administration's decision to shut down the working group with China, can generate mutual distrust, destroying earlier gains from increased cooperation and greatly reducing prospects for future cooperation.

Part II: The Artifactual Commons: Information, Infrastructure, and Public Health

In work initiated with her Workshop colleague Charlotte Hess, Elinor Ostrom also provided foundational contributions to a fast-growing body of work on the "knowledge commons" (see chapter 6 in this volume; Hess and Ostrom 2006, 2007; Ostrom 2010c). Lin's conceptualizations gave impetus to several active, connected areas of research, a few examples of which are included in this volume. Indeed, this may turn out to become the richest "vein" of new research applying Bloomington School ideas and techniques.

In chapter 6, a paper that was originally published four years before their landmark book, *Understanding Knowledge as a Commons* (2007), Charlotte Hess and Elinor Ostrom provide a primer for intellectual property scholars and others interested in the "knowledge" or "information" commons, including lessons from more than 25 years of international studies of natural common-pool resources. They correct confusions and conflations frequently found in writings about the "knowledge commons," including the common conflation of common-pool resources with property systems instituted to manage those resources. Phrases like "common-property resource" are rife in the literature, but they conflate the natural or artifactual resource with the institutional (e.g., property) system humans use to manage it. Pastures, new inventions, and paintings are all resources or "goods." By themselves, they imply nothing about the institutions humans devise to manage them, such as property rights.

Each of the three coauthors of chapter 7 have made signal contributions to the literature on artifactual commons, including Brett Frischmann's brilliant book on *Infrastructure* (2012); Strandburg, Frischmann, and Cui's (2017) work on rare disease networks; and Madison's (2000) work on copyright law. This same team has edited two very important books on knowledge commons generally and the medical knowledge commons in particular (Frischman, Madison, and Strandburg 2014; Strandburg, Frischmann, and Madison, 2017). In chapter 7 of this volume, they establish an analytical framework, based on the Bloomington School's IAD framework, for "constructing" commons in the cultural environment. The term "constructing" is an important recognition that, unlike natural CPRs, in an artifactual world dominated by trade secrets and intellectual property, cultural commons may be deliberately created to solve certain problems. That said, in the "natural intellectual environment," otherwise known as the "public domain" or, more recently, the "creative commons," intellectual property rights do not exist, and a "vast pool of intellectual resources" is available to be shared by all. Some constructed cultural commons may create other problems by remaining too exclusive, which obstructs potentially life-saving and other socially valuable efforts to build on prior knowledge.

The theme of differences between problems in the natural commons and problems in the artifactual commons is picked up by Dan Cole in chapter 8, which originated when he and Lin Ostrom traveled together to a conference at NYU Law School that was organized around a book project (Frischmann, Madison, and Strandburg 2014). Ostrom was originally assigned to write a paper on this topic, but after her death, Cole attempted, as best he could, to write the kind of paper he imagined Ostrom might have written as a caution to scholars working on issues of the knowledge commons. The chief caution relates to the overwhelmingly normative nature of writings on the knowledge and cultural commons, with authors typically advocating for a greater (or lesser) "public domain" of information. However, very little of what Ostrom wrote suggested normative answers to policy problems. Instead, she focused on improving techniques for accurately *analyzing* and *understanding* problems, in all their complexity, which is a necessary precondition to useful policy advice. She and Vincent certainly shared certain normative commitments to methodological individualism, the promise of self-governance, and polycentrism; but Lin (more so than Vincent) was reluctant to promote particular policy options. Though she is sometimes portrayed as an *advocate* for local self-governance, her actual commitment, based on a great deal of empirical and experimental evidence, was to the *idea* that local self-governing systems can sometimes be successful. She never believed in local self-governance as a panacea solution. "There are no panaceas," she would say. So, what value does her work actually have for scholars of artifactual commons? Ostrom's clear conceptual, analytical, and methodological techniques have a great deal to offer scholars who are not only interested in policy outcomes but in *understanding, analyzing, and evaluating* problems in the artifactual commons. The IAD framework, in particular, has great utility for their work.

In chapter 9, Rolf Künneke and Matthias Finger focus on a specific type of artifactual commons that differs significantly from the "knowledge commons." Infrastructure, such as networks of roads (including bridges), electric power grids and transmission lines, oil pipelines, and flight routes for airlines, shares many features with natural commons. Both are congestible and degradable common-pool resources with (relatively) high exclusion costs but rivalrous consumption. Indeed, the kinds of irrigation systems that Lin Ostrom studied for many years as local CPRs could be described as either natural commons or systems of infrastructure, which create collective-action problems relating to maintenance, among others. Especially given the decrepit state of physical infrastructure in the United States (and presumably other places) today, due mainly to a lack of funding for proper maintenance (see, e.g., McBride 2017), the treatment of infrastructure as a CPR makes a great deal of sense, and may generate some insights for better management in the future.

Chapters 10 and 11 offer alternative viewpoints on a very different kind of infrastructure, namely, the scientific, technological, and policy foundations for public health and health care in the United States. In the first,

Robert Cook-Deegan addresses the importance of a "science commons" for continuing innovation in medicine and pharmacology. Genomics, in particular, has been the focus of contestation between intellectual property advocates and those who would keep genomic data in the science commons. As a field that emerged quite recently (the 1980s), it presented new issues that the legal system and the courts had never before confronted. But the conflict raises the traditional issue in intellectual property of balancing the need to provide incentives for innovators, which patents and copyright provide, against the broad public values that "free" scientific information serves by facilitating continued research to update prior knowledge. Where to strike that balance is hotly disputed by economists, the intellectual property bar, and policy wonks. Applying Bloomington tools and techniques, although unlikely to determine the most normatively desired answer, can assist in better framing the question and understanding how various solutions might differentially affect the various private and social interests at stake.

Michael McGinnis, in chapter 11, demonstrates how Bloomington-School analysis might help us better understand and evaluate options for allocating scarce common resources to address complex issues relating to health care, health insurance, and public health. McGinnis's paper, written expressly for this volume, applies Ostrom's "design principles" (from *Governing the Commons* [1990], on which see chapters 8–9 of volume 2 of this series) to certain health care resources that appear to be CPRs, including public access to emergency services, the time physicians allocate to patients, fixed budgets for social insurance programs, and the number of available hospital beds. One major complicating factor of this project is that, in the US health care system, all different types of goods—private, public, club, and CPRs—are interwoven and nearly impossible to disentangle. McGinnis reviews research that suggests that medical professionals and community leaders can effectively manage these common resources, by regularly communicating with one another and building higher levels of mutual trust and cooperation (along the same lines suggested by Cole in chapter 5). McGinnis concludes by imagining what a fully polycentric system of health care might look like, not as a guide to policy so much as a thought experiment of what such a system would require.

Part III: Continuing Projects

Even while breaking new ground, Lin Ostrom never stopped seeking to improve her analytical frameworks—the IAD and SES frameworks—

either in light of new empirical findings or as a result of ongoing discussions with other social and ecological scientists. From the time she published the initial version of the IAD framework in 1982 (Kiser and Ostrom 1982), it was subjected to almost continual improvement. Ostrom published at least ten distinct versions of the IAD framework between 1982 and 2011. Since her death, scholars have continued to apply and revise Ostrom's frameworks as they confront new problems and continue efforts to resolve old ones.

For example, in 2009, Ostrom and Michael McGinnis started a new "Program in Institutional Analysis of Social-Ecological Systems" (see McGinnis and Ostrom 2010). Its purpose was to more clearly combine the IAD and SES frameworks, but, unfortunately, many participants instead treated these frameworks as alternatives. McGinnis continues to pursue this same goal, via a different approach, along with Daniel Cole and Graham Epstein. (See chapter 14 in this volume for an application, by other scholars, of one version of their ongoing efforts to combine the IAD and SES into a common framework.)

Chapter 12 demonstrates how the Bloomington School's analytical frameworks can be used and sometimes misused, and suggests a means for reassessing and correcting previous misunderstandings. After rehearsing the basics of the SES framework, Cole, Epstein, and McGinnis observe that one of Ostrom's initial applications of the framework—to Garrett Hardin's "Tragedy of the Commons" (1968)—participates in a basic mistake Hardin (and most scholars following him) have made about the institutional structure of the common pasture in his allegory. The "Governance Systems" box in Ostrom's SES application was empty, suggesting the complete absence of any institutions. But in other settings, Ostrom expresses her fervent belief that humans, as social animals, could never have been completey preinstitutional. The authors conclude that the absence of institutions in both Hardin's account and Ostrom's illustration was inconstant with the "tragic" outcome so central to the power of Hardin's allegory. They show that the tragedy could not have resulted from open access to the pasture alone. It also required the efforts of ranchers responding to a level of demand for food beyond subsistence levels, the existence of private ownership of the cattle, and markets in which cattle were bought and sold (which in turn required enforceable contracts). Hardin's allegory is replete with assumed and unexplained institutions without which the tragedy of the commons could simply not have occurred. The authors provide a revised SES application to Hardin's pasture that more accurately characterizes the surprisingly complex set of maladjusted (to each other) institutions required to lead to Hardin's "inexorable" tragedy. The chapter also shows that institutional "fit" is not just about how rules align with ecological circumstances but also about how various rules interact with one another.

In chapter 13, Ulrich Frey and Michael Cox take two of Lin Ostrom's basic tenets—the need to take complexity seriously and consequent need to recognize that no panacea solutions exist—and suggest how the use of ontologies—formal frameworks for representing knowledge based on clear, explicit specifications of conceptualized entities populating the world or some domain of knowledge—can help scholars who study social-ecological systems to move beyond diagnosing specific dilemmas to developing more general theories of the interactions of important variables within social-ecological systems. This effort is similar to, but not the same as, earlier attempts by Elinor Ostrom and Sue Crawford to develop an "institutional grammar" (Crawford and Ostrom 1995). It is also consistent with Ostrom's use of analytical frameworks to study social-ecological systems using consistent concepts, and the development of databases, such as the International Forestry Resources and Institutions database, original created at the Ostrom Workshop but now housed at the University of Michigan (see www.ifriresearch.net). But what Frey and Cox suggest is an even more formal approach than either the IAD or SES framework. In fact, they attempt to convert the SES framework into an ontology, mainly by establishing clear relationships between its various tier 1 categories, recognizing that some primary categories are components or attributes of the SES, while others are related by interactions (such as related ecosystems). They similarly subdivide second-tier variables based on various relationships between them. The extent to which Frey and Cox's SES ontology succeeds will depend on applications and refinements over time.

Chapter 14 presents what may appear to be a standard Bloomington School-style case study of a local CPR: irrigation water in Kenyan villages. But this is the first paper to apply a combined IAD-SES framework, as yet unpublished, and still being developed by Dan Cole, Graham Epstein, and Michael McGinnis. In the early version of the combined framework as used here, the primary SES variables simply take the place of the "exogenous variables" or "preexisting conditions" of the original IAD framework (see Figure 14.1(c)). The same or enhanced second-tier SES variables then populate those boxes.

In chapter 14, Paul McCord, Jampel Dell'Angelo, Elizabeth Baldwin, and Tom Evans apply the combined framework to a case involving the social and ecological consequences of Kenya's 2002 Water Law. The authors discuss how reforms under the 2002 law facilitated the rise of a more polycentric system of irrigation water governance. The authors use the combined IAD-SES framework because it provides a clear feedback mechanism that better facilitates multiple observations over time, so that as institutions change, the effects of those changes can more easily be tracked not just as outcomes but also as part of the "preexisting conditions" for future action situations that might lead to other institutional changes. In other words, the combined IAD-SES framework facilitates comparative static or punctuated equilibrium studies of institutions and their social-ecological effects.

As with the ontological approach in chapter 13, it remains to be seen whether the new combined IAD-SES framework will be widely adopted and applied. In any event, the McCord et al. paper stands as a compelling example of Bloomington-School analysis at work, since this case study shows how polycentric governance systems can be institutionally facilitated within nested national, regional, and local governance structures.

Part IV: Persisting Challenges

We had hoped to squeeze in another wide-ranging theoretical essay by Vincent Ostrom (1990), but space constraints would not allow it. For each of the four volumes of this compendium, we had to make very difficult choices about what to leave out. For some parts, we had twice as many papers as we could possibly include. Our guiding principle was to select papers that clearly represent both the diversity and the consistency of the thinking of the Ostroms and the ideas associated with the Bloomington School.

It is only fitting that Lin Ostrom should have the last word on the Bloomington School of Political Economy and the ongoing challenges faced by all social scientists seeking to understand human behavior, both individually and in groups, and for those engaged in policy analysis. Both chapters 15 and 16 address Lin Ostrom's career-long concern about the need for more and better interdisciplinary research and analysis, as well as the structural impediments that need to be overcome to accomplish those goals. This was the central theme of one of Lin's later books, *Working Together* (2010), coauthored with Amy Poteete and Marco Janssen.

As first named by Mitchell (1988), the Bloomington School epitomizes one way of approaching the study of public choice, the others being identified with the University of Virginia and the University of Rochester (see Aligica and Boettke 2009). All developed from an initial 1963 conference that included, among others, James Buchanan, Gordon Tullock, William Riker, Mancur Olson, and Vincent Ostrom. One of the most significant aspects of the Public Choice Society was its interdisciplinary makeup, including from the outset economists, political scientists, legal scholars, and sociologists. Both Ostroms subsequently served as presidents of the Public Choice Society. When the Ostroms created their Workshop in Political Theory and Policy Analysis at Indiana University in 1973, their goal was to establish a place where scholars, from whatever discipline, who shared interests in political theory and/or policy analysis could meet, exchange ideas, develop common research projects, and help to develop a shared vocabulary for conceptualizing and analyzing problems such that scholars from diverse disciplines could more fully understand each other's research studies. Ever since, the quest to facilitate interdisciplinary cooperation and research, in conditions of Tocquevillian voluntary association, has been at the core of the Ostrom Workshop's mission. Nonetheless, impediments remain.

In chapter 15, Lin compares the important contributions made by the New Institutional Economics, Behavioral Economics, Political Science, Political Economy, Sociology, and both Cognitive and Social Psychology to our understanding of individual and group behavior with respect to resources (especially CPRs), under institutionally generated incentives. But in chapter 16, she strikes a less optimistic note, observing that "overcoming disciplinary limits" remains a "great need" (p. 414). She quotes one cynic: "The world has problems, but universities have departments" (p. 414). Cynical or not, that quote is not far from describing Lin's attitude about the negative effects of departmental "silos" on grappling with real-world problems.

As legal scholar Robert Ellickson (1987) explains, in order to develop useful theories of social and social-ecological dilemmas, "a theorist . . . needs a command of psychology, economics, sociology, organization theory, and political science" (quoted on pp. 415–16 of this volume). Of course, no ordinary scholar can hope to gain sufficient expertise in all of these fields (notable exceptions may include the likes of John Stuart Mill, Max Weber, Herbert Simon, and Elinor Ostrom herself). Which is why the ability to work together with other scholars is so fundamentally important to understanding and ultimately resolving complex problems in the world. Any single disciplinary approach may provide, at best, a necessary part of a comprehensive solution. At worst, they offer simple or simplistic policy solutions that cannot possibly explain, let alone resolve, complex problems. As Lin writes, "we need to think about how to overcome the disciplinary walls that have been erected in the contemporary university . . ." (p. 421). One chief purpose of the Ostrom Workshop and associated organizations, such as the Center for the Study of Institutions, Population, and Environmental Change (CIPEC), has been to "cross-train" students, learning not only the basic theories of anthropology, economics, or political science, but also "a heavy dose of ecology, the analysis of spatial metrics, the use of geographic information systems, and the analysis of remotely sensed data" (p. 421). In short, Workshoppers are trained to "analyze complex adaptive systems" (p. 421).

There are precious few places where cross-disciplinary theoretical and multi-methodological training and wide-ranging applications to empirical research projects have been so effectively integrated. Arguably, such spaces are needed now more than ever in a world and time of increasingly complex and interrelated problems. In a 2011 publication, Lin noted that "The research program facing IAD scholars, as they explore new questions, new research methods, and new modes of analysis, is immense!" (p. 24). Indeed, it is. But Lin gave us analytical tools and techniques that we can use to continue her important work. And, as she was known to quip, "What could be more fun than work?"

References

Aligica, Paul Dragos, and Peter J. Boettke. 2009. *Challenging Institutional Analysis and Development: The Bloomington School*. Abington, Oxon, UK: Routledge.

Cole, Daniel H. 2011. "From Global to Polycentric Climate Governance." *Climate Law* 2: 395–413.

———. 2015. "The Problem of Shared Irresponsibility in International Climate Law." In *Distribution of Responsibilities in International Law*, edited by A. Nollkaemper and D. Jacobs, 290–320. Cambridge: Cambridge University Press.

Crawford, Sue E. S., and Elinor Ostrom. 1995. "A Grammar of Institutions." *American Political Science Review* 89(3): 582–600.

Ellickson, Robert C. 1987. "A Critique of Economic and Sociological Theories of Social Control." *Journal of Legal Studies* 26: 67–99.

Frischmann, Brett M. 2012. *Infrastructure: The Social Value of Shared Resources*. Oxford: Oxford University Press.

Frischmann, Brett M., Michael J. Madison, and Katherine J. Strandburg, eds. 2014. *Governing Knowledge Commons*. Oxford: Oxford University Press.

Hardin, Garrett. 1968. "The Tragedy of the Commons." *Science* 162(3859): 1243–48.

Hess, Charlotte, and Elinor Ostrom. 2006. "A Framework for Analyzing the Microbiological Commons." *International Social Science Journal* 58: 333–49.

———, eds. 2007. *Understanding Knowledge as a Commons: From Theory to Practice*. Cambridge, MA: MIT Press.

Keohane, Robert O., and Elinor Ostrom, eds. 1995. *Local Commons and Global Interdependence: Heterogeneity and Cooperation in Two Domains*. London: Sage.

Keohane, Robert O., and David G. Victor. 2011. "The Regime Complex for Climate Change." *Perspectives on Politics* 9(1): 7–23.

Kiser, Larry L., and Elinor Ostrom. 1982. "The Three Worlds of Action: A Metatheoretical Synthesis of Institutional Approaches." In *Strategies of Political Inquiry*, edited by Elinor Ostrom, 179–222. Beverly Hills, CA: Sage.

Leal-Arcas, Rafael. 2011. "Top-Down and Bottom-Up Approaches for Climate Change Negotiations: An Analysis." *The IUP Journal of Governance and Public Policy* 6: 7–52.

Madison, Michael J. 2000. "Complexity and Copyright in Contradiction." *Cardozo Arts & Entertainment Journal* 18: 125–74.

McBride, James. 2017. "The State of U.S. Infrastructure." Council on Foreign Relations. https://www.cfr.org/backgrounder/state-us-infrastructure.

McGinnis, Michael D., and Elinor Ostrom. 2010. "IAD and SES Dynamic Flows: Introducing the Program in Institutional Analysis of Social-Ecological Systems (PIASES) Framework." Unpublished conference paper on file at the Ostrom Workshop. https://dlc.dlib.indiana.edu/dlc/handle/10535/9250.

Mitchell, William C. 1988. "Virginia, Rochester, and Bloomington: Twenty-Five Years of Public Choice and Political Science." *Public Choice* 56:101–19.

Ostrom, Elinor. 1990. *Governing the Commons: The Evolution of Institutions for Collective Action.* New York: Cambridge University Press.

———. 2010a. "Beyond Markets and States: Polycentric Governance of Complex Economic Systems." *American Economic Review* 100: 641–72.

———. 2010b. "Polycentric Systems for Coping with Collective Action and Global Environmental Change." *Global Environmental Change* 20: 550–57.

———. 2010c. "The Institutional Analysis and Development Framework and the Commons." *Cornell Law Review* 95: 807–15.

———. 2010d. "Nested Externalities and Polycentric Institutions: Must We Wait for Global Solutions to Climate Change before Taking Actions at Other Scales?" *Economic Theory* 49: 353–69.

———. 2011. "Background on the Institutional Analysis and Development Framework." *Policy Studies Journal* 39: 7–27.

———. 2014. "A Polycentric Approach for Coping with Climate Change." *Annals of Economics and Finance* 15: 97–134.

Ostrom, Elinor, Roy Gardner, and James Walker. 1994. *Rules, Games, and Common-Pool Resources*. Ann Arbor: University of Michigan Press.

Ostrom, Vincent. 1969. "Operational Federalism: Organization for the Provision of Public Services in the American Federal System." *Public Choice* 6: 1–17.

———. 1990. "Problems of Cognition as a Challenge for Policy Analysts and Democratic Societies." *Journal of Theoretical Politics* 2(3): 243–62.

Ostrom, Vincent, and Elinor Ostrom. 1977. "Public Goods and Public Choices." In *Alternatives for Delivering Public Services: Toward Improved Performance*, edited by E. S. Savas, 7–49. Boulder, CO: Westview Press.

Ostrom, Vincent, Charles Tiebout, and Robert Warren. 1961. "The Organization of Government in Metropolitan Areas: A Theoretical Inquiry." *American Political Science Review* 55: 831–42.

Poteete, Amy R., Marco A. Janssen, and Elinor Ostrom. 2010. *Working Together: Collective Action, the Commons, and Multiple Methods in Practice*. Princeton, NJ: Princeton University Press.

Stewart, Richard B., Michael Oppenheimer, and Bryce Rudyk. 2013a. "Building Blocks for Global Climate Protection." *Stanford Environmental Law Journal* 32: 341–92.

———. 2013b. "A New Strategy for Global Climate Protection." *Climatic Change* 120: 1–12.

Strandburg, Katherine, J., Brett M. Frischmann, and Can Cui. 2017. "The Rare Diseases Clinical Research Network and the Urea Cycle Disorders Consortium as Nested Knowledge Commons." In *Governing Medical Knowledge Commons*, edited by Katherine J. Strandburg, Brett M. Frischmann, and Michael J. Madison, 155–207. New York: Cambridge University Press.

Strandburg, Katherine J., Brett M. Frischmann, and Michael J. Madison, eds. 2017. *Governing Medical Knowledge Commons*. New York: Cambridge University Press.

PART I

Climate Change and Sustainability

1

Organization of Decision-Making Arrangements and the Development of Atmospheric Resources

Vincent Ostrom

The Human Environment and Its Utilization

In beginning an exploration of the human uses of the atmosphere, we might draw upon some of the conceptions used by Pierre Teilhard de Chardin as a point of departure. Teilhard has attempted to distinguish diverse aspects of the human environment by reference to the geosphere, the hydrosphere, the atmosphere, the biosphere, and the noosphere. The geosphere has reference to the earth forms as that part of the human environment found predominantly in an inorganic liquid and solid state.

The hydrosphere refers to the streams and bodies of water that flow over and through the outer crust of the geosphere and constitute the liquid pool and flow resources of the oceans, rivers, lakes, and groundwater supplies. The atmosphere is the outermost concentric layer of the earth, a blanket of air, composed predominantly of the gases, nitrogen and oxygen.

The atmosphere is a dynamic, turbulent gaseous mass held in a position of greatest density at the combined surfaces of the geosphere and hydrosphere and shades into interplanetary space only a relatively few miles beyond the earth's surface.

Teilhard, following the tradition of Jean-Baptiste Lamarck, identifies the biosphere as the film of life forms with its configuration of organisms living in ecological communities that predominantly occupy positions in the upper hydrosphere, in a very shallow mantle at the surface of the geosphere and the lower atmosphere. All forms of life depend upon some slender thread of connection that enables them to make use of the atmosphere in nurturing the organic processes of life, but no form of life, so far as I know, has been able to form a niche by which it can exclusively derive its continued sustenance in the atmosphere. The biosphere is nurtured and sustained by the conjunction of the geosphere, the hydrosphere, and the atmosphere, and by the essential processes of interaction occurring *among* these spheres of the environment.

Human life occupies its position in the life-space of the biosphere; but Teilhard, Huxley, and others have also given human life independent recognition as forming a separate dimension among earth forms. They refer to this human dimension of earth forms as the "noosphere." The noosphere constitutes that part of the earth that has been brought and shaped by human knowledge—by human action or enterprise based upon human knowledge.

The noosphere is represented by the configuration of man-made forms that has reshaped the geosphere, the hydrosphere, the biosphere, and the atmosphere into a productive environment to serve human purposes and to improve the conditions and opportunities for human life.

Evidences of the massive transformations that have been wrought by human endeavor in reshaping the earth into the forms and patterns of a noosphere are at every hand. The forms and patterns of an agriculture (i.e., the cultured biosphere) can be observed as the predominant feature of the landscape through the temperate zones of the earth. Human cities rise like mountains and sprawl with a stark realism that mutes and obliterates the shades and tones of the surrounding biosphere. Networks of highways, railroads, and lighted beacons cross the landscape in diverse sparkling, web-like patterns. These are the artifacts, the instruments, and the products of human action.

The noosphere has other dimensions that are more specifically reflected in the actions of people engaged in their endeavors, the organizations that constitute those endeavors, and the conceptions that lie behind the actions that form the space—time continuum of human enterprise. The political process is that part of the human endeavor concerned with stricturing, regulating, controlling, and generally with ordering the course of human action as each and every individual sustains his life amid the miscellaneous human endeavors that constitute the noosphere.

The raison d'etre of the political process is rooted in the human capability for developing, organizing, and using knowledge. The political process is the basic arrangement for constituting human enterprise. It is the means for translating knowledge into action and thus in transforming the earth into a noosphere. The political process is the method for organizing, guiding, and channeling activity into enterprise in the transformation of a state of nature into a state of human affairs.

Any consideration of the human use of the atmosphere involves an analysis of interaction between two systems—the atmosphere as a resource system and the organization of human endeavor and of human action as a social system concerned with the utilization and exploitation of the resource system. This social system can be viewed as an economy if the analysis is primarily concerned with the production and consumption of goods and services associated with the use, development, and control of a resource system. This same system can also be viewed as a political system or as a polity if the analysis is directed to the process for ordering decision-making arrangements among those involved in the use, development, and control of a resource system. An economy is not functionally independent of a polity, and from a participant's point of view, both might best be conceptualized simply as a political economy. However, different analytical perspectives can be used in considering different properties of a social system as conceptually independent systems even though they are not functionally independent in an experiential sense.

Those involved in the use, development, and control of resource systems must come to terms with the constraints and conditions of the social systems as well as the requirements of the resource system. The technical feasibility of a course of action, that is, the capacity to deal with the requirements of a resource system in relation to its systematic characteristics in order to produce the desired products or changes, is only one set of criteria involved in planning a resource development program. Standards of economic, financial, legal, and political feasibility turn increasingly upon a capability for meeting the terms and conditions reflected in the constitution of a political economy as a social system organized to facilitate productive enterprise in the enhancement of human welfare.

The task of the social scientist, in an analysis of the human use of the atmosphere, is to clarify behavioral regularities or systemic characteristics involved in the organization of the human endeavor. In undertaking an examination of the political dimensions involved in the human use of the atmosphere, I shall sketch in broad outline some of the basic characteristics of political organization and then analyze problems in the development of atmospheric resources in terms of the effect that the political process has and will continue to have upon the organization and conduct of human enterprises concerned with the human use of the atmosphere.

Basic Characteristics of Political Organization

The Political Context

The distinctive quality about human beings that has been so important in the development of the noosphere is their very extensive capacity for learning and their capability for organizing their learning through symbolic representations into complex information systems that can be transmitted from one to another in contemporary or in succeeding generations. The organization of learning in symbolic forms has led to the development of a human capacity for handling an increasing quantity of information as the frontiers of learning are extended and for assuming specialized roles in the development and use of information. New knowledge transformed into new technological capabilities are among the forces at work to shape the noosphere and to reshape the total human environment.

The capability for acquiring, organizing, and handling very large amounts of information imposes a correlative requirement for exercising choices from among the large variety of opportunities that become available for taking alternative courses of action inherent in human knowledge. The problem of ordering the making of choices or the exercise of discretion has been resolved in human experience by the development of complex systems of decision rules assigning certain capabilities (rights, powers, privileges, and immunities) and certain limitations (duties, liabilities, exposures, and disabilities) in relation to the actions that might be taken in the diverse circumstances of life, and by the development of a correlative set of institutional facilities (also organized on the basis of decision rules) for the development, maintenance, enforcement, and revision of decision rules.

My use of the term "decision rules" in this context is synonymous with the concept of law in the broad sense that lawyers would refer to enforceable legal prescriptions, legal norms, or legal propositions as law. This includes public and private law, criminal and civil law, and all other fields of law. Property law, for example, is a system of decision rules assigning differential capabilities and limitations to persons regarding the acquisition, use, allocation, and disposition of the valued objects or events that are subject to a property relationship. By virtue of the law of property, a proprietor (i.e., property owner) is assigned the authority (i.e., formal power or the formal assignment of capabilities and limitations for action) to make decisions commensurate with his lawful use and enjoyment of that property. The use of the term "lawful" implies that one's authority is conditioned by certain limitations in recognition of the commensurate authority of others. The correlative set of facilities for the development, enforcement, and revision of decision rules (i.e., law) are the institutional facilities that constitute the government of a political system.

A political system has reference to all decision-making functions and includes reference to all decision rules concerning the allocation of authority for the exercise of discretion in all human conduct. The substructure of a political system is formed by the allocation and distribution of power to persons to act or to control actions in the realization of diverse values in relation to other persons in a society. The law of property, for example, can be conceived as part of the political formula first in the sense that the law of property governs the assignment of authority applicable to the allocation, use, and reallocation of diverse resources. In addition, property owners are assigned capabilities for instituting certain undertakings to facilitate their mutual interests and for securing remedies to determine and to enforce their lawful interests.

A serf holding a life estate to his cottage, for example, would have occupied an altogether different political position if he had access to the courts of the realm than if he had access only to the lord of the manor in seeking remedies in his situation. Property law is not only a basis for the exercise of productive capabilities in the conduct of economic enterprise but is also a significant basis for the exercise of capabilities in constituting, enforcing, and revising the structure of legal relationships as the enforceable decision rules operative in a social system. The superstructure of a political system is defined by a system of decision rules that provide for the assignment of authority to certain agencies or officers (decision structures) to perform specialized decision-making functions in the government (i.e., maintenance, regulation, enforcement, and revision of legal relationships) of a political system. These decision structures comprise the superstructure or government of a political system. They also perform an assortment of decision-making functions bearing upon the provision of a variety of goods and services for the collective benefit of the community of people served by those instrumentalities in addition to the maintenance of "law and order."

Different political systems have recourse to different structures of authority in defining political relationships and, as a result, give rise to different opportunities for people to make use of their own authority as persons, or as proprietors and to have recourse to other specialized authorities to pursue their individual and collective interests. The assignment of authority, and the terms and conditions applicable to the exercise of authority, affect the feasibility and performance of any human undertaking. For this reason, any consideration of the human dimensions of the atmosphere must have reference to the structure of authority and to the exercise and use of authority in the governance of human affairs.

Any political system can be represented as a structure of authority. Following the work of Harold Lasswell, authority can be defined as formal power, as the assignment of capabilities (with correlative limitations) for action by legal prescriptions or norms. Law can be viewed as a *political formula*, performing the function of *prescribing and describing the social order in detail*. Authorities are formally assigned powers or decision-making capabilities by the political formula. The political formula represented as the formulation of a structure of authority is a formula for the distribution, exercise, and control of decision-making capabilities in political systems.

Where a structure of authority is designed exclusively to control affairs within a specified jurisdiction and to be independent of all other structures of authority, a political system can be represented as being a sovereign state. Matters of mutual interest affecting sovereign states may only be decided by mutual agreement based upon appropriate authorization by those authorities that are assigned responsibility for dealing with such affairs. To the extent that alternative institutional remedies are recognized as controlling in conflicts arising between "sovereign" states, new structures of authority representing broader communities of interest may be taking form.

From Teilhard's perspective, we might characterize the political structure of the noosphere as composed of a large number of independent nation-states (somewhat in excess of 125) claiming to exercise exclusive authority in the regulation and control of human enterprise and conduct within the territorial limits of those states except for such understandings as each has with others in dealing with matters of mutual interest. As a result, the political structures in the noosphere form a configuration quite independent of various other forms and patterns of events that comprise the natural resource systems in the human environment. Many problems associated with the human use of the atmosphere cannot be readily confined to the jurisdiction of single nation-states and thus require international agreement in accordance with the decision rules of international law.

[. . .]

A Political Analysis of Problems in the Development of Atmospheric Resources

The Atmosphere as an Admixture of Goods and Bads

Human use of the atmosphere is no new condition. All species in the biosphere, as indicated in the introduction, maintain some connection with the atmosphere and its resources. Very large numbers of species make direct use of the atmosphere as the source of their essential supply of oxygen. Humans are no different than other species that rely directly upon the atmosphere for their supply of oxygen, and for the discharge of carbon dioxide and other waste products of human metabolism.

Human use of the atmosphere has long included the creation of artificial atmospheric conditions by bounding airspace in some form of "shelter" and then regulating the airspace for control of temperature, humidity, and for the presence of toxic materials including plant pollens. Shelters and their regulated airspace are increasing both in size and in the variety and quality of control. Enclosed malls in large shopping centers today provide protection from different atmospheric "elements" on a continuous basis. Such encapsulated airspaces can be expected to grow both in size and frequency of use.

The contemporary "political" problems associated with the use of atmospheric resources are usually of quite different magnitudes. These are the problems that involve the larger-scale dynamics of atmospheric conditions and the potentialities that control over these large-scale atmospheric conditions have for human welfare.

The atmosphere in a state of nature behaves as a dynamic system that sustains a flow of both goods and bads when measured by the criteria of human evaluation. Hail, lightning, tornadoes, hurricanes, and other atmospheric phenomena can be the source of major destruction to human values. On the other hand, the atmosphere performs the essential work of distilling and transporting nearly all of the potable water supplies found upon the land masses of the earth. A major political question is whether the developing technology of weather modification can be used to modify atmospheric conditions to increase the yield of precipitation under certain conditions and to decrease the magnitude of turbulence and the yield of bads under other conditions. An economic advance in human welfare can occur wherever human intervention increases the yield of goods in excess of aggregate costs or decreases the yield of injuries or bads with the same net result.

Difficulties arise from circumstances that are good at one time and place but may create injuries and losses at another time and place. Increased precipitation at the time of harvest may be as detrimental to agriculture as decreased precipitation during the early growing season. The harvest of one crop, cherries for example, may coincide with the growing season for many other crops. A person may be willing to take the calculated risk and tolerate the losses suffered by an "act of God," while being far less tolerant of losses suffered as a consequence of the actions of other people.

The atmosphere also performs important utilities in regulating temperatures upon the earth within relatively narrow tolerances, and, as a consequence, the atmosphere substantially affects conditions for the habitation of life upon the earth. The extent that weather modification may have a favorable or unfavorable effect upon temperature regulation in relation to increasing precipitation or ameliorating the intensity of storm patterns is a matter for speculation.

Many existing forms of human endeavor have taken account of climatic probabilities in making locational decisions. What are the costs of dislocation if probabilities bearing upon climatic conditions are altered by human action? Who pays for the costs and who reaps the benefits? The atmosphere is used as a transportation and communication media that serves a large variety of other human utilities and disutilities. Much of modern industry is based upon processes of combustion to provide the principal sources of energy and to perform many of the processes of physical and chemical transformation that serve as means of production. These processes normally depend upon the atmosphere as the principal source of oxygen to supply the combustion process and to carry away the load of waste gases and other waste chemicals that can be discharged into the atmosphere.

Humans may have a relatively low threshold in response to some chemicals wasted into the atmosphere and have a relatively high tolerance for other chemicals. Highly toxic compounds discharged by metallurgical industries, for example, may have the effect of producing substantial damages within the immediate vicinity of a plant. In other situations, similar wastes may become toxic only when higher thresholds are reached. Toxic by-products may also be released by photosynthetic chemical transformations that take place under natural atmospheric conditions. Radioactive waste produced by nuclear explosions are but one of the more perplexing problems concerning the pollution of the atmosphere through its function as a medium of transport.

In addition to these transport functions performed by the atmosphere, we should not fail to recognize that "air transport" with the development of the "airplane" has become a major mode of commercial transportation in the movement of persons and products about the earth's surface. The uses of the atmosphere for such purposes must be taken into a proper accounting in dealing with the use and development of atmospheric resources. The development of air transport that moves at supersonic speed will also be accompanied by atmospheric disturbances in the form of high-intensity sound waves that may be capable of causing substantial damages as well as producing inconvenient annoyances.

This incomplete and sketchy inventory of the human uses of the atmosphere merely serves to indicate the lack of conscious self-awareness that exists in relation to the use and development of atmospheric resources. We need a more complete inventory of present uses made of the atmosphere and an assessment of the future potentialities of pending uses that can be derived either from existing technologies or from pending technological developments.

In any such inventory, we need to know something of the magnitude of existing and potential demand in relation to existing and potential conditions of supply for the various different demands and of the pattern of interaction among the different potential uses. What are the relative inelasticities of supply so that an increased demand or use results in an impairment of the conditions of supply? When such a condition is reached, policies of free development must begin to give way to policies of controlled development. A knowledge regarding the conditions of interaction between demand and supply has an important bearing upon the choice of policies to maintain demand-supply equilibrium at the tolerances that permit an optimal pattern of development.

Patterns of Interaction and Interdependency among Potential Uses

We also need to know something of the pattern of interaction among the different potential uses of the atmosphere and the effect that these patterns of interaction have upon the general resource economy of the atmosphere. How, for example, will efforts at weather modification to reduce storm damage affect the atmosphere's yield in the precipitation of water, its regulation of temperatures, its use for air transportation, and its capacity to discharge diverse waste loads? Conversely, how do efforts to increase the atmospheric yield in precipitation of water affect storm patterns and intensities and the other patterns of use that form a part of the total configuration of demands made upon the atmosphere?

The patterns of interaction among diverse uses can either be complementary and facilitative or alternative and conflicting. Other uses might be independent of one another with no interaction between two or more different patterns of use. Where a development or course of action for one purpose increases the available supply conditions for another use, the two uses are complementary or facilitative. Under certain conditions, weather modification programs undertaken for one purpose might be facilitative in increasing yields for other purposes. Conflicting or alternative uses give rise to the circumstances where an increase in one use will impair or partially impair the use of a resource for another purpose.

Interaction among uses implies interdependencies that must be taken into account by any enterprise or agency undertaking progress concerned with the development of atmospheric resources. Where one type of use impairs, excludes, injures, or destroys an alternative use, serious problems of conflict are apt to arise. Where one type of use facilitates another, problems may also arise in assuring the appropriate level of development that will take account of the joint yield or payoff for both purposes. Where one set of users is able to enjoy the benefits of a windfall produced by others, a problem of underinvestment and underexpenditure, and consequently of underdevelopment, may provide an industry.

Questions about levels and elasticities of demand, levels and elasticities of supplies affecting each pattern of use, of the interactions and interdependencies among diverse patterns of use, and of the configuration of beneficial, indifferent, and harmful consequences of different courses of action will abound in any effort to undertake the development of atmospheric resources. Answers to some of these questions can be anticipated in advance. Some questions may only occur as problems arise in the course of experience. It is necessary to proceed with caution, attempting to anticipate the flow of consequences as accurately as possible but with an appreciation that elements of uncertainty and risk will plague any efforts to advance new ventures in the development of atmospheric resources. These problems will have to be solved by appropriate decision-making arrangements in light of experience. But those who venture must know the opportunities and risks inherent in the structure of the political system as well as the probable meteorological consequences of intervening in the atmosphere to affect its potential yield of goods and bads.

The Design and Organization of Institutional Arrangements for the Development of Atmospheric Resources

The atmosphere yields a mixed bag of goods—and bads—of substantial significance for human welfare. We shall now turn to an examination of some of the problems involved in constituting the diverse range of human activities concerned with the use and development of atmospheric resources. The common-pool characteristics of the atmosphere that pose the most fundamental problems will be examined first. We can turn, second, to conception of the common-property relationships involved—to the problems concerning individual use of a common property, and to the conception of the communities of interests inherent in development of common-property resources. Some of the opportunities available within existing structures of institutional arrangements for undertaking the development of atmospheric resources will then be examined.

The Atmosphere as a Common-Pool, Flow Resource

The atmosphere as a natural resource meets all of the conditions of a common-pool, flow resource. The resource is not easily isolable except within the controlled airspace of a shelter, and as a consequence it cannot be easily bounded or packaged. The resource in most of its aspects is subject only to a limited degree of control. Spillover and interdependency effects abound among the diverse joint and alternative uses that can be made of the atmosphere.

The atmosphere as a common-pool, flow resource has some of the most perplexing characteristics of any of the common-pool resource, at least as perplexing as those of the oceans. First, the atmosphere has no distinct and definitive boundaries for distinguishing subunits. Water resource systems are formed into natural watersheds that provide definitive boundary conditions for organizing management programs. There are no such boundaries for easily characterizing microclimates and subsystems in the atmosphere. The concept of an airshed has limited utility even as an analogy. Instead, the atmosphere is a dynamic system subject to changing velocities and patterns of flow under varying conditions of pressure and carrying capacities.

Yet, the field of effects, or scope of the consequences that flow from any course of action affecting atmospheric conditions, is not without limits. It is doubtful that air pollution from Southern California has any appreciable effect upon Santa Fe, New Mexico, for example. Knowledge regarding the field of effects would provide us with the first tools for the specification of proximate boundary conditions applicable to atmospheric resource development. The political process will provide alternative remedies so that those who may be adversely affected can present their case and seek appropriate remedies to take account of their interests. Exposure to such actions are a necessary risk of doing business in a field of endeavor where action is taken with only limited awareness of the likely consequences. While the risks may be high in undertaking programs of atmospheric resource development in the absence of adequate knowledge, the incentives for action may also be high. An aggravated air pollution problem in Southern California may call for alleviation without being able to specify the technical criteria most appropriate for defining the field of effects or for formulating the precise boundaries of the community of interest appropriate to a smog-control program.

The task of specifying boundary conditions appropriate to the field of effect produced by one form of action in the use and development of atmospheric resources may be quite independent of the boundary conditions appropriate to another pattern of use and development. As a result, different scales of organization and different forms of enterprise may be appropriate to different types of development. It is probably not unreasonable to expect that the configuration of enterprises associated with the use and development of atmospheric resources will be at least as highly differentiated as the mixture of enterprises that presently constitute the American water industry.

Common-Property Relationships in the Use and Development of Common-Pool Resources

All common-pool or flow resources that are lawfully subject to use and development by persons making independent claims upon the resource are conceived as common properties. The conception of a common property, as indicated in a previous section, usually includes reference both to the individual interests in the common-pool or flow resource and to the community of interests that are shared in such a resource. One has reference to the elements and relationships comprising the subsets of interests; the other has reference to the universal set of interests associated with a common-pool or flow resource.

The law relating to rights in common property includes reference to concepts that imply significant variations in the methods for conceptualizing the various interests involved. The concept of *res nullius* has usually been applied to the rights of persons to make use of the atmosphere or of the ocean. This concept implies a negative community—an undefined, ambiguous universal set involved in the development of a common-property resource. On the basis of this concept, the property is defined as belonging to no one and as subject to use by everyone. The relationships among different users can, however, be adjudicated under equity jurisprudence allowing for the application of rules of reason in reaching equitable solutions to conflicts of interest. Some such rules were once applied in the location of windmills, for example, where the construction of a new mill might adversely affect the operation of an established mill.

The doctrine of res nullius is a doctrine applicable to the use of a resource as essentially a free good. Willful injury, malfeasance, unreasonable or wasteful uses or methods of use provided the basis for governing relationships among various users without the necessity for defining the community of interests inherent in the common-property situation. Much of the contemporary law regarding the use and development of the atmosphere has not advanced beyond the conceptions inherent in the doctrine of res nullius.

The concept of *res communes* implies an increasing capacity to define and delimit the community of interests shared by those who have established a right to use a common property. Each has a right to use, no one owns the resource in particular, but the universal set is subject to a more finite and less ambiguous relationship. The reciprocal sets of interests including both the rights to use and the limitations and obligations of use are subject to increasing specification. In the relatively simple common-pool problem such as those associated with the use of a definable groundwater basin, the reciprocal property rights may be subject to determinate solution through adjudication. The rights in a common property under such circumstances can be converted into an exclusive right to a divisible share in the common property once the universal set can be discretely defined.

This solution is not readily available under conditions where public solutions are required either to undertake the management of a production program to increase the supply of goods to be derived from a common-pool resource system, to provide some good subject to public provision (i.e., a nondivisible, nonmarketable good or service), or a combination of both these production and consumption characteristics. Under these circumstances, a part of the universal set of interests shared among the community of interests to a common property is subject to public proprietorship in one form or another.

Where public and private interests are shared in a common-property resource, the law of property no longer provides an adequate solution to the organization of institutional arrangements for resource development.

Recourse to public solutions, at least in part, are necessary, and the traditions of public law bearing upon the organization and government of public enterprises become an essential element in institutional framework for shaping public solutions. Circumstances requiring public solutions need not, however, call for exclusive preemption and occupation of a resource system by any single public authority. Concurrent occupation of a resource system by private proprietary interests, as well as diverse public proprietary interests, may be most conducive to an incremental solution of resource problems in light of changing conditions. Solutions need not be devised on the basis of a model postulating ideal solutions. Instead, solutions can be attempted, a step at a time, in light of accumulated experience without attempting to reach ultimate or final solutions.

The field of water resource development provides the most extensive experience in the use of mixed private and public institutional arrangements for the development of common-pool and flow resources. This experience is not directly applicable to problems concerning the development of atmospheric resources. However, many of the basic concepts can be used, subject to appropriate modification to deal with the distinctive circumstances associated with the development of atmospheric resources as distinguished from water resources.

Some Opportunities Available within Existing Institutional Arrangements

In turning to a consideration of some of the opportunities available within existing institutional arrangements for undertaking the development of atmospheric resources, we shall give brief attention to programs concerned with (1) weather modification to increase yields of water supply, (2) weather modification to decrease the extent of storm damage, and (3) air pollution control.

Where institutional arrangements and production facilities are already well developed to assure rather full control over the hydrologic behavior of different river courses and watershed basins, private entrepreneurs should be confronted with minimal difficulty in undertaking weather modification programs. Existing water supply agencies are the potential buyers for such services. More frequently than not, these agencies are organized as public enterprises capable of sustaining a flow of revenues whether through service charges or from tax levies. Where major water producers are not free to levy a tax upon local beneficiaries, these producers are usually parties to contractual arrangements with wholesale or distribution agencies, organized as public water districts or as municipal water supply systems, which can exercise the power of taxation and provide an appropriate flow of revenues. If weather modification programs assure an incremental water supply at less cost than alternative sources of supply, minimal difficulties would be anticipated in accommodating this incremental source of supply into the production schedule of the primary water production agencies in response to normal growths in demand. In many areas of the western United States, where demands for water are relatively high in relation to local supplies, whole watershed areas are held in public ownership where water production is a principal element in the watershed management program. These circumstances should tend to minimize conflict over actions to increase precipitation and the normal operations of diverse landowners. In turn, reservoirs operated by the principal water production agencies would be available to minimize the risks of flooding in the lower floodplains of a river system and of producing damages for which weather modifiers might be held responsible.

Experience gained on the basis of these more fortuitous circumstances should serve as a basis for the expansion of weather modification programs to increase the yield of precipitation under other conditions as the demands for water grow. Private enterprise in weather modification is not precluded as long as public agencies are available to function as the buyers of the increased yield of water produced by weather modification. The problem of dealing with potential holdouts in a highly fragmented water industry composed of numerous individual proprietors would probably preclude effective marketing arrangements until such water producers were organized as some type of public enterprise capable of charging for water services without regard for the willing consent of each and every water producer.

Questions bearing upon conflict and rivalry among competing private entrepreneurs engaged in weather modification efforts would have to be resolved through other institutional facilities in light of increasing experience. Presumably, private proprietors engaged in weather modification might interfere with each other's operations and impinge adversely upon innocent third parties to such an extent that decisions might be taken to preempt the field of weather modification, as a matter of public policy, for exclusive development and control by public agencies directly responsive to control by governmental authorities. Decisions regarding optimal patterns of organization concerning economies of scale among production agencies operating weather modification programs can only be decided in light of much more extensive experience and knowledge. These decisions can be taken in due course as added experience is acquired. In the meantime, the organization of the water industry in many areas of the United States provides an appropriate organizational structure to contract for the service of private entrepreneurs engaged in weather modification.

Similar situations exist regarding the conduct of weather modification programs to alleviate storm damages. Large expanses of areas in the western United States are under the jurisdiction either of the Bureau of Land Management in the U.S. Department of the Interior or of the Forest Service in the U.S. Department of Agriculture. Both agencies operate fire prevention programs in forest and watershed areas. Several large timber companies maintain similar programs on private forestlands, and still other areas are organized as fire prevention districts with authority to tax local landowners for the operation of fire prevention programs.

Agencies operating fire prevention programs on timberlands or on watersheds provide the necessary institutional structures to be able to pay for weather modification programs in order to reduce fire losses produced by lightning strikes. Presumably, such agencies would be prepared to contract for such services wherever a net savings could be demonstrated through the prevention of fire losses.

Still other opportunities may exist regarding potential savings in storm damage insurance as a justification for public expenditures to prevent storm damage associated with hail storms, wind damage, tornadoes, and hurricanes. Where such insurance is provided through private firms, a rating system might be used to calculate insurance risks with reference to the preventative actions being taken to reduce storm damages. Ordinary fire insurance is based upon such a rating system that takes account of publicly operated water supply and firefighting facilities in establishing the price of fire insurance for each locality. Presumably, additional expenditures for weather modification programs would be justified whenever such efforts would result in a net savings in the combined expenditures or outlay for storm prevention and storm insurance.

The same principle can also be applied to public insurance programs concerned with various forms of insurance against the loss of crops by storm damage. Potential savings realized in the costs of crop insurance payments would justify added expenditures for the prevention of storm damages. Within the course of the last two decades, a number of local government agencies have undertaken air pollution control programs. Those usually have been stimulated by public demand in areas where problems of air pollution have been the most aggravated. The experience that has been derived from these programs should be subject to careful evaluation. What alternative strategies have been used to control air pollution? What have been the results of these efforts? What are the economies of scale in the conduct of these programs? Do weather modification programs offer any opportunities to prevent atmospheric stagnation and the consequent diminution of the atmosphere's carrying capacity in the discharge of waste products? Answers to these questions would provide important increments to an expanding knowledge regarding the use of atmospheric resources based upon the experience derived from existing patterns of organizational arrangements. The existing structure of institutional arrangements provides a basis for taking the first steps in the development of atmospheric resources. Concepts associated with the development of common-property resources and the organization of public and mixed enterprise systems will help guide the way to further solutions.

Long-Term Prospects

More than a century ago, pioneers advancing into the arid regions of the American West found it necessary to design and organize new institutional arrangements for the development and use of water resources. Some of their solutions were drawn from the concepts of mining law; some were drawn from the law of municipal corporations and adapted to the problems of human enterprise in a desert region. The institutional arrangements that form the contemporary structure of the California water industry were fashioned as incremental solutions to water problems over the course of more than a century of experience with life in a desert region. The deserts have been watered by human enterprise, and the improbable prospect of a major megapolis developing in a desert has become a reality.

The realm of the noosphere as characterized by Teilhard and Huxley represents the incremental accumulation of piecemeal solutions in the building of civilization as humanity has advanced through time along diverse paths of learning and development. There are no master planners to plot the course of civilization. The most that people can do is to use the best of their capabilities in building upon the knowledge and technology that is available in fashioning a workable environment that affords the promise of a better life. The bits and pieces become a part of a whole fabric by virtue of a coordinated unfolding of the works, the technology and the operations that affect the physical transformation of resource systems, and by virtue of the incremental addition of agreements, decisions, and their implementing actions that affect a social transformation in the organization of human society.

Every new physical solution, every new technological development must be accompanied by a new political solution, a new institutional arrangement. Meeting the criteria of technical feasibility is only one condition to be met in developing any resource system as a part of the human endeavor. The criteria of economic feasibility, financial feasibility, legal feasibility, and political feasibility must all be met. These criteria relate primarily to the coordination and integration of each new enterprise into the institutional configuration of human society as a going concern.

The organization of appropriate institutional arrangements to undertake the development of atmospheric resources will undoubtedly require pioneering into new political realms. In the long run, national arrangements will not suffice. International arrangements will be required to deal with the continental and global dimensions of atmospheric phenomena. These innovations will have to be fashioned from the familiar tools at hand. New institutions must always be fashioned from the old if we are to sustain the continuity of human enterprise and human civilization.

Note

This chapter was originally written in 1986, but it was first published in *The Quest to Understand Human Affairs: Natural Resources Policy and Essays on Community and Collective Choice, vol. 1*, edited by Barbara Allen (Lanham, MD: Lexington Books, 2011), pp. 137–76. The chapter included here is based on that published version, but with editorial notes removed. Also, the symbol "[. . .]" designates our deletion of material from pages 145–63. The deleted sections focused on internal decision-making processes in the United States, which are not directly pertinent to the theme of this volume.

Selected References

Bain, Joe S., Richard E. Caves, and Julius Margolis. 1966. *Northern California's Water Industry: The Comparative Efficiency of Public Enterprise in Developing a Scarce Natural Resource*. Baltimore, MD: Johns Hopkins University Press.

Buchanan, James M., and Gordon Tullock. 1962. *The Calculus of Consent: Logical Foundations of Constitutional Democracy*. Ann Arbor: University of Michigan Press.

Commons, John R. [1924] 1968. *Legal Foundations of Capitalism*. Madison: University of Wisconsin Press.

Lindblom, Charles E. 1965. *The Intelligence of Democracy: Decision Making through Mutual Adjustment*. New York: Free Press.

Olson, Mancur. 1965. *The Logic of Collective Action: Public Goods and the Theory of Groups*. Cambridge, MA: Harvard University Press.

Rousseau, Jean-Jacques. [1762] 1947. *On the Social Contract*. Trans. Charles Frankel. New York: Hafner.

Teilhard de Chardin, Pierre. 1959. *The Phenomenon of Man*. Introduction by Julian Huxley. Trans. Bernard Wall. New York: Harper.

Tocqueville, Alexis de. [1835–1840] 2000. *Democracy in America*. Trans. and ed. with introduction by Harvey Mansfield and Delba Winthrop. Chicago: University of Chicago Press.

Wiel, Samuel C. 1911. *Water Rights in the Western States*. San Francisco, CA: Bancroft-Whitney.

2

Revisiting the Commons: Local Lessons, Global Challenges

Elinor Ostrom, Joanna Burger, Christopher B. Field, Richard B. Norgaard, and David Policansky

Thirty years have passed since Garrett Hardin's influential article "The Tragedy of the Commons" (*1*). At first, many people agreed with Hardin's metaphor that the users of a commons are caught in an inevitable process that leads to the destruction of the very resource on which they depend. The "rational" user of a commons, Hardin argued, makes demands on a resource until the expected benefits of his or her actions equal expected costs. Because each user ignores costs imposed on others, individual decisions cumulate to a tragic overuse and the potential destruction of an open-access commons. Hardin's proposed solution was "either socialism or the privatism of free enterprise" (*2*).

The starkness of Hardin's original statement has been used by many scholars and policy-makers to rationalize central government control of all common-pool resources (*3*) and to paint a disempowering, pessimistic vision of the human prospect (*4*). Users are pictured as trapped in a situation they cannot change. Thus, it is argued that solutions must be imposed on users by external authorities. Although tragedies have undoubtedly occurred, it is also obvious that for thousands of years, people have self-organized to manage common-pool resources, and users often do devise long-term, sustainable institutions for governing these resources (*5–7*). It is time for a reassessment of the generality of the theory that has grown out of Hardin's original paper. Here, we describe the advances in understanding and managing commons problems that have been made since 1968. We also describe research challenges, especially those related to expanding our understanding of global commons problems.

An important lesson from the empirical studies of sustainable resources is that more solutions exist than Hardin proposed. Both government ownership and privatization are themselves subject to failure in some instances. For example, Sneath shows great differences in grassland degradation under a traditional, self-organized group-property regime versus central government management. A satellite image of northern China, Mongolia, and southern Siberia (*8*) shows marked degradation in the Russian part of the image, whereas the Mongolian half of the image shows much less degradation. In this instance, Mongolia has allowed pastoralists to continue their traditional group-property institutions, which involve large-scale movements between seasonal pastures, while both Russia and China have imposed state-owned agricultural collectives that involve permanent settlements. More recently, the Chinese solution has involved privatization by dividing the "pasture land into individual allocations for each herding household" (*8*). About three-quarters of the pasture land in the Russian section of this ecological zone has been degraded and more than one-third of the Chinese section has been degraded, while only one-tenth of the Mongolian section has suffered equivalent loss (*8*, *9*). Here, socialism and privatization are both associated with more degradation than resulted from a traditional group-property regime.

Most of the theory and practice of successful management involves resources that are effectively managed by small to relatively large groups living within a single country, which involve nested institutions at varying scales. These resources continue to be important as sources of sustained biodiversity and human well-being. Some of the most difficult future problems, however, will involve resources that are difficult to manage at the scale of a village, a large watershed, or even a single country. Some of these resources—for example, fresh water in an international basin or large marine ecosystems—become effectively depletable only in an international context (*10*). Management of these resources depends on the cooperation of appropriate international institutions and national, regional, and local institutions. Resources that are intrinsically difficult to measure or that require measurement with advanced technology, such as stocks of ocean fishes or petroleum reserves, are difficult to manage no matter what the scale of the resource. Others, for example global climate, are largely self-healing in response to a broad range of human actions, until these actions exceed some threshold (*11*).

Although the number and importance of commons problems at local or regional scales will not decrease, the need for effective approaches to commons problems that are global in scale will certainly increase.

Here, we examine this need in the context of an analysis of the nature of common-pool resources and the history of successful and unsuccessful institutions for ensuring fair access and sustained availability to them. Some experience from smaller systems transfers directly to global systems, but global commons introduce a range of new issues, due largely to extreme size and complexity (*12*).

The Nature of Common-Pool Resources

To better understand common-pool resource problems, we must separate concepts related to resource systems and those concerning property rights. We use the term common-pool resources (CPRs) to refer to resource systems regardless of the property rights involved. CPRs include natural and human-constructed resources in which (i) exclusion of beneficiaries through physical and institutional means is especially costly, and (ii) exploitation by one user reduces resource availability for others (*13*). These two characteristics—difficulty of exclusion and subtractability—create potential CPR dilemmas in which people following their own short-term interests produce outcomes that are not in anyone's long-term interest. When resource users interact without the benefit of effective rules limiting access and defining rights and duties, substantial free-riding in two forms is likely: overuse without concern for the negative effects on others, and a lack of contributed resources for maintaining and improving the CPR itself.

CPRs have traditionally included terrestrial and marine ecosystems that are simultaneously viewed as depletable and renewable. Characteristic of many resources is that use by one reduces the quantity or quality available to others, or that use by others adds negative attributes to a resource. CPRs include earth-system components (such as groundwater basins or the atmosphere) as well as products of civilization (such as irrigation systems or the World Wide Web).

Characteristics of CPRs affect the problems of devising governance regimes. These attributes include the size and carrying capacity of the resource system, the measurability of the resource, the temporal and spatial availability of resource flows, the amount of storage in the system, whether resources move (like water, wildlife, and most fish) or are stationary (like trees and medicinal plants), how fast resources regenerate, and how various harvesting technologies affect patterns of regeneration (*14*). It is relatively easy to estimate the number and size of trees in a forest and allocate their use accordingly, but it is much more difficult to assess migratory fish stocks and available irrigation water in a system without storage capacity. Technology can help to inform decisions by improving the identification and monitoring of resources, but it is not a substitute for decision-making. On the other hand, major technological advances in assessing groundwater storage capacity, supply, and associated pollution have allowed more effective management of these resources (*15*). Specific resource systems in particular locations often include several types of CPRs and public goods with different spatial and temporal scales, differing degrees of uncertainty, and complex interactions among them (*16*).

Institutions for Governing and Managing Common-Pool Resources

Solving CPR problems involves two distinct elements: restricting access and creating incentives (usually by assigning individual rights to, or shares of, the resource) for users to invest in the resource instead of overexploiting it. Both changes are needed. For example, access to the north Pacific halibut fishery was not restricted before the recent introduction of individual transferable quotas and catch limits protected the resource for decades. But the enormous competition to catch a large share of the resource before others did resulted in economic waste, danger to the fishers, and reduced quality of fish to consumers. Limiting access alone can fail if the resource users compete for shares, and the resource can become depleted unless incentives or regulations prevent overexploitation (*17*, *18*).

Four broad types of property rights have evolved or are designed in relation to CPRs (Table 2.1). When valuable CPRs are left to an open-access regime, degradation and potential destruction are the result. The proposition that resource users cannot themselves change from no property rights (open access) to group or individual property, however, can be strongly rejected on the basis of evidence: Resource users through the ages have done just that (*5–7*, *13*, *15*, *19*). Both group-property and individual-property regimes are used to manage resources that grant individuals varying rights to access and use of a resource. The primary difference between group property and individual property is the ease with which individual owners can buy or sell a share of a resource. Government property involves ownership by a national, regional, or local public agency that can forbid or allow use by individuals. Empirical studies show that no single type of property regime works efficiently, fairly, and sustainably in relation to all CPRs. CPR problems continue to exist in many regulated settings (*17*). It

Table 2.1. Types of property-rights systems used to regulate common-pool resources (*7*)

Property rights	Characteristics
Open access	Absence of enforced property rights
Group property	Resource rights held by a group of users who can exclude others
Individual property	Resource rights held by individuals (or firms) who can exclude others
Government property	Resource rights held by a government that can regulate or subsidize use

is possible, however, to identify design principles associated with robust institutions that have successfully governed CPRs for generations (*19*).

The Evolution of Norms and Design of Rules

The prediction that resource users are led inevitably to destroy CPRs is based on a model that assumes all individuals are selfish, norm-free, and maximizers of short-run results. This model explains why market institutions facilitate an efficient allocation of private goods and services, and it is strongly supported by empirical data from open, competitive markets in industrial societies (*20*). However, predictions based on this model are not supported in field research or in laboratory experiments in which individuals face a public good or CPR problem and are able to communicate, sanction one another, or make new rules (*21*). Humans adopt a narrow, self-interested perspective in many settings, but can also use reciprocity to overcome social dilemmas (*22*). Users of a CPR include (i) those who always behave in a narrow, self-interested way and never cooperate in dilemma situations (free-riders); (ii) those who are unwilling to cooperate with others unless assured that they will not be exploited by free-riders; (iii) those who are willing to initiate reciprocal cooperation in the hopes that others will return their trust; and (iv) perhaps a few genuine altruists who always try to achieve higher returns for a group.

Whether norms to cope with CPR dilemmas evolve without extensive, self-conscious design depends on the relative proportion of these behavioral types in a particular setting. Reciprocal cooperation can be established, sustain itself, and even grow if the proportion of those who always act in a narrow, self-interested manner is initially not too high (*23*). When interactions enable those who use reciprocity to gain a reputation for trustworthiness, others will be willing to cooperate with them to overcome CPR dilemmas, which leads to increased gains for themselves and their offspring (*24*). Thus, groups of people who can identify one another are more likely than groups of strangers to draw on trust, reciprocity, and reputation to develop norms that limit use. In earlier times, this restricted the size of groups who relied primarily upon evolved and shared norms. Citizen-band radios, tracking devices, the Internet, geographic information systems, and other aspects of modern technology and the news media now enable large groups to monitor one another's behavior and coordinate activities in order to solve CPR problems.

Evolved norms, however, are not always sufficient to prevent overexploitation. Participants or external authorities must deliberately devise (and then monitor and enforce) rules that limit who can use a CPR, specify how much and when that use will be allowed, create and finance formal monitoring arrangements, and establish sanctions for nonconformance. Whether the users themselves are able to overcome the higher level dilemmas they face in bearing the cost of designing, testing, and modifying governance systems depends on the benefits they perceive to result from a change as well as the expected costs of negotiating, monitoring, and enforcing these rules (*25*). Perceived benefits are greater when the resource reliably generates valuable products for the users. Users need some autonomy to make and enforce their own rules, and they must highly value the future sustainability of the resource. Perceived costs are higher when the resource is large and complex, users lack a common understanding of resource dynamics, and users have substantially diverse interests (*26*).

The farmer-managed irrigation systems of Nepal are examples of well-managed CPRs that rely on strong, locally crafted rules as well as evolved norms (*27*). Because the rules and norms that make an irrigation system operate well are not visible to external observers, efforts by well-meaning donors to replace primitive, farmer-constructed systems with newly constructed, government-owned systems have reduced rather than improved performance (*28*). Government-owned systems are built with concrete and steel headworks, in contrast to the simple mud, stone, and trees used by the farmers (Figure 2.1). However, the cropping intensity achieved by farmer-managed systems is significantly higher than on government systems (Table 2.2). In a regression model of system performance, controlling for the size of the system, the slope of the terrain, variation in farmer income, and the presence of alternative sources of water, both government ownership and

Figure 2.1. The government-owned Chiregad irrigation system (right panel) was constructed in Nepal to replace five farmer-owned irrigation systems whose physical infrastructures were similar to the Kathar farmer-managed irrigation system (left panel). In planning the Chiregad system, designers focused entirely on constructing modern engineering works and not on learning about the rules and norms that had been used in the five earlier systems. Even though the physical capital is markedly better than that possessed by the earlier systems, the Chiregad system has never been able to provide water consistently to more than two of the former villages. Agricultural productivity is lower now than it was under farmer management (*37*). Not only do the farmers invest heavily in the maintenance of the farmer-owned system on the left, they have devised effective rules related to access and the allocation of benefits and costs. They achieve higher productivity than most government-owned systems with modern infrastructure. [Photographs by G. Shivakoti (left) and E. Ostrom (right)]

Table 2.2. Relationship of governance structures and cropping intensities [(*27*), p. 106]. A crop intensity of 100% means that all land in an irrigation system is put to full use for one season or partial use over multiple seasons, amounting to the same coverage. Similarly, a crop intensity of 200% is full use of all land for two seasons; 300% is full use for three seasons.

Parameter	Farmer-owned systems (N=97)	Government-owned systems (N=21)	F	p
Head-end crop intensities	246%	208%	10.51	0.002
Tail-end crop intensities	237%	182%	20.33	0.004

the presence of modern headworks have a negative impact on water delivered to the tail end of a system, and thus, overall system productivity (*27*).

Imposing strong limits on resource use raises the question of which community of users is initially defined as having use rights and who is excluded from access to a CPR. The very process of devising methods of exclusion has substantial distributional consequences (*29*). In some instances, those who have long exercised stewardship over a resource can be excluded. A substantial distributional issue will occur, for example, as regulators identify who will receive rights to emit carbon into the atmosphere. Typically, such rights are assigned to those who have exercised a consistent pattern of use over time. Thus, those who need to use the resource later may be excluded entirely or have to pay a very large entry cost.

The counterpoint to exclusion is too rapid inclusion of users. When any user group grows rapidly, the resource can be stressed. For example, in the last 10 years the annual sales of personal watercraft (PWCs) have risen in the United States from about 50,000 to more than 150,000 a year. This has placed a burden on the use of surface water and created conflicts with homeowners, other boaters, fishermen, and naturalists. The rapid rise of PWCs has created a burden on the use of shorelines, contributed to a disproportionate increase in accidents and injuries, and caused disturbances to aquatic natural resources *(30)*. Traditional users of the water surface feel threatened by the invasion of their space by a new, faster, and louder boat that reduces the value of surface waters. In many other settings, when new users arrive through migration, they do not share a similar understanding of how a resource works and what rules and norms are shared by others. Members of the initial community feel threatened and may fail to enforce their own self-restraint, or they may even join the race to use up the resource (*31*).

Given the substantial differences among CPRs, it is difficult to find effective rules that both match the complex interactions and dynamics of a resource and are perceived by users as legitimate, fair, and effective. At times, disagreements about resource assessment may be strategically used to propose policies that disproportionately benefit some at a cost to others (*4*). In highly complex systems, finding optimal rules is extremely challenging, if not impossible. But despite such problems, many users have devised their own rules and have sustained resources over long periods of time. Allowing parallel self-organized governance regimes to engage in extensive trial-and-error learning does not reduce the probability of error for any one resource, but dramatically reduces the probability of disastrous errors for all resources in a region.

Lessons from Local and Regional Common-Pool Resources

The empirical and theoretical research stimulated over the past 30 years by Garrett Hardin's article has shown that tragedies of the commons are real, but not inevitable. Solving the dilemmas of sustainable use is neither easy nor error-free even for local resources. But a scholarly consensus is emerging regarding the conditions most likely to stimulate successful self-organized processes for local and regional CPRs (*6*, *26*, *32*). Attributes of resource systems and their users affect the benefits and costs that users perceive. For users to see major benefits, resource conditions must not have deteriorated to such an extent that the resource is useless, nor can the resource be so little used that few advantages result from organizing. Benefits are easier to assess when users have accurate knowledge of external boundaries and internal microenvironments and have reliable and valid indicators of resource conditions. When the flow of resources is relatively predictable, it is also easier to assess how diverse management regimes will affect long-term benefits and costs.

Users who depend on a resource for a major portion of their livelihood, and who have some autonomy to make their own access and harvesting rules, are more likely than others to perceive benefits from their own restrictions, but they need to share an image of how the resource system operates and how their actions affect each other and the resource. Further, users must be interested in the sustainability of the particular resource so that expected joint benefits will outweigh current costs. If users have some initial trust in others to keep promises, low-cost methods of monitoring and sanctioning can be devised. Previous organizational experience and local leadership reduces the users' costs of coming to agreement and finding effective solutions for a particular environment. In all cases, individuals must overcome their tendency to evaluate their own benefits and costs more intensely than the total benefits and costs for a group. Collective-choice rules affect who is involved in deciding about future rules and how preferences will be aggregated. Thus, these rules affect the breadth of interests represented and involved in making institutional changes, and they affect decisions about which policy instruments are adopted (*33*).

The Broader Social Setting

Whether people are able to self-organize and manage CPRs also depends on the broader social setting within which they work. National governments can help or hinder local self-organization. "Higher" levels of government can facilitate the assembly of users of a CPR in organizational meetings, provide information that helps identify the problem and possible solutions, and legitimize and help enforce agreements reached by local users. National governments can at times, however, hinder local self-organization by defending rights that lead to overuse or maintaining that the state has ultimate control over resources without actually monitoring and enforcing existing regulations.

Participants are more likely to adopt effective rules in macro-regimes that facilitate their efforts than in regimes that ignore resource problems entirely or that presume that central authorities must make all decisions. If local authority is not formally recognized by larger regimes, it is difficult for users to establish enforceable rules. On the other hand, if rules are imposed by outsiders without consulting local participants, local users may engage in a game of "cops and robbers" with outside authorities. In many countries, two centuries of colonization followed by state-run development policy that affected some CPRs has produced great resistance to externally imposed institutions.

The broader economic setting also affects the level and distribution of gains and costs of organizing the management of CPRs. Expectations of rising resource prices encourage better management, whereas falling, unstable, or uncertain resource prices reduce the incentive to organize and assure future availability (*34*). National policy also affects factors such as human migration rates, the flow of capital, technology policy, and hence the range of conditions local institutions must address to work effectively. Finally, local institutions are only rarely able to cope with the ramifications of civil or international war.

Challenges of Global Commons

The lessons from local and regional CPRs are encouraging, yet humanity now faces new challenges to establish global institutions to manage biodiversity, climate change, and other ecosystem services (*35*). These new challenges will be especially difficult for at least the following reasons.

Scaling-up problem. Having larger numbers of participants in a CPR increases the difficulty of organizing, agreeing on rules, and enforcing rules. Global environmental resources now involve 6 billion inhabitants of the globe. Organization at national and local levels can help, but it can also get in the way of finding solutions.

Cultural diversity challenge. Along with economic globalization, we are in a period of reculturalization. Increasing cultural diversification offers increased hope that the diversity of ways in which people have organized locally around CPRs will not be quickly lost, and that diverse new ways will continue to evolve at the local level. However, cultural diversity can decrease the likelihood of finding shared interests and understandings. The problem of cultural diversity is exacerbated by "north-south" conflicts stemming from economic differences between industrialized and less-industrialized countries.

Complications of interlinked CPRs. Although the links between grassland and forest management are complex, they are not so complex as those between maintaining biodiversity and ameliorating climate change. As we address global issues, we face greater interactions between global systems. Similarly, with increased specialization, people have become more interdependent. Thus, we all share one another's common interests, but in more complex ways than the users of a forest or grassland. While we have become more complexly interrelated, we have also become more "distant" from each other and our environmental problems. From our increasingly specialized understandings and particular points on the globe, it is difficult to comprehend the significance of global CPRs and how we need to work together to govern these resources successfully. And given these complexities, finding fair solutions is even more challenging.

Accelerating rates of change. Previous generations complained that change occurred faster and faster, and the acceleration continues. Population growth, economic development, capital and labor mobility, and technological change push us past environmental thresholds before we know it. "Learning by doing" is increasingly difficult, as past lessons are less and less applicable to current problems.

Requirement of unanimous agreement as a collective-choice rule. The basic collective-choice rule for global resource management is voluntary assent to negotiated treaties (*36*). This allows some national governments to hold out for special privileges before they join others in order to achieve regulation, thus strongly affecting the kinds of resource management policies that can be adopted at this level.

We have only one globe with which to experiment. Historically, people could migrate to other resources if they made a major error in managing a local CPR. Today, we have less leeway for mistakes at the local level, while at the global level there is no place to move.

These new challenges clearly erode the confidence with which we can build from past and current examples of successful management to tackle the CPR problems of the future. Yet, the lessons from successful examples of CPR management provide starting points for addressing future challenges. Some of these will be institutional, such as multilevel institutions that build on and complement local and regional institutions to focus on truly global problems. Others will build from improved technology. For example, more accurate long-range weather forecasts could facilitate improvements in irrigation management, or advances in fish tracking could allow more accurate population estimates and harvest management. And broad dissemination of widely believed data could be a major contributor to the trust that is so central to effective CPR management.

In the end, building from the lessons of past successes will require forms of communication, information, and trust that are broad and deep beyond precedent, but not beyond possibility. Protecting institutional diversity related to how diverse peoples cope with CPRs may be as important for our long-run survival as the protection of biological diversity. There is much to learn from successful efforts as well as from failures.

References and Notes

This chapter was originally published in *Science* 284(5412) (1999): 278–82. Reprinted with the permission of the American Association for the Advancement of Science. Figure 2.1 reprinted with the permission of G. Shivakoti. Table 2.2 reprinted with the permission of W. F. Lam.

1. G. Hardin, *Science* **162**, 1243 (1968).

2. ———, *ibid.* **280**, 682 (1998).

3. J. E. M. Arnold, *Managing Forests as Common Property* (FAO Forestry Paper 136, Rome, 1998); D. Feeny, S. Hanna, A. F. McEvoy, *Land Econ.* **72,** 187 (1996); F. Berkes and C. Folke, Eds., *Linking Social and Ecological Systems: Management Practices and Social Mechanisms for Building Resilience* (Cambridge Univ. Press, New York, 1998); A. C. Finlayson and B. J. McCay, *ibid.*, pp. 311–337; R. Repetto, *Skimming the Water: Rent-seeking and the Performance of Public Irrigation Systems* (Research Report 4, World Resources Institute, Washington, DC, 1986).

4. D. Ludwig, R. Hilborn, C. Walters, *Science* **260**, 17 (1993).

5. B. J. McCay and J. M. Acheson, *The Question of the Commons: The Culture and Ecology of Communal Resources* (Univ. of Arizona Press, Tucson, AZ, 1987); F. Berkes, D. Feeny, B. J. McCay, J. M. Acheson, *Nature* **340**, 91 (1989); F. Berkes, *Common Property Resources: Ecology and Community-Based Sustainable Development* (Belhaven, London, 1989); D. W. Bromley *et al.*, *Making the Commons Work: Theory, Practice, and Policy* (ICS Press, San Francisco, 1992); S. Y. Tang, *Institutions and Collective Action: Self-Governance in Irrigation* (ICS Press, San Francisco, 1992); E. Pinkerton, Ed., *Co-operative Management of Local Fisheries: New Directions for Improved Management and Community Development* (Univ. of British Columbia Press, Vancouver, Canada, 1989); C. Hess, *Common-Pool Resources and Collective Action: A Bibliography, Vol. 3*, and *Forest Resources and Institutions: A Bibliography* (Workshop in Political Theory and Policy Analysis, Indiana Univ., Bloomington, IN, 1996) (https://ostromworkshop.indiana.edu/resources/library/index.html).

6. R. Wade, *Village Republics: Economic Conditions for Collective Action in South India* (ICS Press, San Francisco, 1994).

7. D. Feeny, F. Berkes, B. J. McCay, J. M. Acheson, *Hum. Ecol.* **18**, 1 (1990).

8. D. Sneath, *Science* **281**, 1147 (1998).

9. C. Humphrey and D. Sneath, Eds., *Culture and Environment in Inner Asia* (White Horse Press, Cambridge, 1996), vol. 1.

10. R. Costanza *et al.*, *Science* **281,** 198 (1998).

11. W. S. Broecker, *ibid.* **278**, 1582 (1997).

12. M. McGinnis and E. Ostrom, in *The International Political Economy and International Institutions*, O. R. Young, Ed. (Elgar, Cheltenham, UK, 1996), vol. 2, pp. 465–493; R. O. Keohane and E. Ostrom, Eds., *Local Commons and Global Interdependence: Heterogeneity and Cooperation in Two Domains* (Sage, London, 1995); S. Buck, *The Global Commons: An Introduction* (Island, Washington, DC, 1998).

13. E. Ostrom, R. Gardner, J. Walker, *Rules, Games, and Common-Pool Resources* (Univ. of Michigan Press, Ann Arbor, MI, 1994).

14. E. Schlager, W. Blomquist, S. Y. Tang, *Land Econ.* **70**, 294 (1994).

15. W. Blomquist, *Dividing the Waters: Governing Groundwater in Southern California* (ICS Press, San Francisco, 1992).

16. R. Norgaard, *Ad. Hum. Ecol.* **4**, 141 (1995); C. Gibson, *Politicians and Poachers: The Political Economy of Wildlife Policy in Africa* (Cambridge Univ. Press, New York 1999); A. Agrawal, *Greener Pastures: Politics, Markets, and Community among a Migrant Pastoral People* (Duke Univ. Press, Durham, NC, 1999).

17. Organisation for Economic Co-operation and Development (OECD), *Towards Sustainable Fisheries: Economic Aspects of the Management of Living Marine Resources* (OECD, Paris, 1997); National Research Council, *Sustaining Marine Fisheries* (National Academy Press, Washington, DC, 1999).

18. H. S. Gordon, *J. Pol. Econ.* **62**, 124 (1954); B. J. McCay, *Coastal Ocean Manage.* **28**, 3 (1995).

19. E. Ostrom, *Governing the Commons: The Evolution of Institutions for Collective Action* (Cambridge Univ. Press, New York, 1990).

20. C. R. Plott, *Science* **232**, 732 (1986); K. A. McCabe, S. J. Rassenti, V. L. Smith, *ibid.* **254**, 534 (1991).

21. See S. Bowles, R. Boyd, E. Fehr, H. Gintis, *Homo reciprocans: A Research Initiative on the Origins, Dimensions, and Policy Implications of Reciprocal Fairness* (working paper, University of Massachusetts, 1997); E. Ostrom and J. M. Walker, in *Perspectives on Public Choice: A Handbook*, D. C. Mueller, Ed. (Cambridge Univ. Press, New York, 1997), pp. 35–72; J. M. Orbell, A. van de Kragt, R. M. Dawes, *J. Personality Soc. Psych.* **54**, 811 (1988); E. Ostrom, *Am. Pol. Sci. Rev.* **92**, 1 (1998). In these experiments, the formal structure of a dilemma is converted into a set of decisions made by subjects who are financially rewarded as a result of their own and others' decisions. See also J. H. Kagel and A. E. Roth, Eds., *The Handbook of Experimental Economics* (Princeton Univ. Press, Princeton, NJ, 1995). The model is also not as robust in explaining exchange behavior in traditional societies where evolved norms still strongly affect behavior.

22. L. Cosmides and J. Tooby, in *The Adapted Mind: Evolutionary Psychology and the Generation of Culture*, J. H. Barkow, L. Cosmides, J. Tooby, Eds. (Oxford Univ. Press, New York, 1992), pp. 163–228; L. Cosmides and J. Tooby, *Am. Econ. Rev.* **84**, 327 (1994); E. Hoffman, K. McCabe, V. Smith, *ibid.* **86**, 653 (1996).

23. R. Axelrod, *The Evolution of Cooperation* (Basic Books, New York, 1984); *Am. Pol. Sci. Rev.* **80**, 1095 (1986).

24. M. A. Nowak and K. Sigmund, *Nature* **355**, 250 (1992); D. M. Kreps, P. Milgrom, J. Roberts, R. Wilson, *J. Econ. Theory* **27**, 245 (1982).

25. H. Demsetz, *Am. Econ. Rev.* **62**, 347 (1967); D. North, *ibid.* **84**, 359 (1994); C. M. Rose, *Property & Persuasion: Essays on the History, Theory, and Rhetoric of Ownership* (Westview, Boulder, CO, 1994); J. E. Krier, *Harvard J. Law Pub. Policy* **15**, 325 (1992); F. Michelman, in *Liberty, Property, and the Future of Constitutional Development*, E. F. Paul and H. Dickman, Eds. (State Univ. of New York Press, Albany, NY, 1990), pp. 127–171; V. Ostrom, *Brigham Young Univ. Law Rev.* **3**, 857 (1990).

26. E. Ostrom, in *Protecting the Commons: A Framework for Resource Management in the Americas*, J. Burger, E. Ostrom, R. B. Norgaard, D. Policansky, B. D. Goldstein, Eds. (Island, Washington, DC, 2001), pp. 17–41.

27. W. F. Lam, *Governing Irrigation Systems in Nepal: Institutions, Infrastructure, and Collective Action* (ICS Press, Oakland, CA, 1998).

28. ———, *World Dev.* 24, 1301 (1996).

29. G. D. Libecap, *J. Instl. Theor. Econ.* **145**, 6 (1989).

30. J. Burger, *Condor* **100**, 528 (1998); in (*26*); L. Whiteman, *National Parks* **71**, 22 (1997).

31. F. G. Speck and W. S. Hadlock, *Am. Anthropol.* **48**, 355 (1946); C. Safina, *Issues Sci. Technol.* **10,** 37 (1994).

32. J.-M. Baland and J.-P. Platteau, *Halting Degradation of Natural Resources: Is There a Role for Rural Communities?* (Clarendon, Oxford, 1996); M. A. McKean, *J. Theor. Pol.* **4**, 247 (1992).

33. J. Buchanan and G. Tullock, *The Calculus of Consent* (Univ. of Michigan Press, Ann Arbor, MI, 1962); J. B. Wiener, *Yale Law J.* **108**, 677 (1999).

34. C. W. Clark and G. R. Munro, in *Investing in Natural Capital: The Ecological Economics Approach to Sustainability*, A. M. Jansson, M. Hammer, C. Folke, R. Costanza, Eds. (Island, Washington, DC, 1994), pp. 343–361.

35. See O. Young, Ed., *Science Plan for Institutional Dimensions of Global Environmental Change* (International Human Dimensions Programme on Global Environmental Change, Bonn, Germany, 1999); *Global Governance: Drawing Insights from the Environmental Experience* (MIT Press, Cambridge, MA, 1997); P. Haas, R. Keohane, M. Levy, *Institutions for the Earth: Sources of Effective Environmental Protection* (MIT Press, Cambridge, MA, 1993).

36. J. B. Wiener, *Georgetown Law J.*, in press.

37. R. M. Hilton, *J. Theor. Pol.* **4**, 283 (1992).

38. This paper profited from ideas discussed at a symposium on "The Commons Revisited: An Americas Perspective" held in conjunction with the X General Assembly of the Scientific Committee on Problems of the Environment (SCOPE), June 1998. We thank the U.S. Environmental Protection Agency, NSF, and NASA for supporting the U.S. National Committee for SCOPE, where this effort began. We thank F. Berkes, A. Blomqvist, P. Dalecki, D. Dodds, K. Dougherty, D. Feeny, T. Hargis-Young, C. Hess, B. J. McCay, M. McGinnis, M. Polski, E. Schlager, N. Sengupta, J. Unruh, O. Young, and anonymous reviewers for their useful comments. Supported by NSF grant SBR–9521918, the U.N. Food and Agriculture Organization (FAO), the Ford Foundation, and the MacArthur Foundation (E.O.) and by U.S. Department of Energy grant AI DE–FC01–95EW55084 to the Consortium for Risk Evaluation with Stakeholder Participation and National Institute of Environmental Health Sciences grant ESO 5022 (J.B.).

3

Earth System Science for Global Sustainability: Grand Challenges

W. Reid, D. Chen, L. Goldfarb, H. Hackmann, Y. Lee, K. Mokhele, E. Ostrom, K. Raivio, J. Rockström, H. Schellnhuber, and A. Whyte

Tremendous progress has been made in understanding the functioning of the Earth system and, in particular, the impact of human actions (*1*). Although this knowledge can inform management of specific features of our world in transition, societies need knowledge that will allow them to simultaneously reduce global environmental risks while also meeting economic development goals. For example, how can we advance science and technology, change human behavior, and inflence political will to enable societies to meet targets for reductions in greenhouse gas emissions to avoid dangerous climate change? At the same time, how can we meet needs for food, water, improved health and human security, and enhanced energy security? Can this be done while also meeting the United Nations Millennium Development Goals of eradicating extreme poverty and hunger and ensuring ecosystem integrity?

Answering these questions will require reorientation toward new research that better allows science and society to address the needs of decision-makers and citizens at global, regional, national, and local scales (*2*). We will have to meet a twofold challenge: (i) develop strategies to respond to ongoing global change while meeting development goals and (ii) deepen knowledge of the functioning of the Earth system and its critical thresholds (*3*). Promoting sustainable development requires research on a wide range of social, economic, cultural, institutional, and environmental issues (*4*). Given that sustainable development is no longer possible without addressing interactions with global change dynamics (*5*), we focus here on an important dimension of this larger sustainability agenda: the need to broaden and deepen Earth system research to encompass the intersection of global environmental change and sustainable development.

Grand Challenges

A great deal of collaborative international research on global environmental change is coordinated through four Global Environmental Change Research Programmes (*6*) and the Earth System Science Partnership. In light of the need for an overarching set of solution-focused and integrated research priorities for these institutions, the International Council for Science (ICSU) and the International Social Science Council (ISSC) carried out a consultative process to rethink the focus and framework of Earth system research (*7*, *8*). Efforts were made to obtain balanced input from developed and developing country experts, young and senior scientists, social and natural sciences, and both researchers and those using the findings of research. This process resulted in five "Grand Challenges" (listed below in italics), a consensus list of the highest priorities for Earth system science that would remove critical barriers impeding progress toward sustainable development (*9*). The challenges meet four criteria: (i) scientific importance, (ii) need for global coordination, (iii) relevance to decision-makers, and (iv) leverage (i.e., would help address multiple problems). For each grand challenge, several important research questions are identified as answerable within a decade.

Improve the usefulness of forecasts of future environmental conditions and their consequences for people. We need to develop what amounts to an enhanced Earth system simulator to improve our ability to anticipate impacts of a given set of human actions or conditions on global and regional climate and on biological, geochemical, and hydrological systems on seasonal to decadal time scales. Most current efforts to build state-of-the-art whole-Earth system models depart from sophisticated geophysical kernels (coupled atmosphere-ocean models based on exact dynamical equations like Navier-Stokes) that are to be complemented by equally powerful tools (once they become available) representing other parts of the planetary makeup. But, for instance, there is no marine-biosphere model available that will match the standards of the fluid-dynamics–based simulators of the atmosphere within the next 5 years, and the situation seems to be even worse when it comes to simulation of economic, social, and cultural processes. Thus, alternative approaches need to be explored, such as distributed simulators, where available models for all relevant Earth system compartments are virtually assembled from institutions around the world, even if those sectoral models differ heavily in predictive power, or an ensembles approach, where a given Earth system module would be represented by an entire set of credible realizations.

Research is also needed to assess the potential impact of environmental changes on regional economic conditions, food security, water supplies, health, biodiversity, and energy security. Furthermore, research is needed to understand how people are likely to respond to such changes in different socio-geographic and cultural contexts, in particular in poor and vulnerable communities.

Develop, enhance, and integrate observation systems to manage global and regional environmental change. Although investments are being made to build and coordinate more effective observation systems (e.g., the Global Earth Observation System of Systems), current systems fall short of addressing the grand challenges and meeting decision-makers' needs for forecasts and other research products. Economic and social science data, for example, are often gathered and reported at scales that are incompatible for analyzing interlinkages between social and natural systems. The paucity of empirical data on changes in social-environmental systems undermines the ability of decision-makers and the public to establish appropriate responses to emerging threats and address the needs of vulnerable groups. To design cost-effective systems that meet these needs, important scientific questions need to be addressed: What do we need to observe, at what scales, in coupled social environmental systems in order to respond to, adapt to, and influence global change?

Determine how to anticipate, avoid, and manage disruptive global environmental change. Human interference will likely trigger highly nonlinear changes in the global environment that will tend to alter the very character of the life-support system in question and be largely irreversible on human time scales. In turn, disruptive changes in social systems can result from such events, as well as from more gradual environmental changes. For example, a relatively gradual decline in annual precipitation or soil fertility could lead to an abrupt change in the social system as residents abandon unproductive lands and become environmental refugees. Social and economic policies and institutions are rarely designed for abrupt nonlinear social and environmental change. Understanding the underlying nonlinear dynamics will require integration of environmental and complexity sciences, two fields that have developed largely separately. To confine global change to tolerable ranges, having a low risk of dangerous thresholds or "tipping points," we will have to identify and track system conditions with respect to key planetary boundaries (e.g., critical levels of ocean acidification) (*10*). To confine the impacts of unavoidable excursions of the system into dangerous ranges, we will have to enhance resilience to change. Such research may explore whether there are also "positive" social tipping points, that is, pioneering action that can tip economic or social dynamics into sustainable regimes.

Determine institutional, economic, and behavioral changes to enable effective steps toward global sustainability. Global change exposes gaps in social institutions for managing emerging problems. Modern systems of governance are much more effective in addressing national and local problems over time scales of years to decades than in addressing global problems that will affect future generations more strongly than current generations. Addressing problems of global change will require a step change in research on fundamental questions of governance, economic systems, and the assumptions, beliefs, and values underlying human behavior. This must involve close integration of social and biophysical sciences. We must understand how more effective environmental governance can be established at a time of weakening confidence in traditional forms of governance. It is insufficient to identify necessary reforms in policies and institutions; research must explore how to catalyze adoption of those reforms.

Encourage innovation (and mechanisms for evaluation) in technological, policy, and social responses to achieve global sustainability. We need to improve our understanding about how to strengthen incentives for technology, policy, and institutional innovation to respond to global environmental change. For example, there is need for transformative changes in the world's energy system, including efforts at an international level (e.g., establishing a global cap-and-trade system or a global tax on carbon). Insights into how best to attain such international policies can be drawn from innovations at local and regional levels, which are important laboratories for assessing how diverse carbon policies affect economic and social development at multiple scales. Just as countries seek to harmonize public sector research, economic incentives for emerging industries, and public policies to stimulate growth of new competitive industries, a mix of incentives will be needed to generate ideas and technologies to address global change in the context of sustainable development. In particular, we need focused efforts, coupled with careful assessment, on such issues as the potentials and risks of geoengineering strategies (including exploration of local to global institutional arrangements needed to oversee them) and options to meet competing demands for scarce land and water over the next half-century.

A Call to Action

These grand challenges provide an overarching research framework to mobilize the international scientific community around a focused decade of research to support sustainable development in the context of global environmental change. This will require new research capacity, including efforts to attract young scientists, particularly in developing countries. Research dominated by the natural sciences must transition toward research involving the full range of sciences and humanities. A more balanced mix of disciplinary and interdisciplinary research is needed that actively involves stakeholders and decision-makers.

These needs will be challenging to address. There is no simple mechanism to fund "global" research. And because research at the intersection of Earth system science and sustainable development has not attracted great attention from either natural or social scientists, it will take time to build this research community. The disciplinary-dominated structure of academia runs counter to the need to address interdisciplinary aspects of these grand challenges.

But, building on ongoing efforts to promote the broader field of "sustainability science," there is a growing effort by Earth system science researchers and research funders to overcome these barriers (*11–13*). For example, discussions are now under way with the Belmont Forum (*13*), a group of leading global-change funding agencies, to design an overarching approach that would (i) coordinate and focus international scientific research to address the grand challenges; (ii) deliver at global and regional scales the knowledge that societies need to effectively respond to global environmental change while meeting economic and social goals; and (iii) engage a new generation of researchers in the social, economic, natural, health, and engineering sciences in the necessary research. An innovative international partnership between researchers, operational agencies, research funders, and users is fundamental to this approach. Ultimately, a coordinated international funding approach is needed to ensure strategic codesign and implementation of the research.

Roughly 30 years ago, establishment of the first global environmental change research programs represented a revolutionary response by the scientific community to coordinate research across countries and continents to understand the functioning of the Earth system. In a similar spirit, we call on the scientific community to continue improving our understanding of the Earth system and human impacts, but also to deliver knowledge that will enable human development in a world facing rapid global change.

References and Notes

This chapter was originally published in *Science* 330 (12 November 2010): 916–17. Reprinted with the permission of the American Association for the Advancement of Science.

1. H. J. Schellnhuber, D. Sahagian, *Global Change Newsl.* **49**, 20 (2002).

2. W. C. Clark, H. J. Schellnhuber, P. J. Crutzen, in *Earth System Analysis for Sustainability*, H. J. Schellnhuber *et al.*, Eds. (MIT Press, Cambridge, MA, 2004), pp. 1–28.

3. The Earth system is the physical, chemical, biological, and social components, processes, and interactions that together determine the state and dynamics of Earth, including its biota and human occupants.

4. R. W. Kates *et al.*, *Science* **292**, 641 (2001).

5. B. Walker *et al.*, *Science* **325**, 1345 (2009).

6. These are the World Climate Research Programme, International Geosphere-Biosphere Programme, International Human Dimensions Programme on Global Environmental Change, and DIVERSITAS.

7. W. V. Reid, C. Bréchignac, Y. T. Lee, *Science* **325**, 245 (2009).

8. For process details, see www.icsu-visioning.org/the-visioning-process.

9. For challenge details, see www.icsu-visioning.org.

10. J. Rockström *et al.*, *Nature* **461**, 472 (2009).

11. B. L. Turner, 2nd *et al.*, *Proc. Natl. Acad. Sci. U.S.A.* **100**, 8074 (2003).

12. E. Ostrom, *Science* **325**, 419 (2009).

13. ICSU analyzed global change research capacity needs on behalf of research donors; www.icsu.org/2_resourcecentre/ICSU_Belmont_report.

14. H.H., K.M., E.O., K.R., W.V.R., J.R., H.J.S., and A.W. were appointed by ICSU to guide the visioning process. We thank the more than 1000 individuals from 85 countries who contributed to the initial online consultation, participants in the September 2009 research priorities workshop, and the more than 200 individuals and 46 institutions that reviewed the draft of the grand challenges report.

4

A Polycentric Approach for Coping with Climate Change

Elinor Ostrom

The Challenge of Climate Change

Richard Meserve, president of the Carnegie Institution of Washington and former chairman of the U.S. Nuclear Regulatory Commission, opened a panel on Global Change at the October 7, 2007, Stated Meeting of the American Academy of Arts and Sciences with several warnings about the severity and diversity of effects that are predicted by the Intergovernmental Panel on Climate Change (2007). Meserve (2008, 31) stressed that "climate change is a severe challenge that no one country can solve." Rosina Bierbaum, Dean of the School of Natural Resources and Environment at the University of Michigan, in her own excellent analysis of the problem, also stressed the imminent dangers that the world was facing due to melting glaciers, rising sea levels, reduced food supplies, as well as the expected increases in extreme events that climate change was stimulating.

Instead of focusing primarily on the need for a global solution, Bierbaum (2008, 34) stressed that adaptation research has been lagging and that we "are not making progress in understanding vulnerability to climate change and its potential impacts on humans, conducting risk analysis, or understanding what stakeholders want from science to aid decision making." In addition to the excellent research agenda outlined by Bierbaum, it is also essential that substantial research reexamine Meserve's view that solutions to global change must be global in scale. I agree with him that "no one country can solve" the global climate change problem by acting alone. If *only* one country in the world tried to solve climate change—even one of the wealthier countries of the world—this would be a grossly inadequate effort.

Must We Wait for a Global Solution?

Waiting for a single worldwide "solution" to emerge from global negotiations is also problematic. The Kyoto Protocol to the United Nations Framework Convention on Climate Change (UNFCCC or FCCC) is an international environmental treaty created and signed at the Conference of the Parties of the UNFCC in Kyoto in 1997. While more than 180 countries have ratified the Protocol, the United States has not. Further, considerable disagreements exist even among the major states that have signed as to how large a reduction in emissions is required (Matthews and Caldeira 2008).

Major debates exist over a number of key issues related to achieving efficient and fair mechanisms at a global level. One relates to who is responsible for the current and immediate future levels of carbon dioxide (CO_2) in the atmosphere (Botsen et al. 2008; Dellink et al. 2009; den Elzen et al. 2005). This is related to who should bear the primary burden of paying for solutions (Najam et al. 2003; Baer et al. 2000; Posner and Sunstein 2008). Other debates relate to whether or not various "remedies" proposed to reduce carbon sequestration contribute to helping solve other environmental concerns. One puzzle is related to whether deforestation contributes to climate change primarily through releases of CO_2 to the atmosphere or whether changes in land cover, evapotranspiration, and cloud cover are as important and must be taken into account when planning afforestation efforts (Bala et al. 2007). Similarly, scholarly concerns have been raised about claims that Payments for Ecosystem Services (PES) can jointly increase carbon sequestration and enhance species conservation on the same landscape (Nelson et al. 2008).

Given the decades-long failure at an international level to reach agreement on efficient, fair, and enforceable reductions of greenhouse gas emissions, continuing to wait may defeat the possibilities of significant adaptations and mitigations in time to prevent tragic disasters. Further, given the importance of technological change, without numerous innovative technological and institutional efforts at multiple scales, we may not even begin to learn which combined sets of actions are the most effective in reducing the long-term threat of massive climate change.

In addition to the problem of waiting too long, "global solutions" negotiated at a global level, if not backed up by a variety of efforts at national, regional, and local levels, however, are not guaranteed to work well. While the level of CO_2 and other greenhouse gases in the atmosphere may be relatively uniformly distributed at a mega-scale, the impacts of climate change differentially affect regions depending on their geographic location, ecological and economic conditions, prior preparation for extreme events, and past investments. The people most hurt by impacts may not have adequate representation at higher levels and may be unable to articulate clear solutions to reduce greenhouse gas emissions and help them adapt to the variety of threats they face (Agrawal 2008).

Further, while many of the effects of climate change are global, the causes of climate change are the actions undertaken by individuals, families, firms, and actors at a much smaller scale. The familiar slogan "Think Globally but Act Locally" hits right at a major dilemma facing all inhabitants of our globe. To solve climate change in the long run, the day-to-day activities of individuals, families, firms, communities, and governments at multiple levels—particularly those in the more developed world—will need to change substantially. Many of those who need to change, however, have not yet accepted the reality of the threat and their need to act locally in a different manner. As Sovacool and Brown (2009a, 318) point out, "Individuals continue to drive alone, so much that single occupancy vehicle trips constitute more than 80 percent of all travel in the U.S. because people see it as more convenient than adjusting their schedules for mass transit or carpooling" (see also Burris and Lei 2006). If families would change their fundamental behavior relating to how they insulate their housing and whether they buy fuel-efficient cars, however, these actions taken at a small scale would cumulatively reduce their greenhouse gas emissions and their energy consumption by around 30 percent (Vandenberg and Steinemann 2007).

The problem of averting massive climate change—or a global "public bad"—would be a global "public good" (Sandler 2004; Carraro 2003). Millions of actors affect the global atmosphere. All benefit from reduced greenhouse gas emissions, but the problem is they benefit whether or not they pay any of the costs. In other words, beneficiaries cannot be excluded from the benefit of cleaner air. Trying to solve the problem of providing a public good is a classic collective-action dilemma—and potentially the largest dilemma the world has ever knowingly faced.

The classic theory of collective action predicts that no one will change behavior and reduce their energy use unless an external authority imposes enforceable rules that change the incentives faced by those involved. This is why many analysts call for a change in institutions at the global level (see Stavins 1997; Miller 2004; Wiener 2007). Given the presumption that any collective-action problem that has global effects must be "solved" globally, several questions need to be addressed as analysts undertake the next round of research on climate change. They include the following:

1. Is the conventional theory of collective action the best theory for analyzing how to reduce the threats of massive climate change?
2. If not, what key assumptions need to be changed related to (a) the basic theory and (b) potentially the assumptions made regarding the scale of effects produced by actions taken at less than global levels?
3. Are only global benefits generated from local efforts to reduce greenhouse gas emissions, or are there potential benefits at multiple scales?
4. Are actions being taken at less than global scale to reduce greenhouse gas emissions, or at least to offer some levels of adaptation?
5. Are large-scale governments usually better equipped to cope with collective-action problems that have outcomes that are large scale themselves?
6. If multiple governments and other organizations work to reduce energy consumption and greenhouse gas emissions, does that only produce leakage, or chaotic systems, and potentially counterproductive processes?
7. How might a polycentric approach be an improvement over relying exclusively on a global approach to cope with global climate issues?

The paper is organized so as to address each of these questions in turn.

The Conventional Theory of Collective Action

The term "social dilemma" refers to settings where uncoordinated decisions motivated by the pursuit of individual benefits generate suboptimal payoffs for others and for self in the long run. Individual maximization of short-term benefits to self leads individuals to take actions that generate lower joint outcomes than could have been achieved. The reason that such situations are considered to be *dilemmas* is that at least one outcome yields higher returns for *all* who are involved, but participants posited as maximizing short-term material benefits make independent choices and are not predicted to achieve this outcome. The socially optimal outcome could be achieved if most of those involved "cooperated" by selecting strategies other than those prescribed by the Nash equilibrium. Since the suboptimal joint outcome is an equilibrium, however, no one is independently motivated to change their choice, given the predicted choices that others will make (Sandler 1997, 2004; Sandler and Arce 2003).

Social dilemmas thus involve a conflict between individual rationality and optimal outcomes for a group (Schelling 1978; Lichbach 1996; Vatn 2005). Even if some individuals cooperate, others are predicted to "free ride" on the contributions of the cooperators. In addition to the assumption regarding the structure of payoffs leading to a deficient equilibrium, further assumptions made in most game-theoretic models of social dilemmas include the following:

1. All participants have complete and common knowledge of the exogenously fixed structure of the situation and of the payoffs to be received by all individuals under all combinations of strategies.
2. Decisions about actions are made independently and simultaneously.
3. Participants do not communicate with one another.
4. No central authority is present to enforce agreements among participants about their choices.

When these assumptions are made for a game that is not repeated, or is finitely repeated, the theoretical prediction derived from noncooperative game theory is unambiguous—zero cooperation (Luce and Raiffa 1957).

The structure of the tragedy of the commons as described by Hardin (1968) is consistent with that of a Prisoner's Dilemma. Game theory gave logical force to Hardin's expectation of noncooperation leading to socially suboptimal outcomes in the regulation of shared natural resources. Mancur Olson's major book, *The Logic of Collective Action* (1965), reinforced the link between Hardin's analysis of the tragedy of the commons and the game-theoretic analysis of the Prisoner's Dilemma. Olson analyzed the problems facing citizens who might wish to achieve a public good through collective action. Olson's theory relates to the problem of overcoming social dilemmas in general. In Olson's analysis, collective action is a problem because the costs of contributing are concentrated while the benefits are diffused. The fundamental problem in both situations is the same: actions taken for individual benefit result in socially suboptimal outcomes. People who pursue individual self-interest are "free riders" in that they enjoy the benefit of others' restraint in using shared resources or others' contribution to collective action.

Olson's logic of collective action is important for the study of climate change as well as for the governance of natural resources and other questions of importance related to human relationships. Many objectives that individuals seek within a family, a neighborhood, a community, a region, a nation, or an alliance of nations may be produced by the actions of others—whether or not a particular actor contributes. If many individuals decide to "free ride" on the actions of others, the "others" may stop contributing to the collective good. If more and more actors pull out, eventually no one contributes. Basically, Olson laid out a theory of collective *in*action. What might be of mutual benefit is not achieved. In the case of climate change, the joint "good" is reducing a joint "bad" caused by increased emissions of greenhouse gases. The joint goal is reducing the threats of massive climate change, of increased ocean levels, of increased variability in climate patterns, and many other global bads.

Without externally imposed regulations at the scale of the potential externalities, the theory predicts that the benefits that might be achieved through collective action are impossible to obtain. Under this view of the world, which became the "conventional" theory for many scholars interested in the sustainability of natural resources at multiple scales, little variance is predicted in the performance of groups jointly affected by their own actions. In the conventional theory, "self-organized groups" that have devised their own policies to achieve a public good or regulate a common-pool resource do not exist at any scale.

On the surface, the conventional theory of collective action appears to be precisely relevant to the analysis of climate change and other social dilemmas with global impacts. While individuals and organizations may not have complete information about the externalities they generate, it is reasonable to assume they have good information about their own immediate costs and benefits. Many of the decisions made that affect the release of greenhouse gases—how and with whom to travel to work and other destinations, the level of energy use, the type of investments in building infrastructure and new technologies for energy production—are made independently by multiple actors without communicating with others making similar decisions. And no central authority exists at the global level making authoritative decisions about payments for energy use and investments in new technologies—and enforcing these decisions.

The applicability of the conventional theory is considered to be so obvious by many scholars that few questions have been raised about whether this is the best theoretical foundation for making real progress toward substantially reducing greenhouse gas emissions and taking other actions to reduce the threat of massive harm brought about by climate change. Two broad grounds exist for doubting whether sole reliance on the conventional theory of collective action is a wise scientific strategy. The first is the weakness of empirical support for the conventional theory of collective action related to small- to medium-size environmental social dilemmas. The second is the existence of multiple externalities at small, medium, and large scales within the global externality that has been of primary concern in the academic and policy literature. The paper discusses each of these issues in turn.

The Lack of Empirical Support for the Conventional Theory of Collective Action

In a major, book-length effort, Poteete, Janssen, and Ostrom (2010) review the empirical support for the theory of collective action related to natural resource problems. They examine the evidence generated by in-depth case studies, meta-analyses of cases, large-scale comparative field studies, laboratory experiments, and agent-based models. The major finding is that the unambiguous predictions of the conventional theory are not supported. While many instances of free riding are observed in the array of empirical research, a surprisingly large number of individuals facing collective-action problems do cooperate.

Contrary to the conventional theory, many groups in the field have self-organized to develop solutions to common-pool resource problems at a small to medium scale (Baland and Platteau [1996] 2000; Agrawal 2000, 2002; McKean 2000; Wade 1994; Schlager 1994; Schlager et al. 1994; Ostrom 1992, 2001; Ostrom et al. 1994; NRC 1986, 2002; Dietz et al. 2003). Rational choice theory was used as a foundation for the conventional theory of collective action. Predictions from this theory are well supported when applied to the analysis of the provision and production of private goods in a highly competitive environment. Predictions from the theory are not well supported when applied to situations involving social dilemmas where participants trust one another to be effective reciprocators (Ostrom 1998). Thus, before analyzing efforts to reduce the threat of massive costs related to climate change, it is essential to update the theory of collective action so that future policies are not made on the basis of a theory that appears to be so reasonable but has not received strong empirical support.

Updating the Theory of Collective Action Related to Climate Change

For future analyses of how individuals relate to natural resources at multiple scales, the conventional theory of collective action needs revision based on a behavioral theory of human action and a recognition of the importance of context in affecting levels of trust and reciprocity of those involved. Further, the application of this theory to climate change also needs to question whether smaller-scale externalities exist from the use of energy by individuals and firms and whether that may form a different foundation for future actions.

Since behavior in social dilemmas varies substantially across individuals as well as across settings, updated theoretical efforts depend on a behavioral theory of the individual (Camerer 2003; Fehr and Gächter 2000, 2002; Fehr and Leibbrandt 2008; Fehr and Rockenbach 2003) as well as on structural features of the particular dilemma that affect the likelihood of voluntary cooperation or relatively high levels of compliance with official rules. A behavioral theory of the individual assumes that while individuals do not possess perfect information, they are capable of learning more accurate information as they interact in a particular setting—especially when the rules enhance the accuracy and rapidity of feedback. It is appropriate to assume that individuals do seek benefits for self, but that individuals vary in their other-regarding preferences and norms about the appropriate actions they should take in particular settings (Sen 1977; Frohlich and Oppenheimer 1992; Cox et al. 2007; Crawford and Ostrom 2005).

The capability of those involved to gain a reputation for being trustworthy and reciprocating the efforts of others to cooperate with their own cooperation turns out to be a central characteristic of settings where moderate to high levels of cooperation are sustained (Milinski et al. 2002; Rothstein 2005; Poteete, Janssen, and Ostrom 2010). To achieve its objects, any policy that tries to improve levels of collective action to overcome social dilemmas must enhance the level of trust by participants that others are complying with the policy or else many will seek ways of avoiding compliance.

At scales less than the global commons, a core finding is that the features of an immediate micro-situation and the broader contextual setting in which individuals interact have a major impact on the likelihood of individuals acting cooperatively in collective-action situations. Empirical studies focusing on common-pool resource dilemmas that are discussed and synthesized in Poteete, Janssen, and Ostrom (2010) have identified a large number of variables that increase the likelihood of cooperation in social dilemmas. Among the most important are the following: (1) reliable information is available about the immediate and long-term costs and benefits of actions; (2) the individuals involved see the common resource as important for their own achievements and have a long-term time horizon; (3) gaining a reputation for being a trustworthy reciprocator is important to those involved; (4) individuals can communicate with at least some of the others involved; (5) informal monitoring and sanctioning is feasible and considered appropriate; and (6) social capital and leadership exist, related to previous successes in solving joint problems. Further, when individuals and groups face rules and sanctions imposed by external authorities, these are viewed as legitimate and enforced equitably on all.

Thus the updated theory of collective action developed in Poteete, Janssen, and Ostrom (2010) is not as pessimistic about the likelihood of diverse organizations at multiple levels finding policies that increase levels of voluntary cooperation or increase compliance with rules established by governmental authorities. Instead of presuming that cooperation related to social dilemmas is an impossibility, the presumption should be that cooperation will occur in settings with several broad characteristics. These include the following:

1. Many of those affected have agreed on the need for changes in behavior and see themselves as jointly sharing responsibility for future outcomes.
2. The reliability and frequency of information about the phenomena of concern are relatively high.
3. Participants know who else has agreed to change behavior and that their conformance is being monitored.
4. Communication occurs among at least subsets of participants.

The exact structure cannot be worked out at a general level, as many specific features of a particular dilemma affect what has a chance of working. The crucial factor is that a combination of structural features leads many of those affected to trust one another and to be willing to do an agreed-upon action that adds to their own short-term costs because they do see a long-term benefit for themselves and others and they believe that most others are complying.

The problem of collective action does not disappear once a policy to deal with an externality is made by a government. Even governmental policies need to rely to a great extent on willing cooperation by citizens. When citizens approve of a governmental policy, think they *should* comply, and this view is complemented by a sense that the governmental policy is effectively and fairly enforced, the costs of that enforcement are much lower than when citizens try to evade the policy. Trust that governmental officials are objective, effective, and fair is more important in enabling a governmental policy to work than reliance on force (Rothstein 1998, 2005).

It is obviously much easier to craft solutions for collective-action problems related to smaller-scale common-pool resources than for the global commons. Many of the policy analyses recommending "solutions" at an international level to be implemented by national governments are based on a fear that unless global solutions are made for global problems, these problems will continue unabated. The third major question addressed above was, Are only global benefits generated from local-level efforts to reduce greenhouse gas emissions, or are there potential benefits at multiple scales? If there are benefits at multiple scales, as well as costs at these scales, applying the updated theory of collective action needs to take these into account for analyzing proposed solutions to climate change.

Are Only Global Benefits Generated from Reducing Greenhouse Gases Emissions?

Greenhouse gas emissions are the result of an extraordinarily large number of actions taken at multiple scales. As mentioned above, decisions within a family as to what form of transportation to use for various purposes, what car to purchase, and what investments to make for power consumption within the home all have small effects on the global atmosphere. Similar decisions within firms are also important, as buildings in general account for "more than 70 percent of the electricity use and almost 40 percent of greenhouse gas emissions in the United States" (Fuller et al. 2009, citing several U.S. Department of Energy reports). Proposals for substantial increases in energy taxes at a national level (to comply with proposed international agreements) are strongly urged as the only way of changing the decisions of individuals and families, as they make decisions based on individual and family household budgets and do not take the external costs they generate into account.

Without shared knowledge about the external costs of these actions, shifts in preference functions to take into account benefits for others, and reduced discount rates, no change at a small scale can be expected. As the scientific community has achieved a higher level of agreement about human impacts on the global atmosphere, knowledge of the effects of individual and family actions is becoming more and more available. Discussions within the family and with neighbors in a community about actions that can be taken locally to reduce greenhouse gas emissions are also important factors leading to the potential for change. Local discussions and meetings generate information about the prevailing unrecognized costs of individual and family activities as well as sometimes leading to a change in the preferences of individuals involved. Even without major taxes imposed on energy at a national level, however, families that decide to invest in better insulation and more efficient furnaces and other appliances, to join a carpool whenever feasible, and to take other energy-conserving actions can save funds over the long run. They may face high up-front investments to achieve some of these benefits, but there are potential benefits to be achieved even at a household level.

Communities that have established power networks that enable households to invest in solar power that is used for household energy use and when not needed is contributed to the network, can potentially reduce local energy costs as well as reducing greenhouse gas emissions. Investments in better waste disposal facilities also generate local benefits as well as helping on global emissions. Efforts to reduce pollution levels in large metropolitan areas focus both on total energy use and on emissions of particulates and thus generate benefits at a metropolitan level as well as globally. Decisions to reduce subsidies to various types of economic development that increase emissions are difficult for any government to make, but some of these decisions can reduce the administrative costs of government as well as improving the environment.

Efforts at a local level are challenging. The Cities for Climate Protection (CCP) campaign (sponsored by the International Council for Local Environmental Initiatives) tried to encourage cities to find ways of controlling greenhouse gas emissions but found it a difficult task. Part of the problem is that "the problem" has been framed so often as a global issue that local politicians and citizens sometimes cannot see that there are things that can be done at a local level that are important steps in the right direction (Betsill 2001). Further, some claims of achievements have been questioned by analysts who have dug into the reports (Eadson 2008). Given that many of the actions generating greenhouse gas emissions are taken at multiple scales, activities could be organized at multiple scales, ranging from households, farms, and cities at a local scale to regions within a state, states, regional units that cross state boundaries and the globe (Kates and Wilbanks 2003).

What Efforts to Reduce Greenhouse Gas Emissions are Being Taken at Less Than a Global Scale?

It is not possible to do a full inventory in this paper of all of the projects going on across the world at multiple scales. What I can do is focus on some of the projects that have been organized at a local level, at the level of state governments in the United States, and at a regional level in Europe, and discuss some of the efforts to reduce emissions substantially.

Local-Level Projects and Alliances to Reduce Local-Level Externalities

One of the most successful efforts made by many local governments across the United States has been to reduce the level of fine-particulate air pollution (which in some cases has reduced greenhouse gas emissions as well). Pope et al. (2009) have just completed a major study of the impact on life expectancy of particulate matter in the air sampled over the period from 1979 to 2000 for 51 metropolitan areas (including more than 200 counties).[1] Metropolitan areas across the nation have reduced air pollution levels by one-third. Pope et al. also found that increased life expectancy during this period was associated with reductions in fine-particulate air pollution after controlling for socioeconomic, demographic, and other variables associated with life expectancy. Their statistical analysis shows that the gain in average life expectancy that could be attributed to reduction in air pollutants was one-third of a year.

Retrofitting buildings to add insulation, solar photovoltaics, and more efficient heating systems is one strategy that can be pursued at a local level and may generate long-term energy cost savings for the firm or family that takes such actions as well as reducing greenhouse gas emissions. The upfront costs of such efforts are frequently daunting, however, even when the private investment will reduce private costs over the long run. By a public ballot approved by 81 percent of the voters, Berkeley, California, has adopted a general policy to reduce emissions substantially over time. One of the programs is called Berkeley FIRST (Financing Initiative for Renewable and Solar Technology) and is designed to reduce the barrier of up-front costs. To participate in the program, the owner of a commercial or residential building asks a contractor for an estimate of the costs of new solar energy equipment or energy-efficiency improvements to the building that would likely cost between $4,000 and $20,000 (Pope et al. 2009). The owner then submits an application to the city, and staff review the estimate and ensure that the owner has clear title.

> After the municipality approves the application, the work is completed, a lien is placed on the property, and a check is issued to the property owner. A special tax is added to future property bills. If the property is sold before the end of the 20-year repayment period, the new owner pays the remaining special taxes as part of their property's annual tax bill. The interest component of the special tax payments will be tax deductible, similar to a home equity line or home mortgage. . . .
>
> The City of Berkeley started accepting applications through its Web site on 5 November 2008, and applications to claim $1.5 million available for the pilot were submitted within 10 minutes. (Pope et al. 2009, 25)

Obviously the demand for making these investments in improving buildings so as to reduce energy consumption is very high. The City of Berkeley plans to increase the funds available to support this program over time.

Other cities have started a variety of "green" initiatives that are prominently displayed on their home pages on the web. The City of Toronto, for example, has set up an "environmental portal" that announces more than a dozen current city policies, related publications, and meetings that are focused on climate change.[2] In 2008, the city allocated $700,000 to renewable energy projects combining major investments averaging around $100,000 each for building rooftop gardens, solar photovoltaic panels on houses, and solar water heating systems, and a dozen smaller projects ranging around $25,000 to support neighborhood efforts to enhance the forested areas of local parks and gardens and for local-level organizations working with communities to hold planning meetings to think through better bicycle paths and other activities that can be undertaken at a small, neighborhood scale. The City of Toronto has increased the budget for its "Live Green Toronto" program to $2.2 million for 2009.

Mayors of large cities are also banding together to discuss actions to reduce carbon emissions that can be taken locally but that if taken jointly can have a much bigger effect. In October 2005, 18 large cities sent representatives to London to examine actions that could be taken at a municipal level; to reexamine urban policies that could be revised, including their own purchasing policies; and to discuss ways of encouraging more investment in climate-friendly technologies in their cities. The mayors reviewed the results of the £8 congestion charge imposed by London on vehicles that drive within the city's central zone during business hours, from 7:00 a.m. to 6:00 p.m.[3] In October 2008, a merger with the Clinton Climate Initiative was arranged to create the C40 Cities Climate Leadership group, whose members have jointly pledged to reduce emissions in each of their cities to meet or even improve on Kyoto standards. The C40 Large Cities Climate Summit was held in May 2007 to exchange information about many policies adopted to reduce emissions and to announce a $5 billion global Energy Efficiency Building Retrofit Program by the Clinton Climate Initiative.[4] A similar league, the World Mayors Council on Climate Change, was initiated by the mayor of the City of Kyoto (Japan) in December 2005, soon after the Kyoto Protocol entered into force. Currently, there are 20 members of this alliance, from all regions of the world.

Other local-level efforts to overtly increase the level of alternative energy production or reduce the level of automobile use have been reported for many cities around the world—including Sorsogon, Philippines; Esmeraldas, Ecuador; Maputo, Mozambique; and Kampala, Uganda, where efforts are supported by the Cities in Climate Change Initiative, funded by the government of Norway and the UN Development Account (UN-Habitat 2008).

A complete inventory cannot be undertaken in this paper, though it would be a good subject for a future research project. But the major point is that many local governments and community organizations have recognized that actions undertaken at a local level are a major source of carbon emissions and that a need exists to tackle these at the local level as well as at higher scales.

State-Level Projects in the United States

The state of California not only is the twelfth largest emitter of greenhouse gases in the world—with emissions comparable to Australia's—but is also now one of the leading states in adopting policies related to climate change

(Engel 2006). For example, in 2006, the California legislature passed the Global Warming Solutions Act, aimed at reducing greenhouse gas emissions in the state by 25 percent by 2020 by requiring drastic reductions in major industries, including oil and gas refineries and utilities.[5] The California Air Resources Board is charged with developing a market-based, cap-and-trade program to implement the required reductions.

The Colorado legislature passed State House Bill 08–1350, signed into law in 2008, to enable local governments within the state to adopt policies similar to the Berkeley FIRST program. The legislation allows municipalities in Colorado to finance approved building improvements and enables property owners to pay off capital investments made to decrease their use of fossil fuels for heating and electricity through repayments over 20 years. In July 2007, Florida Governor Charlie Crist brought together government, business, and scientific leaders from across the state to discuss what actions could be taken by Florida to address climate change issues. At the conclusion of the meeting, several executive orders were signed to set out targets for reducing greenhouse gas emissions in Florida and to change the building code to require increased energy efficiency in new construction.[6]

Efforts are also being made among the states to develop joint policies. The Regional Greenhouse Gas Initiative (RGGI), joined by ten states in the Northeast and mid-Atlantic regions of the United States, plans to reduce CO_2 emissions from the power sector by 10 percent by 2018.[7] Further, RGGI is one of the first market-based efforts in the United States aimed at reducing greenhouse gas emissions by auctioning emission allowances and investing the proceeds in clean energy technologies and the creation of green jobs in each of the states. The third auction occurred on March 18, 2009.[8]

European Efforts

In Europe, interventions tend to combine local, national, and regional levels. The EU Emissions Trading Scheme (EU-ETS) was developed so as to reduce the economic costs of meeting the European Union's Kyoto target of 8 percent CO_2 reduction by 2012. The scheme includes around 10,000 large industrial plants in the power generation, iron and steel, glass, brick, and pottery industries, but not the transport sector. Operators of these facilities receive emission allowances that are good for a one-year period. If an allowance is not fully used by the assigned operator (after verification), the unused portion may be sold to other facilities that cannot yet meet their assigned target. The official data issued by the European Environmental Agency (EEA) in 2006 show that the EU members that had signed the Kyoto Agreement were able to achieve in 2005 a 2 percent cut in CO_2 emissions compared with 1990 levels and that greenhouse gas emissions were projected to decline further by 2010 compared with 2004 levels (EEA 2006, sections 8 and 9).

While a considerable accomplishment has been achieved, some concerns have been raised—which could also be raised regarding the RGGI approach in the United States—that some energy-intensive sectors may relocate to regions that have less stringent policies on climate change or none at all.

> To the extent this happens, the EU-ETS program will be responsible for shifting production to countries that allow a free-for-all with emissions. The risk of carbon leakage is said to be high, for example, for the European chemical and lime industries. The chemical industry is highly energy intensive and competes in a global market where it is not possible to pass on unilateral costs, conditions that are ripe for carbon leakage. . . . Carbon leakage is a risk because of high production costs within the EU including CO_2 costs compared with lower costs of products imported from outside the EU which include transportation costs but no CO_2 costs. (Sovacool and Brown 2009b, 324)

We return to the potential problems of leakage associated with less than global efforts to avert massive climate change in the section below, which discusses the problems and possibilities of organizing efforts to cope with climate change at diverse levels.

Are Large-Scale Governments Usually Better Able to Cope with Collective Action?

While the presumption is made in many policy discussions that global solutions are necessary for coping with the problems of climate change because of the inadequacy of local and regional efforts, few of these analyses examine the problems that large-scale units may face in developing effective policies related to resources. Before making a commitment that the global level is the *only* scale on which to address climate change, one should at least reflect on past efforts to adopt uniform policies by very large entities, efforts intended to correct for problems of collective action. The presumption that locals cannot take care of public sector problems has led to diverse policies to place responsibility for local public services on units of government that are very large, frequently lacking the resources to carry out their assignments, and overwhelmed with what they are assigned to do.

Contemporary assignments to regional, national, or international governments of the *exclusive* responsibility for providing local public goods and common-pool resources remove authority from local officials and citizens to solve local problems that differ from one location to the next. Doug Wilson, Research Director for the Institute for Fisheries Management and Coastal Community Development in Denmark, has recently reflected on the evolution of fisheries policies in the European Union.[9]

> The Common Fisheries Policy (CFP) as it is called is an "exclusive competence" of the European Union (EU), meaning that all decisions are taken at the level of the Union. . . .
>
> The CFP is not only politically important within the overall effort to build a new kind of polity in Europe; it is also failing to do a very good job of maintaining sustainable fish stocks. Fisheries scientists tell us that, in 2003, 22% of the fish caught from stocks managed by the CFP were taken from stocks that were smaller than they should have been for sustainable fishing. Neither scientists, fishers, government agencies, nor marine conservation groups are happy with the CFP, and there are myriad attempts to reform it. The reforms include better policy, better data gathering, a reduction in perverse subsidies to the fishing industry and, finally, 30 years after most other fisheries management agencies had moved beyond top-down management, some serious attempts at stakeholder involvement. (Wilson 2006, 7)

Other fisheries-related policies adopted by large-scale units have also exhibited major problems.[10] The United Nations Conference on the Law of the Sea allocated about one-third of what had been considered international ocean to individual nations because of the inability of international authorities to regulate ocean fisheries effectively (United Nations 1982). Exclusive Economic Zones (EEZs) were created that extend 200 nautical miles along the borders between the ocean and coastal states and extended full sovereign powers to these states to manage coastal fisheries so that they are not overexploited. Instead of reducing overharvesting, however, many national governments subsidized expansions of fishing fleets that increased the demand on coastal fisheries and placed more fishing areas in danger of overexploitation (Walters 1986). The models of fishery dynamics used by national governments tended to be relatively crude and led to inaccurate assessment of fishery stocks (Wilson 2002).

The Department of Fisheries and Oceans in Canada, for example, developed a model of stock regeneration for northern cod that scientists later found to be flawed (Harris 1990). Local cod fishers in Newfoundland raised serious questions in the late 1980s and predicted a near-term collapse, but the Canadian government refused to listen and assured doubters that its model was correct. In 1992, however, the cod stock collapsed and the Canadian government declared a moratorium on all fishing in Canadian waters. This has generated very substantial costs for local fishing villages dependent upon that stock, which they had earlier managed relatively effectively (Finlayson 1994; Finlayson and McCay 1998).

The capability of other large governmental bodies to make scientifically recommended policies related to fishing quotas has also been questioned. The European Union established a 2007 Fishing Quota for the eastern Baltic cod, but ignored the warning issued by the International Council for the Exploitation of the Seas (ICES). ICES had urged the European Union to skip a full year before authorizing *any* catch (Burton 2006). Thus the faith in the capability of very large-scale units to make better scientific judgments and implement them is not fully realized in regard to ocean fisheries, which, while not global in scope, are larger than most territorially based resources.

Problems have also been noted in the way the Clean Development Mechanism (CDM) authorized by the Kyoto Protocol is being implemented. Several CDM processes are involved. One CDM process is supposed to replace carbon-emitting energy production processes with "green energy production."

This process works approximately in this fashion: A developing country decides to forgo the construction of a power plant using coal as the energy source and emitting substantial greenhouse gases as a result. It plans to build a wind farm that is more "carbon friendly." The country applies for credit in the form of Certified Emissions Reductions (CERs) that it can sell to industrialized nations wishing to buy CERs as authorized by the Kyoto Protocol (Lohmann 2008). The income from selling the CERs can then, in principle, be allocated to the construction of the wind farm, which is more expensive as well as being carbon neutral.

The problem with this highly complemented and flexible system is that it can be gamed (Sovacool and Brown 2009). Only 300 of the thousands of CDM projects that are underway have received accreditation by the United Nations. As it turns out, a large proportion of the CERs relate to trifluoromethane, HFC-23, a greenhouse gas that is not associated with transportation or power generation but is used as a refrigerant—and is a highly profitable greenhouse gas to claim to have "averted." As Sovacool and Brown (2009) conclude, the CDM has unfortunately made HFC-23 abatement too profitable.

> The sale of carbon credits generated from CERs for HFC-23 has become far more valuable than its production in the first place. Manufacturers of HFC-23, responding to market demand for CERs, started producing it just to offset it. Researchers at Stanford University have calculated that, at a result, payments to refrigerant manufacturers and carbon market investors to governments and compliance buyers for HFC-23 credits have exceeded €4.7 *billion* when the costs of merely abating HFC-23 would have been about €100 *million*—a major distortion of the market. (Sovacool and Brown 2009, 14, citing Wara 2007 and Wara and Victor 2008)

Other CDM processes relate to efforts to decrease carbon emissions as a result of deforestation. But what exactly is deforestation? In the American West, the kind of fire that counts as "deforestation" is subject to considerable debate among public officials. Small fires may help prevent very large-scale forest fires in regions where the forest ecology has developed in a high-frequency, low-severity fire regime (Covington 2000; Fule et al. 2004; Odion and Hanson 2006).

The California Climate Action Registry,[11] for example, considers all thinning of forests to send carbon to the atmosphere even though thinning reduces the risk of an even greater fire burning down an entire stand. "If, by contrast, that same forest is not thinned and instead experiences a catastrophic fire, the C stock baseline is simply *reduced*, as if no CO_2 emissions had occurred during the fire" (Hurteau et al. 2008). Scientists criticize the carbon accounting methodology as a "one size fits all" policy that does not account for the diversity of ecosystems involved and may penalize actions that help restore forest ecosystems rather than destroy them (*ibid.*). As Boyd (2009, 3) reflects, "solving problems through centralized controls and global blue prints tends to create its own vulnerabilities in the long term."

Since the Bali round of negotiations held in December 2007, efforts to reduce emissions from deforestation and degradation (REDD) have been added to the portfolio of activities authorized under the Kyoto Protocol.

It is undoubtedly very important to recognize that forest ecosystems store an immense quantity of carbon, and that harvesting timber and converting forests to other uses is as important a source of greenhouse gas emissions as power production. Thus the scientific foundation for adopting REDD is quite strong. Designing REDD projects so that new projects do not just lead to further leakage is a substantial problem. Further, ensuring that the rights of indigenous people are at least protected, and ideally enhanced, as a result of support of their management of forest ecologies is a goal that is widely shared by social activists at multiple scales. Accomplishing this goal while expanding the amount of forested land in developing countries would be economically efficient but a difficult challenge.[12] Currently, there is considerable debate about this program, and too few projects have been adopted to make a serious evaluation of the possibilities and threats (see O'Sullivan 2008 and other chapters in Streck et al. 2008 and Corbera and Brown 2008).

The description in this section of problematic policies of large-scale governmental units related to climate change and other environmental issues is not meant to challenge the need for global policies related to climate change. The intent is to balance the major attention that has been given in the policy literature to the need for *global* solutions as the primary strategy for coping with climate change. Many criticisms have been made of policies adopted by smaller-scale private and governmental units as evidence that we must go global. Yet extensive research on institutions related to environmental policies has repeatedly shown that creative, effective, and efficient policies, as well as disasters, have been implemented at all scales. Dealing with the complexity of environmental problems can lead to "negative learning" by scientists and policymakers at all scales (Oppenheimer et al. 2008). Reliance on a single "solution" may be more of a problem than a solution (Pritchett and Woolcock 2003). It is important that we recognize that devising policies related to complex environmental processes is a grand challenge and that reliance on one scale to solve these problems is naïve.

Are There Too Many Actors Working on Climate Change?

One of the criticisms leveled at current efforts to reduce greenhouse gas emissions is that too many projects and activities are operating at multiple scales and that the system is chaotic. Unquestionably, many problems characterize the current efforts and many of these do relate to the lack of effective policies at an international level. Further, some of the projects that are overtly aimed at reducing greenhouse gas emissions may well be ineffective, too costly, and rewarding actors who are not genuinely interested in reducing the threat of climate change but are instead looking for opportunities to gain funds and search for minimal ways of meeting project objectives.

Overall, however, massive disagreements exist about how to achieve a global solution between those who urge a "cap and trade" approach and those who wish to see taxes placed on emissions. Further disagreements exist about how to allocate funds that are derived from large-scale policies. The likelihood of developing an effective, efficient, and fair system to reduce greenhouse gas emissions that can be rapidly initiated at the global level appears to be very low. Given the severity of the threat, simply waiting for resolution of these issues at a global level, without trying out policies at multiple scales because they lack a global scale, is not a reasonable stance.

As discussed above, the benefits from reduced greenhouse gas emissions are not just global in scope. The benefits are distributed across scales—from the household to the globe. Thus, because units smaller than the globe have sought to reduce emissions, at least some marginal reduction of greenhouse gas emissions is likely to result from projects undertaken at multiple scales while waiting for global policies to evolve. Doing nothing simply means increasing the level of greenhouse gases, emitted at an ever greater rate. While not yet the amount of reductions that climate scientists estimate is needed to avert calamity, reduction levels do appear to be growing in at least some parts of the world, which may provide examples to other regions of what can be done and what these actions cost. And better technologies for tracking CO_2 emissions are being developed (Normille 2009) that will help evaluate the effectiveness of all policies in the future.

Currently, it is important that we examine some of the key problems that have been identified as plaguing efforts to control greenhouse gas emissions. Recognition of problems is essential to start serious efforts to find methods to reduce them. The problems raised most frequently are leakage, inconsistent policies, free riding, and inadequate certification.

Leakage

One of the problems frequently identified with subnational projects aimed at reducing carbon emissions is leakage. Two types of leakage can occur from policies adopted at less than global scale: leakage between locations and market leakage (Ebeling 2008, 49–51). Leakage between locations occurs when an activity that would have taken place in X location is shifted to Y location because of a climate change project that occurs in X location. As discussed above, the EU efforts to reduce emissions from industrial producers may, in some cases, simply shift the emissions that would have been produced by a European chemical firm to another location in a developing country. There, the costs of production may be lower, but carbon is still emitted in the production of chemicals and in the transportation of the chemicals to European locations (Chomitz 2002). Similarly, farmers who are forced to leave a location because of a REDD project of planting trees may simply move to a new location and cut down the timber located there unless there are commitments that they must make related to funds they obtain and their activities are monitored for several years after the project is started.

Market leakage refers to changes in price structure that may occur as a result of restrictions placed on harvesting from forests. Such restrictions reduce the volume of timber and other forest products generated in one area. This stimulates an increase in the prices of these products. If everything goes well, higher prices encourage the intensification of agricultural and forest production in other areas, and they do not stimulate more deforestation. "In a less favorable scenario, particularly when land-use regulations are poorly enforced, higher prices provide an additional incentive to clear forests for timber or agriculture elsewhere, thereby reducing the net benefits of the climate mitigation project" (Ebeling 2008, 50).

Inconsistent Policies

Closely related to the problem of leakage is the problem of inconsistent policies. Industrial firms that are trying to develop new technologies to reduce greenhouse gas emissions may find it costly when policies vary in different regions. Potential sales of new technology are limited to areas where the technology fits the policies adopted, and these areas may not be large enough to generate sales warranting the investment in new technology.

Free Riding

Whenever actions taken by some individuals or organizations benefit a larger group, a risk always exists that some participants will free ride on the efforts of others and not contribute at all or not contribute an appropriate share. Currently, there are many governmental and private entities at multiple scales that are increasing their greenhouse gas emissions substantially—especially in the developing world—without adopting any policies to reduce emissions. This is a major problem. And current debates over who caused the great increase in the presence of greenhouse gases in the atmosphere in the first place, and thus who should be paying the most in the future, are legitimate debates at the same time that they may cover up a free-riding strategy by at least some of those involved.

Inadequate Certification

For policies adopted at any scale that provide diverse rewards for projects that reduce greenhouse gas emissions, there is a need for skilled personnel to certify that a project does indeed reduce ambient CO_2 by some specified amount over a defined time period. A very active new industry of "global consultants" has emerged. While many consultants do have good scientific training, the greatly increased need for certification has generated opportunities for at least some contractors lacking appropriate skills to earn money in the new "certification game." Sovacool and Brown (2009, 14) report on one study that evaluated 93 randomly chosen CDM projects and "found that in a majority of cases the consultants hired to validate CERs did not possess the requisite knowledge needed to approve projects, were overworked, did not follow instructions, and spent only a few hours evaluating each case."

What are We Learning?

Debating whether local and national efforts to reduce greenhouse gas emissions undermine global efforts or whether global efforts generate net costs rather than net benefits produces a lot of hot air but not necessarily better solutions. It is essential that we recognize (1) the complexity of causes of climate change; (2) the challenge of acquiring knowledge about causes and effects in a world that is changing rapidly; (3) the wide diversity of policies that can lead to reduced emissions but might also enable opportunistic efforts to obtain a flow of funds by appearing to reduce emissions while not having a real impact or, worse, effectively increasing rather than decreasing emissions; (4) the opportunities that major sources of funding open up for policy experiments if funds are also allocated to monitoring and evaluation of the benefits and costs of the experiments; and (5) that all policies adopted at any scale can generate errors, but that without trial and error, learning cannot occur.

Acknowledging the complexity of the problem, as well as the relatively recent agreement among scientists about the human causes of climate change, leads to recognition that waiting for effective policies to be established at the global level is unreasonable. Rather than only a global effort, it would be better to self-consciously adopt a polycentric approach to the problem of climate change in order to gain the benefits at multiple scales as well as to encourage experimentation and learning from diverse policies adopted at multiple scales. Let us turn to a discussion of what a polycentric approach means.

A Polycentric Approach to the Problem

The title of this paper is "A Polycentric Approach for Coping with Climate Change." I purposely chose the term "polycentric" for the title even though it has not previously been applied to the analysis of climate change. Colleagues associated with the Workshop in Political Theory and Policy Analysis at Indiana University have developed this approach over the years for the analysis of collective-action problems in urban areas that are characterized by diverse public goods and services best provided at multiple scales. Given that multiple benefits at diverse scales are generated from efforts taken to reduce greenhouse gas emissions, as discussed above, I thought it would be a useful approach to take with respect to global change. Let us briefly review the origin of the term.

During the 1950s, massive criticism was leveled at metropolitan areas across the United States and Europe because of the large number of small-, medium-, and large-scale governmental units operating at the same time. Scholars thought this was chaotic. Vincent Ostrom, Charles Tiebout, and Robert Warren wrote a classic article in 1961 entitled "The Organization of Government in Metropolitan Areas: A Theoretical Inquiry." The authors were trying to make scholars aware that a simple dichotomy between "the" market and "the" government was not a good scientific approach to the study of public economies. Further, "the" market is usually composed of many small-, medium-, and large-scale firms, and the expected efficiency of a market disappears if it is consolidated into a monopoly.

There is a lot to learn from economics about the dangers of allocating all capabilities to a single unit, even though one cannot apply *all* lessons derived from the analysis of market economies to the public sector. Drawing on the rich tradition of public sector development in the United States, the authors urged readers to think of the public sector as a polycentric *system* rather than a monocentric *hierarchy*. In a later essay, Vincent Ostrom (1999, 57) defined a polycentric order as "one where many elements are capable of making mutual adjustments for ordering their relationships with one another within a general system of rules where each element acts with independence of other elements." Opening up the discourse about the public sector enables one to analyze and measure how systems with diverse structures perform in the provision and production of different types of public goods.

The early theoretical work on polycentricity stimulated three decades of very intense research on governance of one of the major public goods for urban areas—that of providing public safety across a metropolitan region. Since these findings are not well known by scholars focusing on global change questions, a brief summary of the findings from this research program, as well as more recent studies of public education, is presented in Appendix A. In addition to the specific findings about the efficiency and effectiveness of diverse scales of provision of urban public goods presented in Appendix A, it is also useful to review the basic assumptions of a polycentric approach as applied to the study of urban areas. These are as follows:

1. Public goods and services differ substantially in regard to their production functions and their scale of effects.
2. Policy preferences tend to be more homogeneous within smaller units than across an entire metropolitan area.
3. Citizens who live in areas served by multiple jurisdictions learn more about the performance of any one jurisdiction by seeing or hearing about how problems are handled in other jurisdictions.
4. The presence of large numbers of potential producers of urban goods and services in a metropolitan area allows elected officials more effective choice of producers.
5. Multiple jurisdictions with different scopes and scales of organization allow citizens and officials more choice in selecting modes of providing and producing public goods to try to utilize the best available technology, to achieve economies and avoid diseconomies of scale, and improve performance over time.

6. Producers who must compete for contracts are more likely to search for innovative technologies, to encourage effective team production, as well as citizen coproduction, so as to enhance their own performance (V. Ostrom 2008a, 2008b; E. Ostrom, Parks, and Whitaker 1978).

Polycentric metropolitan regions tend to reduce opportunistic behavior even though no institutional arrangement can totally eliminate opportunism with respect to the provision and production of collective goods. Allowing citizens to form smaller-scale collective consumption units encourages face-to-face discussion and the achievement of common understanding. Creating larger collective consumption units reduces the strategic behavior of the wealthy trying to escape into tax havens where they could free ride on the tax contributions of citizens in other jurisdictions. Larger units also can more effectively cope with urban goods and services that have large-scale effects and real economies of scale.

Some readers of this paper will ask, What is the relevance of the polycentric approach for the analysis of *global* public goods? The initial relevance of the polycentric approach is the parallel between the earlier theoretical presumption that *only* the largest scale was relevant for the provision and production of public goods for metropolitan areas, and the contemporary presumption that only one scale is relevant for policies related to global public goods. Extensive empirical research found, however, that while large-scale units were part of effective governance of metropolitan areas, small and medium-scale units were also necessary components. An important lesson is that simply recommending a single governmental unit to solve global collective-action problems—because of global impacts—needs to be seriously rethought and the important role of smaller-scale effects recognized.

As discussed above, instead of the benefits derived from reducing greenhouse gases existing only at the global level, multiple benefits are created by diverse actions at multiple scales. Potential benefits are even generated at a household level. Better health is achieved by members of a household who bike to work rather than driving. Expenditures on heating and electricity may be reduced when investments are made in better construction of buildings, reconstruction of existing buildings, installation of solar panels, and many other efforts that families as well as private firms can make that pay off in the long run.

Further, the extensive empirical research on collective action discussed above has repeatedly identified a necessary central core of trust and reciprocity among those involved that is associated with successful levels of collective action. If the *only* policy related to climate change was adopted at the global scale, it would be particularly difficult to increase the trust that citizens and firms need to have that other citizens and firms located halfway around the globe are taking actions similar to those being taken "at home." When participants fear they are being "suckers" for taking costly actions while others free ride, more substantial effort is devoted to finding deceptive ways of appearing to reduce emissions while not doing so. A key problem is monitoring.

Diverse Monitoring Strategies

Relying only on preexisting levels of trust and reciprocity among those involved in collective action is not associated with long-term success. This is especially the case when new problems arise that groups have not previously faced. Rules must be enforced in some manner to achieve sustainable systems, but the question of how rules will *actually* be enforced is frequently ignored when a reform is proposed. Our current research on resource regimes is highly relevant (Gibson et al. 2000; Ostrom and Nagendra 2006). In efforts to enhance another large-scale collective good—biodiversity—all too many "comanaged paper parks" have been drafted in the home office of an overseas donor or even in a country's capital city only to be destroyed by illegal harvesting in the specified territory. While many agree that rule enforcement is necessary for creating a sustainable resource over time, considerable disagreement exists about who should be the monitors (see, e.g., Bruner et al. 2001; Wells and Brandon 1992). Simply employing a few guards who cannot get to know the terrain or the people living in an area has not been a successful strategy.

Most long-surviving resource regimes select some of their own monitors, who are accountable to the appropriators or are appropriators themselves and who keep an eye on resource conditions as well as on harvesting activities. By creating official positions for local monitors, a resource regime does not have to rely *only* on local community norms to sanction a rule breaker. The community creates an official position. In some systems, users rotate into this position so that everyone has a duty to be a monitor. In other systems, all participants contribute resources and they jointly hire monitors.

In an analysis of results from a study by the International Forestry Resources and Institutions (IFRI) research network of the conditions of forests used by 178 forest user groups located in 12 countries, Gibson, Williams, and Ostrom (2005) found that the level of local monitoring varies substantially across groups. One of the measures obtained in this study is the frequency with which a local group monitors and sanctions rule-breaking behavior in the forest. We examined the impact of this variable on appropriators' assessment of forest conditions (as well as on a forester's assessment). We also examined the impact of a group's social capital, the group's dependence on forest resources, and whether the group was formally organized or not. The result of the analysis is that regular monitoring by a local group is more important than the other three variables in enhancing forest conditions. Regardless of the levels of social capital, forest dependence, and formal organization, regular monitoring and sanctioning are strongly and statistically associated with better forest conditions (see Hayes and Ostrom 2005; Coleman 2009). Chhatre and Agrawal (2009) have just completed a major empirical study of how local autonomy in rule making and forest ownership are positively associated with increased carbon storage.

Some local utilities in the United States are now seeking to reduce energy consumption by developing local monitoring systems whose results are then reported on the bills that customers receive. The Sacramento Municipal Utility District, for example, has tried various techniques, including rebates for energy-saving appliances, but recently found a more effective technique.

> Last April (2008), it began sending out statements to 35,000 randomly selected customers, rating them according to their energy use compared with that of neighbors in 100 homes of similar size that used the same heating fuel. The customers were also compared with 20 neighbors who were especially efficient in saving energy.
>
> Customers who score high earned two smiley faces on their statements. "Good" conservation got a single smiley face. (Kaufman 2009)

The utility company conducted an initial assessment of this new strategy after using it for six months. The assessment found "that customers who received the personalized report reduced energy use by 2 percent more than those who got standard statements" (*ibid.*). Using various forms of competition among households and groups and feedback on who is doing the best at reducing energy use is a strategy for reducing emissions that is increasingly being adopted by college campuses, small cities, and utility firms around the country.

Contemporary psychological studies have found that framing problems related to resource use in a social context does affect actions. Schultz et al. (2007) and Mumford (2007) have conducted studies finding that messages containing social references are more effective in changing behavior than messages stressing factual information. For example, statements saying that "x% of guests in this hotel recycle towels," instead of specifying the amount of water saved when one recycles, lead to increased levels of recycling.

Complex, Multi-Level Systems to Cope with a Complex, Multi-Level Problem

Given that the recognition of the danger of climate change among citizens and public officials is still relatively recent, and given the debates about who is responsible for causing the problem and for finding solutions, one cannot expect that an effective polycentric system will be constructed in the near future. But given the slowness and conflict involved in achieving a global solution, recognizing the potential of building even more effective ways of reducing energy use at multiple levels is an important step forward.

Further, one of the important strategies for reducing the level of CO_2 in the atmosphere is developing more effective policies for protecting ecosystem services—particularly those related to carbon sequestration. Developing effective and adaptive programs, however, requires selecting appropriate areas and developing plans for leaving some areas untouched and for making major investments in the flora and fauna as well as the technological infrastructure of other areas (Michel 2009). This requires substantial investment in scientific modeling (Nelson et al. 2009). Fortunately, recent breakthroughs in using geographic information systems and in-depth knowledge of the biophysical settings to map ecological systems over time are beginning to provide the tools needed for more careful planning for improvements in ecological systems (Daily et al. 2009). The models, however, need to be developed at multiple scales and decision-making units so that they can then focus at diverse scales to determine which policies can be adopted to improve carbon sequestration in line with the ecology at that particular scale.

Given the complexity and changing nature of the problems involved in coping with climate change, there are no "optimal" solutions that can be used to make substantial reductions in the level of greenhouse gases emitted into the atmosphere. A major reduction in emissions is, however, needed. The advantage of a polycentric approach is that it encourages experimental efforts at multiple levels, as well as the development of methods for assessing the benefits and costs of particular strategies adopted in one type of ecosystem and comparing these with results obtained in other ecosystems. A strong commitment to finding ways of reducing individual emissions is an important element for coping with climate change. Building such a commitment, and the trust that others are also taking responsibility, can be more effectively undertaken in small- to medium-scale governance units that are linked through information networks and monitoring at all levels.

Acknowledgments

Report prepared for the WDR2010 Core Team, Development and Economics Research Group, World Bank, 1818 H Street NW, Washington, DC 20433. Thanks to Jimmy Walker for several discussions of the questions raised in this report, to Patty Lezotte for her excellent editing help, and to the National Science Foundation for research support.

Notes

This chapter was originally published as Policy Research Working Paper 5095, Background Paper to the 2010 World Development Report (Washington, DC: World Bank, October 2009).

1. This study also illustrates the importance of effective monitoring efforts. The U.S. Environmental Protection Agency (EPA) maintained the Inhalable Particle Monitoring Network from 1979 to 1983 for 61 metropolitan areas. The monitoring effort was not continued until the passing of the National Ambient Air Quality Standards for Particle Pollution in 1997. EPA then developed the Aerometric Information Retrieval System, which has continued the monitoring process. The maintenance of reliable, comparative information over time is a very important step in coping with large-scale externalities, both to assess who is complying with policies and to compare the effectiveness of diverse strategies in different units.

2. http://www.toronto.ca/environment/index.htm (accessed February 9, 2009).

3. A *Wikipedia* article on the London Congestion Charge (accessed February 9, 2009) reports that between 2003 and 2006, the CO_2 level in the city fell by 20 percent as a result of reduced traffic levels, better traffic flow, and improved

vehicle technology. The speed of traffic flow and the reliability of bus schedules have also been improved.

4. http://www.c40cities.org/ (accessed February 1, 2009).

5. Global Warming Solutions Act of 2006, Calif. Assembly Bill 32.

6. http://www.dep.state.fl.us/climatechange/ (accessed June 27, 2008).

7. http://rggi.org/home/ (accessed February 7, 2009).

8. http://www.climatetrust.org/solicitations_RGGI.php.

9. Emphasis on top-down planning is certainly not the way that Europe developed. Since the eleventh century, thousands of independent water boards were established in the delta of the Rhine River with their own rules and physical structures. These water boards drained the swampy land and protected the land from being inundated except during extreme storms (Toonen 1996; Andersen 2001). In Switzerland, alpine peasants devised a variety of private and common-property systems to earn income from a diverse ecology (Netting 1981). More than 1,000 free cities with their own charters and legal traditions flourished in Europe during the Middle Ages and were the foundation for modern constitutional democracies (Berman 1983).

10. See Clark (2006) for a review of fisheries-related policies adopted by national governments that initially led to perverse outcomes—some of which were eventually reversed.

11. California Climate Action Registry, *Forest Sector Protocol* (2007), http://www.climateregistry.org/PROTOCOLS (accessed January 15, 2009).

12. John Vidal, in an article in *The Guardian* (October 17, 2008), stressed that recognizing forest community rights would be a more cost-effective mechanism for reducing emissions than paying organizations to plant trees. "A study by Jeffrey Hatcher, an analyst with Rights and Resources in Washington, found that it costs about \$3.50 (€2) per hectare to recognise forest people's land. The costs of protecting forests under REDD have been estimated at about €2,000 per hectare" (https://www.theguardian.com/environment/2008/oct/17/forests-endangeredhabitats) (accessed October 23, 2008).

References

Agrawal, Arun. 2000. "Small Is Beautiful, but Is Larger Better? Forest-Management Institutions in the Kumaon Himalaya, India." In *People and Forests: Communities, Institutions, and Governance*, ed. Clark Gibson, Margaret McKean, and Elinor Ostrom, 57–86. Cambridge, MA: MIT Press.

———. 2002. "Common Resources and Institutional Sustainability." In *The Drama of the Commons*, National Research Council, Committee on the Human Dimensions of Global Change, ed. Elinor Ostrom, Thomas Dietz, Nives Dolšak, Paul C. Stern, Susan Stonich, and Elke Weber, 41–85. Washington, DC: National Academies Press.

———. 2005. *Environmentality: Technologies of Government and Political Subjects.* Durham, NC: Duke University Press.

———. 2008. "The Role of Local Institutions in Adaptation to Climate Change." Report submitted to the World Bank, Washington, DC.

Andersen, M. S. 2001. *Economic Instruments and Clean Water: Why Institutions and Policy Design Matters.* Paris: OECD.

Baer, Paul, John Harte, Barbara Haya, et al. 2000. "Equity and Greenhouse Gas Responsibility." *Science* 289(5488) (September 29): 2287.

Bala, G., K. Caldeira, M. Wickett, T. J. Phillips, D. B. Lobell, C. Delire, and A. Mirin. 2007. "Combined Climate and Carbon-Cycle Effects of Large-Scale Deforestation." *Proceedings of the National Academy of Sciences* 104(16): 6550–55.

Baland, Jean-Marie, and Jean-Philippe Platteau. [1996] 2000. *Halting Degradation of Natural Resources: Is There a Role for Rural Communities?* New York: Oxford University Press.

Barnes, Peter. 2008. *Climate Solutions: A Citizen's Guide.* White River Junction, VT: Chelsea Green Publishing.

Barrett, Scott. 2003. "Global Climate Change and the Kyoto Protocol." In *Environment and Statecraft: The Strategy of Environmental Treaty-Making*, ed. Scott Barrett, 359–98. Oxford: Oxford University Press.

Berman, Harold J. 1983. *Law and Revolution: The Formation of the Western Legal Tradition.* Cambridge, MA: Harvard University Press.

Betsill, Michele M. 2001. "Mitigating Climate Change in US Cities: Opportunities and Obstacles." *Local Environment* 6(4): 393–406.

Bierbaum, Rosina M. 2008. "Energy and Climate Change." *Bulletin of the American Academy* 61(2) (Winter): 32–36.

Botsen, W. J. W., J. M. Gowdy, and J. C. J. M. Van den Bergh. 2008. "Cumulative CO_2 Emissions: Shifting International Responsibilities for Climate Debt." *Climate Policy* 8: 569–76.

Boyd, Emily. 2009. "Governing the Clean Development Mechanism: Global Rhetoric versus Local Realities in Carbon Sequestration Projects." *Environment and Planning A* 41: 2380–95.

Bruner, Aaron, Raymond Gullison, Richard Rice, and Gustavo da Fonseca. 2001. "Effectiveness of Parks in Protecting Tropical Biodiversity." *Science* 291(5501): 125–29.

Brondizio, Eduardo S., and Emilio F. Moran. 2008. "Human Dimensions of Climate Change: The Vulnerability of Small Farmers in the Amazon." *Philosophical Transactions of the Royal Society B* 363 (February): 1803–9.

Burris, Mark W., and Xu Lei. 2006. "Potential Single-Occupancy Vehicle Demand for High-Occupancy Vehicle Lanes: Results from State-Preference Survey of Travelers in High Occupancy Toll Corridors." *Transportation Research Record* 1960: 108–18.

Burton, A. 2006. "What Future for Fish." *Frontiers in Ecology and the Environment* 4(1): 508.

Camerer, Colin F. 2003. *Behavioral Game Theory: Experiments in Strategic Interaction*. Princeton, NJ: Princeton University Press.

Carraro, C. 2003. *Governing the Global Environment.* Cheltenham, UK: Edward Elgar.

Chhatre, Ashwini, and Arun Agrawal. 2009. "Trade-Offs and Synergies between Carbon Storage and Livelihood Benefits from Forest Commons." *Proceedings of the National Academy of Sciences*, early edition, http://www.pnas.org/content/early/2009/10/05/0905308106.

Chomitz, K. M. 2002. "Baseline, Leakage and Measurement Issues: How Do Forestry and Energy Projects Compare?" *Climate Policy* 2: 35–49.

Clark, Colin W. 2006. *The Worldwide Crisis in Fisheries: Economic Models and Human Behavior.* Cambridge: Cambridge University Press.

Coleman, Eric. 2009. "Institutional Factors Affecting Ecological Outcomes in Forest Management." *Journal of Policy Analysis and Management* 28(1): 122–46.

Corbera, Esteve, and Katrina Brown. 2008. "Building Institutions to Trade Ecosystem Services: Marketing Forest Carbon in Mexico." *World Development* 36(10) (October): 1956–79.

Costanza, Robert, John Cumberland, Herman Daley, et al. 1997. *An Introduction to Ecological Economics.* Boca Raton, FL: St. Lucie Press.

Covington, W. W. 2000. "Helping Western Forests Heal." *Nature* 408: 135–36.

Cox, James C., Daniel Friedman, and Steven Gjerstad. 2007. "A Tractable Model of Reciprocity and Fairness." *Games and Economic Behavior* 59: 17–45.

Crawford, Sue E. S., and Elinor Ostrom. 2005. "A Grammar of Institutions." In *Understanding Institutional Diversity*, Elinor Ostrom, 137–74. Princeton, NJ: Princeton University Press. Originally published in *American Political Science Review* 89(3) (September 1995): 582–600.

Daily, Gretchen C., Stephen Polasky, Joshua Goldstein, et al. 2009. "Ecosystem Services in Decision Making: Time to Deliver." *Frontier in Ecology and the Environment* 7(1): 21–28.

Dasgupta, Partha. 2001. *Human Well-Being and the National Environment.* Oxford: Oxford University Press.

Dellink, Rob, Thijs Dekker, Michael den Elzen, et al. 2009. "Sharing the Burden of Adaptation Financing." Amsterdam: Institute for Environmental Studies Newsletter, January.

den Elzen, M. G. J., M. Schaeffer, and P. L. Lucas. 2005. "Differentiating Future Commitments on the Basis of Countries' Relative Historical Responsibility for Climate Change: Uncertainties in the 'Brazilian Proposal' in the Context of a Policy Implementation." *Climate Change* 71: 277–301.

Dietz, Thomas, Elinor Ostrom, and Paul Stern. 2003. "The Struggle to Govern the Commons." *Science* 302(5652): 1907–12.

Eadson, Will. 2008. "Climate Change Mitigation in Local Area Agreements: An Enforced Lack of Ambition?" *People, Place & Policy Online* 2/3: 140–50.

Ebeling, Johannes. 2008. "Risks and Criticisms of Forestry-Based Climate Change Mitigation and Carbon Trading." In *Climate Change and Forests: Emerging Policy and Market Opportunities*, ed. Charlotte Streck, Robert O'Sullivan, Toby Janson-Smith, and Richard Tarasofsky, 43–58. London: Chatham House.

Engel, Kirsten H. 2006. "State and Local Climate Change Initiatives: What Is Motivating State and Local Governments to Address a Global Problem and What Does This Say about Federalism and Environmental Law?" Discussion Paper 06–36. Tucson: University of Arizona, James E. Rogers College of Law, Arizona Legal Studies.

European Environmental Agency (EEA). 2006. *Greenhouse Gas Emission Trends and Projections in Europe 2006.* Luxembourg: Office for Official Publications of the European Communities. EEA Report No. 9, ISSN 1725–9177.

Fehr, Ernst, and Simon Gächter. 2000. "Fairness and Retaliation: The Economics of Reciprocity." *Journal of Economic Perspectives* 14(3): 159–81.

———. 2002. "Altruistic Punishment in Humans." *Nature* 415: 137–40.

Fehr, Ernst, and Andreas Leibbrandt. 2008. "Cooperativeness and Impatience in the Tragedy of the Commons." IZA Discussion Paper 3625, University of Zurich.

Fehr, Ernst, and Bettina Rockenbach. 2003. "Detrimental Effects of Sanctions on Human Altruism." *Nature* 422 (March): 137–40.

Fehr, Ernst, and Klaus Schmidt. 1999. "A Theory of Fairness, Competition, and Cooperation." *Quarterly Journal of Economics* 114(3): 817–68.

Finlayson, A. Christopher. 1994. *Fishing for Truth: A Sociological Analysis of Northern Cod Stock Assessment from 1977–1990.* St. Johns: Memorial University of Newfoundland, Newfoundland Institution of Social and Economic Research.

Finlayson, A. Christopher, and Bonnie J. McCay. 1998. "Crossing the Threshold of Ecosystem Resilience: The Commercial Extension of Northern Cod." In *Linking Social and Ecological Systems: Management Practices and Social Mechanisms for Building Resilience*, ed. Fikret Berkes and Carl Folke, 311–38. Cambridge: Cambridge University Press.

Frey, Bruno S. 2005. "Beyond Traditional Borders: A New Proposal for Federalism." *The Economists' Voice* 2(2): article 9, https://works.bepress.com/bruno_s_frey/1/.

Frohlich, Norman, and Joe A. Oppenheimer. 1992. *Choosing Justice: An Experimental Approach to Ethical Theory.* Berkeley: University of California Press.

Fule, P. Z., J. E. Crouse, A. E. Cocke, et al. 2004. "Changes in Canopy Fuels and Potential Fire Behavior, 1880–2040." *Ecological Modeling* 175: 231–48.

Fuller, Merrian C., Stephen C. Portis, and Daniel M. Kammen. 2009. "Toward a Low-Carbon Economy: Municipal Financing for Energy Efficiency and Solar Power." *Environment* 51(1): 22–32.

Gibson, Clark, Margaret McKean, and Elinor Ostrom, eds. 2000. *People and Forests: Communities, Institutions, and Governance.* Cambridge, MA: MIT Press.

Gibson, Clark, John Williams, and Elinor Ostrom. 2005. "Local Enforcement and Better Forests." *World Development* 33(2): 273–84.

Hardin, Garrett. 1968. "The Tragedy of the Commons." *Science* 162: 1243–48.

Harris, L. 1990. *Independent Review of the State of the Northern Cod Stock*. Prepared for The Honourable Thomas Siddon, Minister of Fisheries. Ottawa: Communications Directorate, Department of Fisheries and Oceans.

Hayes, Tanya, and Elinor Ostrom. 2005. "Conserving the World's Forests: Are Protected Areas the Only Way?" *Indiana Law Review* 38(3): 595–617.

Hess, Charlotte, and Elinor Ostrom, eds. 2007. *Understanding Knowledge as a Commons: From Theory to Practice*. Cambridge, MA: MIT Press.

Hurteau, Matthew D., George W. Koch, and Bruce A. Hungate. 2008. "Carbon Protection and Fire Risk Reduction: Toward a Full Accounting of Forest Carbon Offsets." *Frontiers in Ecological Environment* 6(9): 493–98.

Intergovernmental Panel on Climate Change. 2007. *Climate Change 2007: Mitigation of Climate Change*. Cambridge: Cambridge University Press.

Kates, Robert W., and Thomas J. Wilbanks. 2003. "Making the Global Local: Responding to Climate Change Concerns from the Ground Up." *Environment* 45(3): 12–23.

Kaufman, Leslie. 2009. "A Desire to Keep Up with Neighbors is Spurring Conservation." *New York Times*, January 30.

Lichbach, Mark Irving. 1996. *The Cooperator's Dilemma*. Ann Arbor: University of Michigan Press.

Lohmann, L. 2008. "Carbon Trading, Climate Justice and the Production of Ignorance: Ten Examples." *Development* 51(3): 359–65.

Luce, R. Duncan, and Howard Raiffa. 1957. *Games and Decisions: Introduction and Critical Survey*. New York: Wiley.

Matthews, H. D., and K. Caldeira. 2008. "Stabilizing Climate Requires Near Zero Emissions." *Geophysical Research Letters* 35: 1–5.

McKean, Margaret A. 2000. "Common Property: What Is It, What Is It Good For, and What Makes It Work?" In *People and Forests: Communities, Institutions, and Governance*, ed. Clark C. Gibson, Margaret A. McKean, and Elinor Ostrom, 27–55. Cambridge, MA: MIT Press.

Meserve, Richard A. 2008. "An Introduction to Energy and Climate Change." *Bulletin of the American Academy* (Winter): 29–32.

Michel, David. 2009. "Foxes, Hedgehogs, and Greenhouse Governance: Knowledge, Uncertainty, and International Policy-Making in a Warming World." *Applied Energy* 86: 258–64.

Milinski, Manfred, Dirk Semmann, and Hans-Jürgen Krambeck. 2002. "Reputation Helps Solve the 'Tragedy of the Commons.'" *Nature* 415 (January 24): 424–26.

Miller, Clark A. 2004. "Climate Science and the Making of a Global Political Order." In *States of Knowledge: The Coproduction of Science and Social Order*, ed. Sheila Jasanoff, 46–66. New York: Routledge.

Mintrom, Michael. 2000. *Policy Entrepreneurs and School Choice.* Washington, DC: Georgetown University Press.

Mumford, G. 2007. "Psychology's Ability to Curb Energy Use." *Monitor on Psychology* 38(11): 20–21.

Najam, A., S. Huq, and Y. Sokona. 2003. "Climate Negotiations beyond Kyoto: Developing Countries Concerns and Interests." *Climate Policy* 3: 221–31.

Nelson, Erik, Guillermo Mendoza, James Regetz, et al. 2009. "Modeling Multiple Ecosystem Services, Biodiversity Conservation, Commodity Production, and Tradeoffs at Landscape Scales." *Frontiers in Ecology and the Environment* 7(1): 4–11.

Nelson, Erik, Stephen Polasky, David J. Lewis, et al. 2008. "Efficiency of Incentives to Jointly Increase Carbon Sequestration and Species Conservation on a Landscape." *Proceedings of the National Academy of Sciences* 105(28): 9471–76.

Netting, Robert McC. 1981. *Balancing on an Alp: Ecological Change and Continuity in a Swiss Mountain Community.* New York: Cambridge University Press.

NRC (National Research Council). 1986. *Proceedings of the Conference on Common Property Resource Management.* Washington, DC: National Academies Press.

———. 2002. *The Drama of the Commons.* Committee on the Human Dimensions of Global Change. Elinor Ostrom, Thomas Dietz, Nives Dolšak, Paul Stern, Susan Stonich, and Elke Weber, eds. Washington, DC: National Academies Press.

Normille, Dennis. 2009. "Tracking CO_2's Comings and Goings from Space." *Science* 323 (January 16): 325.

Odion, D. C., and C. T. Hanson. 2006. "Fire Severity in Conifer Forests of the Sierra Nevada, California." *Ecosystems* 9: 1177–89.

Olson, Mancur. 1965. *The Logic of Collective Action: Public Goods and the Theory of Groups.* Cambridge, MA: Harvard University Press.

Oppenheimer, Michael, Brian C. O'Neill, and Mort Webster. 2008. "Negative Learning." *Climatic Change* 89: 155–72.

Opschoor, Johannes Baptist, K. Button, and P. Nijkamp, eds. 1999. *Environmental Economics and Development.* Cheltenham, UK: Edward Elgar.

Ostrom, Elinor. 1990. *Governing the Commons: The Evolution of Institutions for Collective Action.* New York: Cambridge University Press.

———. 1992. "The Rudiments of a Theory of the Origins, Survival, and Performance of Common-Property Institutions." In *Making the Commons Work: Theory, Practice, and Policy*, ed. Daniel W. Bromley et al., 293–318. San Francisco, CA: ICS Press.

———. 1998. "A Behavioral Approach to the Rational Choice Theory of Collective Action." *American Political Science Review* 92(1): 1–22.

———. 2001. "Reformulating the Commons." In *Protecting the Commons: A Framework for Resource Management in the Americas*, ed. Joanna Burger,

Elinor Ostrom, Richard Norgaard, David Policansky, and Bernard Goldstein, 17–41. Washington, DC: Island Press.

———. 2005. *Understanding Institutional Diversity.* Princeton, NJ: Princeton University Press.

———. 2007. "A Diagnostic Approach for Going beyond Panaceas." *Proceedings of the National Academy of Sciences* 104: 15181–87.

Ostrom, Elinor, Roy Gardner, and James Walker. 1994. *Rules, Games, and Common-Pool Resources*. Ann Arbor: University of Michigan Press.

Ostrom, Elinor, and Harini Nagendra. 2006. "Insights on Linking Forests, Trees, and People from the Air, on the Ground, and in the Laboratory." *Proceedings of the National Academy of Sciences* 103(51): 19224–31.

Ostrom, Elinor, Roger B. Parks, and Gordon P. Whitaker. 1978. *Patterns of Metropolitan Policing.* Cambridge, MA: Ballinger.

Ostrom, Vincent. 1999. "Polycentricity—Part 1." In *Polycentricity and Local Public Economies*, ed. Michael McGinnis, 52–74. Ann Arbor: University of Michigan Press.

———. 2008a. *The Intellectual Crisis in American Public Administration.* 3rd ed. Tuscaloosa: University of Alabama Press.

———. 2008b. *The Political Theory of a Compound Republic: Designing the American Experiment.* 3rd ed. Lanham, MD: Lexington Books.

Ostrom, Vincent, Charles M. Tiebout, and Robert Warren. 1961. "The Organization of Government in Metropolitan Areas: A Theoretical Inquiry." *American Political Science Review* 55(4) (December): 831–42.

O'Sullivan, Robert. 2008. "Reducing Emissions from Deforestation in Developing Countries." In *Climate Change and Forests: Emerging Policy and Market Opportunities*, ed. Charlotte Streck, Robert O'Sullivan, Toby Janson-Smith, and Richard Tarasofsky, 179–90. London: Chatham House.

Paavola, Jouni. 2008a. "Science and Social Justice in the Governance of Adaptation to Climate Change." *Environmental Politics* 17(4): 644–59.

———. 2008b. "Governing Atmospheric Sinks: The Architecture of Entitlements in the Global Commons." *International Journal of the Commons* 2(2): 313–36.

Pope, C. Arden, Majid Ezzati, and Douglas W. Dockery. 2009. "Fine-Particulate Air Pollution and Life Expectancy in the United States." *New England Journal of Medicine* 360(4): 376–86.

Posner, Eric A., and Cass Sunstein. 2008. "Justice and Climate Change." Discussion Paper 08–04. Cambridge, MA: Harvard University Project on International Climate Agreements.

Poteete, Amy, Marco Janssen, and Elinor Ostrom. 2010. *Working Together: Collective Action, the Commons, and Multiple Methods in Practice.* (Particularly relevant is chapter 9.)

Pritchett, Lant, and Michael Woolcock. 2003. "Solutions When the Solution Is the Problem: Arraying the Disarray in Development." *World Development* 35(3): 435–61.

Rothstein, Bo. 1998. *Just Institutions Matter: The Moral and Political Logic of the Universal Welfare State*. Cambridge: Cambridge University Press.

———. 2005. *Social Traps and the Problem of Trust.* Cambridge: Cambridge University Press.

Sandler, Todd. 1997. *Global Challenges: An Approach to Environmental, Political and Economic Problems.* Cambridge: Cambridge University Press.

———. 2004. *Global Collective Action.* Cambridge: Cambridge University Press.

Sandler, Todd, and Daniel G. Arce M. 2003. "Pure Public Goods versus Commons." *Land Economics* 79(3): 355–68.

Schelling, Thomas C. 1978. *Micromotives and Macrobehavior*. New York: Norton.

Schlager, Edella. 1994. "Fishers' Institutional Responses to Common-Pool Resource Dilemmas." In *Rules, Games, and Common-Pool Resources*, ed. Elinor Ostrom, Roy Gardner, and James M. Walker, 247–66. Ann Arbor: University of Michigan Press.

Schlager, Edella, William Blomquist, and Shui Yan Tang. 1994. "Mobile Flows, Storage and Self-Organized Institutions for Governing Common-Pool Resources." *Land Economics* 70(3) (August): 294–317.

Schlager, Edella, and Elinor Ostrom. 1992. "Property-Rights Regimes and Natural Resources: A Conceptual Analysis." *Land Economics* 68(3) (August): 249–69.

Schultz, P., J. Nolan, R. Cialdini, et al. 2007. "The Constructive, Destructive, and Reconstructive Power of Social Norms." *Psychological Science* 18(5): 429–34.

Sen, Amartya. 1977. "Rational Fools: A Critique of the Behavioral Foundations of Economic Theory." *Philosophy and Public Affairs* 6(4): 317–44.

Sovacool, Benjamin K. 2008. "The Best of Both Worlds: Environmental Federalism and the Need for Federal Action on Renewal Energy and Climate Change." *Stanford Environmental Law Journal* 27: 397–473.

Sovacool, Benjamin K., and Marilyn A. Brown. 2009a. "Addressing Climate Change: Global and Local?" In *Generating Electricity in a Carbon Constrained World*, ed. Fereidoon P. Sioshansi. New York: Elsevier.

———. 2009b. "Scaling the Policy Response to Climate Change." *Policy and Society* 27(4): 317–28.

Stavins, Robert. 1997. "Policy Instruments for Climate Change: How Can National Governments Address a Global Problem?" *University of Chicago Legal Forum*, volume 1997: Rethinking Environmental Protection for the 21st Century, 293–329.

Stern, Nicholas. 2007. *The Economics of Climate Change: The Stern Review.* Cambridge: Cambridge University Press.

Streck, Charlotte, Robert O'Sullivan, Toby Janson-Smith, and Richard Tarosofsky, eds. 2008. *Climate Change and Forests: Emerging Policy and Market Opportunities.* London: Chatham House.

Toonen, Theo A.J. 1996. "On the Administrative Condition of Politics: Administrative Transformation in the Netherlands." *West European Politics* 19(3): 609–32.

UN-Habitat. 2008. *Cities and Climate Change Adaptation*. Prepared for the UN-Habitat Donors Meeting, Seville, October 15–16, 2008.

United Nations. 1982. *Final Act of the Third Conference on the Law of the Seas*. Montenegro Bay, Jamaica: United Nations.

Vandenberg, Michael P., and Anne C. Steinemann. 2007. "The Carbon-Neutral Individual." *New York University Law Review* 82 (December): 1673–741.

Vatn, Arild. 2005. *Institutions and the Environment*. Cheltenham, UK: Edward Elgar.

Wade, Robert. 1994. *Village Republics: Economic Conditions for Collective Action in South India*. San Francisco, CA: ICS Press.

Walters, Carl J. 1986. *Adaptive Management of Renewable Resources*. New York: Macmillan.

Wara, Michael. 2007. "Is the Global Carbon Market Working?" *Nature* 445 (February 8): 595–96.

Wara, Michael, and David G. Victor. 2008. "A Realistic Policy on International Carbon Offsets." Working Paper 74. Stanford, CA: Stanford University Program on Energy and Sustainable Development.

Wells, Michael, and Katrina Brandon. 1992. *People and Parks: Linking Protected Area Management with Local Communities*. Washington, DC: World Bank.

Wiener, Jonathan B. 2007. "Think Globally, Act Globally: The Limits of Local Climate Policies." *University of Pennsylvania Law Review* 155: 1961–79.

Wilson, Doug. 2006. "Predictions about European Commons." *Common Property Resource Digest* 77: 7–8.

Wilson, James. 2002. "Scientific Uncertainty, Complex Systems, and the Design of Common-Pool Institutions." In *The Drama of the Commons*, National Research Council, Committee on the Human Dimensions of Global Change, ed. Elinor Ostrom, Thomas Dietz, Nives Dolšak, Paul C. Stern, Susan Stonich, and Elke U. Weber, 327–59. Washington, DC: National Academies Press.

Wilson, James, James Acheson, Mark Metcalfe, and Peter Kleban. 1994. "Chaos, Complexity, and Community Management of Fisheries." *Marine Policy* 18: 291–305.

Wilson, James, Liying Yan, and Carl Wilson. 2007. "The Precursors of Governance in the Maine Lobster Fishery." *Proceedings of the National Academy of Sciences* 104(39): 15212–17.

APPENDIX A

A Brief Overview of the Studies of Polycentric Provision of Public Goods in Metropolitan Areas

Among the major public goods provided at an urban level are public safety and education. During the 1970s and 1980s, in response to concerns about police and school effectiveness, proposals to slash the number of police departments and school districts serving urban and rural areas of the United States were placed on the national agenda. Underlying these proposals was the assumption that "bigger is always better." Some proposals recommended the reduction of the more than 40,000 police departments that then existed in the United States to around 400 police departments for the entire country. Other recommendations proposed massive consolidation of school districts, and many efforts to achieve this consolidation were successful even though voters did not approve most of these administrative reforms. *No systematic empirical evidence supported reform proposals related to moving the provision of public goods from smaller-scale units to larger governments.* This appendix provides a brief overview of the findings from a major set of studies conducted by researchers associated with the Workshop in Political Theory and Policy Analysis at Indiana University regarding the polycentric provision of policing in metropolitan areas of the United States and a very brief overview of more recent studies related to other urban public goods.

Polycentricity and Police

Small and Medium-Size Police Agencies are More Effective in Producing Direct Services

One of the first sets of studies measured the performance of diversely sized police agencies serving similar communities in the Indianapolis, Chicago, St. Louis, Rochester, and Tampa–St. Petersburg metropolitan areas. The severe challenge of measuring police performance was met by collecting performance data from interviews with a random sample of households served by small, medium-size, and large departments. Information was obtained about victimization, willingness to call the police, speed of police response, amount of police follow-up, satisfaction levels with police contacts, and general evaluations of the quality of policing in a neighborhood. By studying matched neighborhoods with similar service conditions, we controlled for many of the other factors that can be expected to affect performance.

The consistent finding from this series of studies was that small and medium-size police departments perform more effectively, and frequently at lower costs, than large police departments serving similar neighborhoods (see McGinnis 1999). Victimization rates tend to be lower, police response tends to be faster, citizens tend to be more willing to call the police, citizens tend to more positively evaluate specific contacts with the police, and citizens tend to rate police higher across a series of evaluative questions.

Small Police Agencies Arrange for Indirect Services from Large Police Agencies

In our major study of police organization in 80 metropolitan areas (Ostrom et al. 1978), a total of 1,159 direct-service producers were found to produce services directly for the residents in the areas. Most of these agencies produced general area patrol, traffic patrol, accident investigation, and burglary investigation services. In regard to indirect services, we found that 70 percent of the direct-service producers also produced their own radio communications, but only a small proportion of any of the direct-service producers produced the other indirect services, such as crime labs or entry-level training. In all 80 Standard Metropolitan Statistical Areas, indirect services were made available to *all* direct-service producers.

Police Performance Enhanced in Metropolitan Areas with Larger Numbers of Police Agencies

In order to examine the effect of interorganizational arrangements on police performance, we relied on measures of performance such as the allocation of police personnel to on-the-street assignments and the relative efficiency of agencies in producing response capacity and solving crime. For each of the 80 metropolitan areas, we calculated the number of producers of each type of service (multiplicity) and the proportion of the population being served by the largest producer of each type of service (dominance). Metropolitan areas with low scores in multiplicity and high scores in dominance come closest to approximating the "consolidated" model. Metropolitan areas with high scores in multiplicity and low scores in dominance come closest to approximating the "fragmented" metropolitan area so strongly criticized in the policy literature.

We found a distinct difference in the availability of sworn officers to conduct patrols in the metropolitan areas depending upon the structure of interorganizational arrangements. While more officers per capita were employed in the most consolidated areas, a lower percentage of these officers were actually assigned to patrol divisions in these metropolitan areas. One-third more officers were required in the most consolidated metropolitan areas to place the *same* number of officers on patrol as compared with the least consolidated metropolitan areas. Citizens living in the most fragmented metropolitan areas received more police presence on the streets for their tax expenditures than did citizens living in the most consolidated areas (Parks 1985).

Polycentricity and Other Urban Public Goods

Other research has been undertaken since the early police studies that strongly supports the findings of those studies. In addition to the research on police, scholars have conducted rigorous empirical research that has challenged the presumptions that larger public school districts achieve higher performance (Hanushek 1986; Teske et al. 1993) and that fragmentation of governments leads to higher costs (Dilorenzo 1983; Schneider 1986; Boyne 1992), and that has provided further insights into the way local governments are constituted (Oakerson and Parks 1989; Stephens and Wikstrom 2000). As a result of extensive empirical and theoretical research, the presumed self-evident truth that constructing one government for each metropolitan area is the best way to achieve efficiency and equity has slowly been replaced by a recognition that judging "structure directly on the single criterion of uniformity contributes little to the advancement of research or reform" (Oakerson 1999, 117). Instead of a single best design that would have to cope with the wide variety of problems faced in different localities, a polycentric theory generates core principles that can help in the design of effective local institutions when used by informed and interested citizens and public officials.

In his conclusion to an in-depth study of the adverse effects of urban consolidation efforts in the United States and Canada during the last century, Andrew Sancton (2000, 167) reflected that:

> Municipalities are more than just providers of services. They are the democratic mechanisms through which territorially based communities of people govern themselves at a local level. . . . Those who would force municipalities to amalgamate with each other invariably claim that their motive is to make municipalities stronger. Such an approach—however well-intentioned—erodes the foundations of our liberal democracies because it undermines the notion that there can be forms of self-government that exist outside the institutions of the central government. . . .

Thus scholars, public officials, and citizens who are concerned with solving collective-action problems effectively, equitably, and efficiently, recognize the importance of authorizing citizens to constitute their own local jurisdictions and associations using the knowledge and experience they have about the public problems they face.

References to Appendix A

Boyne, G. 1992. "Local Government Structure and Performance: Lessons from America." *Public Administration* 70: 333–57.

Dilorenzo, T. 1983. "Economic Competition and Political Competition: An Empirical Note." *Public Choice* 40: 203–209.

Hanushek, E. A. 1986. "The Economics of Schooling: Production and Efficiency in Public Schools." *Journal of Economic Literature* 24: 1141–77.

McGinnis, Michael, ed. 1999. *Polycentricity and Local Public Economies: Readings from the Workshop in Political Theory and Policy Analysis.* Ann Arbor: University of Michigan Press.

Oakerson, Ronald. 1999. *Governing Local Public Economies: Creating the Civic Metropolis.* Oakland, CA: ICS Press.

Oakerson, Ronald, and Roger Parks. 1989. "Local Government Constitutions: A Different View of Metropolitan Governance." *American Review of Public Administration* 19(4): 279–84.

Ostrom, Elinor, Roger Parks, and Gordon Whitaker. 1978. *Patterns of Metropolitan Policing.* Cambridge, MA: Ballinger.

Parks, Roger. 1985. "Metropolitan Structure and Systemic Performance: The Case of Police Service Delivery." In *Policy Implementation in Federal and Unitary Systems*, ed. Kenneth Hanf and Theo A. J. Toonen, 161–91. Dordrecht, the Netherlands: Martinus Nijhoff.

Sancton, Andrew. 2000. *The Assault on Local Government.* Montreal: McGill-Queen's University Press.

Schneider, Mark. 1986. "Fragmentation and the Growth of Government." *Public Choice* 48: 255–63.

Stephens, G. R., and N. Wikstrom. 2000. *Metropolitan Government and Governance: Theoretical Perspectives, Empirical Analysis, and the Future.* New York: Oxford University Press.

Teske, Paul, Mark Schneider, Michael Mintrom, and Samuel Best. 1993. "Establishing the Micro Foundations of a Macro Theory: Information, Movers, and the Competitive Local Market for Public Goods." *American Political Science Review* 87(3): 702–13.

5

Advantages of a Polycentric Approach to Climate Change Policy

DANIEL H. COLE

The lack of progress in global climate change negotiations has spurred scholars to examine workable, subglobal policies to reduce anthropogenic emissions of greenhouse gases (GHGs). The late Elinor Ostrom led the way in a report she authored in 2009 for the World Bank, calling for a more 'polycentric' approach to climate governance[1]. Others soon followed suit[2–9]. Whether referring to 'polycentric approaches', 'building blocks', 'regime complexes' or 'bottom-up systems', these authors all agree about the need to pay more attention to existing and potential subglobal climate policies that might, alone or in some combination, substitute for or supplement the existing United Nations (UN) regime and/or provide new impetus to global negotiations. No one has yet offered a sufficient set of reasons for believing that a polycentric approach might produce a better climate outcome. This Perspective attempts to fill that gap.

Some scholars seem to have embraced polycentric solutions to climate change almost in desperation because of the lack of progress in global negotiations, but others have long preferred it as a matter of theory. Victor and Raustiala[10] argued in favour of "regime complexes"—defined as collective[s] of partially overlapping and non-hierarchical regimes—over monocentric international legal systems for plant genetic resources several years before Keohane and Victor[3] made similar arguments about climate policy. Abbott[11], citing Ostrom[12,13], specifically referenced the pre-existing literature on polycentric governance of common-pool resources.

The Polycentric Approach to Policy

Ostrom's[1,13] own approach to climate governance was deeply rooted in the polycentric approach that was pioneered by her husband Vincent[14], and that became a central pillar of the 'Bloomington School' of political economy[15]. Ostrom *et al.*[14] based the polycentric approach on a principle of subsidiarity according to which government services are best provided at the lowest level of government consistent with their effective application. A polycentric system is characterized by "the concurrence of multiple opportunities by which participants can forge or dissolve links among different collective entities. . . . [P]articipants must be able to pick and choose those producers and providers that are most appropriate to each specific issue at hand"[16]. Instead of a 'monocentric hierarchy', where governmental units at higher levels make all collective-choice decisions, and units at lower levels simply follow commands from above, "a polycentric system is one in which governmental units both compete and cooperate, interact and learn from one another, and responsibilities at different governmental levels are tailored to match the scale of the public services they provide"[1,4].

The 'Bloomington School' is associated with the Ostrom Workshop in Political Theory and Policy Analysis at Indiana University. Throughout its 45-year history, the Ostroms and their Workshop colleagues developed theories and conducted empirical tests of collective action for resolving social and combined social-ecological problems based in large part on the theory of polycentric governance. Years before she became famous as a scholar of 'the commons', Ostrom and her colleagues were designing and carrying out studies comparing 'small' (presumptively fragmented) and 'large' (consolidated and presumptively more efficient) police departments in Indianapolis and other cities. Those studies demonstrated that large-scale, consolidated police departments do not always benefit from economies of scale and often suffer performance deficiencies compared with smaller policing units in metropolitan areas. These police studies informed Ostrom's subsequent work on natural common-pool resources, ranging from small forests to large irrigation systems, where the polycentric approach was found to have substantial utility[1,12]. Although much of her work on common-pool resources focused on local resource-management problems, Keohane and Ostrom[17] explored how the polycentric approach to governance might also successfully operate at the international level.

When Ostrom later turned her attention to the problem of climate change[1,13], she summarized the findings of her earlier applications of the polycentric approach to problems of providing public goods (for example, police services) and conserving common-pool resources. A key factor running through several of those findings was that the polycentric approach provides "greater opportunity for experimentation, choice, and learning" across levels of social organization[4]. She also referenced its tendency to "enhance innovation, learning, adaptation, trustworthiness, levels of cooperation of participants, and the achievement of more effective, equitable, and sustainable outcomes at multiple scales. . ."[13]. These conclusions are well established in the 'Bloomington School' literature, but Ostrom's explanation was incomplete. She never fully explained how the polycentric approach could improve climate outcomes by (1) creating more opportunities for experiments and learning, and (2) building the mutual trust necessary for improved climate outcomes. Because much already has been written about experimentation and learning in climate policy[1,13,18], the emphasis here is on the widely neglected issue of trust-building.

Experimentation and Learning in Climate Policy

No one believes that the UN's global climate policy has been successful. Yet it seems remarkably resistant to change, let alone replacement. But it has never been "the only game in town"[19]. Several authors point to numerous climate policies that have been, and are being, implemented at local, state, regional and national governments, and even among private business associations[1,2,4]. These polycentric policies multiply opportunities for communication, trust-building, policy experimentation and learning.

Local-level governments have been experimenting with GHG mitigation policies for many years now, and paying close attention to what others have been doing. Ostrom[13] writes about a 2005 conference in London attended by representatives of 18 large cities. They compared notes on urban mitigation policies and reviewed the congestion tax introduced by the City of London in 2003. Non-exempt motor vehicles entering London's 'Congestion Charge Zone' must pay £11.50 each working day. The primary purpose of the tax is to reduce city traffic and raise funds for London's public transportation system. To the extent that the congestion charge moves more commuters from private to public transport, it also reduces carbon emissions. Virtually all major cities have been watching London's experiment, and several, including Stockholm[20] and Milan[21], have already replicated it. In 2007, when Mayor Michael Bloomberg proposed a congestion charge for New York City, it was blocked in the state legislature despite widespread support[22].

Elinor Ostrom[1] observed that "all policies adopted at any scale can generate errors, but that without trial and error, learning cannot occur." If the Kyoto Protocol were in fact 'the only game in town', the extent of learning, and prospects for improving policies, would be quite narrow. A polycentric system of climate policies necessarily entails a greater number of discrete policy experiments from which policymakers at various levels of governance might learn valuable lessons, including about designing monitoring systems to ensure policy compliance[1]. The growing literature on experimentalist governance, including at the global level, supports Ostrom's arguments[18,23,24].

Relatedly, Ostrom[1] observed that efforts "to improve levels of collective action to overcome social dilemmas must enhance the level of trust of participants that others are complying with the policy or else many will seek ways of avoiding compliance." And she noted that "[i]f the *only* policy related to climate change was adopted at the global scale, it would be particularly difficult to increase the trust that citizens and firms need to have that other citizens and firms located halfway around the globe"[1] are reciprocating.

Building Mutual Trust through a Polycentric Approach

Trust has been absent in the global-level climate negotiations, which Scott Barrett[25] has aptly described as a "free-rider game". Formal and highly structured meetings involving thousands of individuals—the United Kingdom's official delegation to the most recent meeting of the parties in Warsaw reportedly[26] numbered 45—may not always provide the best fora for facilitating communications that lead to trust-building and cooperation. Trust is not the same as blind faith, where parties simply sit down and 'do the right things' according to someone's moral compass. Rather, trust is earned by mutual commitments that are not overly costly to monitor[27]. Thus, Ronald Reagan's famous admonition to "trust, but verify" is redundant. Verifiability is part and parcel of trust.

One hypothesis of the polycentric approach to climate policy is that social-ecological problems can be successfully resolved, whether those problems are conceived as iterated Prisoners' Dilemmas[28,29] or Assurance games[30–32], only if mutual trust among resource users can be cultivated over time through communication and cooperation across a range of issues. This hypothesis is consistent with Keohane's[33] observation that "Intergovernmental relationships . . . characterized by ongoing com-

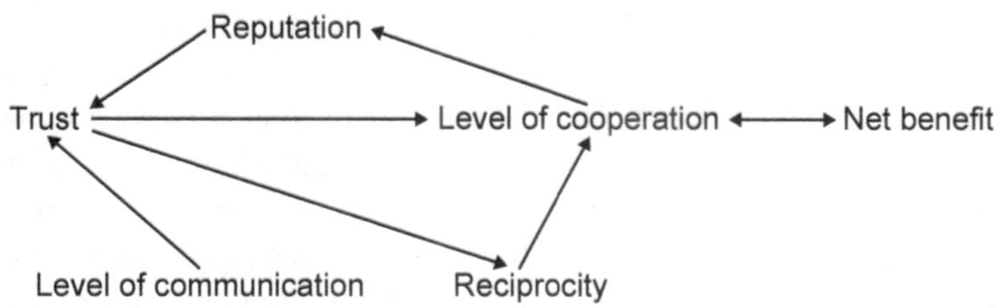

Figure 5.1. Core relations in repeated social dilemmas.

Source: Adapted from Ostrom[34,35].

munication among working-level officials, 'unauthorized' as well as authorized, are inherently more conducive to information-exchange and agreements than are traditional relationships between internally coherent bureaucracies that effectively control their communications with the external world."

The diagram in Figure 5.1, adapted from Ostrom[34,35], describes relations between communication, trust and cooperation in repeated social dilemmas. Similar to Sen's[30] Assurance games, she locates "the core of a behavioural explanation" for mutual cooperation on social dilemmas in the trust individuals place in others, the investment those others make in developing and maintaining reputations for trustworthiness, and the probability that participants adopt norms of reciprocity (such as tit-for-tat strategies)[35]. If initial levels of cooperation are sufficiently high, then individuals learn to trust one another, developing new, or reinforcing existing, norms of reciprocity and establishing reputations for trustworthiness that may lead to higher levels of cooperation in future interactions. This dynamic, reinforcing aspect of the cycle is not entirely clear in Ostrom's original depiction of these 'core relationships'. My own contribution is to make manifest the dynamic process of trust-reinforcement by (1) directly incorporating communication as a variable affecting trust, (2) describing a direct feedback from the level of cooperation to reputation, and (3) describing another direct feedback from 'net benefit' to the 'level of cooperation'. The chief point of the figure is altered only slightly: levels of communication can affect trust levels, which substantially determine levels of cooperation. Positive outcomes of cooperation include enhanced reputations for cooperators, which can lead to increased trust and reciprocity, and subsequently even higher levels of cooperation.

The goal of communicating and developing a reputation for trustworthiness is to build 'relationship capital', as it is known in the literature on international business alliances[36], which can alter a game's expected payoffs by raising the subjectively perceived probabilities of mutual cooperation. Communication does not inevitably lead to higher levels of trust, of course. But simple communication has too often been denigrated as 'cheap talk'[35], which, ironically, can prove extremely valuable for improving cooperation.

The hypothesis about communication, trust and cooperation is further supported by a substantial body of research. In a variety of experimental settings, Ostrom, Gardner and Walker found "communication . . . to be a very effective mechanism for increasing the frequency with which players choose joint income-maximizing strategies, even when individual incentives conflict with the cooperative strategies" [27]. Their experiments confirmed, more generally, "the power of face-to-face communication in a repeated common-pool resource dilemma where decisions are made privately"[27], particularly where costs of communication are low. More recently, a field experiment conducted by Cardenas *et al.*[37] revealed that repeated communications help to establish the identities of 'conditional cooperators' in a group, "who can then develop common knowledge that they will play the cooperative equilibrium in a repeated game." Extraction rates from common pools fell significantly as a direct consequence of the repeated communications.

Although the existing empirical and experimental literatures do not provide much insight into relations between the scale or scope of communications and cooperative outcomes, especially in the context of international negotiations, several discrete studies provide some indication that the scale, scope, duration and context of communications can matter. Aumann and Hart[38], for example, show that 'long cheap talk' (that is, communications over a longer period of time) helps to promote cooperation better than 'short cheap talk'. Barrett[25] suggests that quieter and more confidential conversations might be advantageous, observing that the recent trend toward greater democracy and transparency in international negotiations has not necessarily promoted cooperation. Compromise, he notes, is not so easy when it must be done in full public view. Such assessments warrant the hypothesis that formal or informal, one-on-one, or small-group communications might have a significant positive impact on climate negotiations.

In a literature review of public good and common-pool resource experiments, Ostrom[35] explored six potential reasons that communication increases cooperation. It:

(1) facilitates the development of socially optimal strategies;
(2) allows for exchanges of promises;
(3) "increases mutual trust and thus affects expectations of others' behaviour";
(4) adds value to payoffs;
(5) reinforces norms; and
(6) promotes development of 'group identity'.

Ostrom found "building trust . . . to be a key link in the communication–cooperation connection", and that "the efficacy of communication is related to the capability to talk on a face-to-face basis."

The US–China Climate Change Working Group

But can increasing the frequency and types of interactions among parties increase levels of mutual trust and cooperation in the climate change context? Despite more than two decades of formal meetings under the auspices of the UNFCCC, most major emitting countries including China and the United States have remained (generally speaking) non-cooperators on GHG mitigation. In April 2013, however, those two climate belligerents established a joint US–China Climate Change Working Group with the explicit goal of fostering cooperation and facilitating bilateral and multilateral negotiations[39]. How many people outside the climate policy community have even heard about this group, let alone follow its ongoing negotiations?

The Working Group's first official report[40] enunciated three main goals, the second of which relates directly to the thesis of this Perspective: "both sides appreciate that advancing concrete action on climate change can serve as a pillar of our bilateral relationship, build mutual trust and respect, and pave the way for a stronger overall collaboration." In June 2013, the Working Group picked some low-hanging fruit by agreeing to a 'phase-down' of emissions of hydrofluorocarbons—potent GHGs, but not of great importance to either the United States or the Chinese economy, especially after the European Union prohibited its member states from funding hydrofluorocarbon-based Clean Development Mechanism projects in China, which had been a major source of fraud[4].

No one realistically expected the US–China Climate Change Working Group to yield significant climate-policy benefits in a matter of a few months or even years. But already the regular meetings seem to be paying dividends. On 11 November 2014, US President Obama and Chinese President Xi signed a climate-change agreement, "worked out quietly" over the course of nine months[41]. Pursuant to that agreement, the United States set a new target of reducing its carbon emissions by 26–28% from 2005 levels by 2025, and China committed to peak its carbon dioxide emissions by 2030 (or earlier), while increasing use of non-fossil fuels to 20% of its total energy portfolio[42]. These are, of course, only pledges of future reductions; it remains to be seen whether the pledges will be fulfilled. Future governmental action is especially difficult to guarantee in democratic republics such as the United States, where presidential elections can lead to policy reversals.

An explicit motivating factor for both the United States and China was to "galvanize efforts to negotiate a new global agreement by 2015"[41]. At the very least, the agreement puts more pressure on other non-cooperating countries, including India and Canada. That the world's two largest emitters of carbon, and two of the existing global climate regime's greatest belligerents, entered into a bilateral agreement with the aim of improving global negotiations amounts to an implicit endorsement of the polycentric approach to climate governance, regardless of the ultimate outcome of the global negotiations. And, interestingly, although the deal was done behind closed doors, in complete secrecy, no one seems to be complaining about a 'democracy deficit'.

The US–China climate agreement was not hammered out in the course of a couple of days by the two principals. It was worked out over many months by their agents, lower-level government officials. Unfortunately, trust and cooperation between negotiators does not always translate into trust and cooperation among their principals, the individuals who sign agreements and ratify treaties. Moving trust from the negotiators (that is, agents) to the principals depends on processes of 'intra-organizational bargaining'[43]. But whatever the difficulties of such processes, it remains clear that if trust does not first develop between negotiators, its development among the principals is unlikely. Principal-agent problems are, at least at some level, unavoidable for any proposed solution to a given collective-action problem. The key empirical question is whether principal-agent difficulties are so serious as to undermine any negotiated solutions, whether local, national or global.

Private Actors in Polycentric Governance

The polycentric approach is not solely concerned with cooperation between public agents at different levels of government. It is about governance, not governments, and encompasses private as well as public actors. Those private agents include GHG emitters, non-governmental organizations, small groups of concerned citizens, even families who might decide, for example, to install solar systems at their homes and take other steps to minimize their carbon footprints[1]. It is easy enough to point to private-sector actors that have taken significant actions to reduce GHG emissions. The World Business Council for Sustainable Development (WBCSD) was founded in 1992, just before the Earth Summit in Rio, by a Swiss entrepreneur who "believed that business had an inescapable role to play in sustainable development" (http://www.wbcsd.org/Overview/About-us). Today, the WBCSD represents the CEOs of more than 200 companies globally. Its Executive Committee includes CEOs from multinational corporations such as Unilever, Toyota, Infosys, Royal Dutch Shell and China Petrochemical. Recently, the WBCSD partnered with scientists from the Stockholm Resilience Centre and policy analysts at the World Resources Institute to establish ACTION2020, a programme designed to develop 'business solutions' that will ensure global mean temperatures do not increase by more than 2 °C by 2050. According to its Action2020 Overview (http://www.wbcsd.org/Overview/About-us/Action2020/Resources/Action2020-Overview), those solutions will be measurable, scalable, replicable, beyond business as usual and, ultimately, good for business. On other matters relating to sustainable development, it has partnered with the World Wildlife Fund, the International Union for the Conservation of Nature, and the Earthwatch Institute, among many others.

The WBCSD's activities should not be dismissed blithely as 'greenwash', but should be understood, as Najam[44] has argued, as a serious offer from the private sector to participate in finding effective solutions to problems such as climate change. At the very least, by taking climate science seriously and recognizing a need for private-sector cooperation with regulators and non-governmental organizations on climate solutions, the WBCSD makes it more difficult for other firms and business associations to deny or downplay the climate change problem. In addition, member CEOs of the WBCSD who claim to take the climate change problem seriously and promise to participate in solutions implicitly open themselves and their firms to public and media criticism, should they fail to live up to their promises. Finally, the WBCSD reminds us that no matter who imposes what climate change regulations, the vast majority of actual GHG emission reductions will ultimately come from private actors (at least in countries where most major emitting firms are privately owned). Thus, the role of private actors in the process, whether it is a comprehensive global treaty-making process or some set of polycentric processes, should not be underestimated. Improving levels of trust and cooperation among the individuals who are decision-makers within private enterprises, with both policy advocates and those who establish and implement government policy, would be advantageous for climate policy. To that end, the WBCSD's positive interactions with climate scientists and various environmental groups provide a useful and replicable working model.

Conclusion

If any realistic policy solution (or set of policy solutions) to the climate change problem requires the development of higher levels of mutual trust among the relatively small number of major emitting parties, then how quickly can that happen? The honest answer is probably not quickly enough to avert the need for fairly high levels of adaptation and/or geoengineering. Ostrom[45] observes that mutual trust is "an asset that individuals build over time by engaging in mutually beneficial transactions that cannot be consummated in an immediate quid pro quo exchange." Certainly, the evidence of more than 20 years of UN climate meetings is that little mutual trust has developed so far. Indeed, a review of contemporaneous accounts from recent global climate meetings indicates continuing high levels of distrust, represented not only by lack of progress on mitigation but also by well-publicized conflicts among parties. A headline from the meeting in Warsaw (November 2013) makes the point well: "Bitter recriminations highlight climate-summit rift"[46].

That subglobal negotiations and agreements might not reduce GHG emissions rapidly enough to forestall the need for adaptation and/or geoengineering is no reason to maintain an exclusive focus on global policies that have failed and global negotiations that remain stalled. To the contrary, a polycentric approach to climate governance might provide the best chance we have of accelerating progress toward global climate stabilization by providing more frequent and varied opportunities for major emitting parties to engage in face-to-face communications in bilateral and multilateral fora, including some outside the intense glare of the public spotlight. Those interactions, some of which the UN might even facilitate, could inculcate the kind of mutual trust that seems necessary for greater cooperation at the global level. Thus, a broader focus on bilateral and smaller-scale multilateral negotiations might be not only desirable; it could be a necessary condition for more successful negotiations in the global, UN-based process.

As Prins and Rayner[47] have observed, no silver bullet exists to solve the climate change problem, but a 'silver buckshot approach' might work.

Acknowledgments

Financial support for this project is provided by the Swedish Research Council (FORMAS) grant, COMMONS. My Ostrom Workshop colleagues E. Brondizio and M. McGinnis provided invaluable support and advice. I am grateful to P. Grossman, M. Oppenheimer, B. Rudyk, R. Stewart, M. Vandenbergh, J. Walker and participants in the Workshop on Building Block Strategies for Global Climate Action at NYU Law School (December 2013) for comments and suggestions. Last but certainly not least, P. Lezotte provided exceptional editorial assistance.

Note

This chapter was originally published in *Nature Climate Change* 5(2) (February 2015): 114–18.

References

1. Ostrom, E. *A Polycentric Approach for Coping with Climate Change.* Policy Research Working Paper 5095 (World Bank, 2009).
2. Paavola, J. in *Property in Land and Other Resources* (eds Cole, D. H. & Ostrom, E.) 417–433 (Lincoln Institute of Land Policy, 2012).
3. Keohane, R. O. & Victor, D. G. The regime complex for climate change. *Persp. Polit.* **9,** 7–23 (2011).
4. Cole, D. H. From global to polycentric climate governance. *Clim. Law* **2,** 395–413 (2011).
5. Stewart, R. B., Oppenheimer, M. & Rudyk, B. Building blocks for global climate protection. *Stanford Environ. Law J.* **32,** 341–392 (2013).
6. Heal, G. & Kunreuther, H. in *Climate Change and Common Sense: Essays in Honour of Tom Schelling* (eds Hahn, R. W. & Ulph, A.) 50–60 (Oxford Univ. Press, 2012).
7. Leal-Arcas, R. Top-down versus bottom-up approaches for climate change negotiations: an analysis. *IUP J. Govern. Publ. Policy* **6,** 7–52 (2011).
8. Leal-Arcas, R. A bottom-up approach for climate change: the trade experience. *Asian J. Law Econ.* **2,** 1–54 (2011).
9. Vasconcelos, V. V., Santos, F. C. & Pacheco, J. M. A bottom-up institutional approach to cooperative governance of risky commons. *Nature Clim. Change* **3,** 797–801 (2013).

10. Victor, D. G. & Raustiala, K. The regime complex for plant genetic resources. *Indust. Organ.* **32,** 147–154 (2004).

11. Abbott, K. W. The transnational regime complex for climate change. *Environ. Plan. C: Govern. Policy* **30,** 571–590 (2012).

12. Ostrom, E. Beyond markets and states: polycentric governance of complex economic systems. *Am. Econ. Rev.* **100,** 641–672 (2010).

13. Ostrom, E. Polycentric systems for coping with collective action and global environmental change. *Glob. Environ. Change* **20,** 550–557 (2010).

14. Ostrom, V., Tiebout, C. M. & Warren, R. The organization of government in metropolitan areas: a theoretical inquiry. *Am. Pol. Sci. Rev.* **55,** 831–842 (1961).

15. Aligica, P. D. & Boettke, P. J. *Challenging Institutional Analysis and Development: The Bloomington School* (Routledge, 2009).

16. McGinnis, M. D. in *Polycentricity and Local Public Economies: Readings from the Workshop in Political Theory and Policy Analysis* (ed. McGinnis, M. D.) 1–27 (Univ. Michigan Press, 1999).

17. Keohane, R. O. & Ostrom, E. (eds) *Local Commons and Global Interdependence* (Sage, 1995).

18. De Búrca, G., Keohane, R. O. & Sable, C. Global experimentalist governance. *Br. J. Pol. Sci.* **44,** 477–486 (2014).

19. Michaelowa, A. Global warming policy. *J. Econ. Persp.* **17,** 204–205 (2003).

20. Börjesson, M., Eliasson, J., Hugosson, M. B. & Brundell-Freij, K. The Stockholm congestion charges—5 years on. Effects, acceptability and lessons learnt. *Transp. Policy* **20,** 1–12 (2012).

21. Rotaris, L., Danielis, R., Marcucci, E. & Massiani, J. *The Urban Road Pricing Scheme to Curb Pollution in Milan: A Preliminary Assessment.* Working Paper 122 (Universitá Degli Studi di Trieste, Dipartimento di Scienze Economiciie e Statistiche, 2009).

22. Schaller, B. New York City's congestion pricing experience and implications for road pricing acceptance in the United States. *Transp. Policy* **17,** 266–273 (2010).

23. Sabel, C. F. & Zeitlin, J. *Experimentalist Governance in the European Union: Towards a New Architecture* (Oxford Univ. Press, 2010).

24. De Búrca, G. New governance and experimentalism: an introduction. *Wisconsin Law Rev.* **2010,** 227–238 (2010).

25. Barrett, S. *Environment and Statecraft: The Strategy of Environmental Treaty-Making* (Oxford Univ. Press, 2003).

26. Prynne, M. UK to fly 45 delegates to climate conference despite no deal being expected. *The Telegraph* (1 November 2013).

27. Ostrom, E., Gardner, R. & Walker, J. *Rules, Games, and Common-Pool Resources* (Univ. Michigan Press, 1994).

28. Ledyard, J. in *The Handbook of Experimental Economics* (eds Kagel, J. & Roth, A.) 111–194 (Princeton Univ. Press, 1995).

29. Helm, D. Climate-change policy: why has so little been achieved? *Oxf. Rev. Econ. Policy* **24,** 211–238 (2008).

30. Sen, A. K. Isolation, assurance, and the social rate of discount. *Q. J. Econ.* **81,** 112–124 (1967).

31. Cole, D. H. & Grossman, P. Z. Institutions matter: Why the herder problem is not a Prisoner's Dilemma. *Theory Decis.* **69,** 219–231 (2010).

32. Cole, D. H. in *Distribution of Responsibilities in International Law* (eds Nollkaemper, A. & Jacobs, D.) 290–320 (Cambridge Univ. Press, 2015).

33. Keohane, R. O. The demand for international regimes. *Intl. Organ.* **36,** 325–355 (1982).

34. Ostrom, E. A behavioral approach to the rational choice theory of collective action. *Am. Pol. Sci. Rev.* **92,** 1–22 (1997).

35. Ostrom, E. in *Trust and Reciprocity: Interdisciplinary Lessons from Experimental Research* (eds Ostrom, E. & Walker, J.) 19–79 (Russell Sage Foundation, 2003).

36. Cullen, J. B., Johnson, J. L. & Sakano, T. Success through commitment and trust: the soft side of strategic alliance management. *J. World Business* **36,** 223–240 (2000).

37. Cardenas, J-C., Ahn, T. K. & Ostrom, E. in *Advances in Understanding Strategic Behaviour: Game Theory, Experiments and Bounded Rationality* (ed. Huck, S.) 258–286 (Palgrave Macmillan, 2004).

38. Aumann, R. A. & Hart, S. Long cheap talk. *Econometrica* **71,** 1619–60 (2003).

39. Volcovici, V. US–China climate deal called "breakthrough" but no long-term cuts yet. *Reuters* (11 June 2013); http://go.nature.com/QaELce.

40. Special Envoy for Climate Change. *Report of the US–China Climate Change Working Group to the Strategic and Economic Dialogue* (US Department of State, 10 July 2013); http://www.state.gov/e/oes/rls/pr/2013/211842.htm.

41. Landler, L. U.S. and China reach climate accord after months of talks. *New York Times* (11 November 2014); http://go.nature.com/vdsK6n.

42. Plumer, B. The US and China just reached a major climate deal on cutting emissions. *Vox* (11 November 2014).

43. Walton, R. E. & McKersie, R. B. *A Behavioral Theory of Labor Negotiations: An Analysis of a Social Interaction System* (Cornell Univ. Press, 1965).

44. Najam, A. in *Yearbook of International Co-operation on Environment and Development 1999/2000* (eds Bergesen, H. O., Parmann, G. & Thommessen, Ø. B.) 65–75 (Earthscan, 1999).

45. Ostrom, E. in *Making the Commons Work: Theory, Practice, and Policy* (eds Bromley, D. W. *et al.*) 293–318 (ICS Press, 1992).

46. McCarthy, S. Bitter recriminations highlight climate-summit rift. *Globe and Mail* (22 November 2013).

47. Prins, G. & Rayner, S. Time to ditch Kyoto. *Nature* **449,** 973–975 (2007).

PART II

The Artifactual Commons: Information, Infrastructure, and Public Health

6

Ideas, Artifacts, and Facilities: Information as a Common-Pool Resource

CHARLOTTE HESS AND ELINOR OSTROM

There is an increasing concern about the implications of recent and impending legislation on the future of academic research, open science, traditional knowledge, and the intellectual public domain. The Duke Law School Conference on the Public Domain brought together, for the first time, an interdisciplinary group of leading scholars studying the increasing enclosure[1] of the global information commons. In the past five years, law review articles have described an information arms race from various perspectives, with multiple sides battling for larger shares of the global knowledge pool.[2] Information that used to be "free" is now increasingly being privatized, monitored, encrypted, and restricted. The enclosure is caused by the conflicts and contradictions between intellectual property laws and the expanded capacities of new technologies.[3] It leads to speculation that the records of scholarly communication, the foundations of an informed, democratic society, may be at risk.

This "intellectual land-grab"[4] is an outcome of new technologies and global markets. Distributed digital technologies have the dual capacity to increase access to information while in some instances restricting such access. These technologies have generated greater access to important information about history, science, art, literature, and current events, while at the same time enabling profit-oriented firms to extract value from resources previously held in common and to establish property rights.[5] Multiple forces are vying for capture and restriction of traditionally available knowledge: corporations versus indigenous peoples, such as Monsanto owning the patent on the genetic structure of the neem; federal and state governments versus citizens regarding balancing encryption and digital surveillance with individual privacy; universities versus professors as to whether institutions or individuals will own intellectual property; and publishers versus libraries in the ephemeralization of library collections through licensing, bundling, and withdrawal of information.

This competition for ownership of previously shared resources is not unique to the public domain of knowledge. Given the opening of vast markets for commodities of all kinds, many natural as well as human-made resources are under pressure. The world's fisheries, for instance, are fighting depletion because of the capture capabilities of larger trawlers, wider and finer nets, and larger fleets. Local control of forests throughout the world is being increasingly encroached upon by state and private interests, resulting in alarming rates of deforestation. Resultant forest burning is not only rapidly reducing primary growth forests but is also contributing to the degradation of the global atmosphere as well.[6] Commodification and privatization of natural resources is a trend with virtually all types of resources. And radical changes in the structure and process of all natural and human-constructed resources can occur through the development of new technologies.[7]

The problems are complex, multilayered, and of crucial importance. To direct attention to this evolving situation, James Boyle has called for the recreation of the public domain, drawing from the intellectual construct of the environment. "Like the environment," he writes, "the public domain must be invented before it can be saved."[8] A greater depth of understanding of the public domain requires the concept to be more deeply analyzed and clarified. It is a logical step, therefore, to draw from the fruitful research and analytical methods applied to the study of common-pool resources ("CPRs") and natural resource management.

The goal of this article is to summarize the lessons learned from a large body of international, interdisciplinary research on common-pool resources in the past twenty-five years and consider its usefulness in the analysis of scholarly information as a resource. We will suggest ways in which the study of the governance and management of CPRs can be applied to the analysis of information and the "intellectual public domain." The complexity of the issues is enormous for many reasons: the vast number of players, multiple conflicting interests, rapid changes of technology, the general lack of understanding of digital technologies, local versus global arenas, and a chronic lack of precision about the information resource at hand. We suggest, in the tradition of Hayek, that the combination of time and place analysis with general scientific knowledge is necessary for sufficient understanding of policy and action.[9] In addition, the careful development of an unambiguous language and agreed-upon definitions is imperative.

We focus on the *language*, *methodology*, and *outcomes* of research on common-pool resources to better understand how various types of property regimes affect the provision, production, distribution, appropriation, and consumption of scholarly information. Our analysis will suggest that collective action and new institutional design play as large a part in the shaping of scholarly information as do legal restrictions and market forces.

In [the second section] we present a brief intellectual history of the commons and discuss the development of the understanding of the term. [The third section] discusses key concepts of the terms "commons," "common-pool resources," and "common property." Four frequent areas of confusion are identified and elucidated. [The fourth section] presents a method of analyzing information as a commons. [The fifth section] illustrates the development and change of scholarly information as a shared resource. It focuses on collective action initiatives as a response to the dilemmas of new technological freedoms within an increasing amount of legal constraints.

What is a Commons?

A large body of international, interdisciplinary literature on the commons has grown in the past fifteen to twenty years.[10] It reflects concerted attempts to arrive at unified understandings of the definition of the commons. The recent law literature on the commons, however, presents various different concepts of the commons without reference to this literature. Lawrence Lessig's concept of the commons is one of a universal, open access: "The commons: There's a part of our world, here and now, that we all get to enjoy without the permission of any."[11] Yochai Benkler's concept involves legal constraints against controlling regimes: "The commons refers to institutional devices that entail government abstention from designating anyone as having primary decision-making power over use of a resource. A commons-based information policy relies on the observation that some resources that serve as inputs for information production and exchange have economic or technological characteristics that make them susceptible to be allocated without requiring that any single organization, regulatory agency, or property owner clear conflicting uses of the resource."[12] Litman equates the commons with the public domain: "The concept of the public domain is another import from the realm of real property. In the intellectual property context, the term describes a true commons comprising elements of intellectual property that are ineligible for private ownership. The contents of the public domain may be mined by any member of the public."[13]

Indeed, in the law literature cited throughout this article, a wide variety of concepts and definitions of the commons or public domain is used. We feel there needs to be clarity, shared meanings, and a common language to research this area better. In the legal arena, the term "commons" is often used synonymously with the term "public domain." Is it a given right, a nonassigned right, an unclaimed right, an unmanaged resource, or something that should just be there in a democracy?[14] A survey of law dictionaries does not clear matters up. *Oran's Dictionary of the Law*, for instance, gives two definitions of public domain: "land owned by the government" and "something free for anyone to use or something not protected by patent or copyright."[15] In the first definition, there is an owner—the government. In the second, there is *no* owner. Are scholars trying to protect a realm of government ownership or a realm of no ownership?

In relation to the intellectual public domain, the commons appears to be an idea about democratic processes, freedom of speech, and the free exchange of information. The term "commons," however, has various histories, from property to shared spaces to notions of democratic ideals. It refers to the house of British Parliament representing nontitled citizens, and agricultural fields in England and Europe prior to their enclosure. In the United States, commons refers to public spaces such as the New England town square, campus dining halls, and concepts of the "common" good.[16] In almost all uses, the term has been contested. In the realm of legal property rights, the publication of *Ancient Law* by Henry Sumner Maine[17] in 1861 set off a major debate about the origin of the very concept of property in ancient times.[18] Drawing on his own extensive research in India and the research of others on early European communities, Maine argued that joint ownership by families and groups of kin (in other words, common property) was more likely the initial property regime in most parts of the world than the notion of property owned by a single individual.[19] This great debate was not simply one between historians over whether common property or individual private property came first. Rather, the debate framed a perspective on whether landed proprietors have a special role in society that needed protection and the legitimacy of enclosing properties owned communally. The debate started long ago and is still not fully resolved. A major textbook on property law devotes the entire first chapter to *The Debate over Private Property* and the second chapter to *The Problem of the Commons*.[20]

Social scientists have had their own debates about the consequences of allowing multiple individuals or firms to use jointly a resource system. The debate was kicked off half a century ago by the path-breaking works of H. Scott Gordon in 1954 and Anthony Scott in 1955,[21] which introduced an economic analysis of a natural resource (fisheries) that had, prior to that time, been the domain of biologists. The two articles are credited with outlining the conventional theory of the commons.[22] Gordon and Scott demonstrated that when multiple individuals jointly harvested high-demand fish without a limit on the amount that any fisher could withdraw, the quantity harvested would exceed both the maximum sustainable yield and the maximum economic yield. At that time, the only solution they contemplated to this problem was ownership of the fishery by a single firm or by the government. In 1968, biologist Garrett Hardin crystallized the thinking of many social scientists and policymakers with his metaphoric analysis of the "tragedy of the commons."[23] Hardin argued that individuals who jointly use a commons are hopelessly trapped in an immutable tragedy.[24] Given this inevitable trap of overuse (or, for Hardin, overpopulation), the *only* solution Hardin envisioned was externally imposed government or private ownership.[25] Unfortunately for the development of rigorous thinking, Hardin casually used the example of a pasture "open to all" as if all jointly owned pastures would be "open to all."[26]

Since the work of Gordon, Scott, and Hardin, most theoretical studies by political economists have analyzed simple common-pool resource systems using relatively similar assumptions. In such systems, it is assumed that the resource generates a highly predictable, finite supply of one type of resource unit (one species, for example) in each relevant time period. Appropriators (those who harvest from a resource system, such as fishers and pastoralists) are assumed to be homogeneous in terms of their assets, skills, discount rates, and cultural views. They are also assumed to be short-term, profit-maximizing actors who possess complete information. In this theory, *anyone* can utilize the resource and appropriate resource units. Appropriators gain property rights only to what they harvest. The harvested resource units are then privately owned and can be sold in an open, competitive market. The open-access condition is a given and the appropriators make no effort to change it. Appropriators act independently and do not communicate or coordinate their activities in any way.[27]

Many current textbooks in resource economics and in law and economics still present this conventional theory of a simple common-pool resource as the *only* theory needed for achieving a more general understanding of common-pool resources.[28] With the growing use of game theory, appropriation from common-pool resources is frequently represented as a one-shot or finitely repeated Prisoner's Dilemma game.[29] These models formalize the problem differently, but do not change any of the basic theoretical assumptions about the finite and predictable supply of resource units, complete information, homogeneity of users, their maximization of expected profits, and their lack of interaction with one another or capacity to change their institutions.

A sufficient number of empirical examples exist where the absence of property rights and the independence of actors captures the essence of the problem facing appropriators that the broad empirical applicability of the conventional theory was not challenged until the mid-1980s. The massive deforestation in tropical countries and the collapse of the California sardine fishery and other ocean fisheries confirmed for many scholars the worst predictions to be derived from this theory.

Since appropriators are viewed as being trapped in these dilemmas, repeated recommendations were made that external authorities must impose a different set of political regimes and property rights. Some scholars recommended private property as the most efficient form of ownership.[30] Others, drawing on Hobbes, recommended government ownership and control.[31] Implicitly, theorists assumed that regulators will act in the public interest and understand how ecological systems work and how to change institutions to induce socially optimal behavior.[32]

The possibility that the appropriators would find ways to organize themselves was not considered seriously in the political-economy literature until recently. Organizing to create rules that specify rights and duties of participants creates a public good for those involved. Anyone who is included in the community of users benefits from this public good, whether they contribute or not. Thus, getting "out of the trap" of the free-rider problem is itself a second-level dilemma. Further, investing in monitoring and sanctioning activities to increase the likelihood that participants follow the agreements they have made also generates a public good. Such investments represent a third-level dilemma. Since much of the initial problem exists because individuals are stuck in a setting where they generate negative externalities on one another, it is not consistent with the conventional theory that they solve a second- and third-level dilemma to address the first-level dilemma.

The work of the National Academy of Sciences' Panel on Common Property challenged the application of this conventional theory to all common-pool resources regardless of the capacity of appropriators to communicate, coordinate their activities, and create institutions to allocate property rights and make policies related to a jointly owned resource.[33] The growing evidence from many field studies of common-pool resources conducted by anthropologists[34] and historians[35] called for a serious rethinking of the theoretical foundations for analysis of common-pool resources.[36] The cumulative impact of the extensive empirical studies does not challenge the empirical validity of the conventional theory *where it is relevant*, but rather questions its presumed, universal generalizability.

Clarifying Key Concepts

To develop a broader and empirically verifiable theory that encompassed the dominant "tragedy of the commons" theory as a special case, scholars learned that they had to make some key distinctions between concepts that had previously and casually been treated as the same. Because we feel that a similar effort is needed for the intellectual public domain, we will discuss these distinctions in some depth. There are four basic confusions that need to be untangled. The source of confusion relates to the differences between (1) the nature of the good (common-pool *resources*) and a property regime (common-property *regimes*), (2) resource systems and the flow of resource units, (3) common property and open-access regimes, and (4) the set of property rights involved in "ownership." All four sources of confusion reduce clarity in assigning meaning to terms and retard theoretical and empirical progress.

The Confusion between the Nature of a Good and a Property Regime

The problems resulting from confusing concepts were particularly difficult to overcome given that the term "common-*property* resource" was frequently used to describe a type of economic good that is more appropriately referred to as a "common-*pool* resource." For many scholars, the concept of a property regime and the nature of a good were thus conflated.

One of the key problems in developing a good analytical approach to the effect of diverse institutional arrangements on the incentives, activities, and outcomes of the individuals involved is getting a clear conception of the structure of events involved. The political-economy literature usually refers to the structure of the biophysical events as the nature of the goods.[37]

For some time, economists struggled with classifying goods as either private or public.[38] By labeling all goods as fitting this dichotomy, scholars talked about those things that the market could solve most efficiently and those that would require government provision and production.

In the 1970s, a major breakthrough came with clear identification that there were more than two types of goods.[39] Two attributes have been identified in the political-economy literature that help identify four broad classes of goods. The first attribute is that the benefits consumed by one individual subtract from the benefits available to others.[40] The second attribute is that it is very costly to exclude individuals from using the flow of benefits either through physical barriers or legal instruments. Both attributes vary across a range.

Recognizing a class of goods that shares these two attributes enables scholars to identify the core theoretical problems facing individuals, whenever more than one individual or a group utilizes resources for an extended period of time. Using "property" to refer to a type of good reinforces the impression that goods sharing these attributes tend to share uniformly the same property regime. This is certainly not the case.

As shown in Figure 6.1, common-pool resources share with what economists call "public goods" the difficulty of developing physical or institutional means of excluding beneficiaries. Unless means are devised to keep nonauthorized users from benefiting, a strong temptation to free ride on the efforts of others will lead to a suboptimal investment in improving the resource, monitoring use, and sanctioning rule-breaking behavior. Second, the products or resource units from common-pool resources share with what economists call "private goods" the attribute that one person's consumption subtracts from the quantity available to others. Thus, common-pool resources are subject to the problems of congestion, overuse, pollution, and potential destruction unless harvesting or use limits are devised and enforced. In addition to sharing these two attributes, particular common-pool resources differ in many other attributes that affect their economic usefulness including their extent, shape, and productivity, as well as the value, timing, and regularity of the resource units produced.[41]

Common-pool resources may be owned by national, regional, or local governments, by communal groups, by private individuals or corporations, or used as open-access resources by whomever can gain access. Each of the broad types of property regimes has different sets of advantages and disadvantages, but at times may rely upon similar bundles of operational rules.[42] Examples exist of both successful and unsuccessful efforts by

		SUBTRACTABILITY	
		Low	*High*
EXCLUSION	*Difficult*	**Public Goods** Sunset Common Knowledge	**Common-Pool Resources** Irrigation Systems Libraries
	Easy	**Roll or Club Goods** Dare-Care Centers Country Clubs	**Private Goods** Doughnuts Personal Computers

Figure 6.1. Types of goods.

governments, communal groups, cooperatives, voluntary associations, and private individuals or firms to govern and manage common-pool resources.[43] Thus, no automatic association exists between common-pool resources and common-property regimes—*or, any other particular type of property regime.*

The Confusion between a Resource System and the Flow of Resource Units

The second confusion is related to the relationships between resource systems and a flow of resource units or benefits from these systems.[44] In regard to common-pool resources, the resource system (or alternatively, the stock or the facility) is what generates a flow of resource units or benefits over time.[45] Examples of typical common-pool resource systems include lakes, rivers, irrigation systems, groundwater basins, forests, fishery stocks, and grazing areas. Common-pool resources may also be facilities that are constructed for joint use, such as mainframe computers and the Internet. Examples of resource units from a common-pool resource are water, timber, medicinal plants, fish, fodder, and central processing units. The resource units from a complex facility like the Internet may be the data packets or the computer files (information artifacts), depending upon whether it is being studied as an infrastructure resource or as an information resource.[46] Devising property regimes that effectively allow sustainable use of a common-pool resource requires one set of rules that limits access to the resource system and another set of rules that limits the amount, timing, and technology used to withdraw diverse resource units from the resource system. It is frequently the case that the resource system is jointly owned, while the resource units withdrawn from the system are individually owned by appropriators.

The Confusion between Common-Property and Open-Access Regimes

In a now classic article, Ciriacy-Wantrup and Bishop[47] clearly articulated the difference between property regimes that are *open-access*, where no one has the legal right to exclude anyone from using a resource, and *common property*, where members of a clearly defined group have a bundle of legal rights including the right to exclude nonmembers from using that resource.[48] Legal doctrine has long considered open-access regimes (*res nullius*)—including the classic cases of the open seas and the atmosphere—to involve no limits on who has authorized use. Thus, the work of Gordon, Scott, and Hardin focused on resources that were paired with open-access regimes.[49] If anyone can use a resource—the definition of an open-access resource—then no one has an incentive to conserve its use or to invest in its improvements.

Some open-access regimes lack effective rules defining property rights by default.[50] Either the resources affected by these open-access regimes are not contained within a nation-state or no entity has successfully laid claim to legitimate ownership. Other open-access regimes are the consequence of conscious public policies to guarantee the access of all citizens to use a resource within a political jurisdiction.[51] The concept of *jus publicum* applies to their formal status, but effectively these resources are open-access.[52] Still other open-access regimes result from the ineffective exclusion of nonowners by the entity assigned formal rights of ownership. In many developing countries, the earlier confusion between open-access and common-property regimes paradoxically led to an increase in the number and extent of local resources that are *de facto* open-access.[53] Common-property regimes controlling access to and harvesting from local streams, forests, grazing areas, and inshore fisheries had evolved over long periods of time in all parts of the world, but were rarely given formal status in the legal codes of newly independent countries.[54]

Many common-property regimes do efficiently regulate the joint use and management of a resource. There is, however, nothing inherently efficient or inefficient about such regimes. A modern, private corporation is, after all, a common-property regime that has widespread use throughout the global economy—with both efficient and inefficient consequences. Common-property regimes are essentially share contracts.[55] As such, they face the potential of opportunistic behavior and moral hazard problems. Common-property regimes, however, are much more likely to have beneficial consequences for a resource system and its users than an open-access regime.

As concern for the protection of natural resources mounted during the second half of the last century, many developing countries nationalized all land and water resources that had not yet been recorded as private property.[56] The institutional arrangements that many local users had devised to limit entry and use frequently lost legal standing.[57] The national governments that declared ownership of these natural resources, however, frequently lacked monetary resources and personnel to exclude users or to monitor the harvesting activities of users.[58] Thus, resources that had been under a *de facto* common-property regime enforced by local users were converted to a *de jure* government-property regime, but reverted to a *de facto* open-access regime. When resources that were previously controlled by local participants have been nationalized, state control has usually proven to be less effective and efficient than control by those directly affected, if not disastrous in its consequences.[59]

The Confusion over What Rights are Involved in "Ownership"

A property right is an enforceable authority to undertake particular actions in a specific domain.[60] Within the property regime, different kinds of rights define actions that individuals can take in relation to other individuals regarding some "thing." If one individual has a right, someone else has a commensurate duty to observe that right. Edella Schlager and Elinor Ostrom identify five major bundles of rights that are most relevant for the use of common-pool resources: access, extraction,[61] management, exclusion, and alienation. These are defined as:

Access	The right to enter a defined physical area and enjoy nonsubtractive benefits (for example, hike, canoe, enjoy nature);
Extraction	The right to obtain resource units or products of a resource system (for example, catch fish, divert water);

Management	The right to regulate internal use patterns and transform the resource by making improvements;
Exclusion	The right to determine who will have access rights and withdrawal rights, and how those rights may be transferred; and
Alienation	The right to sell or lease management and exclusion rights.

In much of the economics literature, as well as in legal literature, private property is defined as "holding the right of alienation." Property-rights systems that do not contain the right of alienation are considered by many scholars to be *ill defined*. Further, they are presumed to lead to inefficiency, since property-rights holders cannot trade their interest in an improved resource system for other resources, nor can someone who has a more efficient use of a resource system purchase that system in whole or in part.[62] Consequently, it is assumed that property-rights systems that include the right to alienation will result in the highest-valued use of the resource systems affected. Bruce Larson and Daniel Bromley[63] challenge this commonly held view and show that much more information must be known about the specific values of a large number of parameters before judgements can be made concerning the efficiency of a particular type of property right.

Scholars studying common-property systems have found that it is more useful to examine which of the five bundles of property rights are exercised in the field and what consequences result. In this view, private individuals, private associations or firms, and governments may hold well-defined rights to a resource that include or do not include all five of the rights defined above. This approach separates the question of whether a particular right is well defined from the questions of which rights are possessed and who possesses them. While not the conventional view of lawyers, analysis of resources can benefit from viewing these rights bundles as diverse forms of property rights. In this respect, the analysis of distributed digital information would particularly benefit from a close examination of these bundles of rights.

"Authorized entrants" include most recreational users of national parks who purchase an operational right to enter and enjoy the natural beauty of the park, but do not have a right to harvest forest products. Those who have both entry and withdrawal use-right units are "authorized users." The contents of the bundle of rights of an authorized user may vary substantially in regard to the quantity, timing, location, and use of resource units appropriated from a resource system. The presence or absence of constraints upon the timing, technology used, purpose of use, and quantity of resource units harvested is usually determined by operational rules devised by those holding the collective-choice rights (or authority) of management and exclusion over the resource system.[64] An external authority, however, may mandate that the owner of a resource system must allow some access or withdrawal rights to another individual or group than the proprietor or owner of the resource system.

"Claimants" possess the operational rights of access and withdrawal plus a collective-choice right of managing a resource that includes decisions concerning the construction and maintenance of facilities and the authority to devise limits on withdrawal rights. Fishing territories are a frequent form of property for indigenous, inshore fishers.[65] Farmers on large-scale government irrigation systems frequently devise rotation schemes for allocating water on a branch canal.[66]

"Proprietors" hold the same rights as claimants with the addition of the right to determine who may access and harvest from a resource. Most of the property systems that are called "common-property" regimes involve participants who are proprietors and have four of the above rights, but do not possess the right to sell their management and exclusion rights even though they most frequently have the right to bequeath it to members of their family and to earn income from the resource.

"Full owners" possess the right of alienation—the right to transfer a good in any way the owner wishes that does not harm the physical attributes or uses of other owners—in addition to the bundle of rights held by a proprietor. An individual, a private corporation, a government, or a communal group may possess full ownership rights to any kind of good including a common-pool resource.[67] The rights of owners, however, are never absolute. Even private owners have responsibilities not to generate particular kinds of harms to others.[68]

What is particularly important in the context of the intellectual public domain about this view of property rights is that property rights to the flow of units from a resource system are frequently held by different actors than those who hold rights related to the system itself. Further, empirical studies of common-property institutions have found that proprietors (as contrasted to full owners) have sufficient rights to make decisions that promote long-term investment in, and sustainable harvesting from, a resource.[69]

A key finding from multiple studies is that *no* set of property rights works equivalently in all types of settings. For private-property systems in land to make a difference in productivity gains, one needs (1) a somewhat dense population so competition for use is present and (2) the existence of effective markets related to credit, inputs, and the sale of commodities. In a series of studies of inshore fisheries, self-organized irrigation systems, forest user groups, and groundwater institutions, proprietors tended to develop strict boundary rules to exclude noncontributors, established authority rules to allocate withdrawal rights, devised methods for monitoring conformance, and used graduated sanctions against those who did not conform to these rules.[70]

The world of property rights is far more complex than simply government, private, and common property. These terms better reflect the status and organization of the *holder* of a particular bundle of rights. All of the above rights can be held by single individuals or by collectivities. Some communal fishing systems grant their members all five of the above rights, including the right of alienation.[71] Members in these communal fishing systems have full ownership rights. Similarly, farmer-managed irrigation systems in Nepal, the Philippines, and Spain have established transferable shares to the systems. Access, withdrawal, and maintenance responsibilities may be allocated by the amount of water shares owned rather than by the amount of land owned.[72] On the other hand, some proposals to "privatize" inshore fisheries through the device of an Individual Transferable Quota ("ITQ") allocate transferable use rights to authorized fishers, but do not allocate rights related to the management of the fisheries, the determination of who is a participant, nor the transfer of management and exclusion rights. Thus, proposals to establish ITQ systems, which are frequently referred to as forms of "privatization," do not involve full ownership.

Most of the CPR examples discussed so far have been natural resource systems and human-made resources, such as irrigation systems. In the past five years, interdisciplinary researchers are finding great benefit in applying CPR analysis to a number of new or previously ignored common-pool resources.[73] Studies that have been written to date on the Internet as a common-pool resource[74] tend to focus on the technology infrastructure and the social network issues rather than the institutions developed about the distributed information per se. Addressing scientific information, some of the most useful works in recent years have been those based on Michael Heller's groundbreaking work on anticommons.[75] Heller's work demonstrates that among the usual outcomes of a shared resource (particularly overuse,[76] but also depletion, congestion, pollution, etc.), the occurrence of "underprovision" of a traditionally available resource is not only possible, but of growing concern because of increasing commodification of information through new legislation, competing markets, and the recent run on patents.[77]

Ideas, Artifacts, Facilities: The Ecological Makeup of Scholarly Information

In CPR research, the distinction between resource system and resource units has proved helpful in analyzing the impact of diverse property rights on the incentives of participants in regard to resource systems and resource units related to water, fisheries, and other natural resources. When water rights to a groundwater basin are adjudicated, litigants receive defined quantities or shares of the flow to the system. They are not receiving a portion of land that goes down below their surface land. That much earlier conception proved to be inadequate in the adjudication of groundwater rights. So, where water rights have been adjudicated and privatized, what has been privatized is the *flow*. The resource system itself is a *facility* that holds the flow and is not privately owned by a single person or organization unless there is a single overlying owner that owns all the surface land over a groundwater basin. Similarly, with individual transferable quota systems that are extensively used in regard to fisheries, what has been privatized is either a proportion of the estimated yield or an amount of fish that is assigned to each boat for a season.

In struggling with the application of the evolving theory of common-pool resources to the study of information and the intellectual public domain, we would like to pose that this two-way distinction is not as useful as a three-way distinction between the *artifact*, the *facility*, and *ideas*.

- An *artifact* is a discreet, observable, nameable representation of an idea or set of ideas. In regard to scholarly information, examples of artifacts include articles, research notes, books, databases, maps, computer files, and web pages. Artifacts vary in their durability. Physical artifacts can be used in a sequential fashion by multiple readers. Digital artifacts can be used concurrently by multiple users. Artifacts are the physical flow units from an information facility. Users can usually be excluded from using physical artifacts, but the process of excluding potential users has become more complex and less transparent with digital artifacts.
- A *facility* stores artifacts and makes them available. It is a resource system storing the artifacts and their ideas. Prior to the development of digital artifacts, traditional facilities were public and private libraries and archives that stored physical artifacts. A facility had a physical limit on the number and type of artifacts that could be stored. While the cost of excluding users was not usually extremely

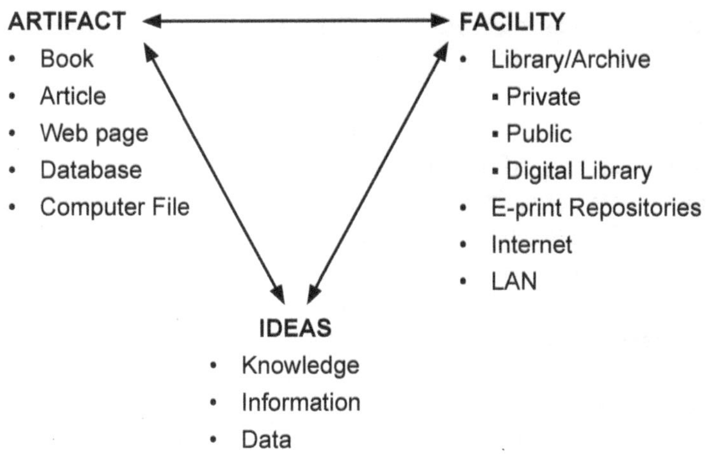

Figure 6.2. Forms of information.

high, many libraries and archives did invest in the development of well-defined rules regarding who would be considered legitimate users, how long individuals could legally remove artifacts from the facilities, and the practices that were to be followed within the facility (silence, no dancing) and in the use of the artifacts (no highlighting, tearing out pages, etc.) as well as guards for monitoring and enforcing these rules. The facilities themselves were subject to deterioration if a substantial investment was not made in their maintenance. Private collections were usually not open to the public.

- The *ideas* contained in an artifact can be understood to mean the creative vision, the intangible content, innovative information, and knowledge. Ideas are the nonphysical flow units contained in an artifact. This is the element that copyright does not protect.[78] Analytically, one person's use of an idea does not subtract from the corpus of that idea for use by others. It may, however, be possible to exclude others from knowing an idea by keeping it a secret.

It is our sense that in analyzing information in the public domain, developing a more careful understanding of the processes of providing and producing the information and artifacts, providing and producing information facilities, distributing artifacts to facilities and to users, and the various forms of consuming and using the information content of these artifacts is needed before one can begin to develop a better legal structure for these processes as they are challenged by new technologies in a global environment.

"Information" is a difficult term to define.[79] To economists, it can mean complete or incomplete knowledge, true or inaccurate knowledge; to governments, it can mean knowledge ranging from public to top-secret. In legal terms, it can mean that the conduit of information is currently owned, previously owned, or as yet unclaimed. Non-Governmental Organizations and donor agencies see access to information as the key ingredient for economic development. Referring to the multiple types of information issues, James Boyle has written: "Is there anything, apart from the *word* information, that holds these issues together? If there is some useful link, is it new to our society?"[80]

"Information" and "knowledge" as raw terms have been dissected and defined in several ways. Fritz Machlup introduced the division of data-information-knowledge, with data being raw bits of information; information as organized data in context; and knowledge as the assimilation of the information and understanding of how to use it.[81] Jerome Reichman and Jonathan Franklin discuss the "dual function of information," which has high value as a commodity and as "the foundation of knowledge in the information economy."[82] Peter Lyman writes that the "the definition of the concept of information must be at the heart of any information policy."[83] Karl Popper earlier stressed that the knowledge contained in scientific reports, articles, and books comes to have an autonomous existence as it affects the thinking and research of the next generation of scientists.[84]

Sandra Braman presents a thorough survey of ways to look at information for policymakers, pointing out that the argument over how to define information is critical.[85] Examined are information as a commodity, as a perception of pattern, as a constitutive force in society.[86] Her analysis of information as a resource emphasizes how people *use* information rather than information's effect upon people.[87] For the purposes of our paper, Hayek's classic analysis of the two types of knowledge essential to bringing a clear understanding remains crucially relevant in the construction of scientific knowledge and information policy. He wrote in 1945 that while we are used to respecting scientific knowledge gathered by experts, it is only in combination with "local knowledge" that the knowledge takes on a real value. All of the valid research on common-pool resources involves this combination of scientific knowledge with time and place analysis, or as Hayek puts it, the "special knowledge of circumstances."[88]

In any discussion of information (including digital software), it is useful to remember that information is a human artifact, with agreements and rules, and strongly tied to the rules of language itself.[89] Thus, information has an important cultural component as well as intellectual, economic, and political functions. As such, it is a "flow resource" that must be passed from one individual to another to have any public value.[90]

Intellectual property and contract laws are only a few of the complex issues facing scholarly communication. Current and future dilemmas extend much further than the legal questions of formal ownership and regulation. Other important areas include informal rights, agreements and standards, transaction costs, new user communities, globalization, growing international collaborative research, language, interdisciplinarity, interoperability, reliability, and accessibility.

But analyzing the whole ecosystem of scholarly information is much more tenuous than in *Governing the Commons*,[91] where (1) the boundaries were clear, (2) the resource systems studied were small and easy to observe, (3) solving problems was of high salience to appropriators, (4) institutions were long-enduring and had evolved over time, and (5) extensive field observation was available. The CPR resources were analyzed by examining the physical characteristics of that resource, the community of users and the actors involved in a situation, along with the rules in use that determine actions taken, the costs of those actions, the outcomes that can be achieved, how those actions are linked to outcomes, what information is available, how much control individuals can exercise, and what payoffs are to be assigned to particular combinations of actions and outcomes.[92]

Information, on the other hand, often has complex tangible and intangible attributes: fuzzy boundaries; a diverse community of users on local, regional, national, and international levels; and multiple layers of rule-making institutions. Until the invention of digital technologies, the flow of most scholarly information was easy to follow. One typical flow pattern was [Figure 6.3].

Each of the arrows in Figures 6.3 through 6.5 represents a transition where property rights may change in regard to the person or organization who holds the rights and/or in regard to the specific bundle of rights held. While the author retained copyright protection for her unique expression of ideas in a book or journal, the publishers owned reproduction rights to the work, and sold copies of the artifacts to decentralized facilities (in this case, local libraries). The libraries owned their individual copies of the book, took responsibility for the organization, storage, preservation, and distribution of their "resource units." Working within the parameters of the formal rules of copyright, first sale, and fair use, the individual facilities designed the rules in use regarding the distribution and the qualified community of users.

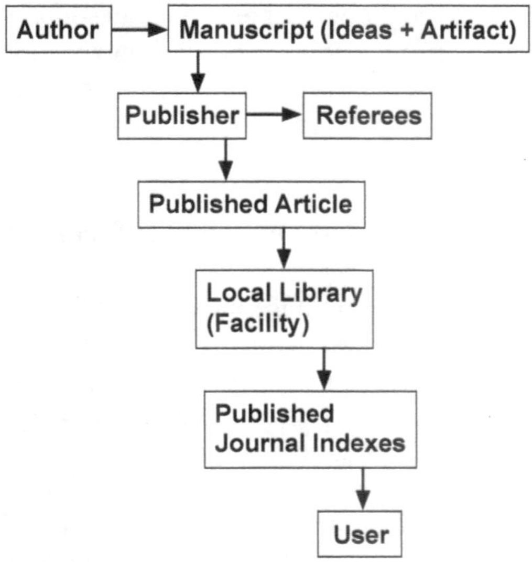

Figure 6.3. Traditional flow pattern of ideas → artifact → facility → user.

The journal volumes, like books, are only temporarily subtractable during one person's use, and are, thus, renewable resources over time. If the artifact is stolen or destroyed, replenishment is possible through repurchase or through interlibrary loan. Journal articles are less subtractable because photocopying allowed through fair use lessens the competition for the resource. The ideas contained within the works are generally nonsubtractable.

The rules and flow patterns are different with digital information. John Perry Barlow pointed out several years ago that digitization, which converts information to ones and zeroes as a conduit of ideas, has obfuscated the "wine from the bottle";[93] that is, the physical characteristics and the boundaries of the resource are no longer clear. Digital artifacts are increasingly being licensed rather than sold, which means that publications are becoming more and more centralized. Centralization creates less stable and more "fugitive" artifacts, in that the publishers have the right of withdrawal. Libraries' distribution rights are increasingly limited by their contracts.

Distributed digitized information, such as that on the Internet, adds more layers of complexity to the flow. And, as with all common-pool resources, when technology changes the capture and use of the resource, the rules in use and the community of users will also change. On the other hand, digital information, though subject to congestion, is generally non-subtractive; thus, the resource flow is not subject to erosion (deterioration) in the same way that physical information artifacts are (books, journals, newspapers, etc.).[94]

The Evolution of Scholarly Information

Prior to thirty years ago, the primary information facilities for scholarly information were public and academic libraries. These facilities were in charge of preserving "the scholarly record and the materials for future research"[95] by collecting, storing, preserving, and making available scholarly artifacts—primarily books and journal articles. Rules such as the fair use and first sale doctrines allowed libraries to provide access to the scholarly community.[96] Librarians consulted with university scholars and mainly purchased published scientific and academic books and journals. They made the distribution rules or lending policies and defined the eligible community of users. At that time, it was clear who was included in their community. For a state university library, for example, this usually included the faculty, students, and staff at that university, and any citizen of that state. The library owned its collection and was responsible for the storage, organization, and long-term preservation of the artifacts. The scholarly community sent their articles off for publication and depended on library personnel to meet their needs.

Interlibrary Loan ("ILL")[97] was enhanced in the 1970s through the proliferation of new technology—the photocopy machine,[98] which allowed for duplication and easy lending of journal articles. It was further developed by the organization of the Online Computer Library Center ("OCLC"), the first electronic union catalog. ILL changed the user communities from local to local-regional-national (and later international) communities. With the costs of books and journals skyrocketing, the focus of library services changed from *owning collections* to serve present and future needs, to *accessing materials* for use upon demand.

Since 1995, the development of distributed digital information through network browsers has radically changed many of the traditional institutions of scholarly communication. Research information is moving much faster and much farther, often bypassing the normal publication process. While it is true that recent commodification and privatization of research information threatens the future of libraries' freedom to collect and distribute information, it is only one part of the story. Recent legislation, such

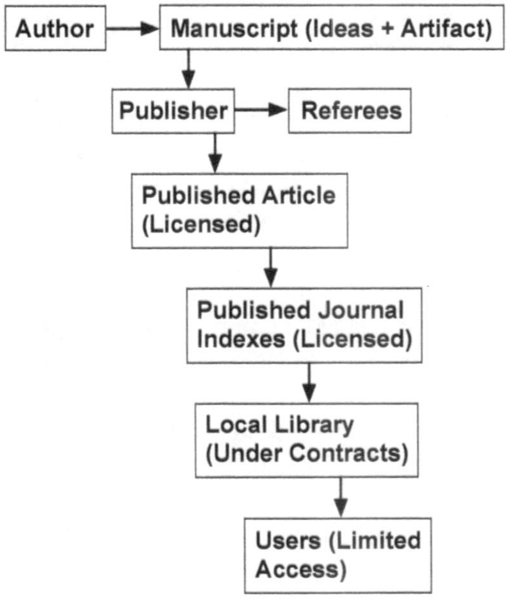

Figure 6.4. Traditional flow of digitized information today.

as the Digital Millennium Copyright Act,[99] the Sonny Bono Copyright Term Extension Act,[100] the proposed legislation of the Uniform Computer Information Transactions Act ("UCITA"),[101] may all adversely affect the costs, access, and availability of scholarly information.[102] This focus of the intellectual public domain literature on commodification and privatization (along with issues of privacy and encryption) concentrates almost solely on the history, interpretation, and possible outcomes of such legislation on copyrighted works that have been *published.* But formal publication is only one type of scholarly communication.

With distributed digitized information, there are various flow patterns of the artifacts with varying property rights or contract arrangements at different points of the process. A sample flow pattern is shown in Figure 6.4. In this scenario, many of the rules in use are now determined by the publisher rather than the library. The facility, in other words, must now license access rights rather than purchase the artifacts. This change from property rights to contracts has multiple impacts on the distribution of scholarly information. The publisher may insist on a pay-per-view agreement, limiting the number of times the artifact can be accessed. Or, it may arbitrarily decide to withdraw certain journals that were formerly available. Frequently, publishers are "bundling" journals in a license package so that individual subscriptions cannot be cancelled by the libraries under that license agreement. At the same time, some contracts allow the publishers to make changes to the bundles at their discretion.[103] Because of the enormous costs of these bundles, there is a growing inequity between the capacity of small versus large libraries to participate in these deals. The license agreements also raise questions about the future of interlibrary loan (which would be a remedy for smaller libraries) since most of the licenses will not allow the copying of digital information.

A major spokesperson for the complexities of digital information for libraries, Clifford Lynch, noted in 1994 that if libraries did not make major changes in their collection practices, their role in store-housing scholarly information would be called into doubt.[104] One of the primary worries is the centralization of digital information:

> We have also yet to encounter the electronic analog of the burning of the great library at Alexandria (either due to natural disaster and inept off-site backup procedures or out of malice or cold, commercial calculation), which was so devastating precisely because in a pre-printing-press world there was such centralization of information at a single site. In a post-printing-press world, we run the danger of returning to the vulnerabilities inherent in such centralization. And it is not only publishers (both commercial and nonprofit) who are moving to centralized storage sites: government at all levels as well is exploiting the potential for low-cost distribution of information through computer networks.[105]

Libraries seem to be at the mercy of the publishers of scholarly digital information. They are dependent on digital publishers not only for the primary journals but also for the indexing and cataloging of scholarly journals. Because they add and delete journal titles from journal indexes, publishers have enormous power to shape the appearance and availability of research. Hence, libraries are able to provide only limited access, rather than the previous open access to journals in their collection. Even with the constraints of the new formal rules, however, library and information specialists are designing new institutions to deal with some of these problems. For instance, to tackle the problem of the precariousness or "fugitiveness" of digital information, one collective action initiative to counteract the loss of control over information is Lots of Copies Keep Stuff Safe ("LOCKSS"), which allows facilities to give permanence to the digital journals to which they subscribe.[106] If license agreements are cancelled, the libraries will still have digital copies of the journals to which they previously subscribed.

Public and academic libraries are also struggling with the possible ramifications of new intellectual property legislation, which more and more often contradicts the very nature of digital information.

> [C]opying occurs with all digital information. Use your computer to read a book, look at a picture, watch a movie, or listen to a song, and you inevitably make one or more copies. Contrast this with the use of traditional media: Reading a book does not involve making a copy of it, nor does watching a movie or listening to a song.
>
> This intimate connection between access and copying has considerable significance in the context of intellectual property protection. One of the essential elements of copyright—the right to control reproduction—works as expected in the world of traditional media, where there is an obvious distinction between access and reproduction and where the copyright owner's control of reproduction provides just that. But in the digital world, where no access is possible except by copying, complete control of copying would mean control of access as well.[107]

One type of action in response to the "digital dilemmas" is the increased monitoring, reporting, and educating to inform the public and information professionals about proposed legislation that may affect the access, costs, and distribution of scholarly information. Professional groups such as the American Library Association ("ALA"),[108] EDUCAUSE, and the Association of Research Libraries ("ARL") are taking on proactive roles to promote continued access to scholarly information. In ARL's May 2001 Membership Meeting Proceedings, Jean-Claude Guédon stressed that "mapping effective counterattacks" against journal publishers who have transformed scholarly publication into big business "will require a fuller understanding of the situation and its roots."[109]

One of the most important sources of information on the developments of digital scholarly communication and research since December 2001 has been *The Free Online Scholarship (FOS) Newsletter*[110] written and compiled by Peter Suber, a professor of philosophy at Earhlam College. The newsletter presents a wide range of news and discussion on the migration of print scholarship to the Internet and efforts to make scholarly information available to readers free of charge. Its broader purpose is "to explore how the internet is transforming scholarly research and how researchers can realize its full potential."[111]

Libraries face many complex issues pertaining to the future of academic scholarly materials and its availability. Jessica Litman[112] and Lawrence Lessig,[113] among others, have discussed the precariousness of the fair use and first sale doctrines as applied to licensed digital information.[114] As authors and information providers design new institutions to disseminate scholarly communication, library professionals must redefine many of their own institutions. Librarians can no longer build viable collections by selecting materials out of publishers' catalogs. They are becoming more actively involved in working with scholars, technologists, and policymakers to build trusted, reciprocal digital archive and repository systems.

The international e-prints "revolution" makes scholarly research freely available in unprecedented ways, in great contrast with the new legislation that increases copyright and patent restrictions, and encourages contract over property law through the constraints of embedded licensing agreements. The movement officially began with the mounting of arXiv.org at Los Alamos National Laboratory.[115] Developed in 1991 by physicist and information specialist Paul Ginsparg, arXiv.org was designed to serve as a repository for digital papers in physics and mathematics. By 1993, the site had received around 500 submissions. By September 24, 2002, the site had received 209,565 submitted papers.[116] Importantly, around 70% of the submissions came from outside of the United States.[117] The numbers reflect a better balance with much greater provision and access to international information, particularly in developing countries. The papers are free but unrefereed, requiring scholars to judge for themselves the accuracy and quality of the work. This archive is the first that actually changes the representation and visibility of the scholarly record.[118] The average number of site users range from 60,000 to 130,000 per day depending upon the day of the week.[119]

There are hundreds of other digital archives.[120] Some, like EconWPA,[121] are devoted to self-archiving and free distribution of working papers in economics. It is an impressive archive because of the number of other participating institutes. Others, like the Oxford Text Archive,[122] make available historical scholarly materials that are in the public domain and make the authorized, full-text versions universally available for free. BioMed Central[123] is the site of a commercial publisher that offers all its medicine and biology journal articles free of charge and provides a systematic pre-print service for research reports.[124] The Digital Library of the Commons[125] is both an e-print repository for self-archiving as well as a traditional/digital library.

An example of an effective grassroots initiative is that taken by the Public Library of Science ("PLS"), a nonprofit organization of scientists dedicated to making the world's scientific and medical literature freely accessible "for the benefit of scientific progress, education and the public good."[126] PLS has so far encouraged over 30,888 scientists from 182 countries to sign its open letter to publishers to make their publications freely available on the website PubMed Central.[127] By September 2002, there were over eighty full-text journals available at this site.[128] Another new collective action initiative is the Creative Commons[129] founded by Lawrence Lessig, James Boyle, and others to promote "the innovative reuse of all sorts of intellectual works."[130] Their first project is to "offer the public a set of copyright licenses free of charge."[131]

A breakthrough for alternative publishing initiatives came only two years ago with the development of new technologies, data and metadata standards, and information provision communities. The Open Archives Initiative ("OAI") and the development of the free E-prints software[132] are already reshaping the direction of scholarly publication by establishing "low-barrier" interoperable standards.[133] OAI was established in October 1999 by an international group of information scholars to develop and promote interoperability standards that aim to facilitate the efficient dissemination of scholarly communication through the establishment of archives for e-prints and other digital materials. In OAI terminology, the information artifact is a "record." The protocol developed by OAI provides access to the metadata of all OAI-compliant repositories by all networked servers (not limited to e-print servers).[134]

In this scenario [Figure 6.5], the author takes on a self-governing role in the distribution of scholarly information by submitting her digital file to an E-print repository (facility), such as CogPrints,[135] a repository for cognitive science, psychology, neuroscience, philosophy, linguistics, and biology. If the article has been, or is to be, published, she may get permission from the publisher,[136] amend the copyright transfer agreement with the publisher,[137] or submit the preprint (the refereed version) or a postscript (a subsequent revision to the published version).

What is new in the self-archiving initiative is that authors are participating, independently of governments and markets, in an international epistemic community that is committed to building an interoperable global scholarly library—a universal public good for which the more who have access, the greater the benefit for everyone.

Earlier we mentioned a prevalent view (particularly of Hardin advocates) that if anyone can use a resource, no one will have an incentive to conserve its use or to invest in improvements.[138] This does not seem to be the case for scholarly information. There are several incentives for taking

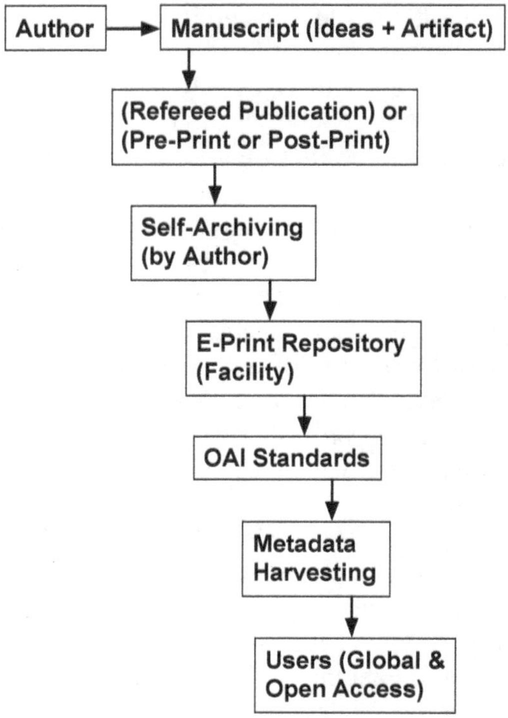

Figure 6.5. Self-archiving digital information flow using the Internet.

an active role in these new information production institutions. Cost is one. Paul Ginsparg estimates the average cost per published journal article to be between $1000 and $2000, compared with the average cost of putting a self-archived paper on the web between $1 and $100.[139] Universities have incentives to support such self-archiving initiatives. Stevan Harnad points out that such action would free libraries from the increasing burden of their serials budgets. "This would be a small investment with an eventually huge return (reduction and eventual elimination of all annual Subscription/Site-License/Pay-Per-View ("S/L/P") expenditure)."[140] Rebecca Eisenberg points to scientific recognition and credibility that comes with public disclosure and increased visibility of information.[141] Global distribution of information facilitates better scholarly collaborative research. And, of course, a primary incentive is the sheer timeliness of distributed digital information with its ability to publish instantly and disseminate information, obviating the long delays of traditional publications.

A further development in building new standards, rules, and cooperative institutions to create resilience for the global knowledge resource is the growing movement to create Trusted Digital Repositories. A recent report by the Research Libraries Group and OCLC defines the required actions and rules for such systems as having: (1) audibility, security, and communication; (2) compliance and conscientiousness; (3) certification, copying controls, and following rules; (4) backup policies and avoiding, detecting, and restoring lost/corrupted information; (5) reputation and performance; (6) agreements between creators and providers; (7) open sharing of information about what it is preserving and for whom; (8) balanced risk, benefit, and cost; (9) complementarity, cost-effectiveness, scalability, and confidence; and (10) evaluation of system components.[142] These design principles point to the kinds of cooperative behaviors and system resilience that are needed to sustain scholarly information as a common-pool resource in an increasingly digital world.

The purpose of this section has been to give examples of collective action initiatives that create new institutions to manage and disseminate scholarly information. We have not discussed the risks and costs that may be involved. There are concerns among some academics that self-archiving may drive academic publishers out of business. Others question whether peer-review will be as respected and authoritative outside of commercial publications. There is also a delicate balance between a possible decline in the well-managed files that have been provided by library professionals in the past and the advantages of increased online accessibility. Confusion over versions and provenance of artifacts is inevitable without standards like the Machine-Readable Catalogue ("MARC")[143] record format. In addition, the fugitive nature of digital archives where authors usually have the right to submit *and* unsubmit is very different from traditional libraries where authors and editors are not permitted to remove their articles and books at whim.

Conclusion

Governments, market forces, publishers, and traditional academic libraries can influence, but are not able to stop, the international movement of distributed information. The physical and virtual characteristics of distributed digital information have created a completely new type of information artifact.

The community of users—the international scholarly community—has grown increasingly aware that its shared resource of scholarly information is at risk. Growing international collaborative research necessitates immediate access and exchange of communication. Groups of scholars and information specialists have begun coordinating strategies to obtain higher joint benefits and to reduce their joint harm. Many of these collective action initiatives are at the experimental stage, but the success of arXiv.org gives reason to believe in the success of other efforts to sustain the intellectual public domain.

We have described a gravitation of scholars' roles from passive *appropriator* of information to active *provider* of information by contributing directly into the common pool. Their multiple goals include not only sustaining the resource (the intellectual public domain) but building equity of information access and provision, and creating more efficient methods of dissemination through informal, shared protocols, standards, and rules among the local and global scholarly community.

Acknowledgments

This paper was initially presented at the Conference on the Public Domain, held at the Duke University School of Law on November 9–11, 2001, and the Workshop in Political Theory and Policy Analysis, March 25, 2002. We would like to thank Gerry Bernbom, James Boyle, Julie Cohen, John Daly, Laura Gassaway, Shubha Ghosh, James Hanley, Tobias Klaus, Harini Nagendra, Robert Najlis, Vincent Ostrom, Enrico Schaar, Peter Suber, James Walker, and Wang Jianxun for their helpful and insightful comments. We are eternally grateful to Patty Zielinski for her expert technological, editorial assistance as well as her perseverance and patience. We also wish to thank the Ford Foundation for its essential support.

Notes

This chapter was originally published in *Law and Contemporary Problems* 66(1&2) (Winter/Spring 2003): 111–45.

1. *See* James Boyle, *The Second Enclosure Movement and the Construction of the Public Domain*, 66 LAW & CONTEMP. PROBS. 33 (Winter/Spring 2003).

2. There is a rapidly growing legal literature on the ramifications of recent intellectual property legislation and its impact on the intellectual public domain. Some of the works that seem particularly relevant to the question of the information commons are: JAMES BOYLE, SHAMANS, SOFTWARE, AND SPLEENS: LAW AND THE CONSTRUCTION OF THE INFORMATION SOCIETY (1996); Yochai Benkler, *Free as the Air to Common Use: First Amendment Constraints on Enclosure of the*

Public Domain, 74 N.Y.U. L. REV. 354 (1999); Dan L. Burk, *Muddy Rules for Cyberspace*, 21 CARDOZO L. REV. 121 (1999); Julie E. Cohen, *Copyright and the Jurisprudence of Self-Help*, 13 BERKELEY TECH. L.J. 1089 (1998); Mark A. Lemley, *Beyond Preemption: The Law and Policy of Intellectual Property Licensing*, 87 CAL. L. REV. 111 (1999); Michael J. Madison, *Complexity and Copyright in Contradiction*, 18 CARDOZO ARTS & ENT. L.J. 125 (2000); Robert P. Merges, *Property Rights Theory and the Commons: The Case of Scientific Research*, 13 SOC. PHIL. & POL'Y 145 (1996); J.H. Reichman & Jonathan A. Franklin, *Privately Legislated Intellectual Property Rights: Reconciling Freedom of Contract with Public Good Uses of Information*, 147 U. PA. L. REV. 875 (1999); Carol M. Rose, *Expanding the Choices for the Global Commons: Comparing Newfangled Tradable Allowance Schemes to Old-Fashioned Common Property Regimes*, 10 DUKE ENVTL. L. & POL'Y F. 45 (Fall 1999); Paul A. David, A Tragedy of the Public Knowledge "Commons"? Global Science, Intellectual Property and the Digital Technology Boomerang (SIEPR Discussion Paper no. 00–02, Stanford Institute for Economic Policy Research, 2000), *available at* http://siepr.stanford.edu/papers/pdf/00-02.html (last visited Oct. 10, 2002); Lawrence Lessig, Reclaiming a Commons, Keynote Address at Harvard University (May 20, 1999), *available at* http://cyber.law.harvard.edu/events/lessigkeynote.pdf [hereinafter Lessig, Harvard].

3. *See* BOYLE, *supra* note 2, at 6–7; Yochai Benkler, *Overcoming Agoraphobia: Building the Commons of the Digitally Networked Environment*, 11 HARV. J.L. & TECH. 287 (Winter 1998); Jane C. Ginsburg, *Copyright and Control of New Technologies of Dissemination*, 101 COLUM. L. REV. 1613 (2001).

4. Boyle, *supra* note 1; James Boyle, *A Politics of Intellectual Property: Environmentalism for the Net?*, 47 DUKE L.J. 87, 94 (1997).

5. Many new common-pool resources have "remained unclaimed due to a lack of technology for extracting their value and for establishing and sustaining property rights." Elinor Ostrom, *Foreword*, *in* SUSAN J. BUCK, THE GLOBAL COMMONS: AN INTRODUCTION xiii (1998).

6. *See* J.E. Michael Arnold, *Devolution of Control of Common Pool Resources to Local Communities: Experiences in Forestry*, *in* ACCESS TO LAND, RURAL POVERTY, AND PUBLIC ACTION 163, 16465 (Alain de Janvry et al. eds., 2001).

7. *See, e.g.*, Stephen R. Palumbi, *Humans as the World's Greatest Evolutionary Force*, SCIENCE, Sept. 7, 2001, at 1786, *available at* http://www.sciencemag.org/cgi/content/full/293/5536/1786.

8. *See* Boyle, *supra* note 1, at 19.

9. F. A. Hayek, *The Use of Knowledge in Society*, 35 AM. ECON. REV. 519, 521 (1945).

10. *See* CHARLOTTE HESS, A COMPREHENSIVE BIBLIOGRAPHY OF COMMON-POOL RESOURCES (CD-ROM, 1999). This bibliography contains 22,500 citations of works on the commons. A searchable version of this bibliography is available at http://www.iascp.org/cprbibs.html (last updated Dec. 16, 1999). A new edition with 35,000 citations is forthcoming.

11. Lawrence Lessig, Code and the Commons, Keynote Address at the Conference on Media Convergence, held at Fordham University Law School (Feb. 9, 1999), *available at* http://cyber.law.harvard.edu/works/lessig/fordham.pdf (last visited Sept. 1, 2002).

12. Yochai Benkler, The Commons as a Neglected Factor of Information Policy, Remarks at the Telecommunications Policy Research Conference (Sept. 1998), *available at* http://www.law.nyu.edu/benklery/commons.pdf (last visited Sept. 1, 2002).

13. Jessica Litman, *The Public Domain*, 39 EMORY L.J. 965, 975 (1990).

14. Boyle, *supra* note 2, at xiv (pointing out the institutional nature of a commons: "Even a conventional economic analysis supports the idea that it is in the interest of those who are exploiting a 'commons' to make sure that the commons continues to exist.").

15. DANIEL ORAN, ORAN'S DICTIONARY OF THE LAW 392 (3d ed. 2000).

16. Charlotte Hess, Is There Anything New Under the Sun?: A Discussion and Survey of Studies on New Commons and the Internet, *presented at* Constituting the Commons: Crafting Sustainable Commons in the New Millennium, the eighth biennial conference of the International Association for the Study of Common Property (May 31–June 4, 2000), *available at* http://dlc.dlib.indiana.edu/documents/dir0/00/00/05/12/dlc-00000512-00/iascp2000.pdf (last visited Dec. 3, 2002).

17. HENRY SUMNER MAINE, ANCIENT LAW (Raymond Firth ed., Beacon Press 1963) (1861).

18. *See* PAOLO GROSSI, AN ALTERNATIVE TO PRIVATE PROPERTY: COLLECTIVE PROPERTY IN THE JURIDICAL CONSCIOUSNESS OF THE NINETEENTH CENTURY 15 (1981).

19. Maine, *supra* note 17, at 252.

20. PERSPECTIVES ON PROPERTY LAW (Robert C. Ellickson et al. eds., 2d ed. 1995).

21. H. Scott Gordon, *The Economic Theory of a Common-Property Resource: The Fishery*, 62 J. POL. ECON. 124 (1954); Anthony D. Scott, *The Fishery: The Objectives of Sole Ownership*, 63 J. POL. ECON. 116 (1955).

22. *See* David Feeny et al., *The Tragedy of the Commons: Twenty-Two Years Later*, 18 HUM. ECOLOGY 1, 2 (1990).

23. Garrett Hardin, *The Tragedy of the Commons*, SCIENCE, Dec. 13, 1968, at 1243.

24. *Id.* at 1244–45.

25. *Id.* at 1245.

26. *Id.* at 1244.

27. Commenting on Gordon and Scott's work, David Feeny says: "In this setting, as the incisive analysis of Gordon and Scott demonstrates, each fisherman will take into account only his own marginal costs and revenues and ignores the fact that increases in his catch affect the returns to fishing effort for other fishermen as well as the health of future fish stocks. . . . [E]conomic rent is dissi-

pated; economic overfishing, which may also lead to ecological overfishing, is the result." David Feeny et al., *Questioning the Assumptions of the "Tragedy of the Commons" Model of Fisheries*, 72 LAND ECON. 187, 189 (1996).

28. *But see* JEAN-MARIE BALAND & JEAN-PHILIPPE PLATTEAU, HALTING DEGRADATION OF NATURAL RESOURCES: IS THERE A ROLE FOR RURAL COMMUNITIES? 25–35 (1996).

29. *See* PARTHA DASGUPTA & GEOFFREY M. HEAL, ECONOMIC THEORY AND EXHAUSTIBLE RESOURCES (1979); Robyn M. Dawes, *The Commons Dilemma Game: An N-Person Mixed-Motive Game with a Dominating Strategy for Defection*, 13 OR. RES. BULL. (1973).

30. *See* RICHARD A. POSNER, ECONOMIC ANALYSIS OF LAW 28–30 (2d ed. 1977); Harold Demsetz, *Toward a Theory of Property Rights*, 57 AM. ECON. REV. 347 (1967); Randy T. Simmons et al., The Tragedy of the Commons Revisited: Politics vs. Private Property (Center for Private Conservation, Competitive Enterprise Institute, Washington, D.C., 1996).

31. William Ophuls, *Leviathan or Oblivion?*, *in* TOWARD A STEADY STATE ECONOMY 214, 219 (Herman E. Daly ed., 1973) ("Hobbes's answer to the tragedy of the commons then is a benevolent form of autocracy. . . .").

32. Feeny et al., *supra* note 27, at 195.

33. *See* PROCEEDINGS OF THE CONFERENCE ON COMMON PROPERTY RESOURCE MANAGEMENT (National Research Council ed., 1986).

34. *See, e.g.*, ROBERT McC. NETTING, BALANCING ON AN ALP: ECOLOGICAL CHANGE AND CONTINUITY IN A SWISS MOUNTAIN COMMUNITY (1981); THE QUESTION OF THE COMMONS: THE CULTURE AND ECOLOGY OF COMMUNAL RESOURCES (Bonnie J. McCay & James M. Acheson eds., 1987); Robert McC. Netting, *Territory, Property, and Tenure*, *in* BEHAVIORAL AND SOCIAL SCIENCE RESEARCH: A NATIONAL RESOURCE 446, 446 (R. McC. Adams et al. eds., 1982).

35. *See, e.g.*, THOMAS F. GLICK, IRRIGATION AND SOCIETY IN MEDIEVAL VALENCIA (1970) (focusing on the conflict arising from an irrigation system that necessitated cooperation); ARTHUR MAASS & RAYMOND L. ANDERSON, . . . AND THE DESERT SHALL REJOICE: CONFLICT, GROWTH, AND JUSTICE IN ARID ENVIRONMENTS (1986) (observing irrigation systems in a number of the world's deserts, including southeastern Spain and the western United States).

36. *See* COMMON PROPERTY RESOURCES: ECOLOGY AND COMMUNITY-BASED SUSTAINABLE DEVELOPMENT, at ix, 2 (Fikret Berkes ed., 1989); MAKING THE COMMONS WORK: THEORY, PRACTICE, AND POLICY, at xi, 4 (Daniel W. Bromley et al. eds., 1992); ELINOR OSTROM, GOVERNING THE COMMONS 2 (1990); ROBERT WADE, VILLAGE REPUBLICS: ECONOMIC CONDITIONS FOR COLLECTIVE ACTION IN SOUTH INDIA xiv (1994). *See also generally* NIRMAL SENGUPTA, MANAGING COMMON PROPERTY: IRRIGATION IN INDIA AND THE PHILIPPINES (1991); A SEA OF SMALL BOATS (John C. Cordell ed., 1989); THE TRADITIONAL KNOWLEDGE AND MANAGEMENT OF COASTAL SYSTEMS IN ASIA AND THE PACIFIC (Kenneth Ruddle & Robert E. Johannes eds., 1985).

37. *See* Paul Samuelson, *The Pure Theory of Public Expenditure*, 36 REV. ECON. & STAT. 387 (1954).

38. *See generally* RICHARD A. MUSGRAVE, THE THEORY OF PUBLIC FINANCE: A STUDY IN PUBLIC ECONOMY (1959).

39. Vincent Ostrom & Elinor Ostrom, *Public Goods and Public Choices*, *in* ALTERNATIVES FOR DELIVERING PUBLIC SERVICES: TOWARD IMPROVED PERFORMANCE 7, 9–14 (E. S. Savas ed., 1977).

40. *Id.* (describing this attribute as jointness of use or consumption); RULES, GAMES, AND COMMON-POOL RESOURCES 6 (Elinor Ostrom et al. eds., 1994) [hereinafter RULES].

41. *See* Edella Schlager et al., *Mobile Flows, Storage, and Self-Organized Institutions for Governing Common-Pool Resources*, 70 LAND ECON. 294 (1994).

42. Feeny et al., *supra* note 22, at 5–9.

43. Bromley et al., *supra* note 36, at 4; KATAR SINGH, MANAGING COMMON POOL RESOURCES: PRINCIPLES AND CASE STUDIES 314–19 (1994).

44. William Blomquist & Elinor Ostrom, *Institutional Capacity and the Resolution of a Commons Dilemma*, 5 POL'Y STUD. REV. 383, 383 (1985).

45. *See, e.g.*, Dean Lueck, *Property Rights and the Economic Logic of Wildlife Institutions*, 35 NAT. RESOURCES J. 625, 636 (1995).

46. *See* Gerald Bernbom, Analyzing the Internet as a Common Pool Resource: The Problem of Network Congestion, *presented at* Constituting the Commons: Crafting Sustainable Commons in the New Millennium, the eighth biennial conference of the International Association for the Study of Common Property (May 31–June 4, 2000), *available at* http://dlc.dlib.indiana.edu/documents/dir0/00/00/02/18/index.html.

47. Siegfried V. Ciriacy-Wantrup & Richard C. Bishop, *"Common Property" as a Concept in Natural Resource Policy*, 15 NAT. RESOURCES J. 713, 715 (1975).

48. *See* DANIEL W. BROMLEY, ENVIRONMENT AND ECONOMY: PROPERTY RIGHTS AND PUBLIC POLICY 22–23 (1991); Daniel W. Bromley, *The Commons, Property, and Common-Property Regimes*, *in* MAKING THE COMMONS WORK: THEORY, PRACTICE, AND POLICY 3, 3–4 (Daniel W. Bromley et al. eds., 1992).

49. *See supra* text accompanying notes 21–27.

50. *See* JOHN H. DALES, POLLUTION, PROPERTY, AND PRICES: AN ESSAY IN POLICY-MAKING AND ECONOMICS (1968).

51. As is the case for works in the public domain, works that are uncopyrightable, unprotectable, or for which copyright has expired. *See* Litman, *supra* note 13, at 967.

52. This point is well illustrated in Robert Higgs, *Legally Induced Technical Regress in the Washington Salmon Fishery*, *in* EMPIRICAL STUDIES IN INSTITUTIONAL CHANGE 247, 251 (Lee J. Alston et al. eds., 1996). The article outlines the case where the state governments of Oregon and Washington intervened in the early twentieth century to prevent local salmon fishermen from devising rules that would have limited entry and established harvesting limits. Fishing unions along

U.S. coastal areas tried to organize inshore fisheries to limit entry and establish harvesting limits during the 1950s. Even though their efforts could not have had a serious impact on prices due to the presence of an active international market for fish, the fishing unions were prosecuted by the U.S. Department of Justice and found in violation of the Sherman Antitrust Act. Ronald N. Johnson & Gary D. Libecap, *Contracting Problems and Regulation: The Case of the Fishery*, 72 AM. ECON. REV. 1005, 1007–08 (1982). Thus, U.S. inshore fisheries have effectively been open-access resources during much of the twentieth century as a result of governmental action to prevent local fishing groups from establishing forms of common-property regimes within those political jurisdictions. In more recent times, however, both the national and state governments have reversed their prior stands and have actively sought ways of creating forms of co-management in inshore fisheries. *See* Evelyn Pinkerton, *Where Do We Go From Here? The Future of Traditional Ecological Knowledge and Resource Management in Native Communities*, *in* TRADITIONAL ECOLOGICAL KNOWLEDGE AND MODERN ENVIRONMENTAL ASSESSMENT 51, 56–58 (P. Boothroyd & B. Sadler eds., 1994); Evelyn Pinkerton, *Local Fisheries Co-Management: A Review of International Experiences and Their Implications for Salmon Management in British Columbia*, 51 CANADIAN J. FISHERIES & AQUATIC SCI. 2363 (1994); James A. Wilson, When are Common Property Institutions Efficient? (working paper, Department of Agriculture and Resource Economics, University of Maine, Orono, 1995) (on file with authors).

53. J.E. Michael Arnold & J. Gabriel Campbell, *Collective Management of Hill Forests in Nepal: The Community Forestry Development Project*, *in* PROCEEDINGS OF THE CONFERENCE ON COMMON PROPERTY RESOURCE MANAGEMENT 425, 425 (National Research Council ed., 1986).

54. Fikret Berkes & Carl Folke, *Linking Social and Ecological Systems for Resilience and Sustainability*, *in* LINKING SOCIAL AND ECOLOGICAL SYSTEMS: MANAGEMENT PRACTICES AND SOCIAL MECHANISMS FOR BUILDING RESILIENCE 1, 13–20 (Fikret Berkes & Carl Folke eds., 1998).

55. THRÁINN EGGERTSSON, ECONOMIC BEHAVIOR AND INSTITUTIONS 223–28 (1990); Thráinn Eggertsson, *The Economic Rationale for Communal Resources*, *in* Vol. I, A CONFERENCE ON COMMON PROPERTY REGIMES: LAW AND MANAGEMENT OF NON-PRIVATE RESOURCES 41 (Erling Berge ed., 1993); Dean Lueck, *Common Property as an Egalitarian Share Contract*, 25 J. ECON. BEHAV. & ORG. 93, 93–108 (1994).

56. *See, e.g.*, CLARK C. GIBSON, POLITICIANS AND POACHERS: THE POLITICAL ECONOMY OF WILDLIFE POLICY IN AFRICA 153–63 (1999).

57. *See, e.g.*, MINOTI CHAKRAVARTY-KAUL, COMMON LANDS AND CUSTOMARY LAW: INSTITUTIONAL CHANGES IN NORTH INDIA OVER THE PAST TWO CENTURIES 12–15 (1996).

58. *See* William Ascher, *Coping with Complexity and Organizational Interests in Natural Resource Management*, 4 ECOSYSTEMS 742 (2001), *available at* http://www.fish.washington.edu/people/naiman/Watershed/readings/ascher.pdf (last visited Dec. 3, 2002).

59. WILLIAM ASCHER, COMMUNITIES AND SUSTAINABLE FORESTRY IN DEVELOPING COUNTRIES 10–14 (1995); *see also* Rita Hilton, *Institutional Incentives for Resource Mobilization: An Analysis of Irrigation Schemes in Nepal*, 4 J. THEORETICAL POL. 283 (1992). The harmful effects of nationalizing forests that had earlier been governed by local user-groups have been well documented for Thailand, the Niger, Nepal, and India. Arnold, *supra* note 53, at 430–31; David Feeny, *Agricultural Expansion and Forest Depletion in Thailand, 1900–1975*, *in* WORLD DEFORESTATION IN THE TWENTIETH CENTURY 112, 125–26, 129 (John F. Richards & Richard P. Tucker eds., 1988); Madhav Gadgil & Prema Iyer, *On the Diversification of Common-Property Resource Use by Indian Society*, *in* COMMON PROPERTY RESOURCES: ECOLOGY AND COMMUNITY-BASED SUSTAINABLE DEVELOPMENT 240, 247–49 (Fikret Berkes ed., 1989); N.S. Jodha, *Depletion of Common Property Resources in India: Micro-Level Evidence*, *in* RURAL DEVELOPMENT AND POPULATION: INSTITUTIONS AND POLICY 261, 270–78 (Geoffery McNicoll & Mead Cain eds., 1990); James T. Thomson et al., *Institutional Dynamics: The Evolution and Dissolution of Common-Property Resource Management*, *in* MAKING THE COMMONS WORK: THEORY, PRACTICE, AND POLICY 129, 154–55 (Daniel W. Bromley et al. eds., 1992); *see also* Donald A. Messerschmidt, *People and Resources in Nepal: Customary Resource Management Systems of the Upper Kali Gandaki*, *in* PROCEEDINGS OF THE CONFERENCE ON COMMON PROPERTY RESOURCE MANAGEMENT 455 (National Research Council ed., 1986). Similar results have occurred when inshore fisheries were taken over by state or national agencies from local control. *See* PARTHA DASGUPTA, THE CONTROL OF RESOURCES 13–40 (1982); Wilfrido D. Cruz, *Overfishing and Conflict in a Traditional Fishery: San Miguel Bay, Philippines*, *in* PROCEEDINGS OF THE CONFERENCE ON COMMON PROPERTY RESOURCE MANAGEMENT 115, 115 (National Research Council ed., 1986); *see also* John C. Cordell & Margaret A. McKean, *Sea Tenure in Bahia, Brazil*, *in* MAKING THE COMMONS WORK: THEORY, PRACTICE, AND POLICY 183 (Daniel W. Bromley et al. eds., 1992).

60. *See* JOHN R. COMMONS, LEGAL FOUNDATIONS OF CAPITALISM (1968).

61. In Schlager and Ostrom, the term used for *extraction* is *withdrawal*. Edella Schlager & Elinor Ostrom, *Property-Rights Regimes and Natural Resources: A Conceptual Analysis*, 68 LAND ECON. 249, 250 (1992).

62. *See* Demsetz, *supra* note 30.

63. Bruce A. Larson & Daniel W. Bromley, *Property Rights, Externalities, and Resource Degradation: Locating the Tragedy*, 33 J. DEV. ECON. 235 (1990).

64. The operational rights of entry and use may be finely divided into quite specific "tenure niches" that vary by season, by use, by technology, and by space. JOHN W. BRUCE, LEGAL BASES FOR THE MANAGEMENT OF FOREST RESOURCES AS COMMON PROPERTY 12–14 (1999). Tenure niches may overlap when one set of users owns the right to harvest fruits from trees, another set of users owns the right to the timber in these trees, and the trees may be located on land owned by still others. *See* John W. Bruce et al., *Tenures in Transition, Tenures in Conflict:*

Examples from the Zimbabwe Social Forest, 58 RURAL SOC. 626 (1993). Operational rules may allow authorized users to transfer access and withdrawal rights either temporarily through a rental agreement, or permanently when these rights are assigned or sold to others. *See* Allen Adasiak, *Alaska's Experience with Limited Entry*, 36 J. FISHERIES RES. BOARD CAN. 770 (1979) (describing the rights of authorized users of the Alaskan salmon and herring fisheries).

65. E. Paul Durrenberger & Gisli Palsson, *The Grass Roots and the State: Resource Management in Icelandic Fishing*, *in* THE QUESTION OF THE COMMONS: THE CULTURE AND ECOLOGY OF COMMUNAL RESOURCES 370, 374–75 (B. J. McCay and J. M. Acheson eds. 1987). Another example is the net fishers of Jambudwip, India, who annually regulate the positioning of nets to avoid interference, but do not have the right to determine who may fish along the coast. *See* BIKASH RAYCHAUDHURI, THE MOON AND NET: STUDY OF A TRANSIENT COMMUNITY OF FISHERMEN AT JAMBUDWIP (Government of India Press, Anthropological Survey of India 1980).

66. *See generally* PAUL BENJAMIN ET AL., INSTITUTIONS, INCENTIVES, AND IRRIGATION IN NEPAL (1994).

67. *See generally* ROBERT A. DAHL & CHARLES E. LINDBLOM, POLITICS, ECONOMICS AND WELFARE: PLANNING AND POLITICO-ECONOMIC SYSTEMS RESOLVED INTO BASIC SOCIAL PROCESSES (1963); JOHN MICHAEL MONTIAS, THE STRUCTURE OF ECONOMIC SYSTEMS (1976).

68. *See* Demsetz, *supra* note 30, at 355–57.

69. Frank Place and Peter Hazell conducted surveys in Ghana, Kenya, and Rwanda to ascertain if indigenous land-right systems were a constraint on agricultural productivity. They and others found that having the rights of a proprietor as contrasted to an owner in these settings did not affect investment decisions and productivity. *See* Frank Place & Peter Hazell, *Productivity Effects of Indigenous Land Tenure Systems in Sub-Saharan Africa*, 75 AM. J. AGRIC. ECON. 10 (1993). In densely settled regions, however, proprietorship over agricultural land may not be sufficient. *See* GERSHON FEDER ET AL., LAND POLICIES AND FARM PRODUCTIVITY IN THAILAND (1988); Terry L. Anderson & Dean Lueck, *Land Tenure and Agricultural Productivity on Indian Reservations*, 35 J.L. & ECON. 427 (1992). As land is densely settled, the absence of a title reduces the options for farmers to sell their land and reap a return on this asset. Without a title, farmers lack collateral to obtain credit to invest more intensively in the productive potential of their land. *See* Lee J. Alston et al., *The Determinants and Impact of Property Rights: Land Titles on the Brazilian Frontier*, 12 J.L. ECON. & ORG. 25 (1996).

70. *See generally* Arun Agrawal, *Rules, Rule Making, and Rule Breaking: Examining the Fit between Rule Systems and Resource Use*, *in* RULES, *supra* note 40, at 267; WILLIAM BLOMQUIST, DIVIDING THE WATERS: GOVERNING GROUNDWATER IN SOUTHERN CALIFORNIA (1992); WAI FUNG LAM, GOVERNING IRRIGATION SYSTEMS IN NEPAL: INSTITUTIONS, INFRASTRUCTURE, AND COLLECTIVE ACTION

(1998); Edella Schlager, *Fishers' Institutional Responses to Common-Pool Resource Dilemmas*, *in* RULES, *supra* note 40 at 247; Shui-Yan Tang, *Building Community Organizations: Credible Commitment and the New Institutional Economics*, 13 HUMAN SYS. MGMT. 221 (1994).

71. David Miller, *The Evolution of Mexico's Caribbean Spiny Lobster Fishery*, *in* COMMON PROPERTY RESOURCES: ECOLOGY AND COMMUNITY-BASED SUSTAINABLE DEVELOPMENT 185 (Fikret Berkes ed., 1989).

72. *See* Robert Yoder & Edward Martin, *Water Rights and Equity Issue: A Case from Nepal*, *in* SEARCHING FOR EQUITY: CONCEPTIONS OF JUSTICE AND EQUITY IN PEASANT IRRIGATION 133 (R. Boelens & G. Dávila eds., 1998); *see also* ROBERT Y. SIY, JR., COMMUNITY RESOURCE MANAGEMENT: LESSONS FROM THE ZANJERA (1982); MAASS, *supra* note 35.

73. Some of these include studies of surfer's waves, sports, national budgets, public radio, traditional music, knowledge and information, air slots, campus commons, urban commons (apartment communities and residential community associations, streets, parking places, playgrounds, reclaimed buildings etc.), highways and transboundary transportation systems, the Internet (domain names, infrastructure, acceptable use policies), tourism landscapes, cultural treasures, car-sharing institutions, garbage, and sewage. For citations to these works, see Hess, *supra* note 16.

74. *See* P. Kollock & Marc Smith, *Managing the Virtual Commons: Cooperation and Conflict in Computer Communities*, *in* COMPUTER-MEDIATED COMMUNICATION: LINGUISTIC, SOCIAL AND CROSS-CULTURAL PERSPECTIVES 109 (S. C. Herring ed., 1996); Douglas S. Noonan, *Internet Decentralization, Feedback, and Self-Organization*, *in* MANAGING THE COMMONS 188 (John A. Baden & Douglas S. Noonan eds., 1998); B. A. Huberman & Rajan M. Lukose, *Social Dilemmas and Internet Congestion*, SCIENCE, Jul. 25, 1997, at 535.

75. Michael A. Heller, *The Tragedy of the Anticommons: Property in the Transition from Marx to Markets*, 111 HARV. L. REV. 621 (1998).

76. *See generally* Elinor Ostrom et al., *Revisiting the Commons: Local Lessons, Global Challenges*, SCIENCE, Apr. 9, 1999, at 278.

77. *See, e.g.*, Keith Aoki, *Neocolonialism, Anticommons Property, and Biopiracy in the (Not-So-Brave) New World Order of International Intellectual Property Protection*, 6 IND. J. GLOBAL LEGAL STUD. 11 (1998); Michael A. Heller & Rebecca S. Eisenberg, *Can Patents Deter Innovation? The Anticommons in Biomedical Research*, SCIENCE, May 1, 1998, at 698.

78. "The copyright will protect the expression in the work from being copied without permission, but will give *no protection whatsoever to the underlying ideas, facts, systems, procedures, methods of operation, principles, or discoveries*." JESSICA LITMAN, DIGITAL COPYRIGHT 17 (2001) (emphasis added).

79. A recent *New York Times* article reported on an informal meeting of physicists and computer scientists to debate the meaning of the technology revolution. "[The scholars] found instead that they could not even agree on useful definitions

of their field's most common terms, like 'information' and 'complexity,' let alone the meaning and future of this revolution." Dennis Overbye, *Time of Growing Pains for Information Age*, N.Y. TIMES, Aug. 7, 2001, at F3.

80. BOYLE, *supra* note 2, at 6 (emphasis added).

81. *See* Fritz Machlup, *Semantic Quirks in Studies of Information, in* THE STUDY OF INFORMATION: INTERDISCIPLINARY MESSAGES 641 (Fritz Machlup & Una Mansfield eds., 1983).

82. Reichman & Franklin, *supra* note 2, at 884.

83. *See* Peter Lyman, *The Article 2B Debate and the Sociology of the Information Age*, 13 BERKELEY TECH. L.J. 1063, 1068 (1998).

84. "The world of language, of conjectures, theories, and arguments—in brief, the universe of objective knowledge—is one of the most important of these man-created, yet at the same time largely autonomous, universes." Karl Popper, *Epistemology Without a Knowing Subject, in* OBJECTIVE KNOWLEDGE: AN EVOLUTIONARY APPROACH 118 (1972).

85. Sandra Braman, *Defining Information: An Approach for Policymakers, in* THE ECONOMICS OF COMMUNICATION AND INFORMATION 3, 4 (D. M. Lamberton ed., 1989).

86. *Id.* at 6–11.

87. *Id.* at 6.

88. Hayek, *supra* note 9, at 521.

89. Vincent Ostrom has repeatedly emphasized the artifactual nature of knowledge and institutions: "Every development—street sweeping, production of fertilizers, irrigation works, the development of new seed stocks—has a component to it that is concerned with how the activities of people are organized in relation to one another." Vincent Ostrom, Organization (working paper, Workshop in Political Theory and Policy Analysis, Indiana University, Bloomington, Indiana, 1969) (on file with author).

90. *See* Mark Cooper, *Symposium Overview: Part II: Unbundling and Open Access Policies: Open Access to the Broadband Internet: Technical and Economic Discrimination in Closed, Proprietary Networks*, 71 U. COLO. L. REV. 1011, 1047–49 (2000) (discussing the problem of *flow control* or filtering the flow of distributed information).

91. OSTROM, *supra* note 36.

92. This methodological tool, called the *Institutional Analysis and Development (IAD) Framework*, is discussed at length in Chapter 2 of RULES, *supra* note 40, at 23–50.

93. *See* John Perry Barlow, *The Economy of Ideas: Selling Wine Without Bottles: The Economy of Mind on the Global Net.*, WIRED, Mar. 1994, at 86, *available at* http://www.wired.com/wired/archive/203/economy.ideas_pr.html ("[T]he bottle was protected, not the wine."). In the same vein, Jessica Litman points out "copyright protects a painting or photograph of an automobile, but gives no protection to the automobile itself." LITMAN, *supra* note 78, at 18.

94. See Madison, *supra* note 2, for a discussion of the essential problems with the architecture and boundaries of digital information. "Digital computer network architecture, the substrate of cyberspace, has physical, virtual, and conceptual embodiments." *Id.* at 133.

95. Clifford A. Lynch, *The Transformation of Scholarly Communication and the Role of the Library in the Age of Network Information*, SERIALS LIBRARIAN, Summer 1993, at 5, 14.

96. *See* LITMAN, *supra* note 78, at 80, 81, 83.

97. Interlibrary Loan was formally proposed in the United States in 1898 by the University of California-Berkeley. The Library of Congress first began lending books in 1902. *See* http://www.loc.gov/rr/loan/ (last visited Oct. 17. 2002).

98. The first office copier was introduced in 1959. *See* Chip Holt, *Working Knowledge: Photocopiers*, SCI. AM., Oct. 1996, at 128.

99. 17 U.S.C. §§ 512, 1201–1205, 1301–1332; 28 U.S.C. § 4001 (1998).

100. Pub. L. No. 105–298, Title I, 112 Stat. 2827 (1998).

101. UNIF. COMPUTER INFO. TRANSACTIONS ACT (UCITA) (2001), *available at* http://www.law. upenn.edu/bll/ulc/ulc.htm. For discussions of "technological locks" for information proposed by UCITA, see Lyman, *supra* note 83 and Hannibal Travis, *Pirates of the Information Infrastructure*, 15 BERKELEY TECH. L.J. 777 (2000).

102. *See* Arnold Lutzker, *What the DMCA and the Copyright Term Extension Act Mean to the Library Community: Primer* (Mar. 8, 1999), *available at* http:// www.ala.org/washoff/primer.html.

103. Kenneth Frazier gives as prime example Reed Elsevier, publishers of Lexis-Nexis, who have "both added and deleted content from their database at their discretion." Kenneth Frazier, *The Librarians' Dilemma: Contemplating the Costs of the "Big Deal,"* D-LIB MAG., Mar. 2001, *available at* http://www.dlib. org/dlib/march01/frazier/03frazier.html.

104. Clifford A. Lynch, *Rethinking the Integrity of the Scholarly Record in the Networked Information Age*, EDUCOM REV. (1994) *at* http://www.educause. edu/pub/er/review/reviewArticles/29238.html; *see also* Pamela Samuelson & R. Davis, The Digital Dilemma: A Perspective on Intellectual Property in the Information Age, *presented at* the Telecommunications Policy Research Conference (2000), *available at* http://www.sims.berkeley.edu/~pam/papers/digdilsyn.pdf (last visited Oct. 11, 2002).

105. Lynch, *supra* note 104, at 39.

106. *See* http://lockss.stanford.edu/projectdescfaq.htm (last visited Oct. 10, 2002). This voluntary system developed at Stanford in 2000 "permits libraries to cache content they can access. If a library cancels a subscription and has not cached the content, they cannot get access to that content in the future. If a library caches content and then cancels their subscription, they continue to have access to the content they cached." *Id.* Over forty major libraries worldwide are now running the beta tests on this software. http://lockss.stanford.edu/projectstatus.htm (last visited Oct. 11, 2002).

107. COMMISSION ON PHYSICAL SCIENCES, MATHEMATICS, AND APPLICATIONS, THE DIGITAL DILEMMA: INTELLECTUAL PROPERTY IN THE INFORMATION AGE 31 (2000), *available at* http://www.nap.edu/html/digital_dilemma/index.html (last visited Sept. 6, 2002) [hereinafter DIGITAL DILEMMA].

108. *See, e.g.*, ALA's Washington Office homepage *at* http://www.ala.org/washoff/index.html (last visited Sept. 8, 2002); ARL's pages on its Scholarly Publishing and Academic Resources Coalition (SPARC) *at* http://www.arl.org/sparc/home/ (last visited Sept. 8, 2002); EDUCAUSE's Washington Office on information technology Policy Issues *at* http://www.educause.edu/policy/policy.html (last visited Sept. 8, 2002).

109. *See* Jean-Claude Guédon, *In Oldenburg's Long Shadow: Librarians, Research Scientists, Publishers, and the Control of Scientific Publishing*, *at* http://www.arl.org/arl/proceedings/138/guedon.html (last visited Sept. 8, 2002).

110. *See* http://www.earlham.edu/~peters/fos/index.html (last visited Sept. 8, 2002).

111. *Id.*

112. *See* Litman, *supra* note 78; Litman, *supra* note 13.

113. *See* LAWRENCE LESSIG, CODE AND OTHER LAWS OF CYBERSPACE 134 (1999).

114. *See Individual Behavior, Private Use and Fair Use, and the System for Copyright*, DIGITAL DILEMMA, *supra* note 107 at 123–51.

115. The administration of arXiv.org was moved to the Cornell University Library site in September 2001; the main site hardware operations were transferred in December 2001. *See* http://arxiv.org/new (last visited Sept. 7, 2002).

116. *See* http://arxiv.org/show_monthly_submissions (last visited Sept. 7, 2002).

117. Figures from Paul Ginsparg, Creating a Global Knowledge Network, *presented at* UNESCO-HQ, Paris (Feb. 19–23, 2001), *available at* http://arXiv.org/blurb/pg01unesco.html.

118. A 1995 survey revealed that the main index of scientific journals, the *Science Citation Index*, indexes more than 3,300 journals of the roughly 70,000 that are published worldwide. *See* W. Wyat Gibbs, *Lost Science in the Third World*, SCI. AM., Aug. 1995, at 92, 92. A mere 2% of the journals indexed are written by authors from developing countries (with 80% of the world's population). *Id.* at 96. The author writes that the "near invisibility of less developed nations may reflect the economics and biases of science publishing as much as the actual quality of Third World research." *Id.* at 92. On the other hand, scientific research collaboration is rapidly increasing on an international scale. According to the National Science Board's *Science and Engineering Indicators*—2000, "growth in U.S. co-authorship reflects increases in international collaboration. By the mid-1990s, nearly one of every five U.S. articles had one or more international co-authors, up from 12 percent earlier in the decade." NATIONAL SCIENCE BOARD, SCIENCE AND ENGINEERING INDICATORS 2000 6–4, *available at* http://www.nsf.gov/sbe/srs/seind00/access/c6/c6h.htm (last visited Sept. 6, 2002).

119. *See* http://arxiv.org/show_weekdays_graph (last visited Sept. 6, 2002).

120. For statistics on increased usage of electronic papers, journals, and citations, see Andrew Odlyzko, *The Rapid Evolution of Scholarly Communication*, LEARNED PUBLISHING, Jan. 2001, at 7, *available at* http://www.dtc.umn.edu/~odlyzko/doc/rapid.evolution.pdf (last visited Sept. 7, 2002).

121. *See* http://econwpa.wustl.edu/ (last visited Sept. 6, 2002).

122. *See* http://ota.ahds.ac.uk/ (last visited Sept. 6, 2002).

123. *See* http://www.biomedcentral.com (last visited Sept. 8, 2002).

124. Publisher Jan Velterop wrote in the online Free Online Scholarship Forum that BioMed Central differs from other, conventional, publishers, in that "authors are not 'giving' their article to us. They keep all the rights to their article, are not asked to transfer copyright, and are totally free to distribute their article in any way they like. What we provide, and what authors' institutions are paying for (a fraction, by the way, of what they collectively pay for articles published conventionally), is the service of organising and handling the process of having the article peer-reviewed, and, if accepted, published (given a unique bibliographic journal citation, DOI and URL) in open access, presented in various standardised formats (PDF and XML-generated HTML) and hotlinked (via CrossRef and others) and indexed (PubMed, Biosis and others) to enable optimum findability, citeability, dissemination, and 'embedding' in the network that science literature is." Posting of Jan Velterop to FOS Forum, http://www.topica.com/lists/fos-forum/index.html (Aug. 25, 2002) (copy on file with Law & Contemporary Problems).

125. *See* http://dlc.dlib.indiana.edu/index.html (last visited Sept. 6, 2002).

126. *See* http://www.publiclibraryofscience.org (last visited Oct. 29, 2002).

127. *Id.*

128. *See* http://www.pubmedcentral.nih.gov/index.html (last visited Oct. 29, 2002).

129. http://www.creativecommons.org/index.html (last visited Oct. 10, 2002).

130. *Id.*

131. *Id.*

132. *See* http://www.eprints.org (last visited Sept. 7, 2002).

133. *See, e.g.*, Carl Lagoze & Herbert Van De Sempel, *The Open Archives Initiative: Building a Low-Barrier Interoperability Framework* (2001) *at* http://www.openarchives.org/documents/oai.pdf (last visited Sept. 6, 2002).

134. *See* Clifford A. Lynch, *Metadata Harvesting and the Open Archives Initiative*, ARL BIMONTHLY REPORT, Aug. 2001, at 217, *at* http://www.arl.org/newsltr/217/mhp.html (last visited Sept. 6, 2002).

135. *See* http://cogprints.soton.ac.uk/ (last visited Sept. 7, 2002).

136. As happened with a published paper submitted to the Digital Library of the Commons ("DLC"), Jesse Ribot, *Theorizing Access: Forest Profits Along Senegal's Charcoal Commodity Chain*, 29 DEVELOPMENT AND CHANGE (1998), *available at* http://dlc.dlib.indiana.edu/documents/dir0/00/00/04/43/index.html.

In this case, the publisher granted the author the right to self-publish the paper on the DLC website.

137. *See* Stevan Harnad, *For Whom the Gate Tolls? How and Why to Free the Refereed Research Literature Online through Author/Institution Self-Archiving, Now*, *at* http://www.cogsci.soton.ac.uk/~harnad/Tp/resolution.htm (last visited Sept. 4, 2002). Harnad, leader of the Self-Archiving Initiative, recommends that authors amend their copyright transfer agreements with their publishers as follows: "I hereby transfer to [publisher or journal] all rights to sell or lease the text (on-paper and online) of my paper [paper-title]. I retain only the right to distribute it for free for scholarly/scientific purposes, in particular, the right to self-archive it publicly online on the Web." *Id.*

138. *See supra* [section on "The Confusion between the Nature of a Good and a Property Regime"].

139. *See* Ginsparg, *supra* note 117.

140. Stevan Harnad, *Free at Last: The Future of Peer-Reviewed Journals*, D-Lib Mag., Dec. 1999, *available at* http://www.dlib.org/dlib/december99/12harnad.html.

141. Rebecca S. Eisenberg, The Public Domain in Genomics (paper presented at New York University School of Law, Mar. 31–Apr. 2, 2000), *available at* http://www.law.nyu.edu/ili/conferences/freeinfo2000/abstracts/eisengberg.html (last visited Dec. 3, 2002).

142. Research Libraries Group, *Attributes of a Trusted Digital Repository: Meeting the Needs of Research Resources: An RLG-OCLC Report* (Aug. 2001), *at* http://www.rlg.org/longterm/attributes01.pdf (last visited Dec. 3, 2002).

143. *See* MARC Standards, http://www.loc.gov/marc/index.html (last visited Oct. 4, 2002).

7

Constructing Commons in the Cultural Environment

MICHAEL J. MADISON, BRETT M. FRISCHMANN, AND KATHERINE J. STRANDBURG

The Maine lobster fishery has been recognized as a successful example of a managed natural resource commons. To ensure an ongoing supply of lobster in the face of threats to the fishery from unregulated overfishing, over a period of years Maine lobster fishermen crafted a set of formal and informal rules to determine "who gets the lobster." By design, the product of their efforts is a commons, a managed-access property regime that allows both lobsters and the lobster industry to flourish.[1]

This article confronts the theoretical challenge of understanding the governance of what we refer to as constructed commons in the *cultural* environment, in which the resources to be produced, conserved, and consumed are not crustaceans but pieces of information: copyrighted works of authorship, patented inventions, and other forms of information and knowledge that may, but need not, be aligned with formal systems of intellectual property (IP) law. The phrase "constructed cultural commons," as we use it, refers to environments for developing and distributing cultural and scientific knowledge through institutions that support pooling and sharing that knowledge in a managed way, much as a natural resource commons refers to the type of managed sharing environment for natural resources that the Maine lobster fishery represents. These environments are designed and managed with limitations tailored to the character of those resources and the communities involved rather than left to evolve via market transactions grounded solely in traditional proprietary rights. Just as research on the Maine lobster fishery is grounded in the case study approach used by Elinor Ostrom and her colleagues, this article develops and argues for the use of a theoretical framework to systematize case study-based research exploring the construction of the cultural commons. We borrow from Ostrom in developing our framework, but we necessarily adapt, extend, and distinguish her approach to account for important differences between constructed cultural commons and natural resource commons.

Our approach provides a framework to systematize and unify analyses of various constructed cultural commons that until now have been regarded largely as separate species. We do not claim that all cultural commons work in exactly the same way or that they all solve exactly the same problems or that they all produce exactly the same benefits (or costs). Our claim is precisely the opposite: by aligning case studies of related but distinct commons phenomena, over time we will be able to identify those features of commons that are more and less significant to the success and failure of a commons enterprise. Aligning the empirical study of constructed cultural commons via a framework of structured inquiry will facilitate the development of and choice among theories to explain the existence and structure of the commons currently in existence and provide insights into the interplay between IP law and commons arrangements. Some initial illustrations make the point more vivid.

Intellectual property pools. A patent pool is an agreement by two or more patent holders to aggregate and share their patents by cross-licensing.[2] The patents in question typically relate to complementary technologies, where one holder's exercise of patent rights "blocks" a different holder's exercise of related rights. Pooled patents are typically available to all members of the pool and are available to nonmembers on standard licensing terms.[3] A well-known example of an early patent pool in the United States is the Manufacturer's Aircraft Association (MAA), which formed in 1917 and encompassed nearly all American aircraft manufacturers.[4] The Wright Company and Curtiss Company held major patents on aircraft technology, but Wright and Curtiss did not hold all the relevant patents, and for any given manufacturer the cost of licensing a single needed patent from a competitor might have made manufacturing an airplane prohibitively expensive. During World War I, the United States government needed airplanes at reasonable costs and in a short time. As a result, the government facilitated the implementation of the MAA, a private corporation. The MAA entered into an agreement with airplane manufacturers, through which the manufacturers pooled their patents and their potential claims for exploitation of the patents by rivals and agreed to cross-licensing of the patents to one another on what was, essentially, a royalty-free basis.[5] Largely because of this functioning commons of patented inventions, airplanes were built, and the war was won.

Open source software. The Linux operating system, an alternative to Windows and Mac OS (the Macintosh operating system), was produced and is still maintained by a volunteer collaborative of individual programmers.[6] The Linux collaborative is linked loosely by communications technologies, by members' voluntary allegiance to the project, and by the terms of an open source license. Unlike proprietary computer programs, which are distributed to users in object code or executable format only, open source programs such as Linux are made available in source code form so that members of the community may modify their copies and, under the terms of the governing license, publish their modifications for use by others. Members of the community may also volunteer their modifications for inclusion in the standard Linux code base. Thus, each member of the Linux community may use material in the Linux commons and may contribute material back to the Linux commons. Each individual member of the community contributes code to the accumulated archive of the Linux kernel, which is the core of the operating system. The rules governing the use of open source material and contributions to the open source commons are partly formal and partly informal. Formally, the software is governed by copyright law, and its use is managed by the terms of the General Public License. Informally, the integrity of Linux as an identifiable and stable program depends on a thin hierarchy of informal authority, which extends from Linus Torvalds at the top to the body of individual developers at the bottom.[7] The result is a complete, complex, and successful industrial product that is built and maintained not by a traditional, hierarchical, industrial firm, but by a loose-knit community.

Wikipedia. This free, online encyclopedia is widely read and cited. It resembles an open source software project in many respects. Volunteer authors create and edit Wikipedia entries; anyone with Internet access can read and use the contents of Wikipedia.[8] Wikipedia is not the product of unregulated, potentially chaotic openness, however.[9] A governance structure exists among "Wikipedians" that modulates the openness of the project and operates as a kind of law.[10] For example, not all additions and edits to Wikipedia are automatically added to the site. Moreover, the GNU Free Documentation License, the copyright license that governs the contents of Wikipedia, restricts the use of the contents of the site.[11] Wikipedia also has a dispute-resolution system that plays an important role in sustaining the commons.[12] The site is open, but with limits.

The Associated Press. For more than a century, the Associated Press (AP) has been the leading American wire service for newspapers.[13] It offers a compelling example of a constructed cultural commons that is not grounded in formal IP rights. As factual material, the news itself cannot be copyrighted (though there is an important but narrow "hot news misappropriation" tort rule[14]). Local newspapers could not afford to cover all of the stories that their readers wanted to read, yet the ease with which news stories can be appropriated served as a disincentive to invest in reporting—a classic free-rider dilemma. The solution was a not-for-profit cooperative, owned by the participant news organizations, which partnered originally with Western Union.[15] Co-operative members could both upload to the wire service material that they originated locally and download from the wire service material that other members produced.[16] Local papers were able to carry AP reports on national and international news that they otherwise could not have afforded to produce. The AP itself was a structured commons managed by its members.

Jamband fan communities. Musical groups known as jambands "jam," or improvise heavily, during live performances. Beginning with fans of the first and best-known jamband, the Grateful Dead, jamband fan communities have long been encouraged by the artists themselves to produce and share their own concert recordings. These recordings initially were shared via physical media and now are shared using online archives (organized via the website and organization etree.org).[17] The bands encourage this sharing, provided that the fans comply with informal rules that are set by the bands and honored and policed by the fan communities themselves.[18] For example, as Mark Schultz describes in his detailed case study of the jamband phenomenon, fan communities generally undertake not to interfere with commercial exploitation of the bands' own concert recordings.[19] The commons of jamband recordings is structured not merely by fan expectations that norms will be honored but also by file sharing and archiving technologies that reinforce the commercial/noncommercial distinction, by intermediary institutions that host jamband archives, and by the bands, which cooperate with and nurture their fan communities.[20]

These examples are illustrative of constructed cultural commons phenomena studied in isolation from each other.[21] At first glance, these examples may appear to be disparate and unrelated—like comparing apples to oranges to plums to pears, and so forth. Standing alone, each example is important and worth studying. Nonetheless, a systematic, comprehensive, and theoretically informed research framework offers significant potential for learning within and across these commons phenomena.[22]

The framework described in this article provides a means to investigate the social role and significance of cultural commons institutions. This investigation is relevant to property law, in particular, and social ordering, more generally. The conventional view of property scholars, particularly those with interests in IP law, is that resource production and consumption are—and ought to be—characterized primarily by entitlements to individual resource units, held individually and allocated via market mechanisms.[23] To the extent that those market mechanisms are inadequate to optimize the welfare of society—in other words, in the event of market failure—government intervention may be appropriate. Intellectual property rights themselves are generally justified on precisely this basis.[24] Creative works and new inventions are characterized as public goods, whose intangibility prevents their originators from excluding potential users and thus recouping their investments via pricing.[25] Copyright and patent laws create artificial but legally sanctioned forms of exclusion, restoring a measure of market control to creators and innovators. Communal and collectivist institutions, particularly those that blend informal normative structures with formal government rules, are generally regarded as exceptional and dependent upon preexisting property entitlements.[26]

The framework for collecting and analyzing case studies of constructed cultural commons across a wide range of domains that we describe below offers a method for assessing the validity of this property-focused narrative. We suspect that over time the constructed cultural commons framework will yield a far larger and richer set of commons cases in the cultural context than one might discover by focusing only on patent law or scientific research or software development. We anticipate that social ordering both depends on and generates a wide variety of formal and informal institutional arrangements, and that the logical and normative priority assigned to proprietary rights and government intervention may turn out to be misplaced.

[The first] part of this article describes prior approaches to theoretical understanding of intellectual production based on juxtaposition of IP regimes with a conception of the public domain. It highlights how recent case studies demonstrate the need for a more textured theoretical approach. [The second] part introduces the Institutional Analysis and Development (IAD) framework pioneered by Elinor Ostrom in the natural resources context and presents our proposed adaptation of the framework to constructed cultural commons.

The Backdrop: Intellectual Property Theory, Commons, and the Need for a Research Framework

This part reviews our motivation to produce the constructed cultural commons framework and highlights the key theoretical regimes to which the framework connects. We explain why a research framework is needed in this domain and justify the type of framework and case study-driven approach we develop in [the second] part. We begin with a discussion of IP law and the theoretical problems and solutions that typically characterize IP regimes. In particular, we explain the conventional functionalist account of intellectual property, highlight some of its flaws, and suggest that a more nuanced functional account is needed to better understand the cultural environment. Next, we explain why the functionalist approach of Ostrom and her colleagues, developed in the context of the natural environment, provides a useful starting point but needs adjustment to account for differences between the natural environment and the cultural environment. Finally, we suggest that narrative and metaphorical accounts of property institutions and social ordering might complement a functional approach and enrich the constructed-cultural-commons framework we develop in [the second] part.

Functionalist Intellectual Property Theory and Its Limits

Intellectual property law scholarship has typically viewed invention, creative expression, innovation, and related or subsidiary activities (such as research and development) as a special set of practices for which extra encouragement is warranted. Despite considerable variation and nuance, these activities all can be understood to present a simple core problem: as public goods, the "output" from these activities—whether described as information, expression, invention, innovation, research, ideas, or otherwise—is naturally nonrivalrous, meaning that consumption of the resource does not deplete the amount available to other users, and nonexcludable, meaning that knowledge resources are not naturally defined by boundaries that permit exclusion of users.[27] As a result, such resources

> face the well-known supply-side problem, common to public goods: the inability to (cheaply) exclude competitors and nonpaying consumers (free riders) presents a risk to investors perceived ex ante (prior to produc-

> tion of the good), and this risk *may* lead to undersupply. Essentially, in the absence of [some institutional solution], there would be a significant underinvestment in (some types of) [intellectual resources] because of the risk that competitors would appropriate the value of the [resources].[28]

Two standard solutions to this problem are IP rights and government subsidies. These solutions heavily influence the framing and perception of the cultural environment.

As a result, the conventional functionalist approach to information law and policy divides the information environment into two domains. First, there is the domain of exclusion, in which producers of creative and innovative things employ proprietary rights sanctioned by law to control their development, distribution, and exploitation. Private rights and private market exchange serve to limit, by law, the natural shareability of knowledge and innovation. At the core of IP law, as traditionally conceived, is the right to exclude, without which it is assumed that some producers would abandon their efforts for fear of free riding (unlicensed sharing) by competitors.[29] Without exclusion, competition facilitated by sharing would undermine incentives to invest in the production, development and/or dissemination of some resources in the first place. Intellectual property law constructs and assigns these exclusive rights and encourages their exploitation through market exchange.

Second, there is the public domain, a vast collection of openly accessible resources for which exclusion is disallowed under existing intellectual property systems (for example, due to express exclusion from the system[30] or expiration of rights[31]) or not practiced (for example, because potential owners dedicate their resources to the public or because exclusion is practically impossible).[32] For some types of resources, overconsumption and underinvestment problems associated with unlicensed sharing are solved through direct or indirect provisioning by the public sector using a combination of grants to researchers; tax credits or subsidies to researchers and enterprises that employ them; prizes; and production and distribution of knowledge and innovation by the government itself, either by organizing research enterprises or by purchasing and distributing private research. These alternative solutions often, though not always, supply resources to the public domain.[33]

The conventional functionalist paradigm is woefully inadequate as a descriptive matter.[34] Essentially, it is a caricature—an oversimplified account that roughly describes some cultural practices and productive activities but leaves much too much out of frame, unexamined, and unaccounted for. (Consider, for a moment, how many creative and inventive activities involve much more than "public goods production" or how often participation in such activities is outside of and inexplicable in terms of IP incentives or government subsidies.) We further explain this view below, but first we must emphasize how much rests on the descriptive account: it shapes—if not determines—the set of baseline premises that undergird the legal and social institutions that structure the cultural environment and shape normative outcomes. Although our undertaking is emphatically positive and descriptive, we believe significant normative implications should flow from a better understanding of the cultural environment.[35]

Over the last decade, scholars increasingly have recognized that many of the most interesting and important aspects of the information environment exist in the area between these private and public extremes precisely because of what Brett Frischmann and Mark Lemley characterize as "spillovers": social benefits that flow from uses and reuses of information resources and sustain the dynamic character of the information environment.[36] The information environment is riddled with so-called "semicommons"[37]—complex combinations of private rights and commons, some of which are constructed at the "macro, system level" of law,[38] and some of which are constructed at the "micro, contextual level" of cultural commons.

At the macro level, the rights of exclusion that comprise the default regimes of patent and copyright law are, by design, not absolute. Intellectual property regimes moderate their exclusionary principles with limitations and exceptions. In part, those limitations and exceptions are designed to construct a public domain of resources that are open and freely available to all,[39] and in part, they support public capabilities to use resources in ways that generate spillovers.[40]

In addition to these macro-constructions, intellectual property rules also are used at a micro-level, in conjunction with contracts and social norms, to construct a wide variety of semicommons or limited commons of cultural resources that are partly open and partly closed, usable by members and sometimes by the public at large, though not always on a purely "free" basis. Examples include such diverse institutions as public lending libraries and open source software programs. Default rules of intellectual property thus may be combined with licenses and contracts, with social norms, and with cultural and other institutional forms to construct these cultural commons, which depend on—but are built alongside and on top of—the basic forms of knowledge and culture, on the one hand, and intellectual property rules, on the other hand.

Commons in Culture and the Need for a Research Framework

Our focus on constructed cultural commons emerges from the proposition that cultural production is an inherently social phenomenon, taking place over a wide range of scales and within a complex, overlapping variety of formal and informal institutional structures.[41] Indeed, social production of cultural goods has become more salient and more economically important as a result of globalization and the communications revolution symbolized by the Internet.[42] We are thus beginning to grapple with the realization that legal facilitation of innovation and creative production is not—and cannot—be confined to a simple set of property rules to incentivize individual innovative and creative efforts. Innovation and creativity are matters of governance of a highly social cultural environment. The question for both public policy and legal theory becomes how best to use legal and other tools to encourage the growth and persistence of creative, sustainable, and equitable cultural environments.[43]

Much of the scholarly debate in IP law has pitted proponents of privatization as a means of incentivizing production of intellectual goods against proponents of a widely available public domain upon which cultural goods can be built. The discussion has often devolved into a disagreement over the relative importance of incentives and access for production of ideas and creative expression.[44] As technology has evolved to facilitate an increasingly extensive, varied landscape of social and cooperative projects that enable creativity and innovation, a third perspective has emerged. Books, articles, and scholarly discussion of such projects, of which open source software has become the poster child, increasingly extol community production as a solution to the free-rider problems of cultural production.[45] The danger is that the amorphous idea of "community production" will become the new one-size-fits-all panacea approach in rivalry with privatization, public subsidy, and the public domain.

Fortunately, ours is not the first scholarly enterprise to confront the realization that common-property regimes are more complex and various than had been appreciated. A group of scholars of commons regimes in the natural environment, spearheaded by Ostrom and her collaborators, has eschewed a simplistic approach and developed a framework for synthesizing studies of various and diverse natural resource commons. We argue that now is the time to recognize that the lessons learned by these scholars of the natural environment caution against an overly simplistic view of community cultural production.[46] The primary lesson of their years of case studies of commons regimes, which culminated in Ostrom receiving the 2009 Nobel Prize in Economic Sciences,[47] is that the devil is in the details. Complex environments demand a more contextual empirical and theoretical approach.[48] The complexity of natural and cultural environments and the futility of analyzing them with one-size-fits-all theories or legal approaches create the challenge of developing appropriate conceptual understanding and policy prescriptions. Here is where and why we think that an adaptation of Ostrom's approach to the systematized study of natural resource commons may be particularly helpful for intellectual property scholarship.

As we describe in detail in [the second] part, Ostrom's approach represents a starting point, but one that requires significant modifications. Those modifications, discussed in [the second] part, are woven into the baskets of questions we propose to use to interrogate constructed cultural commons. Those baskets of questions reflect an intentional reliance on two approaches to intellectual property that are sometimes thought to conflict: a functionalist account and a metaphorical or narrative approach.

The functionalist aspect of our proposed framework mirrors the functionalist approach that Ostrom and her colleagues take with respect to regimes governing the sharing and exploitation of natural resources. Despite the many virtues of functionalist accounts, their focus on a handful of variables or factors often limits them. A focus on excludability as a solution to public goods problems can lead to isolated analysis of boundary problems.[49] A focus on appropriability mechanisms may lead to narrow analysis of resource definition issues. A focus on transaction costs may lead to myopic consideration of information-forcing and limiting mechanisms. Such approaches can effectively highlight strengths and weaknesses of policy prescriptions in their respective domains, but these approaches frequently fail to deal adequately with systemic issues or with dynamic changes. Ostrom's approach to natural resource commons addresses the limitations of functionalism by expanding the number of variables considered.

In the context of the cultural environment, the sharing/exclusion and cooperation/competition dichotomies present especially interesting and challenging puzzles to a functionalist approach. This is so for three reasons.

First, those who create, invent, innovate, and participate in similar intellectually driven, productive activities necessarily borrow from or share with others.[50] It is impossible to divest oneself of that to which one has been exposed. Inevitably, the intellectual products of past and contemporary "producers" (a term that we use as a shorthand to refer to creators, inventors, innovators, thinkers, and the like) serve as inputs into each of our own productive activities. We necessarily borrow and share. Second, as discussed above, the resources that shape the cultural environment are by their nature naturally nonrivalrous and nonexcludable, meaning that knowledge resources are not naturally defined by boundaries that permit exclusion of users.[51] Third, unlike resources in the natural world, resources of information and expression must be created before they can be shared. Because of the public goods character of these resources, a cultural commons must manage both use and production of cultural resources.

These features of cultural resources, practices, and environment add to the range of variables that must be considered when studying commons institutions. Moreover, although natural resource management often focuses on sustainability, in the cultural commons the goal generally goes beyond sustainability to innovation, growth, and progress.[52] This shift in focus means that in assessing any particular constructed-cultural-commons arrangement, we must expand the framework used in studying natural resources to consider not only how resources are managed and shared within the community but also how and if resources are *created within* and *transferred outside of* the community. Dynamic effects are central to this analysis. The constructed-cultural-commons framework we propose in [the second] part reflects these functionalist distinctions between Ostrom's approach to natural resource commons and our modified approach to intellectual-resource institutions.

A second and equally important way to address the limitations of functionalist theory in the cultural commons context is to examine a system of social ordering in expressive terms rather than purely functional terms, looking to the construction and evolution of meaning in the system, as reflected in symbol and narrative. In proper proportion, a humanistic and metaphorical inquiry into information policy, on the one hand, and a functional approach grounded in social science models, on the other hand, are complementary and can be effectively unified in a framework of research questions to yield accurate descriptive summaries of commons phenomena and eventual policy prescriptions.

We draw on narrative and metaphorical approaches to legal and sociological questions, specifically by examining the metaphorical dimensions of the information "environment" and the knowledge "commons."[53] The environmental metaphor for information law and policy—focusing on cultural and knowledge resources rather than physical or natural resources—offers an especially illuminating and useful starting point for our project. Relying on this metaphor offers the ability to explore connections within and between interconnected and interdependent natural and constructed resource systems; to differentiate growth and progress from stewardship, conservation, and sustainability; to describe the differences between natural and constructed environments and the differences between open and closed or "gated" or "managed" environments; to describe different versions of concepts based on adjacent metaphors, such as the public domain and the commons; to identify and describe important patterned behaviors that correspond to different kinds of environments; and to draw lessons from a variety of regulatory and governance structures in other environmental contexts (public and private, legislative and administrative, oriented toward individual entitlements and collectivist, and so forth).

The environmental metaphor also illuminates the importance of the nesting process that Ostrom identifies as a salient feature of commons.[54] By "nesting," we mean that a particular commons phenomenon might be analyzed at many levels; these levels may interact strongly with one another. One of the issues that must be resolved in any particular inquiry is the appropriate level of complexity at which a particular commons should be studied. Ostrom analogizes this nested analysis to a set of maps at different levels of detail,[55] such as one sees when using the zoom function in Google Maps.[56] All of these maps are accurate, but the usefulness of a particular map depends on the question one seeks to answer. Moreover, some questions can be answered by focusing only at street level, while others may require zooming back and forth to different levels. Similarly, analyzing a commons institution may require more or less detailed knowledge of the larger cultural institutions within which it resides.

This article begins to explore how this nesting process can and should be examined in the cultural context. Our combined functionalist and expressive framework is deliberately intended for application to the cultural commons in environments that are structured not only by IP law but also by other legal rules, such as the rules of contract and license, and by informal cultural institutions and social practices. A structured inquiry is needed to make progress in understanding the complex and diverse commons arrangements that may be constructed in the cultural environment.

Developing a Framework for the Study of Commons in the Cultural Environment

This part sets out our proposed framework for analyzing constructed cultural commons using a case study approach.

Learning and Building from Ostrom's Institutional Analysis and Development Framework

As discussed above, we base our proposed framework on the work of the political scientist Ostrom and her colleagues, who have for decades been studying commons in the natural resource environment.[57] Examples include not only the lobster fishery with which we began the article but also numerous instances of grazing pastures, forests, and irrigation systems.[58] In each case, a similar underlying problem was diagnosed: what property scholars, following Garrett Hardin, refer to as a "tragedy of the commons."[59] Given a pool of physical resources that is presumptively open to all comers, such as a meadow for grazing sheep, and absent a mechanism for coordinating the actions of resource users, that is, the owners of the sheep, resources are likely to be overconsumed and underproduced.[60] Eventually, the pool will collapse under the weight of individuals acting rationally in pursuit of their own self-interest, without regard for the costs imposed on other existing and future resource users. The tragedy of the commons illustrates a standard externality problem that manifests a failure of collective action.[61]

This argument is often coupled with an argument that such "tragic" situations give rise to solutions grounded in regimes of exclusionary property rights.[62] The leading alternative to privatization and allocation of property rights via markets is government intervention and regulation.[63] A key insight of Ostrom's approach to the natural environment was recognition of the important role for institutions intermediate between private property and the state in solving problems of collective action.[64] These intermediate institutions are sometimes called "common property" or "limited commons" and generally are collective (but not necessarily governmental or even formal) means for sharing and making productive and sustainable use of resources such as fish, water, trees, and so forth.[65] The research of Ostrom and other scholars demonstrates that solutions to these resource-sharing problems are various and highly contextual. Standard theoretic models, whether or not grounded in the presumption that a tragedy of the commons is present, can therefore be only the beginning of a much more complex analysis. The temptation to seek out regulatory panaceas based on universal models, whether through private property, state action, or even notions of community, must be resisted in favor of a more nuanced approach.[66]

In response to the inadequacy of one-size-fits-all approaches, Ostrom's method for systematizing the investigation of commons regimes focuses on the nested, multitier character of the natural resource commons.[67] Her Institutional Analysis and Development (IAD) framework is used to structure a common set of research questions to apply in diverse contexts, with the eventual goal of coming to some conclusions about the significance and interactions of various factors in facilitating effective management of common resources.[68] Our objective is to do the same in the cultural context.

To implement the IAD framework, Ostrom and her collaborators employed a three-pronged approach:

- First, they engaged in a broad range of case studies of natural resource commons to form a basis for a bottom-up practice-based taxonomy of successful and unsuccessful approaches to resource management.
- Second, they developed a framework, based on the initial case studies, for identifying the variables that are significant in determining the success or failure of a commons enterprise and of the viability of institutions in particular contexts.
- Third, they preserved flexibility in their framework so that it could be adapted and revised in response to learning derived from the case studies.[69]

Based on the information obtained by applying their framework to structured case studies, they developed theories and models for particular commons situations, designed experiments to test those theories, and advanced a set of design principles for successful natural resource commons.[70]

The framework approach recognizes the crucial importance of the interplay between the characteristics of a commons resource and the social, political, economic, and institutional arrangements for its governance in which it is embedded.[71] This approach also walks the difficult line between overly simplistic theoretical models, which paper over important complexities, and a fragmented taxonomy of diverse situations. As Ostrom explains, frameworks, theories, and models have different roles to play:

> The development and use of a general *framework* helps to identify the elements (and the relationships among these elements) that one needs to consider for institutional analysis. Frameworks . . . provide the most general set of variables that should be used to analyze all types of settings relevant for the framework. . . . They attempt to identify the *universal* elements that any relevant theory would need to include. . . .

> The development and use of *theories* enable the analyst to specify which components of a framework are relevant for certain kinds of questions and to make broad working assumptions about these elements. Thus, theories focus on parts of a framework and make specific assumptions that are necessary for an analyst to diagnose a phenomenon, explain its processes, and predict outcomes. . . . Microeconomic theory, game theory, transaction cost theory, social choice theory, public choice, constitutional and covenantal theory, and theories of public goods and common-pool resources are all compatible with the IAD framework discussed in this book.
>
> The development and use of *models* make precise assumptions about a limited set of parameters and variables. Logic, mathematics, game theory models, experimentation and simulation, and other means are used to explore the consequences of these assumptions systematically on a limited set of outcomes. Multiple models are compatible with most theories. . . .
>
> One needs a common framework and family of theories in order to address questions of reforms and transitions. Particular models then help the analyst to deduce specific predictions about likely outcomes of highly simplified structures. Models are useful in policy analysis when they are well-tailored to the particular problem at hand. Models are used inappropriately when applied to the study of problematic situations that do not closely fit the assumptions of the model.[72]

In the cultural environment context, the need for a framework to systematize theoretical and empirical research is readily apparent. The conventional functionalist explanation of public goods leads to a rather constrained set of theories and models and a consequently constrained set of prescriptions and knowledge. The theories and models work well for some observed phenomena but not for many other phenomena. Yet identifying or developing other relevant theories or models (or even knowing when to look outside the proverbial box) can be difficult.[73] A framework can help researchers to develop and choose among different theories. For example, club theory may be helpful in understanding the dynamics of patent pools but poorly suited to understanding Wikipedia. Patent pools are less open in terms of membership, and they manage shared resources in a fashion that is much less focused on sustaining joint production. Wikipedia, by contrast, is quite open in terms of membership, contributions, and participation in various aspects of the project largely because it focuses on sustaining joint production. Consequently, club theory is not likely to be particularly helpful for a researcher studying Wikipedia. Other theories of cooperation might be better suited to the task. A research framework such as ours aims to systematize the investigation, facilitate a more rigorous evaluation by matching and testing of theories and models with observed phenomena, and, most generally, enable learning over time. By design, the IAD framework remains a work in progress in the natural resource domain,[74] which is one of its strengths. We follow that tradition.

The IAD framework for natural resource commons is illustrated in Figure 7.1.[75] It divides the investigation of a commons regime into a set of inquiries into groups of underlying factors. The first group, including biophysical characteristics, community attributes, and what Ostrom and her collaborators denote "rules-in-use," or governance mechanisms, are denoted by Ostrom as "exogenous variables." These attributes of a particular commons are fixed, at least with respect to the analysis of a particular situation.[76] In the case of the lobster fishery, for example, these attributes might include the relevant biological characteristics of lobsters, such as the rates at which they age and reproduce; attributes of the community of fishermen, such as the proximity in which they live to others, the existence of familial relationships, and the skill sets needed for lobster fishing; and the rules—explicit or informal—that govern fishing.[77] The second group focuses on what Ostrom calls the "action arena." An action arena "refers to the social space where participants with diverse preferences interact, exchange goods and services, solve problems, dominate one another, or fight (among the many things that individuals do in action arenas)"[78]—in other words, the place at which the exogenous variables combine in particular instances, leading over time to observed patterns of interactions and outcomes.

Ostrom's work emphasizes the diversity of possible combinations of exogenous variables that determine what actually happens in particular instances and, hence, the outcomes that result.[79] The rules governing lobster fishing contribute to the activity's long-term sustainability, for example, but the patterns of interaction actually observed depend on the richness of the particular environment for lobsters, the degree to which rules are actually enforced, seasonal factors such as weather, and interaction with outside influences such as pollution[80] and the state of the larger economy.[81] Understanding the observed success or failure of a commons enterprise such as a lobster fishery may require accounting for all of these factors, even though it may turn out that outcomes are relatively impervious to some of them.

A simple illustration of the framework might be a soccer league. The formal rules of soccer are fixed, but the rules-in-use clearly vary somewhat

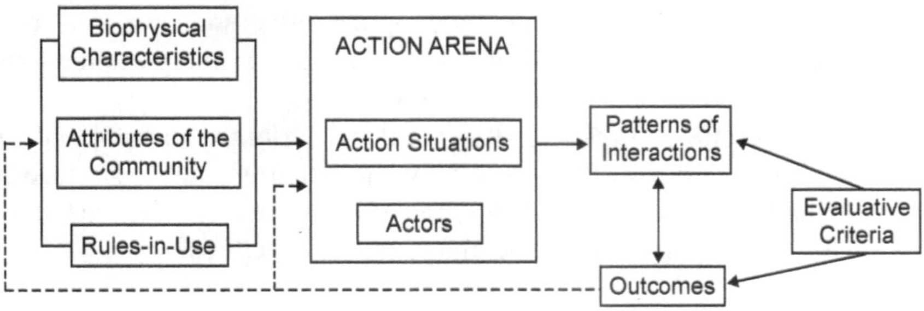

Figure 7.1.[82]

between a professional league and a recreational league, between a children's league and an adult league, and so forth. A specific soccer league is also characterized by the relationships among the players (whether neighbors, professional competitors, or friends), by the attributes of the fields on which games are played, and even by the climate of the places where the games take place. The action arena—soccer games—depends on complex and specific interactions among all of these characteristics. Nonetheless, the outcomes over time in a particular league are the patterns of interaction that are clearly identifiable as "professional soccer," "friendly weekend game," "children's soccer league," and the like. Moreover, some leagues will be successful, lasting for years even as players come and go, while others will fail. The goal of applying the Ostrom framework of analysis in this context would be to use studies and analysis of many different soccer leagues to come to an understanding of success and failure as a function of specific context.

The foundation of the Ostrom analysis is asking related questions in clusters about the exogenous variables, the action arena, and the patterns of interactions and outcomes.[83] Questions about the biophysical characteristics, attributes of the community, and rules-in-use, for example, include the following:

- What boundaries define the resource pool? What is the source of supply and sustainability of the resource units? Under what conditions may resource units be appropriated from the pool?
- How does the population monitor and enforce rules regarding contribution and appropriation? What sorts of sanctions are available, and what sanctions are actually used? What conflict-resolution mechanisms are in place?

- If the community relies on other populations in some respects, or if the population delegates some functions to subsidiary populations, what is the character of these relationships?
- In all instances, to what extent are these attributes inscribed in formal institutions of the state? To what extent are they inscribed in other formal, legal institutions, and to what extent are they inscribed in social norms or other social or cultural structures?

We think that the IAD concept has proven sufficiently fruitful to make it worth adapting for our purposes.[84] The nested, multi-tiered character of sustainable cultural environments and the diversity of attributes that contribute to successful governance regimes are keys to understanding cultural commons as mechanisms for knowledge production, collection, and distribution in the context of modern information and IP law regimes.

Ostrom and her colleagues have taken preliminary steps toward understanding how these methods might be relevant to investigating certain cultural commons.[85] Ostrom and Hess have analyzed the management of digital collections of existing knowledge resources, an admirable first step that signals the need for and plausibility of extending the IAD framework to the cultural environment.[86] As our discussion of the categories of questions below reveals, we argue that the IAD framework must be extended to account adequately for the wide variety of constructed commons in the cultural environment.[87]

Most importantly, unlike commons in the natural resource environment, cultural commons arrangements usually must create a governance structure within which participants not only share existing resources but also engage in *producing* those resources.[88] This characteristic of cultural commons produces a more intertwined set of exogenous variables because separating the managed resources from the attributes and rules-in-use of the community that produces them is impossible. Cultural commons are also *nested* within and interact with more complex systems of natural and socially constructed environments.

To see the point, consider a copyright or patent pool, such as the MAA described in the introduction, to which IP rights holders agree to contribute patents or copyrights that those same holders may exploit on standardized terms specified as part of the construction of the pool.[89] This arrangement creates an environment for pool members that facilitates sharing and use internally and interacts simultaneously with the external environment and shapes relationships with nonmembers. In other words, patent and copyright laws construct particular environments with default boundar-

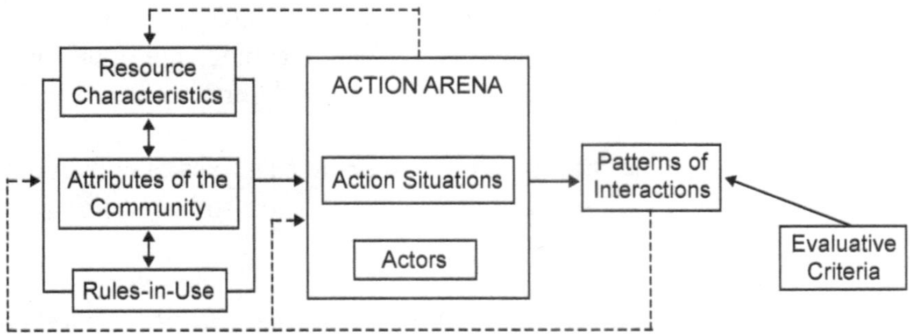

Figure 7.2

ies governing access to and use of certain forms of knowledge. Commons arrangements grounded in those laws involve contextually specific deviations from the default given by IP law. These constructed cultural commons may lead to creativity, innovation, and improvement that would not be attainable either in the so-called "natural" state of information without intellectual property protection or in the state of information with "full" intellectual property protection.

Our proposed modified framework for constructed cultural commons, which reflects the iterative and constructed character of the commons community, its cultural resources, and its governing "rules-in-use," is illustrated in Figure 7.2. Figure 7.2 differs from Figure 7.1 in that it illustrates the interactions among and constructed nature of the cultural resources themselves.

Figure 7.2 also reflects a second modification to Ostrom's IAD framework, the collapse of the distinction between outcomes and "patterns of interaction" that results from the intersection between the commons "action arena" and community attributes, resource attributes, and rules-in-use. We argue that given the role of both formal law and informal rule systems in commons governance, these patterns of interactions are inseparable from the outcomes of commons systems. How people interact with rules, resources, and each other, in other words, is itself an outcome that is inextricably linked with the form and content of the knowledge or informational output of the commons. In an open source software project, for example, the existence and operation of the open source development collaborative, the identity of the dynamic thing called the open source software program, and the existence and operation of the relevant open source software license are constitutive of one another.[90] Because of the more complex relationships among resources, participants, and governance structures in cultural commons, relevant attributes may not divide as neatly into categories as they do when one is describing a pooling of natural resources. Nonetheless, as we describe in the next section, we believe that a structured interrogation of specific examples of constructed cultural commons is both possible and likely to be fruitful.

Specifying the Framework for Studying Constructed Cultural Commons

This section describes in greater detail our proposed framework for approaching case studies of particular constructed cultural commons, building on the concepts reflected in Figure 7.2 and focusing on the character of the questions that should guide any specific investigation. We begin in [the first] section with some comments on important distinctions between our framework and the IAD framework for natural resource commons, namely that the cultural environment itself differs in certain fundamental respects from the natural resource environment. In [the second] section, we describe how those distinctions drive the appropriate set of inquiries into basic characteristics of the commons. This section is the heart of our analysis. In [the third] section, we briefly discuss how the expansion of the framework affects the analysis of patterns of interaction and outcomes of the action arenas arising in culturally constructed commons.

The Background Environment: An Initial Conundrum

When seeking to apply the Ostrom approach to constructed cultural commons, we immediately confront a conceptual challenge. Ostrom's inquiry begins by asking questions about the "biophysical characteristics" of the resources involved in the limited commons in question. This inquiry assumes, implicitly, a natural environment containing natural resources that are to be shared and managed. In describing a constructed cultural commons, we must take a step back before describing the relevant characteristics of the shared resources to ask how we should define the environmental backdrop against which a commons is constructed. As is generally true for understanding constructed cultural commons, there may not be one correct answer to this question. There is no clean way to separate a particular cultural commons from the "natural" cultural background, because cultural activity is always grounded in human social interaction, the material environment, laws, and norms. Although there may not be one right answer, it is important to choose a starting point for investigation in a particular case. Asking the question ensures the salience of the choice of the background against which further description is made. Importantly, that choice frames the larger environment within which a particular commons and related institutions and practices are nested, leading to a better description of the sources and significance of the social, political, and economic aspects of commons.[91]

We identify two reasonable points of "natural environment" reference for the investigation of constructed cultural commons: a "natural" cultural environment without intellectual property and a "default" intellectual-property-based cultural environment. These two starting points correspond roughly to the public domain and to a propertized environment, respectively. Which starting point is most appropriate to use for a particular inquiry will depend on which most closely approximates the cultural commons in a particular case. In a context such as a patent pool[92] or the jamband phenomenon that emerged around the recorded performances of the Grateful Dead,[93] for example, describing a constructed cultural commons according to how it deviates from the default IP regime may be the most useful approach. In other contexts, such as the shared journalism resource constructed by the AP,[94] describing a cultural commons according to its differences from a completely open public domain may be the most useful approach. In still other contexts, such as the sharing of magic tricks among the community of magicians,[95] secrecy may provide the most natural backdrop. Here we comment briefly on the "natural" cultural environment and on the copyright and patent law default propertized environments before moving on to suggest additional questions that should be pursued in analogy to Ostrom's framework.

The "Natural" Cultural Environment

Despite what appears to be the expanding scope of IP law, a significant range of activities, practices, and intellectual resources remain outside the intended scope of even the most expansive IP regimes. When cultural commons are constructed in these arenas, the most appropriate choice for the "natural environment" is a cultural environment unmediated by rights of exclusion or other regulation. This "natural" cultural environment may also be the appropriate starting point for discussing constructed cultural commons in which IP rights, though available, play a marginal role.

The contours of the "natural" cultural environment are not uncontested. The major IP regimes exclude many different types of intellectual resources based on many different criteria and doctrines. Some would describe the complete set of nonenclosed resources as the public domain, including not only matter excluded on subject-matter grounds but also matter subject to rights of fair use or fair dealing,[96] or as to which IP rights have expired.[97] The "natural" environment then can be seen as a vast pool of cultural resources that are openly accessible and openly usable by anyone without the permission of anyone else.[98]

Julie Cohen has argued that a purely natural resources conception of the public domain, and one that relies on the distinction between permitted use and use that does not require a rights owner's permission, may lead to a misleading follow-on analysis too closely tied to geographic concepts—that is, a conception of the public domain as a separate place.[99] Cohen argues persuasively for a more contextual understanding of the "common in culture," a cultural landscape that is informed and shaped by cultural practices.[100]

Our conception of the "natural" environment relates to Cohen's cultural landscape model as it similarly integrates a more dynamic and contextual understanding of intellectual resources. We might say that the "natural" cultural environment encompasses all that we *inherit* and *experience.* We *inherit* the natural physical environment—live within, use, interact with, and change it—and we pass it on to future generations. Similarly, we inherit, live within, use, interact with, change, and pass on an intellectual and cultural environment, which is itself comprised of many overlapping sub-environments of science and art, among other things. *Experience* constitutes an important intellectual resource that simultaneously relates human beings to their inherited and evolving environment(s) and constitutes a resource that may shape the intellectual environment. Experience (or perception or observation) is not enclosed within IP regimes except when expressed and embodied in a particular qualifying form, such as a copyrightable work of authorship or a patentable invention.[101]

In sum, the natural intellectual environment consists of a vast pool of open intellectual resources within which and with which we experience life and engage in a wide variety of activities and practices. The salience of specific features of a "natural" background will depend on the context of the inquiry. In many cases, constructed cultural commons arrangements build directly on this nonpropertized "natural" background. Examples of constructed cultural commons for which the "natural" environment is the most appropriate baseline likely include the commons of scientific research results and tools in the basic sciences, the facts and related information that are compiled not only by journalists via the AP but also in online creations such as Wikipedia, and devices invented by and shared among sports enthusiasts.[102]

The "natural" environment may be the most appropriate baseline for viewing a cultural commons even if intellectual property protection is available for the resources contributed to the commons, and even if IP law plays some role in its construction. For example, the AP, which was constructed initially as a means of managing the sharing of an intellectual resource (news) that was not protected by the standard forms of IP law (the First Amendment generally precludes copyright protection for facts) was the plaintiff in the leading case that established an intellectual-property-like "hot news" doctrine regulating a very specific type of misappropriation of factual information important to the AP constructed commons.[103] The importance of a constructed cultural commons analysis is that it recognizes that creative environments are constructed by deviating from both the purely "natural" and the purely propertized extremes. Indeed, once we have identified the background environment and shared resources of a particular cultural commons, the bulk of the analysis will focus on the institutions that are constructed to govern deviations from that background structure.

THE DEFAULT PROPRIETARY ENVIRONMENTS

The two principal regimes of IP law—patent and copyright law—are the most salient alternatives to the "natural" environmental baseline described above.

Patent grants are justified generally on the ground that the natural shareability of technological ideas undermines incentives to produce and distribute more and superior forms of innovation.[104] This basic conception highlights an important difference between constructed cultural commons and commons in the natural resource context. Constructed cultural commons must be concerned not only with managing and sustaining existing resources but also with providing institutions to encourage the creation of new resources.

Patent rules vary somewhat from country to country, but generally time-limited patent rights are granted to the developers of an "invention" after an appropriate government agency examines a patent application.[105] The applicant must demonstrate to the satisfaction of the patent examiner that the innovation represented by the invention is new (or "novel," in the language of patent law) in that no one has invented the device before; useful; nonobvious (in the language of American patent law) or possessing an "inventive step" (in most European systems), such that the invention represents a technical advance over the existing art;[106] and adequately described in the application for the benefit of future adopters and adapters of the technology.[107] The holder of a valid patent possesses a statutory right to exclude all others from producing or selling the invention,[108] subject to extremely limited exceptions for experimentation and research on the subject matter of the patent.[109] Notably, however, patent rights expire after a relatively short term, typically twenty years.[110] The material covered by the patent then passes into the public domain. An example of a constructed cultural commons for which a patented environment serves as an appropriate baseline is a patent pool.

Copyright law departs from the "natural environment" norm for the cultural environment in ways that resemble patent law, and for the same reasons, but with respect to material forms of artistic and creative cultural expression rather than technological and technical innovation. As with patent law, copyright statutes vary in their details from country to country yet generally embody a set of core principles.[111] The author of an "original" or creative work is granted a statutory entitlement to exclude others from reproducing, adapting, performing, or distributing copies of that work to the public. Unlike patent law, copyright generally embeds a broad range of exceptions and exclusions, including exclusions of subject matter that is functional rather than expressive (and therefore the subject of patent law) or that is too broad or abstract to be identified clearly as the specific product of a specific author. In the United States, the copyright holder is subject to a user's power to engage in "fair use" of copyrighted material.[112] In the Commonwealth countries, a copyright typically is subject to a somewhat more limited "fair dealing" exception.[113] Other countries specify a range of exceptions, exclusions, and compulsory licenses for a variety of specific purposes.[114] Finally, as with patents, expiration of the copyright delivers the covered material to the public domain. In general, the term of copyright lasts far longer than the term of patent—the life of the author plus fifty years, in most countries, and the life of the author plus seventy years in the United States and European Union countries.[115] Examples of constructed cultural commons for which copyright is an appropriate baseline are the General Public License (GPL) for open source computer software[116] and open access repositories for academic publishing.[117]

Basic Characteristics of the Constructed Cultural Commons

The next step after choosing an appropriate characterization of the "natural" environment in which a particular cultural commons resides is to identify basic characteristics relevant to the function of that commons in producing, managing, and disseminating intellectual goods. Here we suggest, as a starting point, a series of nested inquiries that we hope, when applied to and refined by a series of case studies, will assist researchers to identify the attributes that define successful and sustainable cultural-commons regimes and distinguish them from unsuccessful regimes.

By analogy to Ostrom's inquiries, we propose and discuss in this section the following initial inquiries, which we refer to as "baskets" of research questions:

- particular subject matter, resources pooled and so forth;
- particular activities undertaken and the actors who perform them;
- goals and objectives of the cultural commons;
- degree of "openness" of the cultural commons; and
- governance or "rules-in-use" of the cultural commons.

These inquiries are related to the Resource Characteristics, Attributes of Community, and Rules-in-Use section of Figure 7.2.[118]

RESOURCES AND COMMUNITY

After choosing an appropriate baseline environment, the next step in investigating a constructed cultural commons is to identify the set of resources being pooled and the relevant community of actors. The resources might appear to be obvious, such as patents in a patent pool, news items for a news service, recordings for a database of music, or recipes shared within the community of French chefs.[119] Or, it may take some consideration to identify the most salient description of the relevant resources. What resources are pooled and shared in an open source software community? Ideas? Code? Coding expertise? Debugging opportunities? In many contexts, and perhaps even in patent pools and French cooking, multiple types of resources are being shared within a community. The dynamic character of intellectual and knowledge resources means that shared resources may not be fully independent of one another both in the sense that the value of one shared resource may depend on its relationship to other shared resources, and in the sense that any shared resource may arise from or be developed from a different shared resource. The multiple contributions to a single open source software project demonstrate both features. The durability of shared resources must be considered. Patents and copyrights expire; tangible objects may wear out or be consumed. Our framework aims to be inclusive and thus aware of the variety of resources collected in cultural commons. We avoid a myopic focus on intellectual property assets.

Similarly, the identity of community members may be clear—as it is in a patent pool—or questions may exist about how the community is constituted. Does the open source software community consist of programmers alone? Does it include users of the code? People who submit comments or assist with debugging? Entrepreneurs who initiate meetings and dialogue or organize the community? People who develop, disseminate, and manage the relevant licenses? Those who monitor compliance with license terms? People who develop tools, host websites, and otherwise support the community?[120] Rather than seeking a single answer, our inquiry leads us to identify each of these constituencies and describe their specific roles. Critically, asking who is part of a particular constructed cultural commons sharpens the inquiry and helps pave the way for inquiries into institutions, governance, and sustainability.

Cultural commons exist on a spectrum. At one end of this spectrum are collective organizations that manage copyrights or patent pools. This subset is useful to work with because the set of pooled resources is easily identifiable, as is the relevant community of actors. Specifically, the set of resources is comprised of rather discrete, propertized, intellectual works, such as patented inventions, and the community is comprised of those who own those works and wish to reuse them.[121] At the other end of the spectrum are more complex examples. For example, the sharing and development of ideas, skills, tacit knowledge, and even the intellectual and cultural components of social capital within a university research community constitutes a constructed cultural commons.[122] This example invites significant variation among case studies based on the particular resources and subset of the university community targeted for study. Depending on the resources under investigation, the relevant community may be defined broadly in terms of the university as an institution, more narrowly in terms of a particular university or academic discipline, or most narrowly in terms of a specific academic unit, department, or school. Even something as seemingly mundane as an academic conference or scholarly presentation or an e-mail listserv among colleagues in a specific discipline might be usefully analyzed using our constructed cultural commons framework.

Identifying Goals and Objectives

Before describing the "rules-in-use" or governance structure of a constructed cultural commons, it is important to identify the particular problem or problems that a given commons is constructed to address. In the natural resource context, this question does not often come to the fore because common-pool resources are defined by the problem of subtractability or rivalrousness (e.g., removing lobsters from the pool results in fewer lobsters for everyone else) and the risk that a common-pool resource will be exhausted by uncoordinated self-interested activity (e.g., unmanaged harvesting may jeopardize the sustainability of the lobster population).[123]

Intellectual commons address different problems, which are defined initially by the fact that, as public goods, intellectual resources are not rivalrously consumed.[124] A copyrighted work or patented invention can be "used" simultaneously by many people while it is part of a commons without diminishing its availability for others. For example, the news remains available on the AP wire even after a particular member newspaper publishes an AP-generated story. The various problems that cultural commons institutions solve are not merely, or even primarily, problems of overuse. The problems addressed by cultural commons include the production of intellectual goods to be shared, the overcoming of transaction costs leading to bargaining breakdown among different actors interested in exploiting the intellectual resource, the production of commonly useful platforms for further creativity, and so forth.[125]

More generally, we can distinguish among different types of cultural commons based on their core purposes. Some such commons arise as solutions to collective action, coordination, or transactions cost problems that exist apart from IP rights (and perhaps would not be solvable without these rights). These solutions might involve instances of cooperative behavior where members construct an open environment to pool resources and use those resources themselves for some specific purpose. Open source software projects, mediated by formal free and open source licenses and by informal communal structures for determining what code becomes part of the "authorized" code base, are examples of this type.[126] Standard-setting enterprises also fit into this category,[127] as do joint ventures for scientific research and development.[128] These cultural commons depend on each member's possessing certain intellectual property interests as a facilitator of participation.

A second type of commons or pooling arrangement is intended to solve collective action, coordination, or transactions cost problems that exist only because of the IP rights themselves.[129] In some of these cases, a commons is constructed as a defense against potential privatization of commonly useful resources. Examples of such arrangements might include constructed commons for basic biological building blocks such as the Single Nucleotide Polymorphism (SNP) consortium[130] or the publicly available databases of genomic sequences that are part of the Human Genome Project.[131] Formal licenses and related agreements assure that participants in the commons become part of what amounts to a mutual nonaggression pact that is necessary precisely because of the possibility that intellectual resources may be propertized. So long as the resource is in the commons, it can be shared among commons members, and neither commons members nor outsiders are able to appropriate that resource, patent it, and then assert a patent claim against a commons member. Within the commons, research proceeds more or less as it otherwise would, according to informal disciplinary norms and free of (or at least, less burdened by) undue anxiety about propertization and potential holdup.

A third type of cultural commons may be designed to mediate among communities with different default norms. Technology transfer institutions, which enable universities and other nonprofit research enterprises to deliver information resources (such as the technical knowledge described in patent specifications) to the private market, are examples of this type of commons.[132] The cultural environment inside the university is typically characterized by information sharing not governed by IP rights, even if IP rights are present as matters of form.[133] The environment outside the university is governed largely by IP rights. Technology transfer institutions may constitute an institutional pool or commons that mediates these two regimes.[134] Similarly, open source projects have developed "boundary organizations" to mediate their relations with commercial firms.[135]

By specifying these distinct types of cultural commons, we are probably setting up a more sharply delineated field of institutions than is really obtained in practice. In any given commons, it may be the case—and may even likely be the case—that the motivation for the pool arises from a variety of considerations, that is, some do not arise from the character of intellectual property interests themselves, and some do.

Pooling arrangements also may exist for less socially salutary reasons. Most obvious is the case of members colluding to restrict competition, and it is certainly within the purview of our approach that commons should be evaluated in part by reference to the possibility of anticompetitive behavior and other possible costs. But by requiring as an initial matter that an intellectual commons operate via sharing of intellectual resources, we distinguish this project from investigations of cartels as such, which operate by sharing price and output information and which pose significant and obvious risks of anticompetitive behavior without offsetting welfare benefits.[136] The functional purpose of cartels is different from the cultural commons arrangements noted above; that is, cartels are not designed to create an open environment within which resources may be shared and productively used by members or to sustain individual members. But just as the line between different types of intellectual commons may be difficult to draw consistently, the line between commons and cartels similarly may be difficult to draw. Antitrust regulators have long faced the challenge of identifying illegitimate cartels disguised as legitimate patent pools and other knowledge-sharing institutions.[137]

DEGREES OF OPENNESS AND THE CHARACTER OF CONTROL

Commons regimes are defined both by the *degree of openness and control* that they exhibit with respect to contributors, users, and resources, and by the *assignment of control, or custody of the power to administer access.* The rules-in-use of a constructed cultural commons will delineate its degree of openness, particularly with respect to use of the resources by outsiders who do not contribute to resource creation. Again, this inquiry is less relevant to natural resource commons arrangements. Natural resources generally are finite, potentially rivalrous in consumption, often congested, and subject to tragic overconsumption.[138] Consequently, it is often necessary to limit access to a common-pool resource to a defined community. The boundaries of the community sharing a resource tend to be coextensive with the boundaries of commons self-governance.[139] Thus, in many cases, the commons is open to members and closed to everyone else, and that is the end of the story. Intellectual resources, by contrast, are not subject to the same natural constraints and are naturally shareable without a risk of congestion or overconsumption. Rarely does "too much information" diminish the value of individual items of information.[140] It is entirely possible and desirable for a community to produce and/or manage a cluster of cultural goods that is accessible to outsiders.[141] One of the measures of the social benefit of a constructed cultural commons may be the degree to which it disseminates the intellectual goods it produces to a wider audience.

Openness as Applied to Resources

What do we mean by openness? Little ambiguity exists in most everyday contexts (e.g., an open door), but openness can be a confusing concept when used to describe an intellectual resource. Openness describes our capacity to relate to a resource by accessing and using it. In other words, openness describes the extent to which there are barriers to possession or use. Openness varies according to the costs of surmounting barriers (in terms of money, conditions, or other restrictions) to exploitation. Openness in this sense may encompass joint or shared access to and use of the resource.[142]

Barriers to possession or use of a resource may be natural or constructed. A resource may be open naturally because its characteristics prevent it from being possessed, owned, or controlled by anyone.[143] Frischmann provides one example:

> [F]or most of the earth's history, the oceans and the atmosphere were natural commons . . . [b]ecause, for example, exercising dominion over such resources was beyond the ability of human beings or simply was unnecessary because there was no indication of scarcity.
>
> A resource also may be open . . . as the result of social construction. That is, laws or rules may prohibit ownership or ensure [a certain degree of openness]. . . .[144]

For example, copyright law grants protection over creative expression but excludes protection for ideas in order to maintain open access and use of ideas. Patent law likewise excludes abstract ideas from patentability. Openness may arise through norms and customs among owners and users and through institutional design.[145]

Openness and the vesting of control over openness are related. In part, both concepts may simply reflect choices regarding how best to manage resources. In the context of intellectual property pools, for example, management of the pooled resources may be vested in a central institution created specifically for that purpose, or it may be decentralized and vested in the hands of individual IP rights holders.[146]

Openness and the sources of control also reflect power and its distribution among potential possessors and users. Openness may be measured by the degree of control over the terms of access and use of a specific resource. Such control is exercised by human beings on human beings. Openness is relational, and it relies on social institutions.

In sum, openness is a functional variable that describes the degree to which possession and use of a resource is controlled, and it is a relational variable that describes the structure of relationships among potential resource users.

Openness as Applied to a Community

As a resource or set of resources may have an open character, so may a community. As openness is applied to resources, openness of a community is defined partly in functional terms, by natural and constructed attributes that define membership in the community, and partly in terms of power and other bases for relations among participants.[147] Above, we defined the cultural environment as a set of interdependent and interconnected systems and resources.[148] As with openness applied to resources, openness with regard to a community describes our capacity to relate to that community as a contributor or user of resources that comprise in part the cultural commons. Thus, openness describes the extent to which there are criteria for or barriers to membership or participation in the creative or innovative processes that the cultural commons is intended to support. Openness also describes the extent to which a particular community is accessible to and interconnected with related context, institutions, and social practices.

Openness with respect to a community has an internal dimension as well as an external one, as it reflects the degree to which participants in the cultural commons collaborate with one another or otherwise share human capital as well as (or rather than) resources. For example, the participants in an intellectual property pool may specify rules regarding how resources are contributed to and withdrawn from the pool. The General Public License for open source computer programs specifies that membership in the community defined by users of the program is open to anyone.[149] Anyone may add to, use, or redistribute the licensed program. Redistributors, however, must abide by the license term that they make the full source code of the program accessible to further users of the program. Moreover, in most open source software projects, only certain contributions are accepted into "official" versions of the code.[150] Thus, although use and modification of the code for personal use are open to anyone, the ability to contribute to the shared resource is regulated.

In describing and assessing the degrees of openness and control that characterize a cultural commons or pool, one should bear in mind more than just the conventional producer perspective by which information and knowledge shareability problems often are analyzed. Hardin's "tragedy of the commons"[151] is typically understood as challenging markets and governments to offer ways to supply resources in the face of cooperation and competition problems.[152] In analyzing openness with respect to resources and communities, accordingly, it is tempting to limit the analysis to openness with respect to actual and potential resource producers.

In information and knowledge environments, those resources are "naturally" given only in part. The cumulative and aggregative character of knowledge is fundamental to human culture. Producers of knowledge and culture resources are therefore simultaneously users and consumers. In analyzing openness, it is important to consider the degree to which openness expresses the interests of users, as matters of both function and relation. In particular, a constructed commons in the cultural environment may function as infrastructure.[153] In the cultural environment, the tragedy of the commons that Hardin described may refer not to an undersupply of a resource prompted by overconsumption but instead to an undersupply prompted by the failure of the private market to aggregate user or consumer preferences for certain fundamental or "infrastructural" resources. This situation occurs, for example, in the context of basic research conducted within and across universities.[154] To the extent that the Internet itself constitutes a commons, it is likely better characterized as an infrastructural resource that solves certain problems of consumption rather than problems of production.

Governance or "Rules-in-Use"

Having identified a cultural commons, chosen an appropriate description of the background environment within which the commons is nested, and assessed the characteristics of associated resources and populations, goals and objectives, and the degree and character of openness and control, the next task is to investigate more specifically the characteristics of the cultural commons that relate to its governance and the way it functions. Here we identify several relevant clusters or "buckets" of variables that will be important to explore:[155]

- history and narrative;
- entitlement structures and resource provisions;
- institutional setting (including markets and related firm and collective structures, social structures that describe the roles and interests of individual actors in the commons, and boundary organizations or mechanisms mediating internal governance of the commons with external markets, the public domain, and other institutions);
- legal structures (including intellectual property rules, subsidies, contract and licensing law, antitrust provisions); and
- governance mechanisms of the commons (membership rules, resource contribution or extraction standards and requirements, conflict resolution mechanisms, sanctions for rule violation).

History and Narrative

What is the relevant history and narrative of a given commons? Above, we noted the importance of language and metaphor in understanding the information environment.[156] Any given knowledge pool depends in an important sense on its creation narrative. That narrative depends in turn on a variety of linguistic and metaphor resources: the vocabulary and syntax that participants and observers use in describing the construct are keys to unlocking its origins, its operation, and even its future. Carol Rose has written of property as a story.[157] Michael Madison[158] and Jessica Silbey[159] have both described the creation myths that accompany default regimes of intellectual property. The very phrase "patent pool," for example, itself has come to signify a specific set of legal expectations and criticisms. If one says "patent pool," an informed commentator thinks immediately of (i) a self-governing arrangement and (ii) antitrust considerations, rather than intellectual property problems and solutions. (In part, we aim to realign that point of view.) Calling something a "knowledge commons," or recharacterizing certain patent pools as solutions to "anticommons" problems, triggers a different set of expectations. The rhetorical frame shifts primarily to dynamic problems in information and information property, rather than to largely static output concerns. A commons is a rhetorically open place. A "pool" emphasizes the resources themselves and how those resources are bounded.

Explicitly giving attention to creation narratives also encourages attention to evolutionary processes. Changes in the narrative over time, or conflicts embedded within a narrative, can illustrate debates over purpose, which can illuminate the normative foundations of commons and highlight points of conflict. Looking at history can help answer the question of how the commons changes and adapts over time, in light of changes in firm structure, market structure, and resources (such as emergent legal structures, background legal entitlements, and temporal features like limitations on duration) that are built into those entitlements. History and narrative also emphasize the importance of contextual details that are ignored or marginalized in an overly rationalist account of institutional design. For example, within this cluster, we would like to uncover details concerning the influence of power, politics, and personalities that are often necessary to understanding commons. This cluster of questions provides an important link back to the earlier discussion of community and objectives.[160]

Entitlement Structures and Resource Provisions

In any resource pool, the resources that are part of the commons have to come from somewhere. This cluster is intended to capture an array of questions concerning the boundaries around the resources themselves and how those boundaries are socially constructed. Thus, moving beyond, or at least complicating, the initial set of questions concerning *what* resources are contributed and subject to the commons arrangement, we would like to better understand *how* the resources are delineated and *how* they are contributed and made part of the commons.

The "natural" information environment contains an abundance of raw information resources, including inherited and experienced knowledge. Those resources often become information "works" and, therefore, resources in the pool via some cultural construct, such as the default copyright or patent law systems, via some other institution, such as a publishing industry producing books, films, or songs, or via some combination of these and other things, such as cultural practices or norms. Understanding the construction of cultural commons therefore requires understanding the mechanisms by which resources are provisioned to the commons, whether via legal entitlements or otherwise, and the nature of entitlements to use and consume those resources while they are part of that commons. A patent pool offers an obvious example. The patents themselves are resources constructed via rights of exclusion offered by patent law. As pool members develop follow-on inventions based on the pooled resources, the agreement by which the pool is constituted may obligate members to contribute patents covering those inventions to the pool.[161]

As with some natural resource pools that (when suitably managed) are self-sustaining and thus supply their own resources, in the cultural context the commons resources themselves may be sources of additional resources. The follow-on invention is an obvious example. An essential attribute of the governance of a cultural commons, therefore, is the way in which it allocates resources as they are produced dynamically.

Boundaries in an information environment are likewise more obviously culturally constructed than their counterparts in the field of natural resources. Oceans, lakes, and rivers have beds and shores; forests yield to fields. Boundary maintenance is an important part of commons management in natural resources, but the maintenance question often has a reference point in naturally occurring boundaries. In the information environment, all boundaries ultimately depend on cultural constructs.[162] Accordingly, this cluster is intended to help flesh out the connections between the construction of both resources and commons governance systems and the situatedness (or nestedness) of both resources and commons in broader systems. The cluster provides an important link back to the earlier discussion of baselines and degrees of openness.[163]

Institutional Setting

Pools and commons in the cultural environment are functional entities; they often serve markets, industries, and firms. It is important to understand the identities and roles of those institutions and how their own functions relate to the pool and its members. What are those markets, and how do they relate to the pool? The MAA, an example of an early, well-known patent pool, was organized in large part to facilitate the production of aircraft for military use during World War I.[164]

The institutional and social setting of a cultural commons may include related collectivist enterprises. Members of a pool may be part of a network structure that extends to related collectives, firms, individuals, groups, and social structures, including disciplines and social norms.[165] Research scientists may be organized formally into pools or commons structures within firms and other formal institutions, such as universities. Their functional network will include both members of their own technical art and related arts and other researchers in different arts who share a related but distinct set of social norms related to sharing of information and knowledge. Networks in not-for-profit or educational research settings will overlap to a degree with related networks in commercial environments. Researchers in university science departments will be interested in sharing information resources with researchers in corporate research-and-development groups.[166] Pools may bridge gaps created by the edges of formal institutional structures.[167]

Constructed cultural commons are often situated in nonhierarchical and distributed institutional settings, in which participants are only loosely connected and sometimes are connected only by their participation in a particular project.[168] The range of institutional settings likely to be observed in case studies of cultural commons is thus likely to be considerably broader than the range observed in natural resource commons. The institutional setting will, of course, constrain and determine the ways in which rules for production and sharing of resources are both put into place and applied.

Legal Structures That Affect the Pool Itself

Although industry, market, and networked institutional structures are essential reference points for many knowledge commons, positive law and direct government involvement with a particular cultural commons are likewise keys to understanding it. We distinguish between law that creates and enforces the entitlements that create and sustain information works, on the one hand, and law that is specifically addressed to cultural commons themselves, on the other hand. Here, legislators and judges often find that law can reinforce and sustain a pool that is determined to be welfare-enhancing. An exemption or more deferential treatment from antitrust scrutiny for parties engaged in a form of concerted activity, or intended to engage in concerted activity, may be adopted.[169] Market conditions or technologies may develop to the point where observers recognize that some kind of information collective would be useful, but fear of prosecution under antitrust law or relevant IP law may be a barrier to the emergence of the pool. A safe harbor of a sort may emerge, either via legislation or judicial decision. The 1984 judgment of the Supreme Court of the United States in *Sony Corp. of America v. Universal City Studios, Inc.*,[170] upholding the legality of distributing videotape recorders over the objection that they facilitated copyright infringement, may be characterized as creating a form of judicial safe harbor for innovative technologies for reproducing and distributing copyrighted works.

Legal rules may create subsidies or safe harbors in ways other than relieving at-risk parties from potential liability. For example, income-tax regimes may permit (or limit) the deductibility of research expenses by firms, nonprofit enterprises, and/or research collectives. In the United States patent statute, the section that bars patenting inventions that are "obvious" in light of prior art in the relevant technical field includes a subsection that suspends the rule if the inventor and the producer of the relevant prior art are part of a common "joint research agreement."[171] Laws designed for one purpose may contribute differently to promoting collaborations or collectives in ways not intended by the drafters of the law. Such a rule becomes part of the constitution of a commons, even if it was not designed to do so in the first place. Jessica Litman uses this proposition to analyze the persistence of a legal regime subsidizing jukeboxes in American copyright law.[172] A compulsory license permitting owners of coin-operated record players to use copyrighted American music was initially incorporated into the copyright statute to prevent holders of those copyrights from monopolizing adjacent markets for performances.[173] Over time, the rationale for the subsidy became less significant, but the statute was retained because a new collective emerged to support its continued existence—companies that manufactured and distributed jukeboxes.

Governance Mechanisms

A constructed commons is an alternative to proprietary exclusion and to direct government intervention as a means of addressing market failures associated with public goods, externalities, and the tragedy of the commons. Accordingly, understanding the mechanism of governance of a particular commons, in the context of its legal and institutional setting, is at the heart of the analysis. In Ostrom's work, the degree of self-governance is an important characteristic of a resource pool.[174] Members have rights not only to contribute to and extract from the pool but also to govern themselves by adopting and modifying the relevant rules of participation.

The attributes to be considered here overlap to some extent with those addressed in the context of determining the scope of the openness of the pool. The focus shifts, however, from access to the resources of the commons to participation in decision making about how the resources will be produced and managed. Who is a member, and who decides who may be a member? How is resource contribution and extraction monitored and, if necessary, limited? What sanctions and dispute resolution mechanisms are provided for misconduct? To what extent do these self-governance mechanisms rely on or incorporate formal legal mechanisms, and to what extent do they rely on or incorporate other, nonlegal institutions or social structures?

For example, in the context of the General Public License for open source computer programs, membership in the commons defined in part by the license is further defined by use of the program itself, which, according to the terms of the license that accompanies the programs, constitutes assent to its terms.[175] Violation of those terms, such as onward distribution of a copy of a program without including a copy of the program's source code, constitutes a license violation and automatically terminates that membership.[176] Actual enforcement of that regime, however, typically is not pursued by individual contributors to the open source commons but instead by an independent entity, the Free Software Foundation, which operates as a freestanding nonprofit organization dedicated to advocacy on behalf of "free" software and accompanying open source license terms.[177]

Research on natural resource pools emphasizes that effective self-governance typically requires formal access to public sanctioning and/or enforcement mechanisms. Without the threat of seizure or attachment or injunction, community-based or purely norm-based mechanisms may lack sufficient bite to sustain the pool. In the context of cultural commons, effective connections between self-governing collectives and formal sanctioning authorities have not yet been identified. In the open source computer software area, only recently have courts begun to consider the enforceability of the licenses.[178] Conflict resolution mechanisms within a pool depend on monitoring mechanisms. Before the emergence of the Internet, research on self-governing communities emphasized size and distance as key variables in a monitoring system. As Benkler[179] and Cohen[180] each argue, networking technology offers not only the potential for community development and resource aggregation but also the potential for monitoring and enforcement. Examination of a pool should include assessment of whether and how it is embedded in network technologies that perform some or all of the pool's governance functions.

Patterns and Outcomes Emanating from a Particular Action Arena

Finally, as when analyzing natural resource commons, the analysis should include an inquiry into patterns of interactions and outcomes, including:

- solutions to the underlying collective action problem and benefits delivered by the commons (including innovations and creative output, and production, sharing, and dissemination of those innovations and output to a broader audience), along with the dynamics of the social practices that emerge from the interaction of commons resources and commons participants; and
- costs and risks associated with the commons, including, for example, any negative externalities.

A cultural commons should be assessed not only in light of its ostensible purposes but also in light of its consequences. This aspect of the case study approach should both identify the consequences and describe relevant criteria for evaluating them.

The consequences themselves typically will take at least two forms, which in a particular case often will be inextricably linked. With respect to intellectual resources, a cultural commons usually will produce some intellectual or knowledge-related (or material) output. The MAA enabled the production of airplanes. The Linux open source project supports the Linux computer program. Wikipedia produces Wikipedia.org. The AP enables the production of newspapers.

In the case of most cultural-commons examples, moreover, the social patterns that emerge from the construction and governance of the commons may themselves constitute ongoing, constantly refreshed commons outcomes. Many of the companies that were parties to the original MAA agreement combined via merger and acquisition by 1929 to form the Curtiss-Wright Corporation, which is still a significant defense contractor today.[181] The Linux project and Wikipedia are notable not only for the production of complex industrial-scale products but also for the governance of networks of loosely aligned contributors, distributed broadly in space and time.[182] The AP and other wire services have cultivated and retained identities as distinct and productive enterprises in their own right despite the fact that much of what they publish is created by their members.[183] The jamband community is a recognized community that defines itself partly via its practices of archiving and sharing jamband performances.[184]

Solutions and Benefits

We defined constructed commons in the cultural environment as solutions to collective action or other transactions cost problems not arising from the character of intellectual property entitlements themselves, as solutions to problems that do arise from those entitlements, as solutions to boundary-spanning dilemmas, and as reactions to an "infrastructure"-type problem—the market's inability to aggregate individual demand for standards or platform resources—that is the inverse of the standard tragedy-of-the-commons diagnosis.

For any specific cultural commons, the questions involve not only the type of problem that it appears to be designed to solve and precisely how the combination of legal rules and other "openness" constructions propose to solve it, but also the success of the commons in sustaining and generating spillovers and a dynamic cultural environment. Quantifying or otherwise documenting that success is particularly difficult in the cultural environment, because the desired benefits often accrue to populations other than those in direct producer/consumer relationships. Commons can enable spillovers,[185] the dynamic benefits that an information environment can be designed to enable whether in its "natural" state, via the "default" variations on that state as described earlier,[186] or via some pool or other constructed environment. One beneficiary of the MAA patent pool was the American government, which purchased aircraft during World War I.[187] The beneficiaries of an online jamband archive may include ordinary music lovers, who are able to listen to jamband recordings even though they may not count themselves among the jamband community itself.[188] Under some circumstances, the very persistence of an institution may be evidence of the success of a commons regime.[189]

Costs and Risks Associated with a Cultural Commons

Any cultural commons may engender a trade-off between the benefits anticipated from the commons in terms of dynamic welfare enhancements and the costs and risks associated with that commons. In conventional law-and-economics terms, these costs and risks are fairly well understood (and, importantly, they are generally better understood and easier to describe and quantify in many instances than the downstream benefits that commons may supply). Enabling collaboration and cooperation among firms sharing access to pooled information resources facilitates cooperation along lines that may be anticompetitive and therefore socially harmful: agreements to raise and fix costs and agreements to reduce output.[190] Pools, like other collective arrangements, also involve administrative costs associated with constructing, monitoring, and enforcing compliance with the rules of the pool. From a welfare standpoint, the level of those costs must be compared to the level of administrative costs associated with a system that provisions information resources in the absence of the pool.

In sum, we offer the framework described in this part as a template for ongoing case study investigations of constructed cultural commons across a broad variety of domains. In many contexts, the existing scholarly literature has undertaken case study investigations of phenomena grounded in social norms,[191] transactions cost economics,[192] and even history and anthropology,[193] all of which may be profitably aggregated and recast as examples of cultural commons. One step in that direction is an application of the framework to analyze universities as cultural commons.[194] Collecting and reconstructing this literature using the clusters of questions listed above will, in our estimation, yield new insights into the emergence and effective functioning of cultural commons.

Going forward, we anticipate developing an inventory of new commons case studies, perhaps beginning with more detailed investigations of some of the examples discussed in the introduction. We also hope other scholars will consider using this framework as part of their own work. Over time, we anticipate that the results of further case studies will yield not only better information regarding commons themselves but also refinements to the constructed cultural commons framework and to the above baskets of questions. In a real sense, the study of commons is itself a constructed cultural commons, and our own three-part collaboration is a nested commons within the scholarly community that studies commons.

Conclusion

The theoretical discussion of intellectual property policy has been myopically focused on extremes of exclusion and open access, ignoring a wide range of cultural commons that persist between the extremes. It is often divorced from empirical studies of creative and inventive communities. To the extent that case studies are undertaken, they tend to be done in isolated areas (such as open source software or academic publishing) and consider a limited number of descriptive variables. This narrow focus makes integration and learning from a body of case studies quite difficult, which in turn discourages people from pursuing further case studies. Scholars appear to be aware of the need for a more nuanced and structured approach to these questions but have not yet developed a framework for studying them.

This article offers precisely such a framework. Applying the environmental metaphor that is increasingly common in studies of information and intellectual property policy, we analogize information and knowledge resources in the cultural environment to physical resources in the natural environment. We identify a set of constructed cultural commons, or pools of information resources, that serve functions in the cultural environment similar to the functions provided by common-pool resources in the natural environment. Those functions consist largely of serving as alternatives to purely private rights of exclusion and to government intervention in solving underproduction and overconsumption problems associated with an unmanaged or "natural" resource. Although constructed commons in the cultural environment exist for a variety of purposes, in general we hypothesize that they are often welfare-enhancing in regard to promoting valuable spillovers of information and knowledge distribution.

Borrowing from Ostrom, we argue that understanding the origins and operation of beneficial cultural commons requires detailed assessments that recognize that they operate simultaneously at several levels, each nested in a level above, and that each level entails a variety of possible attributes that cannot, at this stage of the inquiry, be specified in detail in advance. We suggest a set of buckets or clusters of issues that should guide further inquiry, including the ways in which information resources and resource commons are structured by default rules of exclusion, and the ways in which members of these pools manage participation in the collection, production, preservation, and extraction of information resources. Case studies across disciplines and reviews of existing literature that addresses cultural commons will help specify relevant attributes within each cluster. These variables will help scholars and eventually policymakers assess the level of openness associated with a given commons and determine the extent to which "openness" is, as we hypothesize, associated with pools that are welfare-enhancing.

Beyond our proposal of a framework for studying them, our consideration of constructed cultural commons has highlighted a number of points that are important in the study of intellectual property going forward. Considering constructed cultural commons helps to elevate collective, intermediate solutions to their possible place of significance in accounts of property regimes and should diminish the skepticism of many scholars that collective, norm-driven solutions can work beyond narrowly defined situations. Case studies will also call our attention to the constructed, designed character of both the cultural and the legal environment in regard to knowledge and information policy problems. Finally, as they have done in the study of natural resource management, systematic analyses of cultural commons across a wide range of collected case studies should lead us to doubt panacea prescriptions drawn from overly simplistic models.

Acknowledgments

The authors especially wish to thank Thráinn Eggertsson, Wendy Gordon, Gregg Macey, Robert Merges, Elinor Ostrom, and Lawrence Solum for their incredibly insightful and constructive comments, which are included in this issue. We also thank Mario Biagioli, Dan Burk, Julie E. Cohen, Doug Kysar, Karim Lakhani, Mark Lemley, Lawrence Lessig, Joseph Scott Miller, Pam Samuelson, Joel West, and reviewers and commenters at the 12th Biennial Conference of the International Association for the Study of the Commons; the Intellectual Property Scholars Conferences at DePaul and Stanford; the Open Source and Proprietary Models of Innovation Conference at the Washington University School of Law; the Science & Technology Studies (STS) and IP Law Conference held in St. Helena, California; the Workshop on Intellectual Property Law and Open & User Innovation at MIT; and Faculty Workshops and Colloquia at Cornell, DePaul, USC, and Washington & Lee Law Schools and the ETH Zurich Professorship for Intellectual Property for criticisms and suggestions.

Notes

This chapter was originally published in *Cornell Law Review* 95(4) (May 2010): 657–709.

1. *See generally* JAMES M. ACHESON, CAPTURING THE COMMONS: DEVISING INSTITUTIONS TO MANAGE THE MAINE LOBSTER INDUSTRY (2003) (describing the success of the Maine lobster industry).

2. *See* Carl Shapiro, *Navigating the Patent Thicket: Cross Licenses, Patent Pools, and Standard Setting*, *in* 1 INNOVATION POLICY AND THE ECONOMY 119, 127–28, 134 (Adam B. Jaffe et al. eds., 2000).

3. *See id.*

4. *See id.* at 127–28.

5. *See* Mfrs. Aircraft Ass'n, Inc. v. United States, 77 Ct. Cl. 481, 483–87 (1933); Harry T. Dykman, *Patent Licensing within the Manufacturer's Aircraft Association (MAA)*, 46 J. PAT. OFF. SOC'Y 646, 648–50 (1964); Robert P. Merges, *Contracting into Liability Rules: Intellectual Property Rights and Collective Rights Organizations*, 84 CAL. L. REV. 1293, 1343–46 (1996).

6. Some of these programmers contribute to the Linux project at the behest of their corporate employers and thus are not volunteers in the strict sense. They

are volunteers with respect to the Linux project, however. Their relationship to the Linux community is governed by the same rules as apply to those who participate for other reasons. For an exploration of the governance issues involved in the relationship between open source software projects and commercial firms, see Siobhán O'Mahony & Beth A. Bechky, *Boundary Organizations: Enabling Collaboration among Unexpected Allies*, 53 ADMIN. SCI. Q. 422, 440 (2008).

7. A recent book thoroughly examines the organizational structure of open source software projects. *See* CHRISTOPHER M. KELTY, TWO BITS: THE CULTURAL SIGNIFICANCE OF FREE SOFTWARE (2008).

8. *See* Wikipedia, http://www.wikipedia.org (last visited Mar. 15, 2010). For discussions of this and other examples of collective production, see OPEN SOURCES 2.0: THE CONTINUING EVOLUTION (Chris DiBona et al. eds., 2005); Michael J. Madison, *Social Software, Groups, and Governance*, 2006 MICH. ST. L. REV. 153.

9. In part due to perceptions of Wikipedia as unregulated, open, and chaotic, Wikipedia presents a puzzle for scholars. "The most common criticism of Wikipedia over the years stemmed from simple disbelief: 'That can't work.'" CLAY SHIRKY, HERE COMES EVERYBODY: THE POWER OF ORGANIZING WITHOUT ORGANIZATIONS 115 (2008). As David Hoffman and Salil Mehra note, "Wikipedia is 'the canonical bee that flies despite scientists' skepticism that the aerodynamics add up.'" David A. Hoffman & Salil Mehra, *Wikitruth through Wikiorder*, 59 EMORY L.J. 151, 155 (2009) (quoting JONATHAN ZITTRAIN, THE FUTURE OF THE INTERNET—AND HOW TO STOP IT 148 (2008)).

10. *See* ZITTRAIN, *supra* note 9, at 143–46 (2008).

11. *See* Wikipedia: Text of the GNU Free Documentation License, http://en.wikipedia.org/wiki/Wikipedia:Text_of_the_GNU_Free_Documentation_License (last visited Mar. 9, 2010).

12. *See* Hoffman & Mehra, *supra* note 9, at 163–75 (examining the Wiki dispute-resolution system).

13. *See* REPORTERS OF THE ASSOCIATED PRESS, BREAKING NEWS: HOW THE ASSOCIATED PRESS HAS COVERED WAR, PEACE, AND EVERYTHING ELSE 18 (2007).

14. *See* Int'l News Serv. v. Associated Press, 248 U.S. 215, 239–43 (1918); *see also* Wendy J. Gordon, *Harmless Use: Gleaning from Fields of Copyrighted Works*, 77 FORDHAM L. REV. 2411, 2421–23 (2009) (discussing the structure of the tort doctrine).

15. *See* Stephen Shmanske, *News as a Public Good: Cooperative Ownership, Price Commitments, and the Success of the Associated Press*, 60 BUS. HIST. REV. 55, 56–57, 59 n.3 (1986).

16. For histories of the AP, see REPORTERS OF THE ASSOCIATED PRESS, *supra* note 13; Shmanske, *supra* note 15; The Associated Press, AP History/Corporate Archives, http://www.ap.org/pages/about/history/history.html (last visited Mar. 11, 2010). The thumbnail sketch presented above necessarily omits important details about the history of the AP, including allegations that its content was biased politically and that it behaved monopolistically, as well as information

about its current, troubled state. On its history, see ALEXANDER JONES, HISTORICAL SKETCH OF THE ELECTRIC TELEGRAPH: INCLUDING ITS RISE AND PROGRESS IN THE UNITED STATES (New York, George P. Putnam, 1852), and Margaret A. Blanchard, *The Associated Press Antitrust Suit: A Philosophical Clash over Ownership of First Amendment Rights*, 61 BUS. HIST. REV. 43 (1987). On its current struggles, see Richard Pérez-Peña, *Some Papers in Financial Trouble are Leaving the A.P. to Cut Costs*, N.Y. TIMES, Oct. 20, 2008, at B1. Any accounting of the history of the AP should include its rivalry with United Press and the International News Service, which merged in the 1950s to form United Press International. *See* RICHARD M. HARNETT & BILLY G. FERGUSON, UNIPRESS: COVERING THE 20TH CENTURY (2003).

17. *See* Mark F. Schultz, *Fear and Norms and Rock & Roll: What Jambands Can Teach Us about Persuading People to Obey Copyright Law*, 21 BERKELEY TECH. L.J. 651, 674, 679 n.116 (2006); *see also* etree.org, http://www.etree.org (last visited Mar. 18, 2010).

18. *See* Schultz, *supra* note 17, at 653, 658.

19. *See id.* at 675–76.

20. *See id.* at 679–80.

21. To illustrate the potential breadth of the concept of the constructed cultural commons, we note a few additional examples, such as (i) medieval guilds, which provided a structured environment for sharing expert trade knowledge among members, see Robert P. Merges, *From Medieval Guilds to Open Source Software: Informal Norms, Appropriability Institutions, and Innovation* 14 (Conference on the Legal History of Intellectual Property, Working Paper, 2004), *available at* http://ssrn.com/abstract=661543; (ii) the modern research university and the departmental and disciplinary structures that lie within it and above it, see Michael J. Madison, Brett M. Frischmann & Katherine J. Strandburg, *The University as Constructed Cultural Commons*, 30 WASH. U. J.L. & POL'Y 365 (2009); and (iii) the Request for Comments (RFCs) series that defines the technical protocols of the Internet, see RFC Editor Homepage, http://www.rfc-editor.org (last visited Mar. 11, 2010). For other historical examples of technological commons, see Robert C. Allen, *Collective Invention*, 4 J. ECON. BEHAV. & ORG. 1 (1983).

22. *See infra* [first] part. Likewise, pomology, the study of fruit, offers something more than studying apples, oranges, plums, and pears independently.

23. *See* Merges, *supra* note 21, at 4–7.

24. *See* Mark A. Lemley, *Property, Intellectual Property, and Free Riding*, 83 TEX. L. REV. 1031, 1073 (2005).

25. *See id.* at 1050–55.

26. Carol M. Rose, *Big Roads, Big Rights: Varieties of Public Infrastructure and Their Impact on Environmental Resources*, 50 ARIZ. L. REV. 409, 423–28 (2008) [hereinafter Rose, *Big Roads*] (emphasizing the idiosyncratic character of "community-based property rights structures"); Carol Rose, *The Comedy of the Commons: Custom, Commerce, and Inherently Public Property*, 53 U. CHI.

L. REV. 711, 718–23 (1986) [hereinafter Rose, *Comedy*] (describing "inherently public property" in the context of an "exception to the general rule favoring private property").

27. On the public-good nature of intellectual resources (ideas, information, expression, and knowledge), see Brett M. Frischmann & Mark A. Lemley, *Spillovers*, 107 COLUM. L. REV. 257, 272–73 (2007). On how those resources generate different types of externalities, see Brett M. Frischmann, *Speech, Spillovers, and the First Amendment*, 2008 U. CHI. LEGAL F. 301, 310–21; Frischmann & Lemley, *supra*, at 258–61. On public goods and externalities generally, see RICHARD CORNES & TODD SANDLER, THE THEORY OF EXTERNALITIES, PUBLIC GOODS, AND CLUB GOODS 40–43 (2d ed. 1996) (describing externalities as the absence of markets and the effect of externalities on property rights).

28. Brett M. Frischmann, *The Pull of Patents*, 77 FORDHAM L. REV. 2143, 2156 (2009) (footnote omitted).

29. *See id.*

30. *See, e.g.*, 17 U.S.C. §§ 102, 107 (2006) (providing for limits on the scope of copyrightable subject matter and for the fair use defense); 35 U.S.C. §§ 101, 102, 103 (2006) (providing for limits on the scope of patentable subject matter); Diamond v. Chakrabarty, 447 U.S. 303, 309 (1980) (noting that the laws of nature, physical phenomena, and abstract ideas are not patentable); *see also* WILLIAM M. LANDES & RICHARD A. POSNER, THE ECONOMIC STRUCTURE OF INTELLECTUAL PROPERTY LAW 147–66, 302–10 (2003) (discussing limits on copyright and patent); Frischmann & Lemley, *supra* note 27, at 284–93 (same).

31. *See* U.S. CONST. art. I, § 8, cl. 8 ("limited times"); 17 U.S.C. § 302 (establishing the duration of a copyright); 35 U.S.C. § 154(a)(2) (establishing the duration of a patent).

32. *See* Pamela Samuelson, Lecture, *Enriching Discourse on Public Domains*, 55 DUKE L.J. 783, 816–28 (2006) (exploring dedication to the public domain).

33. Consider, for example, university patenting of federally funded research. *See, e.g.*, CAPITALIZING KNOWLEDGE: NEW INTERSECTIONS OF INDUSTRY AND ACADEMIA (Henry Etzkowitz et al. eds., 1998); INDUSTRIALIZING KNOWLEDGE: UNIVERSITY-INDUSTRY LINKAGES IN JAPAN AND THE UNITED STATES (Lewis M. Branscomb et al. eds., 1999); Ajay Agrawal, *University-to-Industry Knowledge Transfer: Literature Review and Unanswered Questions*, 3 INT'L J. MGMT. REV. 285 (2001); Wesley M. Cohen et al., *Industry and the Academy: Uneasy Partners in the Cause of Technological Advance*, *in* CHALLENGES TO RESEARCH UNIVERSITIES 171 (Roger G. Noll ed., 1998); Rebecca S. Eisenberg, *Public Research and Private Development: Patents and Technology Transfer in Government-Sponsored Research*, 82 VA. L. REV. 1663 (1996); J.H. Reichman & Paul F. Uhlir, *A Contractually Reconstructed Research Commons for Scientific Data in a Highly Protectionist Intellectual Property Environment*, 66 LAW & CONTEMP. PROBS. 315 (2003).

34. *See, e.g.*, Julie E. Cohen, *Creativity and Culture in Copyright Theory*, 40 U.C. DAVIS L. REV. 1151, 1155–62 (2007).

35. *See* Brett M. Frischmann, *Cultural Environmentalism and* The Wealth of Networks, 74 U. CHI. L. REV. 1083, 1084–85 (2007) (reviewing YOCHAI BENKLER, THE WEALTH OF NETWORKS: HOW SOCIAL PRODUCTION TRANSFORMS MARKETS AND FREEDOM (2006)).

36. *See* Frischmann, *supra* note 27, at 310–21; Frischmann & Lemley, *supra* note 27, at 268–71, 282–84.

37. *See* Henry E. Smith, *Semicommon Property Rights and Scattering in the Open Fields*, 29 J. LEGAL STUD. 131 (2000). Henry Smith gives the example of a highway, which is a commons in that its most significant aspect is its openness to all users—yet the individual driver has private rights with respect to the moving portion that his vehicle occupies. *Id.* at 132.

38. Frischmann and Lemley explain how copyright and patent law are semi-commons. *See* Frischmann & Lemley, *supra* note 27, at 282, 284–85, 290–91.

39. On the public domain, see generally Samuelson, *supra* note 32 (exploring various conceptions of the public domain).

40. *See* Frischmann & Lemley, *supra* note 27, at 286–88 (explaining fair use in these terms); Michael J. Madison, *Rewriting Fair Use and the Future of Copyright Reform*, 23 CARDOZO ARTS & ENT. L.J. 391, 409 (2005) ("Fair use is fair, after all, because (we assume) that it generates social benefits that the market can't otherwise produce.").

41. Cultural works and information goods have always been socially constructed in many senses, meaning that they do not arise "naturally" or inevitably but, instead, are the products of human actions and interactions with each other, social institutions and systems, and the physical environment. The traditional, economically inspired realm of production around which intellectual property protection is designed cannot be treated as independent of the larger cultural environment within which it is situated. On the legal construction of cultural things, see Michael J. Madison, *Law as Design: Objects, Concepts, and Digital Things*, 56 CASE W. RES. L. REV. 381, 447–63 (2005).

42. *See* BENKLER, *supra* note 35, at 466–67 (2006); Frischmann, *supra* note 35, at 1107–10 (reviewing BENKLER, *supra* note 35).

43. We use the term "cultural environment" advisedly, following the work of James Boyle. *See* James Boyle, *A Politics of Intellectual Property: Environmentalism for the Net?*, 47 DUKE L.J. 87, 108–12 (1997). The environmental metaphor should not lead scholars to rely uncritically on the assumption that there is anything "natural" about the cultural environment. As we discuss, one of the most important differences between natural resource commons and cultural commons is the degree to which cultural resources are manufactured, both by humans and by law. Natural resources, typically, are given. Yet we also caution against going too far in the other direction. Although the natural environment is given and not made by humans, it is continuously and unavoidably affected by humans and, in a sense, made and remade and unmade with irreversible consequences through those interactions. And although the cultural environment is always made

by humans, it is also inherited, subject to considerable path dependencies that can have irreversible consequences, and contingent on human interactions with the physical environment.

44. *See, e.g.*, LANDES & POSNER, *supra* note 30, at 11–12.

45. *See, e.g.*, BENKLER, *supra* note 35, at 36–37; SHIRKY, *supra* note 9, at 240–53.

46. *Cf.* Elinor Ostrom et al., *Going Beyond Panaceas*, 104 PROC. NAT'L ACAD. SCI. U.S. 15176 (2007) (arguing against oversimplification and reflexive appeal of panaceas).

47. Professor Ostrom's citation in connection with her recent receipt of the 2009 Nobel Memorial Prize in Economic Sciences focuses on "her analysis of economic governance, especially the commons." The Nobel Foundation, The Sveriges Riksbank Prize in Economic Sciences in Memory of Alfred Nobel 2009, http://nobelprize.org/nobel_prizes/economics/laureates/2009/index.html (last visited Mar. 9, 2010).

48. Our point coincides well with J.B. Ruhl's work on the uses of complexity theory in environmental regulation. *See* JOHN COPELAND NAGLE & J.B. RUHL, THE LAW OF BIODIVERSITY AND ECOSYSTEM MANAGEMENT 335–61 (2d ed. 2006); J.B. RUHL ET AL., THE LAW AND POLICY OF ECOSYSTEM SERVICES 18–20 (2007); J.B. Ruhl, *Complexity Theory as a Paradigm for the Dynamical Law-and-Society System: A Wake-Up Call for Legal Reductionism and the Modern Administrative State*, 45 DUKE L.J. 849, 867–73 (1996).

49. In a recent article, Frischmann argued that a myopic focus on excludability leads to biased analyses: "[P]ossible free riding drives analysts to focus on supply-side considerations, and more specifically, to correct market-driven supply problems by designing property-based institutions to lessen the costs of exclusion and minimize free riding. As I have argued elsewhere, nonexcludability is not a necessary condition for market failure; markets may fail for many other reasons. Nor, however, does exclusion fix all market failures. In fact, exclusion may aggravate other failures of the market. Even if an owner can exclude users from a nonrival resource and therefore meter use by charging a fee, dynamic inefficiencies still may abound. Simply put, property rights and other institutions that lessen the costs of exclusion and facilitate market-driven provision of nonrival goods are no panacea." Brett M. Frischmann, *An Economic Theory of Infrastructure and Commons Management*, 89 MINN. L. REV. 917, 948–49 (2005) (footnotes omitted).

50. Frischmann & Lemley, *supra* note 27, at 258–61.

51. On the point that these resources have no natural boundaries and that, as a result, boundaries are necessarily constructed, see Frischmann & Lemley, *supra* note 27, at 274; Madison, *supra* note 41, at 401–04.

52. Progress in the cultural environment should not be equated with innovation or economic growth. Progress may encompass much more. *See* Margaret Chon, *Postmodern "Progress": Reconsidering the Copyright and Patent Power*, 43 DEPAUL L. REV. 97, 101–03 (1993) (arguing that the definition of "progress" is socially constructed and should be shaped by social values and human priorities);

Frischmann, *supra* note 35, at 1095–96 (arguing that "we know too little about that which we seek to promote" with intellectual property, that the functionalist approach to intellectual property follows from an impoverished view of the cultural environment, and that "[w]e might, for example, imagine Progress as measured by the degree of participation in creative and inventive activities").

53. Scholars of many stripes have focused increased attention over the last decade on the role of language and metaphor in structuring analysis of legal and policy problems, both in connection with IP law and otherwise. For a recent review of the Law and Literature movement, see Bernadette Meyler, *The Myth of Law and Literature*, 8 LEGAL ETHICS 318 (2005) (reviewing THANE ROSENBAUM, THE MYTH OF MORAL JUSTICE: WHY OUR LEGAL SYSTEM FAILS TO DO WHAT'S RIGHT (2004)) (suggesting that Law and Literature should focus on the role of literature in understanding the institutions of law). Other scholars have emphasized connections between language and metaphor, on the one hand, and cognitive processes that drive behavior and experience, on the other hand. *See* GEORGE LAKOFF & MARK JOHNSON, METAPHORS WE LIVE BY 3–6 (1980). James Boyle focuses on the rhetoric of authorship and invention metaphors in order to expose the political character of property law. *See* Boyle, *supra* note 43, at 87–91. Carol Rose focuses on narratives of property law to demonstrate the essentially social character of the law. *See* CAROL M. ROSE, PROPERTY AND PERSUASION: ESSAYS ON THE HISTORY, THEORY, AND RHETORIC OF OWNERSHIP 35–42 (1994). A number of intellectual property scholars draw on environmental and spatial metaphors in their discussions of information law and policy. *See, e.g.*, Frischmann, *supra* note 35, at 1084–85, 1088–97 (reviewing the use of cultural environmentalism as a metaphor in information policy discussions and arguing that, to be analytically useful, "we need to know more about what the cultural environment is, how it works, how it is constructed, how we interact with it, how we change it, how we are a part of it, and how it relates and interacts with other environments"); David Lange, *Recognizing the Public Domain*, 44 LAW & CONTEMP. PROBS. 147, 158–59 (1981) ("[T]he law of trademarks . . . has begun to spill over its boundaries and encroach into territories in which trademark protection amounts to trespass."); Michael J. Madison, *Legal-Ware: Contract and Copyright in the Digital Age*, 67 FORDHAM L. REV. 1025, 1029 (1998) (discussing "open space"); Samuelson, *supra* note 32, at 804–05 (describing the public domain).

54. ELINOR OSTROM, UNDERSTANDING INSTITUTIONAL DIVERSITY 58–62 (2005).

55. *Id.* at 8.

56. *See* Google Maps, http://maps.google.com (last visited Mar. 26, 2010).

57. *See, e.g.*, Elinor Ostrom, *A Diagnostic Approach for Going Beyond Panaceas*, 104 PROC. NAT'L ACAD. SCI. U.S. 15181, 15181 (2007) (studying the problems of overuse or destruction of resources in social-ecological systems).

58. *See, e.g.*, ELINOR OSTROM, GOVERNING THE COMMONS: THE EVOLUTION OF INSTITUTIONS FOR COLLECTIVE ACTION 58–88 (1990) (describing commons case studies).

59. *E.g.*, Rose, *Big Roads*, *supra* note 26, at 411; *see also* Garrett Hardin, *The Tragedy of the Commons*, 162 SCIENCE 1243 (1968).

60. *See* Hardin, *supra* note 59, at 1244.

61. The tragedy of the commons can be explained in terms of externalities, as a collective-action problem, or in game-theory terms as a prisoners' dilemma. *See, e.g.*, Wayne Eastman, *Telling Alternative Stories: Heterodox Versions of the Prisoners' Dilemma, the Coase Theorem, and Supply-Demand Equilibrium*, 29 CONN. L. REV. 727, 749–51 (1997) (describing the tragedy of the commons as a "multi-person Dilemma").

62. *See* Harold Demsetz, *Toward a Theory of Property Rights*, 57 AM. ECON. REV. 347, 348 (1967); Brett M. Frischmann, *Evaluating the Demsetzian Trend in Copyright Law*, 3 REV. L. & ECON. 649, 660 (2007); Harold Demsetz, *Frischmann's View of "Toward a Theory of Property Rights,"* 4 REV. L. & ECON. 127, 127–28 (2008); *see also* R.H. Coase, *The Problem of Social Cost*, 3 J.L. & ECON. 1, 43–44 (1960) (adding well-defined property rights to the menu of options for dealing with externalities).

63. *See* CORNES & SANDLER, *supra* note 27, at 68, 72–78; ARTHUR CECIL PIGOU, THE ECONOMICS OF WELFARE 29–30 (Transaction Publishers 2002) (1952).

64. *See* OSTROM, *supra* note 58, at 103.

65. *See id.* at 88–90.

66. *See generally* Elinor Ostrom & Charlotte Hess, *A Framework for Analyzing the Knowledge Commons*, *in* UNDERSTANDING KNOWLEDGE AS A COMMONS: FROM THEORY TO PRACTICE 41 (Charlotte Hess & Elinor Ostrom eds., 2007) (describing relevance of Institutional Analysis and Development framework to studies of knowledge and information commons); Ostrom et al., *supra* note 46.

67. *See* Ostrom et al., *supra* note 46.

68. *See* Ostrom, *supra* note 57, at 15181–82.

69. *See id.*

70. *See* COMM. ON THE HUMAN DIMENSIONS OF GLOBAL CHANGE, NAT'L RESEARCH COUNCIL, THE DRAMA OF THE COMMONS *passim* (Elinor Ostrom et al. eds., 2002); OSTROM, *supra* note 54; OSTROM, *supra* note 58.

71. *See* Ostrom, *supra* note 57, at 15182–83.

72. OSTROM, *supra* note 54, at 28–29.

73. Recent study of peer production in online environments provides a promising example of efforts to move beyond the conventional set of theories. *See supra* notes 9, 35, 42, and accompanying text.

74. Ostrom, *supra* note 57, at 15186.

75. This illustration is modeled on Ostrom & Hess, *supra* note 66, at 44 fig. 3.1.

76. Of course, as Ostrom herself recognizes, variables that are treated as exogenous or fixed for the analysis of a particular institution (laws relating to a fishery, for example) may be the outcomes of another (a legislature, for example). *See* OSTROM, *supra* note 54, at 13.

77. *See* Ostrom, *supra* note 57, at 15184–85.

78. *See* OSTROM, *supra* note 54, at 14.

79. *See* Ostrom, *supra* note 57, at 15181.

80. *See id.* at 15184–85.

81. *See* Abby Goodnough, *Seeking Salve for the Wound of an Ailing Industry*, N.Y. TIMES, Aug. 23, 2009, at A16 (describing conflicts among fishermen arising from the recent economic crisis).

82. *See* OSTROM, *supra* note 54, at 15.

83. *See id.* at 13–14.

84. *See, e.g.*, *Commons Sense*, ECONOMIST, Aug. 2, 2008, at 76 (paying tribute to the commons research of Ostrom and her colleagues and emphasizing the need for a study of "new commons" of the sort we focus on here).

85. *See* Ostrom & Hess, *supra* note 66.

86. *See id.* at 54–59.

87. Frischmann presented an earlier draft of this paper at the 12th Biennial Conference of the International Association for the Study of the Commons in 2008, and this was a topic of extensive discussion.

88. *See* Madison, Frischmann & Strandburg, *supra* note 21, at 368–69.

89. *See* Dykman, *supra* note 5, at 648–51.

90. *See* Jacobsen v. Katzer, 535 F.3d 1373, 1381–82 (Fed. Cir. 2008) (concluding that violations of an open source software license can be remedied by injunction, in order to preserve the productive character of the open source community).

91. *See supra* notes 54–55 and accompanying text (noting the role of nesting in Ostrom's framework).

92. *See supra* notes 2–5 and accompanying text.

93. *See supra* notes 17–20 and accompanying text.

94. *See supra* notes 13–16 and accompanying text.

95. *See* Jacob Loshin, *Secrets Revealed: Protecting Magicians' Intellectual Property Without Law*, *in* LAW AND MAGIC: A COLLECTION OF ESSAYS 123, 135–37 (Christine A. Corcos ed., 2010).

96. *See* Samuelson, *supra* note 32, at 798.

97. *See id.* at 789–90.

98. On different versions of the public domain, see *id.* at 789–813.

99. *See* Julie E. Cohen, *Copyright, Commodification, and Culture: Locating the Public Domain*, *in* THE FUTURE OF THE PUBLIC DOMAIN: IDENTIFYING THE COMMONS IN INFORMATION LAW 121, 135–37 (Lucie Guibault & P. Bernt Hugenholtz eds., 2006).

100. *See id.* at 157–66.

101. Commenting on an earlier draft of this paper after a presentation, Mario Biagioli offered a metaphor grounded in the work of Edward Young. *See* EDWARD YOUNG, CONJECTURES ON ORIGINAL COMPOSITION 9–12 (Scolar Press Ltd. 1966) (1759). Biagioli suggested that the cultural environment might be seen as a garden and the processes of inheritance and experience as cultivation. Nevertheless, he cautioned against taking the notion of a "natural" cultural environment too far.

Our discussion of choosing an appropriate baseline should make clear that we have heeded his advice.

102. *See, e.g.*, Nikolaus Franke & Sonali Shah, *How Communities Support Innovative Activities: An Exploration of Assistance and Sharing among End-Users*, 32 RES. POL'Y 157, 169 (2003) (studying how individuals in a community of sports enthusiasts share information freely).

103. *See supra* note 14 and accompanying text.

104. *See, e.g.*, ROBERT P. MERGES ET AL., INTELLECTUAL PROPERTY IN THE NEW TECHNOLOGICAL AGE 119 (rev. 4th ed. 2007) (explaining incentive justification).

105. For an overview of U.S. patent doctrine, see *id.* at 124–27.

106. *See* Convention on the Grant of European Patents art. 52(1), Oct. 5, 1973, 13 I.L.M. 270 (as amended by Revision Act of Nov. 29, 2000), *available at* http://www.epo.org/patents/law/legal-texts/epc.html [hereinafter European Patent Convention] ("inventive step").

107. *See* MERGES ET AL., *supra* note 104, at 124.

108. *See id.* at 126.

109. *See id.* at 321–25.

110. *See id.* at 126.

111. For an overview of copyright doctrine, see *id.* at 388–89.

112. *See* 17 U.S.C. § 107 (2006).

113. *See, e.g.*, Copyright, Designs and Patents Act, 1988, c. 48, § 29 (Eng.).

114. *See* European Patent Convention, *supra* note 106, art. 52; INT'L CTR. FOR TRADE AND SUSTAINABLE DEV. & U.N. CONFERENCE ON TRADE AND DEV., EXCEPTIONS TO PATENT RIGHTS IN DEVELOPING COUNTRIES, Issue Paper No. 17, at 19–42 (Oct. 2006) (prepared by Christopher Garrison), *available at* http://ictsd.net/i/publications/11716/ (reviewing exceptions to patent rights).

115. *See* Council Directive 2001/29, 2001 J.O. (L 167) (EU); MERGES ET AL., *supra* note 104, at 388.

116. For an explanation of the basic principles of the GPL, see Brett Smith, *A Quick Guide to GPLv3*, Jan. 8, 2009, http://www.fsf.org/licensing/licenses/quick-guide-gplv3.html. For the terms of the GPL, see Free Software Foundation, GNU General Public License (June 29, 2007), http://www.fsf.org/licensing/licenses/gpl.html. A preliminary examination of the open source license as a managed environment appears in Michael J. Madison, *Reconstructing the Software License*, 35 LOY. U. CHI. L.J. 275 (2003).

117. For a discussion of open access publishing in the context of the norms of an academic community, see Michael J. Madison, *The Idea of the Law Review: Scholarship, Prestige, and Open Access*, 10 LEWIS & CLARK L. REV. 901 (2006) (exploring open access in legal scholarship).

118. We refer to these as "basic characteristics" rather than Ostrom's "exogenous variables" because, as discussed above, here, much more than in the natural resources context, it is unreasonable to regard important characteristics of the resources themselves as "exogenous" to the commons structure. *See* OSTROM, *supra* note 54, at 13.

119. *See* Christopher J. Buccafusco, *On the Legal Consequences of Sauces: Should Thomas Keller's Recipes Be* Per Se *Copyrightable?*, 24 CARDOZO ARTS & ENT. L.J. 1121, 1151–55 (2007); Emmanuelle Fauchart & Eric von Hippel, *Norms-Based Intellectual Property Systems: The Case of French Chefs*, 19 ORG. SCI. 187 (2008).

120. For studies of open source software, see STEVEN WEBER, THE SUCCESS OF OPEN SOURCE (2004).

121. *See supra* note 2 and accompanying text.

122. *See* Brett M. Frischmann, *Commercializing University Research Systems in Economic Perspective: A View from the Demand Side*, *in* 16 UNIVERSITY ENTREPRENEURSHIP AND TECHNOLOGY TRANSFER: PROCESS, DESIGN, AND INTELLECTUAL PROPERTY 155, 169–73 (Gary D. Libecap ed., 2005); Madison, Frischmann & Strandburg, *supra* note 21, at 378–402.

123. *See supra* note 1 and accompanying text.

124. *See supra* note 27 and accompanying text.

125. *See* Merges, *supra* note 5, at 1295–1301; Robert P. Merges, *A Transactional View of Property Rights*, 20 BERKELEY TECH. L.J. 1477, 1515–19 (2005).

126. *See* Merges, *supra* note 21, at 19 (noting that "[i]ndividual contributions [to open source software projects] are evaluated and integrated by a central organization or informal group entrusted with maintaining and authorizing 'official' versions of the software").

127. *See* 2 HERBERT HOVENKAMP ET AL., IP AND ANTITRUST: AN ANALYSIS OF ANTITRUST PRINCIPLES APPLIED TO INTELLECTUAL PROPERTY LAW § 35.4 (Supp. 2009); Merges, *supra* note 125, at 1515–16; Shapiro, *supra* note 2, at 136–42.

128. *See* HOVENKAMP ET AL., *supra* note 127, § 36; JEAN TIROLE, THE THEORY OF INDUSTRIAL ORGANIZATION 413–14 (1988).

129. *See* Michael A. Heller, *The Tragedy of the Anticommons: Property in the Transition from Marx to Markets*, 111 HARV. L. REV. 621, 625 (1998) (noting that "[g]overnments can create too many property rights and too many decisionmakers who can block use").

130. *See, e.g.*, DON TAPSCOTT & ANTHONY D. WILLIAMS, WIKINOMICS: HOW MASS COLLABORATION CHANGES EVERYTHING 166–69 (2006); Michael Morgan, *New Paradigms in Industry: The Single Nucleotide Polymorphism Consortium*, *in* THE ROLE OF SCIENTIFIC AND TECHNICAL DATA AND INFORMATION IN THE PUBLIC DOMAIN: PROCEEDINGS OF A SYMPOSIUM 194, 194–97 (Julie M. Esanu & Paul F. Uhlir eds., 2003).

131. For discussions of "open source" approaches to biology, see, for example, Sapna Kumar & Arti Rai, *Synthetic Biology: The Intellectual Property Puzzle*, 85 TEX. L. REV. 1745 (2007); Arti K. Rai, *"Open and Collaborative" Research: A New Model for Biomedicine*, *in* INTELLECTUAL PROPERTY RIGHTS IN FRONTIER INDUSTRIES: SOFTWARE AND BIOTECHNOLOGY 131 (Robert W. Hahn ed., 2005).

132. *See* Patrick L. Jones & Katherine J. Strandburg, *Technology Transfer and an Information View of Universities: A Conceptual Framework for Academic*

Freedom, Intellectual Property, Technology Transfer and the University Mission 13–17 (Feb. 22, 2010) (unpublished manuscript, on file with authors).

133. *See* Madison, Frischmann & Strandburg, *supra* note 21, at 378–89; John P. Walsh et al., *Where Excludability Matters: Material Versus Intellectual Property in Academic Biomedical Research*, 36 RES. POL'Y 1184, 1199–1200 (2007).

134. *See* Philip E. Auerswald & Lewis M. Branscomb, *Start-ups and Spin-offs: Collective Entrepreneurship between Invention and Innovation*, *in* THE EMERGENCE OF ENTREPRENEURSHIP POLICY: GOVERNANCE, START-UPS, AND GROWTH IN THE U.S. KNOWLEDGE ECONOMY 61, 79–80 (David M. Hart ed., 2003).

135. *See* O'Mahony & Bechky, *supra* note 6; Siobhán O'Mahony & Fabrizio Ferraro, *Managing the Boundary of an 'Open' Project* 18 (IESE Bus. Sch., Univ. of Navarra, Working Paper No. 537, 2004).

136. *See, e.g.*, W. KIP VISCUSI ET AL., ECONOMICS OF REGULATION AND ANTITRUST 116–32 (4th ed. 2005); Peter Z. Grossman, *Introduction: What Do We Mean by Cartel Success?*, *in* HOW CARTELS ENDURE AND HOW THEY FAIL: STUDIES OF INDUSTRIAL COLLUSION 1, 1–7 (Peter Z. Grossman ed., 2004).

137. *See* HOVENKAMP ET AL., *supra* note 127, §§ 30.4, 34.2.

138. Complications arise here because of distinctions between "natural resources" like oil, wood, and other purely rivalrous resources that are necessarily depleted and nonrenewable, and "natural resources" like forests, lakes, or other common-pool resources that are not necessarily depleted and are potentially renewable if managed sustainably. *See* RUHL ET AL., *supra* note 48, at 52, 64–65 (describing a "threshold of irreversibility," noting that "once thresholds are crossed, it can take enormous spans of time to rebuild natural capital through ecological processes," and describing the risk of congestion); Brett M. Frischmann, *Environmental Infrastructure*, 35 ECOLOGY L.Q. 151, 155, 166–68 (2008) (examining differences in the degree of rivalrousness for different natural resources and distinguishing between rival natural resources like oil and partially (non)rival natural resources like the atmosphere).

139. *See* OSTROM, *supra* note 58, at 61–88 (describing various examples illustrating this point).

140. *See* Dennis S. Karjala, *Congestion Externalities and Extended Copyright Protection*, 94 GEO. L.J. 1065 (2006) (critiquing William M. Landes & Richard A. Posner, *Indefinitely Renewable Copyright*, 70 U. CHI. L. REV. 471, 484–88 (2003) (suggesting some instances of congestion)); *see also* Frank Pasquale, *Copyright in an Era of Information Overload: Toward the Privileging of Categorizers*, 60 VAND. L. REV. 133, 166–71 (2007) (considering congestion effects associated with information overload). Trademark dilution is a controversial area in which overuse of a particularly famous and distinctive mark arguably leads to congestion-type effects. *See* LANDES & POSNER, *supra* note 30, at 222–28; Giovanni B. Ramello, *What's in a Sign? Trademark Law and Economic Theory*, 20 J. ECON. SURVEYS 547, 555–56 (2006).

141. Frischmann refers to this as "leveraging" the "nonrivalry" of intellectual resources. Brett Frischmann, *Spillovers Theory and Its Conceptual Boundaries*, 51 WM. & MARY L. REV. 801, 810 (2009) ("In the context of intellectual property law, society [encourages participation in activities that generate spillovers] through a variety of legal arrangements that enable sharing and productive use of nonrival resources—in essence, *leveraging nonrivalry*.").

142. *See* Joel West, *Seeking Open Infrastructure: Contrasting Open Standards, Open Source and Open Innovation*, 12 FIRST MONDAY (2007), http://firstmonday.org/htbin/cgiwrap/bin/ojs/index.php/fm/article/view/1913/1795 (discussing the various meanings of "open" in system-based industries).

143. Frischmann, *supra* note 49, at 936.

144. *Id.* at 936–37 (footnotes omitted).

145. *See id.*

146. *See supra* notes 2–5 and accompanying text.

147. Accordingly, we focus much less on whether some social context is or is not a "community" according to predefined criteria and much more on the functional characteristics of that context.

148. *See supra* text accompanying note 48.

149. *See supra* note 116 and accompanying text.

150. *See* KELTY, *supra* note 7, at 27–31 (describing open source software collectives as "recursive publics").

151. *See supra* note 59 and accompanying text.

152. *See* Elinor Ostrom, *Tragedy of the Commons*, *in* THE NEW PALGRAVE DICTIONARY OF ECONOMICS (Steven N. Durlauf & Lawrence E. Blume eds., 2d ed. 2008), *available at* http://www.dictionaryofeconomics.com/article?id=pde2008_T000193.

153. *See* Frischmann, *supra* note 49, at 974–78.

154. *See* Frischmann, *supra* note 28; Katherine J. Strandburg, *Curiosity-Driven Research and University Technology Transfer*, *in* 16 UNIVERSITY ENTREPRENEURSHIP AND TECHNOLOGY TRANSFER: PROCESS, DESIGN, AND INTELLECTUAL PROPERTY 93, 97–99 (2005); sources cited *supra* note 33; *supra* note 122 and accompanying text.

155. The clusters of questions that follow are analogous to Ostrom's inquiries into the descriptive characteristics of a commons regime. *See* Ostrom & Hess, *supra* note 66.

156. *See supra* text accompanying notes 53–55.

157. *See* CAROL M. ROSE, *Property as Storytelling: Perspectives from Game Theory, Narrative Theory, Feminist Theory*, *in* PROPERTY AND PERSUASION: ESSAYS ON THE HISTORY, THEORY, AND RHETORIC OF OWNERSHIP 25, 25–45 (1994).

158. *See* Michael J. Madison, *Comment: Where Does Creativity Come From? And Other Stories of Copyright*, 53 CASE W. RES. L. REV. 747 (2003).

159. *See* Jessica Silbey, *The Mythical Beginnings of Intellectual Property*, 15 GEO. MASON L. REV. 319 (2008).

160. *See supra* text accompanying notes 119–23.

161. Such grantbacks may raise antitrust concerns. *See* U.S. DEP'T OF JUSTICE & FED. TRADE COMM'N, ANTITRUST GUIDELINES FOR THE LICENSING OF INTELLECTUAL PROPERTY § 5.6 (1995), *available at* http://www.usdoj.gov/atr/public/guidelines/0558.pdf.

162. For a study of boundary maintenance in the open source software context, see O'Mahony & Bechky, *supra* note 6, at 431–50.

163. *See supra* text accompanying notes 138–41.

164. *See supra* text accompanying notes 4–5.

165. *See* Katherine J. Strandburg et al., *Law and the Science of Networks: An Overview and an Application to the "Patent Explosion"*, 21 BERKELEY TECH. L.J. 1293, 1301 (2006).

166. *See* Katherine J. Strandburg, *User Innovator Community Norms: At the Boundary between Academic and Industry Research*, 77 FORDHAM L. REV. 2237 (2009) (discussing the sharing of research tools and materials between researchers in academic and industrial settings); *Norms and the Sharing of Research Materials and Tacit Knowledge*, *in* WORKING WITHIN THE BOUNDARIES OF INTELLECTUAL PROPERTY (Rochelle C. Dreyfuss et al. eds.) (2010).

167. *Cf.* Frischmann, *supra* note 28; Peter Lee, *Interface: The Push and Pull of Patents*, 77 FORDHAM L. REV. 2225 (2009) (examining the role of patents as an "interface" between universities and industry).

168. *See, e.g.*, BENKLER, *supra* note 35, at 59–90 (providing various examples of "commons-based peer production").

169. *See* HOVENKAMP ET AL., *supra* note 127, § 36 (discussing research joint ventures).

170. 464 U.S. 417 (1984).

171. 35 U.S.C. § 103(c)(2) (2006).

172. *See* Jessica Litman, *War Stories*, 20 CARDOZO ARTS & ENT. L.J. 337, 351–53 (2002).

173. *See id.* at 352–53.

174. *See* OSTROM, *supra* note 58, at 29–55.

175. *See* Free Software Foundation, GNU General Public License, *supra* note 116, § 9.

176. *See id.* § 8.

177. *See* Free Software Foundation, What Is Free Software and Why Is It So Important for Society?, http://www.fsf.org/about/what-is-free-software (last visited Mar. 12, 2010).

178. *See, e.g.*, Jacobsen v. Katzer, 535 F.3d 1373, 1381–82 (Fed. Cir. 2008). In *Jacobsen*, the open source collective was represented by one of its members, Jacobsen, as assignee of copyright interests in the open source program at issue. *See id.* at 1375–76.

179. *See* Benkler, *supra* note 35, at 2–7, 29–127.

180. *See* Julie E. Cohen, *Pervasively Distributed Copyright Enforcement*, 95 GEO. L.J. 1, 37–43 (2006).

181. *See* DONALD M. PATTILLO, PUSHING THE ENVELOPE: THE AMERICAN AIRCRAFT INDUSTRY 35, 80–81 (1998).

182. *See* Benkler, *supra* note 35, at 65–74.

183. An adjunct AP product, the Associated Press Stylebook, is published by the AP itself and is something of a bible for newspaper editors across the industry.

184. *See supra* notes 17–20 and accompanying text.

185. *See* Frischmann & Lemley, *supra* note 27, at 258.

186. *See supra* [second] part.

187. *See supra* notes 4–5 and accompanying text.

188. *See* Schultz, *supra* note 17, at 676–77 (describing the free distribution of jamband music).

189. *See supra* note 1 and accompanying text (describing the success of the commons that developed around the Maine lobster industry).

190. *See, e.g.*, HOVENKAMP ET AL., *supra* note 127, § 34.2.

191. *See* Schultz, *supra* note 17.

192. *See* Merges, *supra* note 5.

193. *See* KELTY, *supra* note 7.

194. *See* Madison, Frischmann & Strandburg, *supra* note 21.

8

Learning from Lin: Lessons and Cautions from the Natural Commons for the Knowledge Commons

DANIEL H. COLE

Legal scholars who write about information and intellectual property (IP), especially those concerned with drawing appropriate boundaries between private and public domains, understandably have been mining the voluminous writings of the late Elinor ("Lin") Ostrom for valuable lessons. Ostrom spent a lifetime studying the wide variety of property regimes used anywhere in the world for governing common-pool resources, primarily (but not exclusively) in the natural world (E. Ostrom 2010a, 2010c). Later in her career, Ostrom contributed applications of her frameworks, theories, and models to what she called the "knowledge commons" (Hess & E. Ostrom 2007). She recognized the knowledge commons as a separate realm from the natural commons, which would not admit simple transfer of lessons learned from her earlier work, but required systematic study of its own resources, actors, institutions, action situations, and so forth. Each chapter in this book contributes to that systematic study.

This chapter offers guidance to IP scholars who are seeking to adapt, analogize to, or otherwise use Ostrom's work to inform their own research. The main lessons are two: (1) those looking for *normative* guidance from Ostrom as to the proper structure of IP law are bound to be disappointed (or dishonest); but (2) those looking for conceptual, analytical, and methodological guidance will find it in Ostrom's Institutional Analysis and Development (IAD) framework, which can (a) improve IP scholars' understanding of information and information flows under alternative institutional arrangements;[1] (b) diagnose problems (or dilemmas) in existing institutional arrangements; and (c) in select cases predict outcomes under alternative institutional arrangements. Even then, normative implications will remain scarce (to nonexistent), and all predictions will be contingent and contestable. No panacean solutions to social dilemmas relating to information will be discovered (Frischmann 2013).

Even analytical lessons from Ostrom's work for IP scholars will be limited, as Madison, Frischmann, & Strandburg (2010 [chapter 7 in this volume]) have observed, by an important distinction between natural common-pool resources and information or knowledge commons, which too often goes unremarked: they are very different kinds of goods, implying different governance mechanisms. Suffice it to say, at this point, that for natural common-pool resources "open access" is nearly always a problem requiring an institutional remedy, whereas in information commons it is a viable (though not necessarily preferable) institutional means of achieving social goals.

IP Scholars Seeking Normative Support from Ostrom's Work Will Not Find It

Legal scholarship, including in the field of intellectual property (IP), is overwhelmingly normative. Scholars argue about what sets of rules *should* apply, and who should apply them, to interactions among individuals in society. In IP, nearly all of the biggest questions are normative: What constitutional limits should apply to copyright terms? What should be the scope of private ownership under copyright and patent laws? How best to resolve the tension between creating incentives to innovate, for example, by providing exclusive property rights, and facilitating market competition for the benefit of consumers? What should be the scope of "fair use"? How best to prevent the proliferation of IP rights from creating tangled webs that perversely impede further innovations? Which, if any, innovations that contribute to the stock of useful knowledge fall immediately into the "knowledge commons"? Which should *never* do so?

That IP law is dominated by such normative issues is not surprising. After all, laws *are* (or embody) norms.[2] Few other academic disciplines are so heavily normative in focus as legal studies. Most social-scientific disciplines, and scholars within those disciplines, tend to be more analytical than normative in their approaches and methods.[3]

Elinor Ostrom's work provides a veritable model of social-scientific analysis. She focused on constructing empirically informed frameworks, theories, and models that were (1) conceptually clear; (2) thickly descriptive (embracing complexity); (2) diagnostic; (3) analytically rigorous;

and (4) integrative of configural interactions among explanatory factors, suggesting patterns of social interactions and their social-ecological consequences—as with the "design principles" from *Governing the Commons* (E. Ostrom 1990). The integration of explanatory factors might sometimes allow for (tentative) predictions about the (relative) success or failure of similar institutional applications in similar social-ecological circumstances. But rarely, if ever, will a reader of her work come across an expressly normative argument (unless one considers to be "normative" her frequent arguments about the importance of conceptual clarity and interdisciplinary cooperation using multiple methods).

Throughout much of her work, Ostrom evinced one substantive normative commitment to the principle of self-governance, as reflected in the "polycentric approach" pioneered by her husband, the political theorist Vincent Ostrom (V. Ostrom 1999; V. Ostrom, Tiebout, & Warren 1961; E. Ostrom 2009a, 2009b, 2010b, 2010c, 2010d, 2012). That approach embodies a normative principle of subsidiarity according to which governance is a "coresponsibility" of units at central (or national), regional (subnational), and local levels (see *Decentralization: A Sampling of Omissions*). But even that commitment to polycentricism was contingent, context-specific, and focused on matching the scale of governance to the scale of operations appropriate for the particular production or provision problem under investigation. For example, in her early studies of municipal versus neighborhood policing in Indianapolis, Indiana, Ostrom hypothesized that smaller police departments would function more effectively (according to a variable of criteria) than would highly consolidated, metropolitan police departments. But her empirical research revealed that medium-size police departments overall outperformed both smaller (neighborhood) and larger (municipal-level) units (E. Ostrom, Parks, & Whitaker 1978).[4] Thus, polycentricism itself was not immune to Ostrom's oft-repeated injunction that there are no institutional panaceas for resolving complex social dilemmas (E. Ostrom 2007).

Aside from her strong (but contingent) commitment to polycentricism, the relevance of which is unclear in the context of the information or knowledge commons, the goal of Ostrom's work never was to promote specific social outcomes. Though she is sometimes portrayed as an "advocate" for local self-governance using common-property regimes, she really was only a proponent of the *idea* that such governance systems are *sometimes* successful according to some evaluative criterion, such as sustainability of the resource base over time. As such, she argued that scholars should not summarily exclude, as Garrett Hardin (1968) did, common-property regimes from comparative analyses of alternative institutional solutions to social-ecological dilemmas.[5] Ostrom did not believe local self-governance was *the* answer to resource overuse problems any more than public ownership/regulation or private ownership/markets (E. Ostrom, Janssen, & Anderies 2007; Frischmann 2012). Again, there are no panaceas—no universal, first-best, institutional solutions to inevitably complex social dilemmas (E. Ostrom 2011–2012; Acheson 2011).

That Elinor Ostrom, like many other social scientists, elevated analytical and methodological considerations over normative arguments creates an insuperable problem for legal scholars who would appropriate her frameworks, theories, and models to further their own normative policy preferences, whether in natural resources law or IP law. It just won't work. No one can point to anything in any of Ostrom's voluminous writings that would support arguments that, for example, IP rights should be more restricted than they are at present or the scope of "fair use" should be broader (or narrower).[6] Ostrom might (or might not) have agreed personally with those normative assertions, but nothing in her work on local common-property regimes, including the "design principles" she derived in *Governing the Commons*, supports normative conclusions.

That might seem odd, given that Ostrom's famous IAD framework, which predated *Governing the Commons*, has a box devoted to "Evaluative Criteria." The purpose of that box was to adjudge, as people inevitably do, social and ecological outcomes of social interactions in which actors, holding designated positions, behave strategically but in general accordance with "rules-in-use."[7] It would seem that any such evaluative criteria must themselves be normative or at least imply normative consequences. Tellingly, Ostrom herself paid scant attention to the "Evaluative Criteria" box in her IAD framework, but recognized that the box might be populated by various (not necessarily consistent) criteria. For example, she referred to alternative evaluative criteria, including (1) economic efficiency, (2) fiscal equivalence, (3) redistributional equity, (4) accountability, (5) conformance to values of local actors, and (6) sustainability, and noted the need to make trade-offs among evaluative criteria (E. Ostrom 2011). Ostrom's decision to avoid committing to a specific evaluative criterion or set of criteria was quite intentional. Her goal was to provide a framework for analysis consistent with a wide variety of theories and models, which might embody varying normative commitments. Indeed, she contended that her IAD framework was congenial to microeconomic theory, game theory, transaction cost theory, social cost theory, public choice, and constitutional and covenantal theory, along with theories of public goods and common-pool resources (E. Ostrom 2005: 28; Madison, Frischmann, & Strandburg 2010 [chapter 7 in this volume]). Such a diversity of theories could only be compatible with the IAD framework if the framework itself was not tilted to favor one or more of them to the detriment of others. Moreover, as recognized by the editors of this book and incorporated into their adapted version of the IAD framework, Evaluative Criteria often are, or can be, based on the relevant community's explicit (and sometimes implicit) objectives.

The most that can be said is that, in a social-ecological systems context, Ostrom *assumed* that more robust and resilient resource-management regimes tended to be more successful (perhaps by definition) and, therefore, better. From that point, we might legitimately argue that the "design principles" from *Governing the Commons* were informed by an implicit normative commitment to long-run sustainability of social-ecological systems—hardly a controversial policy goal in the context of natural resources. Indeed, the widespread agreement about that implicit normative goal of sustainability, among diverse scholars with varying normative commitments, may have enabled Ostrom to pay less attention to "evaluative criteria" than would have been necessary in the absence of such consensus.

What IP Scholars *Can* Learn from Ostrom: Conceptual, Analytical, and Methodological Lessons

Setting normative considerations to one side, Ostrom's work has a great deal to offer IP scholars seeking to understand and diagnose IP problems, and possibly (just possibly) to predict outcomes from interactions under alternative IP arrangements. Indeed, unlike many of her fellow political scientists who have fallen in love with abstract models and statistical analyses for their own sakes, Ostrom was never satisfied if her research did not yield policy-relevant insights. Indeed, she possessed a unique ability to simultaneously combine scientific rigor with policy relevance. But she always was more interested in *informing* policy, than pushing it in one direction or another.

In the remainder of this chapter, I will suggest that Ostrom's work offers (at least) two useful and applicable *analytical* and *methodological* lessons for IP scholars, including (1) the importance of conceptual clarity, particularly in distinguishing between resource attributes, institutions, and actors; and (2) the IAD framework (or some variant of it) for understanding social interactions structured in substantial part by IP rights.[8] Using the IAD framework and comparing cases, models, and experimental outcomes might allow scholars eventually (after several years of research design, implementation, data collection, and analysis) to develop something like the "design principles" Ostrom derived for local common-property regimes used to govern common-pool resources.[9] Such principles might (or might not) facilitate *predictions* of circumstances in which one combination of public, common, and private rights (and duties) in "common pools" of information might work better (or worse) than alternative combinations. Her primary purpose in setting them out was not to enable prediction but merely to identify "underlying regularities" in local common-property regimes (E. Ostrom 2010a: 16).[10]

The Paramount Importance of Conceptual Clarity

Legends abound of three-hour (or longer) meetings at Vincent and Elinor Ostrom's Workshop in Political Theory and Policy Analysis at Indiana University devoted entirely to defining a single term or concept. These were not mere scholastic exercises but practical and important efforts to facilitate cross-disciplinary understanding, so that scholars from diverse academic backgrounds (including, but not limited to, anthropology, economics, game theory, history, law, philosophy, political science, psychology, public administration, and sociology), using different analytical tools and methods, could work together effectively to describe, diagnose, analyze, and possibly resolve commons problems. In the absence of an agreed vocabulary—or, at least, clearly defined terms—cross-disciplinary communication suffers, and progress toward resolving social dilemmas of shared concern is obstructed.[11] That concern motivated creation of the Institutional Analysis and Development (IAD) framework, which is addressed in the following subsection. Scholars adopting that framework essentially commit to "a common set of linguistic elements that can be used to analyze a wide diversity of problems," including potentially those relating to the information or knowledge commons (E. Ostrom 2010b).

Ostrom was not an IP scholar; nor am I. So I will not presume to recommend that IP scholars simply adopt or adapt the shared vocabulary that Ostrom "Workshoppers"[12] developed over the course of many years of long and often contentious discussions. Despite Ostrom's goal of generating a shared vocabulary and framework for analysis universally applicable over the wide range of social dilemmas (E. Ostrom 2005: 6), it is entirely possible that the different attributes and issues of the knowledge commons will require deviations from or emendation of existing frameworks and vocabularies. Indeed, the editors of this book have undertaken to adapt Ostrom's IAD framework to the problems of the information or knowledge commons (Madison, Frischmann, & Strandburg 2010 [chapter 7 in this volume]), and this book continues that project. Undoubtedly, however, similar interdisciplinary problems can be expected to arise (if they have not arisen already) among scholars in the "IP wars," who make up an even broader group coming not just from the traditional social sciences and the law but also from informatics, computer science, engineering, and biotechnology.

A few examples might suffice to indicate the types of conceptual issues that require, if not consensus, then at least clarification to allow those various scholars (and non-scholar stakeholders) to understand one another.[13] For one, IP scholars surely will want to heed Ostrom's caution about the potential for confusing or conflating resource systems (which, in the case of IP scholars, are the information, data, or knowledge) with either the humanly devised institutional settings for managing those resources (e.g., property and regulatory systems) or with the actors who (a) create, innovate, or discover new information (re)sources and/or (b) structure the institutional structures for managing information.[14] In the natural commons context, we are careful to distinguish common-pool resources (CPRs)—naturally existing systems with various biophysical attributes—and common-property regimes (also CPRs), which are human-created sets of institutions for managing common-pool resources (among others). In the case of the information or knowledge commons, it is equally important to distinguish the information itself, with whatever attributes it might have, from whatever system(s), including IP laws, humans set up to control or manage it and its flow.

Another issue requiring careful attention and clarification is specification of different kinds or types of information and information flows, with diverse characteristics and attributes, perhaps warranting differential governance. Already we have a substantially different governance system, patents, for dealing with certain kinds of scientific information, as compared with artistic information, which is governed by copyright law (or sometimes placed in the "creative commons"). Trade names, trade secrets, fiduciary and other privileged communications, evidence submitted under oath, computer code, and many other types of information and flows are all dealt with in various ways in the legal system.

Likewise various fora of information exchange, such as e-mail, telecommunications, police interrogations, court sessions, legislative and administrative committee hearings, face-to-face business meetings (with or without written minutes), and personal communications are subject to very different kinds of procedural and sometimes substantive rules (not to mention informal social norms). Much has been written already about all of these types of information and information-exchange by scholars and advocates (occasionally one and the same) from various disciplines and a variety of perspectives. Much work remains to be done, however, to systematize and meta-analyze this vast quantity of "data" so as to develop the kinds of theories and "design principles" that Ostrom and her colleagues painstakingly developed and applied over the course of decades, with some measure of success, to specifying and diagnosing problems of the natural commons. The existing IAD framework (or some variation on it) could be very useful to such an effort, and the adapted IAD framework developed and applied in this book paves the way.

Potential for Applying the IAD Framework to the Information or Knowledge Commons

As noted earlier, the IAD framework originally was created in large part to facilitate scholarly cooperation by providing a common framework based on a shared vocabulary that would be amenable to diverse assumptions, theories, and models of social interaction. The framework itself is deceptively simple in design, but allows for detailed analyses of highly complex interactions of however many variables (and subvariables) are of interest. It is the most widely used framework in studies of the natural commons (Constantinidis 2012), and has been cited as one of the most important analytical tools of the policy process (Sabatier 2007). As a legal scholar, I have long wondered why a framework so obviously congenial to legal analysis has not found wider application in my own field (including, I confess, in my own work). Perhaps it is due to the overwhelming normativity of legal scholarship, discussed earlier. Regardless, IP scholars (lawyers and nonlawyers alike) should find the IAD framework an immensely useful tool for disentangling the various elements that make up social problems relating to information and information flows, understanding those elements, and diagnosing more precisely where the roots of problems lie, enabling (but never guaranteeing) collective action to resolve those problems via new or amended institutions.

Several, marginally different, versions exist of the IAD framework. The version discussed below is fairly standard, and comes from Elinor Ostrom and Charlotte Hess's initial efforts to extend the commons framework to the "knowledge commons."

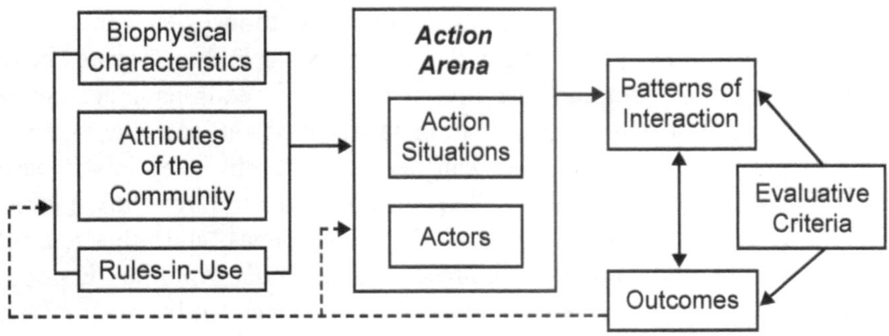

Figure 8.1. Institutional Analysis and Development framework.

Source: Ostrom & Hess (2007: 44, Fig. 3.1).

Biophysical Characteristics and Different Types of Goods

Starting with the three boxes vertically aligned along the left side of the framework, the "Biophysical Characteristics" of the resource probably have less significance for information than for a natural commons. After all, ideas have no biophysical attributes (unless we treat them purely as electrical or chemical outputs of cognition via neurotransmission). Nevertheless, Ostrom and co-author Charlotte Hess identified several bases for distinguishing varying physical characteristics of information: *facilities* through which information is accessed, including bookstores, libraries (public, academic, or private), newspapers, the Internet (including both open-access and subscription-based sources of various kinds); *artifacts*, which are the discreet physical forms through which information flows and in which it is accessed, including maps, books, and computer files (to name just a few); *ideas* themselves, which are the "nonphysical flow units" of the resource (E. Ostrom & Hess 2007: 47–48). Obviously, much more work remains to be done elaborating on these tentative categories, and IP scholars (along with others who work in fields diverse as cognitive psychology, informatics, and semiotics) are better positioned to carry out this work than those of us who focus on natural resources.

Related to the discussion of "biophysical characteristics" is a tricky problem of defining just what kind of good (if it *is* a single kind of good) information actually is. Widespread agreement seems to exist that *ideas*, once they are released into the world from any source, are in the nature of *pure public goods*. They meet the strict conditions of nonrivalrousness in consumption and nonexcludability. Very few other public goods (or goods with public attributes) are so pure. Even goods traditionally thought to be virtually pure public goods, such as sunlight, lighthouses, and the atmosphere, are less *pure* public goods than ideas. Solar access disputes have shown that sunlight can, in some circumstances, be rivalrous in consumption.[15] Ronald Coase has argued that, in special cases at least, the external benefits provided by lighthouses can be recaptured by suppliers (Coase 1974; but see Van Zandt 1993[16]). And since the industrial revolution it has become clear that the atmosphere, like waters, forests, and other natural resources, is at best an *impure, subtractable, or congestible* public good. As such, these resources fall somewhere on the spectrum between public goods, as technically defined, and club or toll goods. It is such *impure* public goods to which Ostrom assigned the label "common-pool resources" (Ostrom & Ostrom 1999: 75). She spent no time studying *pure* public goods, which by definition are not candidates for the "tragedy of the commons" because they would survive, undiminished, regardless of whatever institutional structures were introduced to sustain or exploit them. It is doubtful, however, that any natural resources actually meet the strict requirements of nonrivalrousness and nonexcludability.

To the extent information (in the raw form of "ideas") is a pure public good, the implications for governance are quite different from the case of common-pool natural resources, where "open access" (at least where demands on the resource are increasing relative to supply) leads inexorably to "tragedy," as Hardin surmised. All solutions to the "tragedy of the commons" involve the replacement of open access with restricted access and use via private property, common property, or public property/regulatory regimes (Cole 2002). Open access (signifying the absence of restraints on access and use) is *always* the socially optimal governance system for *existing* pure public goods simply because it is inevitable under conditions of nonrivalrousness and nonexcludability. Consequently, if IP scholars were concerned only about information in its purest form—as ideas—then neither Ostrom's analytical framework nor any other approach would be at all useful because no social dilemmas (or governance problems) would exist. However, that is not the prevailing situation.

In fact, IP institutions matter a great deal not because of the ideas themselves (although IP policy rightfully is concerned with *incentives* for the production of ideas, especially those that contribute to the "stock of useful knowledge" (Kuznets 1965: 85–87)) but with what we might call, to borrow a phrase from mythology and semiotics, "ideas-in-form"—ideas as represented in texts, pictures, symbols and marks, scores or recordings, codes, and so forth. These are what Ostrom and Hess call "artifacts." In contrast to the ideas they contain, the artifacts are not pure public goods;

in fact, some of them, such as closely held secrets (think of the formulae for the original Coca-Cola or Kentucky Fried Chicken), are more nearly pure private goods than any kind of public goods.[17] Other artifacts, such as books, are not so easily subjected to institutional control because, even though exclusion is relatively easy, they remain relatively nonrivalrous in consumption. Books are easy to resell, gift, or lend, so that the ideas they contain can be freely accessed by many (with no diminution in the amount available for anyone else to consume, so long as the book itself remains intact). Nonetheless, institutional arrangements can, with greater or lesser success, control the flow of ideas themselves by controlling access to and use of the artifacts that contain them as well as the "facilities" through which information is accessed. In addition, by controlling the flow of ideas, institutions (including IP rights and duties) can impact the rate of production, and/or the direction, of new ideas, as in the case of alleged "patent trolls" (compare Magliocca 2013 and McDonough 2006).

Attributes of the Community

The middle box on the left of the IAD framework, labeled "Attributes of the Community," arguably requires fewer adjustments in the move from the natural commons to the knowledge commons. As already noted, the relevant community of the information or knowledge commons is much larger than most of the communities with whom scholars of the natural common-pool resources have dealt. Indeed, moving the IAD framework from the resource commons to the knowledge commons involves a wholly new participant of central concern: the creator (or producer). Typically, a natural common-pool resource has no human producer.[18] Thus, the position of "creator" has not been encountered by scholars employing the IAD framework. The various other "actors" are more familiar, including providers, financers, distributors, millions of potential or actual users, and of course policy makers who establish "rules of the game" for information production, provision, distribution, and consumption.

It is, to repeat, an unusually large community compared to those traditionally studied by Ostrom and other students of the natural commons. Although, problems of the global commons, such as climate change, certainly would challenge the information commons for size and variety of attributes, including number of actors. It is worth observing that Ostrom wrote a good deal about climate change in her later years, but never attempted to apply the IAD framework to that problem of the global commons (see E. Ostrom 2010a, 2012). Was she daunted by the scale of the application?[19] If so, might her reluctance signify the scale of the challenge

IP scholars face in applying the framework to the information commons? It is worth noting in this context that the few efforts to apply the IAD framework in the realm of the information or knowledge commons so far have focused on discrete subparts of the problem or applied only subparts of the IAD framework, which seems sensible and perhaps inevitable (see Tenenberg 2008 (a full application of the IAD framework to a case study of student software teams in an undergraduate course at the University of Washington, Tacoma); Schewik & Kitsing 2010 (an application of one important aspect of the IAD framework, the various kinds of rules that apply in action arenas or situations, to open-source governance systems)). This book reflects the most significant effort yet to adapt, extend, and apply the IAD framework to the knowledge commons, and in doing so, much more attention is directed toward analysis of the various communities involved.

Rules-in-Use

Little needs to be explained to legal scholars (at least) about the box at the bottom-left of the IAD framework, other than that the concept of "rules-in-use" occasionally misleads some social scientists into believing that the "rules-in-form"—the formal legal rules—do not matter at all, as if they could not even influence the rules-in-use (Kinston & Caballero 2009: 158 (mistakenly but approvingly attributing to Ostrom a belief that rules-in-form are "dead letters," while rules-in-use are "rules which are actually followed")). Certainly since Robert Ellickson's famous book on the cattle ranchers of Shasta County, California (Ellickson 1991), if not earlier (Pound 1910; Llewellyn 1949; Friedman 1975), legal scholars have understood the important and highly variable relations between formal legal norms and informal social norms. IP scholars have noted, for example, a disjunction between formal legal rules barring Internet file sharing and social norms of sharing among Internet users (Feldman & Nadler 2006). But no legal scholar doubts that the formal legal rules remain very important (if not always the most important institutional variables).

The question remains, where do the rules (in form or in use) come from? They are the outcomes (or outputs) of prior action situations taking place at various levels. Constitutional-level interactions result in meta-rules (which may or may not be codified in a single document called a "constitution"), rules that establish processes and procedures for adopting collective choice–level rules (statutes, decisions, administrative rules, etc.). Collective choice–level arenas include (but are not limited to) courts, legislative bodies, administrative agencies, corporate board rooms, club committees, school boards, church conclaves and synods, faculty meetings, and the family kitchen. Rules adopted in those arenas structure everyday interactions at the "operational level." Even at that level, however, rule making goes on. Social norms, which may be as or more powerful than formal legal rules, emerge from regularized patterns of interaction in operational-level situations. The scholar's task, in applying the IAD framework, is to determine, and diagnose perceived problems with, the rules-in-use that govern day-to-day ("operational-level") interactions in the action situations under study. In the IP context, this might be a slightly easier chore than in many natural commons contexts, where determining the rules requires close observation of, and interaction with, local communities for long periods of time. As a highly top-down system of governance, the basic contours of the rule-structure governing various types of information can be discerned from studying national statutes and cases brought under those statutes. In other words, the relative lack of polycentricity in the IP governance system should make it, all else being equal, an easier governance system to comprehend.

In 2005, Ostrom and her Workshop colleague, Sue Crawford, classified (functionally) various types of rules that apply in action situations (E. Ostrom & Crawford 2005: 186–215) including the following (incomplete list):

Position rules	Define positions that actors hold, including as owners of property rights and duties.
Boundary rules	Define: (1) Who is eligible to take a position; (2) The process for choosing who is eligible to take a position; (3) How actors can leave positions; (4) Whether anyone can hold multiple positions simultaneously; (5) Succession to vacant positions.
Choice rules	Define what actors in positions must, must not, or may do in their position and in particular circumstances.
Aggregation rules	Determine whether a decision by a single actor or multiple actors is needed prior to acting at a decision point in a process.
Information rules	Specify channels of communication among actors, as well as the kinds of information that can be transmitted between positions.
Payoff rules	Assign external rewards or sanctions for particular actions or outcomes.

Ostrom (2005: 189, Fig. 7.1) provides the following graph to illustrate how the various rules affect activity within the action arena or situation.

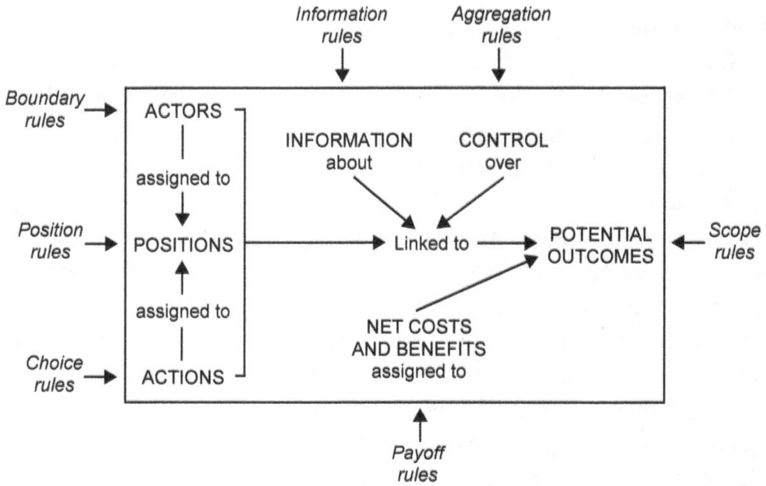

Figure 8.2. Rules as exogenous variables directly affecting the elements of an action situation.

Source: Ostrom (2005: 189, Fig. 7.1).

Among the more significant positional rules, for both natural commons and the information or knowledge commons, are property rights and duties. In 1992, Ostrom and Edella Schlager identified several components of private property ownership (Schlager & E. Ostrom 1992: 250–51; compare with Honoré 1961: 107, identifying nine distinct rights and two duties in the full, "fee simple" ownership):

Access	Right to enter a defined area and enjoy its benefits without removing any resources.
Withdrawal	Right to obtain specified products from a resource system and remove that product from the area for prescribed uses.
Management	Right to participate in decisions regulating resources or making improvements in infrastructure.
Exclusion	Right to participate in the determination of who has, and who does not have, access to and use of resources.
Alienation	Right to sell, lease, bequeath, or otherwise transfer any or all of the preceding component rights.

Not "Exogenous Variables" but "Initial Conditions"

One further point of clarification about the three boxes on the left side of the IAD framework needs to be made before we bring them, as inputs, into the action arena or situation: Ostrom sometimes referred to those three boxes as "exogenous variables" (E. Ostrom 2005: 15, Fig. 1.2). But that is inaccurate. Because of the recursive nature of the framework—feedback from outcomes of action situations effects, either directly or mediated through evaluative criteria, resource attributes, community attributes, and rules-in-use—they are endogenized within the framework. At best, they constitute sets of "initial conditions" immediately preceding any particular social interaction. It might make even more sense to say that they are the prevailing conditions (or "entry conditions") upon a social interaction.[20]

The Action Arena (or Situation): Where Collective Action Happens (or Not)

The action arena (or situation) is where social interactions occur. It is the place—often these days a *virtual* place—where: individual actors make decisions that affect social welfare; collective action succeeds or fails; rules are made; entitlements to resources are allocated; exchanges take place (or not); and disputes are adjudicated. If and when institutional change occurs, it occurs in action arenas or situations (Hess & E. Ostrom 2007: 54).

As already noted, action arenas or situations exist at three different levels of governance in the IAD framework: the constitutional-choice level, the collective-choice level, and the operational level. And what happens in various action arenas at those different levels impacts on relevant resources (e.g., how information is provided, to whom, and under what circumstances), attributes of the relevant community, and the rules-in-use (both formal and informal). Ostrom and Hess, for example, have used the creation of digital repositories of scholarship to exemplify how rule systems are created through collective-choice interactions, and affect the *incentives* of individual actors in operational-level interactions (Hess & E. Ostrom 2007: 54–57).

The individual actors participating in action arenas or situations are typically presumed to be either completely or boundedly rational (following Herbert Simon, who greatly influenced Ostrom's work) (Simon 1972: 161), depending on the theory-based preference of the analyst; either way, actors can be expected to behave strategically to further their own interests (as subjectively determined). This feature makes Ostrom's IAD framework almost uniquely compatible with multiple theories and models, including: neoclassical theory, game theory, public choice theory, and behavioral economics, with the exception of (usually deterministic) models of irrational behavior (see, e.g., Berridge 2003: 17).

Pursuant to rules discussed above, actors in action arenas hold a variety of "positions," depending on the choice-level (constitutional, collective-choice, or operational). At the constitutional level, they may be appointed members of the constitutional convention, members of state ratifying conventions, journalists, scholars, members of interest groups attempting to affect the outcomes of constitutional negotiations, judges determining compliance with constitutional process rules, and so forth. At the collective-choice (or policy) level, positions include legislators (junior and senior) with various congressional or party leadership roles, as well as committee assignments and positions, legislative and committee staff members, lobbyists, hearing witnesses, parliamentarians, official reporters, and journalists, among others. In operational-level action arenas, participants include buyers, sellers, owners, renters, contractors, disputants, fiduciary, beneficiary, player, coach—the whole panoply of roles that humans take on in social interactions of all kinds in everyday life.

Operating within the scope of their respective positions (that is, according to the rules), and strategically according to their own (boundedly) rational interests and preferences (as they subjectively see them), actors choose among available action alternatives in light of information they possess about how potential actions (as well as inaction) link to potential outcomes, including costs and benefits (McGinnis 2011: 173–74). In addition to the costs and benefits internalized to the individual actors, their individual decisions may well have social consequences, entailing significant net costs or benefits for the community. Indeed, if that were not the case, society would not confront any social-cost or public-goods problems (broadly put, social dilemmas) requiring collective action.

Studying social interactions at constitutional, collective-choice, and operational levels allows scholars to observe regularities (and irregularities) in patterns of interaction. In many cases, regularized patterns of interaction will represent an equilibrium (although not necessarily a unique, efficient, or Nash equilibrium) for the actors. In other cases, the equilibrium might be difficult to discern or, in especially conflicted and contested situations, might not actually exist (even over long periods of time). When an equilibrium or regularized pattern of interactions is observed, *patterns* of interaction themselves may constitute or reflect *norms* of social behavior previously known (from the "rules-in-use" box) or unknown. Most importantly, apparent equilibria may be subject to shocks (exogenous or endogenous) that can alter patterns (or norms) of interaction, depending on their robustness and resilience.

Outcomes

In a sense, observed patterns of interaction are *outcomes* of social interactions. For example, in the legal action situation of automobile accident disputes, out-of-court settlements are both an observed regularity of interactions among actors (or parties) and outcomes of the proceedings (Ross 1980: 179 (2,123 of 2,216 cases disposed of by settlement before trial)). Similarly, in the legislative action arena of Congress, the so-called "Mickey Mouse rule" of IP policy, whereby Congress extends copyright terms retroactively whenever the Disney character Mickey Mouse is about to fall into the public domain, reflects an observed regularity of interactions (among players including legislators, lobbyists, and expert witnesses), amounting to an equilibrium situation (which is not to say the equilibrium necessarily is efficient) (see, e.g., Posner 2003). That pattern of interaction is itself a predictable *outcome* of the structure of interests and incentives created by existing sets of institutions (pursuant to theories of public choice) (Landes & Posner 2004). Meanwhile, the equilibrium patterns of interaction yield *predictable* outcomes of specific legislative processes to extend the copyright law at regular intervals.

Importantly, outcomes of interactions frequently entail effects that extend beyond the interacting parties to the broader society. So, in a natural commons setting outcomes frequently include consequences for the resource systems and resource units themselves, as well as for those who use the resources (on a broad interpretation of the word "use"). A collective choice–level interaction that displaces "open access" governance with "regulated access and use" naturally would entail outcomes for the relevant resources and users beyond any observed pattern of social interactions in the action arena. In the same vein, a collective-action decision to enclose completely the information commons (e.g., by prohibiting the creation or maintenance of a "creative commons") would produce various predictable and unpredictable outcomes relative to the production and dissemination of information.

Ostrom and Hess provide an unfortunately misleading table of "potential positive or negative outcomes in various knowledge commons" (Hess & E. Ostrom 2007: 61, Table 3.1), which conflates outcomes with *normative* evaluations of those outcomes. For example, they treat enclosure as a "negative" outcome and maintenance of an information commons as a "positive" outcome. This is presumptuous (and as noted above, contrary to their usual practice). It certainly is true that enclosure is an *outcome* of a proprietary (and gated) scientific database, and "open access" likewise is a consequence of an "open access research library." However, whether one institutional arrangement is "positive," "negative," or preferable is a decidedly normative evaluation for which Ostrom and Hess provided no analysis. They should have been more circumspect. Normative assessments of outcomes as "positive" or "negative" will always be in the eye of the beholder, depending on her or his preferences, interests, and subjectively chosen (but hopefully expressly manifest) "evaluative criteria." Even from a social perspective, a normative assessment of outcomes depends on the selection and application of inherently contestable evaluative criteria.

In other words, the IAD framework itself provides no greater basis for normative presumptions about alternative governance systems for information than it provides for normative presumptions about alternative governance systems for natural common-pool resources. Depending on what function we are trying to maximize, it is entirely possible that neither entirely closed-access nor entirely open-access information systems would maximize it. From a social welfare perspective, some combination of open- and closed-access is overwhelmingly likely to be more socially efficient than complete open- or close-access (David 2003: 19). The trick, of course, would be getting the combination just right. And, again, the IAD framework itself will not help that determination, except to the extent applications of the framework result in meta-analyses that yield something like the "design principles" Ostrom derived in *Governing the Commons*. In addition, the IAD framework can be said to facilitate evaluation by making it easy for evaluators to separate out the various elements that combine to affect outcomes.

Evaluative Criteria

In applying the IAD framework, we should not simply assume one or another social goal. It might or might not be social efficiency (on some definition). The "evaluative criteria" box in the IAD framework has long been the most neglected and underdeveloped element of the framework. Even in her most elaborate account of the IAD framework, in *Understanding Institutional Diversity*, Ostrom devotes only three pages to a discussion of the "evaluative criteria" box, and offers only some general contenders for populating it, including (1) economic efficiency; (2) fiscal equivalence; (3) redistributional equity; (4) accountability; (5) conformance to values of local actors; and (6) sustainability. In the more specific context of the knowledge commons, Ostrom and Hess suggest (without citation) that six evaluative criteria are "frequently used": (1) increasing scientific knowledge; (2) sustainability and preservation; (3) participation standards; (4) economic efficiency; (5) equity through fiscal equivalence; and (6) redistributional equity (Hess & E. Ostrom 2007: 63). They devote a paragraph to describing each discrete criterion (or set of criteria), amounting to just over three pages, without any detailed analysis of how any of the criteria would actually operate within the context of action situations, either separately or in combination with other evaluative criteria.

Ostrom's lack of detailed and critical attention to the "evaluative criteria" in the IAD framework may reflect, more than anything else, her focus on natural common-pool resources, where little (if any) disagreement existed among diverse scholars about the ultimate goal, which was universally assumed to be long-run resource sustainability. Ostrom, Hardin, Demsetz, and virtually every other scholar writing about common-pool resources concurs in ultimate aim, no matter how strongly they disagree about institutional means of achieving it. Consensus about ends makes for easier agreement on evaluative criteria for assessing alternative means (including privatization, public/state regulation of access and use, or local, common-property management) in various circumstances.

In other realms to which the IAD framework might usefully be applied, including the information or knowledge commons, there is unlikely to be agreement with respect to ultimate social goals. Some may argue that the ultimate goal of IP law is to reward innovators, in accordance with well-established property theories based on labor and just deserts, regardless of social welfare (Hughes 1988). Others might argue that the ultimate goal is to build the stock of useful knowledge to facilitate economic growth (representing a social-welfare function) (Kuznets 1965). Still others might assert that *the* goal is to disseminate knowledge as widely as possible for its own sake (Hettinger 1989; Boyle 2003; but see Wagner 2003 (arguing that strong IP rights are *more* likely to ensure a flourishing public domain of ideas)).

In the absence of consensus about ultimate ends, agreement on evaluative criteria for assessing means is unlikely (to say the least). As a consequence, individual scholars have greater freedom to select from among alternative evaluative criteria (at least within some conventional range) for adjudging the outcomes of social interactions. However, that freedom should be constrained by the general scientific principle that evaluative criteria must be clearly specified along with *reasons* for preferring them, either across the board or in the circumstances, so that the basis for evaluation can be understood and/or contested.

Somewhat more hopefully, scholars of the information commons, like scholars of the natural common-pool resources, might achieve consensus on a certain maximand (e.g., an agreed social-welfare function) for information and information-flows in society, which would enable a more fruitful focus on alternative institutional means of achieving that goal. Alternative presumptions and hypotheses about relations between institutional means and social outcomes could then be subject (at least potentially) to testing and comparison across runs of cases, as Ostrom did in *Governing the Commons* and her earlier studies of police department performance relative to size.

Finally, the evaluative criteria (however chosen) provide a basis for *interpreting* as well as evaluating outcomes. Those interpretations and evaluations become part of the feedback loop into resource systems, community attributes, and rules-in-use. When members of the relevant community evaluate outcomes of social interactions as "bad" (according to whatever criteria), they may push (successfully or unsuccessfully) for further action in subsequent action situations at the collective-choice level, to alter or curtail "bad" outcomes. Thus, the recursive aspect of the IAD framework accounts for institutional change (or inertia) over time (even though the framework cannot by itself determine, ensure, or even predict institutional change).

Conclusion

IP scholars already have begun applying the IAD framework to good effect. Charlotte Hess, writing with Elinor Ostrom and on her own, has been a pioneer in calling for application of the framework to problems of the information or knowledge commons (see, e.g., Hess & E. Ostrom 2003, 2006, 2007; Hess 2005, 2008). Charles Schweik has applied the IAD framework to "software commons" (Schweik 2005; Schweik & English 2007). Josh Tenenberg has applied it to study software development teams (Tenenberg 2008). And Jorge Contreras, in this volume and elsewhere, applies the IAD framework to the "genome commons" (Contreras, this volume, ch. 4; Contreras 2011). Other scholars might examine these groundbreaking efforts to assess whether the framework might usefully be applied to their own problems and projects.

These are still early days in the social-scientific study of information as a good, whether public, common, or private. But, as noted earlier, students of the information or knowledge commons should not expect quick and decisive results about appropriate governance institutions. That is one of the chief lessons of the large and growing literature on natural common-pool resources. After several decades of data collection and careful construction of analytical frameworks, theories, and methods to analyze and diagnose commons problems, much has been learned but probably not nearly as much as remains to be learned.

Thanks primarily to Elinor Ostrom and her colleagues at the Ostrom Workshop in Political Theory and Policy Analysis, we have learned that common-property regimes are a viable third category of governance regimes for successfully managing natural common-pool resources over long periods of time.[21] And we have gained some idea of the conditions under which common-property regimes seem more or less likely to succeed based on the "design principles" Ostrom derived from her meta-analyses of hundreds of individual cases. Since then, despite increasing data collection and efforts to improve analytical methods, further progress toward understanding and diagnosing (let alone resolving) commons problems has been marginal (though hardly insignificant).

Scant reason exists to expect easier and more rapid progress toward describing, diagnosing, and explaining issues relating to information and information-flows. Indeed, as noted earlier, important questions remain about just how applicable the existing literature of natural common-pool resources is to the information commons. Even when information arises or is placed in common pools, it may not have the same kinds of attributes of natural resources found in common pools. As defined many years ago by Vincent and Elinor Ostrom, common-pool resources share certain attributes with public goods, but are not themselves pure public goods. Specifically, they lack nonrivalrousness in consumption, which is to say they are subtractable or congestible. This is not true of information (though it may be true of the various vehicles by which information is provided or disseminated). Thus, whereas "open access" is potentially tragic, and only very rarely preferable,[22] for a natural resource commons, IP scholars often make arguments promoting "open access" (see, e.g., Willinsky 2006; Swan 2007). And those arguments make sense in that context (even if they are not completely convincing) to the extent that information approximates a *pure* public good.

Even if the natural resource commons and the information commons were more similar than they are, IP scholars hoping to find support for normative arguments about the preferability of common-property management (let alone full-blown open access) will not find much in the work of Elinor Ostrom and others employing her frameworks, theories, and models. As argued in the first part of this chapter, Ostrom's own normative commitments were few and contingent; her work on natural common-pool resources *never* argued as a general rule that common-property regimes were preferable to private, individual property systems or public property/regulatory systems. It was only in specific circumstances that we might (or might not) find that one type of property/regulatory regime functioned as well as or better than others. She would surely caution IP scholars not to expect to find panacea solutions for problems of the information or knowledge commons.

Acknowledgments

In 2011, Lin Ostrom and I traveled together to the conference that resulted in this book. This chapter, though a poor substitute for what was to have been Lin's contribution to the volume, is dedicated to her memory. I am grateful to Brett Frischmann and Mike McGinnis for several helpful comments and suggestions.

Notes

This chapter was originally published in *Governing Knowledge Commons*, edited by Brett M. Frischmann, Michael J. Madison, and Katherine J. Strandburg (New York: Oxford University Press, 2014), pp. 45–68. Reprinted with the permission of Oxford University Press. Figures 8.1 and 8.2 reprinted with the permission of MIT Press and Princeton University Press, respectively.

1. By "institutional arrangement," I mean sets of rules implemented through some organizational structure. I generally follow Douglass North's definition of an "institution" as a human-devised rule—whether a formal legal rule or an informal social norm—for structuring social interactions (North 1990: 3). For North, organizations are not institutions, but amalgams of actors. Elinor Ostrom defined "institutions" variously, but not inconsistently, in her works (see Cole 2013: 390–391). Moreover, as Ostrom points out, her own definitions were consistent with North's understanding of the distinctions between "institutions" and "organizations" (see E. Ostrom 2005: 179). However, in Ostrom's analytical framework, it might sometimes at least be more useful to consider organizations as "action arenas" rather than as actors. For more on "action arenas" as part of Ostrom's analytical framework, see infra.

2. More specifically, they are the *formal* "rules of the game," which, together with informal social norms, structure social interactions (see North 1990: 3).

3. The recent rise of empirical legal scholarship and other applications of social-scientific methodologies to law have reduced, but not eliminated, the domi-

nance of normative legal scholarship. On the rise of empirical legal scholarship, see, e.g., Heise (2002). On more general applications of social-scientific methodologies to law, see, e.g., Lempert & Sanders (1986); Monahan & Walker (2009); Baird, Gertner, & Picker (1998).

4. More generally, Ostrom and her co-authors found little empirical support for conventional presumptions of constant economies of scale in provision of public services. They found both economies of scale and diseconomies of scale, depending on the types of public services being provided and the circumstances (e.g., community attributes) in which they were being provided.

5. On comparative institutional analysis, see, e.g., Cole (2013); Komesar (1994); Aoki (2001).

6. One arguable exception is mentioned in section ["Outcomes"] below, where I claim that Ostrom (and co-author Charlotte Hess) simply (perhaps "casually" would be a better word) erred in implying that open-access information repositories invariably are a "positive" outcome of collective action and proprietary information systems with gated access invariably are a "negative" outcome. If anything, this example is so exceptional that it proves the rule that Ostrom was exceedingly reluctant to make or support sweeping normative generalizations.

7. The IAD framework is set out in much more detail, infra.

8. The value of the IAD framework already has been recognized by IP scholars writing from various disciplinary perspectives about the information or knowledge commons. See, e.g., Madison, Frischmann, & Strandburg (2010 [chapter 7 in this volume]); Tenenberg (2008); and Schweik & English (2007).

9. Ostrom's phrase "design principles" can be misleading. She did not mean necessarily to imply either the implementation of a strategic plan or a designer. See Becker & Ostrom 1995: 122 ("one should not presume that there was a conscious overall plan to develop institutions that met the design principles. Rather, the design principles are an effort of careful observers to identify commonalities that help to account for sustainability of fragile resources over very long periods of time."). Ostrom, herself, has regretted confusion arising from the phrase "design principles" and has suggested "best practices" as an alternative (E. Ostrom 2010c: 14, n.5). However, given the normative implication of the word "best," the substitute phrase might prove just as misleading as "design principles." In any case, a recent meta-analysis testing the "design principles" from *Governing the Commons* found them robust overall (see Cox et al. 2010).

10. Perhaps the phrase "underlying regularities" (or "regularly observed characteristics") might be more fitting than either "design principles" or "best practices" for denoting the attributes of successful commons-management regimes.

11. What is achieved in the absence of a clearly defined and agreed-upon vocabulary is what the philosopher David Lewis (1969) referred to as a "babbling equilibrium" (see also Ostrom 2005: 176).

12. A "Workshopper" is an affiliated faculty member, visiting scholar, graduate student, or staffer in Indiana University's Workshop in Political The-

ory and Policy Analysis, which in 2012 was named for its founders, Vincent and Elinor Ostrom.

13. Ostrom insisted that everyone should use each term of art, such as "institution," in precisely the same way. For example, Hess & E. Ostrom (2003: 114) stress the need for "shared meanings." In my view, legitimate reasons exist for scholars to use the same term in different ways, depending on what *functions* those terms are serving in their analysis. See Cole (2013). However, if social scientists and legal scholars are to tolerate diverse meanings of similar terms, it becomes imperative for individual scholars to define with utmost care terms amenable to multiple meanings in every paper they write. Moreover, even if Ostrom's insistence on "shared meanings" is unduly strict, her goal of achieving widespread, or even universal, agreement of a common framework for analysis and of variables within that framework remains crucial for enabling meta-analyses of case studies and coding for quantitative empirical analysis.

14. Indeed, some IP scholars already have heeded this lesson. See Madison, Frischmann, & Strandburg (2010) and this volume.

15. See, e.g., Prah v. Maretti, 108 Wis. 2d 223, 321 N.W.2d 182 (1982); Fountainebleau Hotel Corp. v. Forty-five Twenty-Five Inc., 114 So. 2d 357 (Fla. App. 1959).

16. Van Zandt claims that Coase was describing a special case because such a high percentage of global shipping traffic used the Port of London during the period Coase was describing, and notes that the government subsidized private provision of lighthouse services by giving lighthouse owners taxation powers in the Port of London.

17. The ideas contained in the formulae are public goods, but the formulae themselves (the "artifacts") are private goods because of ease of excludability, even if they might in theory be nonrival in consumption.

18. Artificially created "natural" commons do exist; think of stocked fisheries. Moreover, I can easily imagine a philosopher arguing that even what counts as a "natural resource" is, in part, a product of human conceptualization. Thus, all common-pool resources would be at least coproduced or co-created by humans. But I suggest we cabin such issues for purposes of the current discussion, where the distinction between humans as creators of natural and creators of artificial resources seems important regardless of the relation between humans and natural resource systems.

19. I hasten immediately to cast doubt on the implicit assertion by observing that Elinor Ostrom was not daunted by much of anything during the course of her long career. It is entirely possible that she did not apply the IAD framework to the problem of the "climate commons" merely for lack of sufficient time, given her other innumerable obligations.

20. Madison, Frischmann, & Strandburg (2010 [chapter 7 in this volume]) modify the IAD framework in part to account for the complex feedback mechanisms and interactions across the framework components in the knowledge commons context.

21. That is, of course, the primary lesson of Ostrom's *Governing the Commons* (1990).

22. Arguably, "open access" is optimal (that is, preferable to all alternative property/regulatory systems) for natural resource commons only so long as the rate of demand remains quite low relative to the supply—that is to say, prior to some known or presumed congestion point. See Cole (2002); Frischmann (2012: ch. 11).

References

Acheson, James M., *Ostrom for Anthropologists*, 5 INT'L J. COMMONS (Sept. 5, 2011), http://www.thecommonsjournal.org/index.php/ijc/article/view/245/209.

Aoki, Masahiko, TOWARD A COMPARATIVE INSTITUTIONAL ANALYSIS (MIT Press 2001).

Baird, Douglas G., Robert H. Gertner, & Randall C. Picker, GAME THEORY AND THE LAW (Harvard University Press 1998).

Becker, C. Dustin & Elinor Ostrom, *Human Ecology and Resource Sustainability: The Importance of Institutional Diversity*, 26 ANN. REV. ECOLOGY & SYSTEMATICS 113 (1995).

Berridge, Kent C., *Irrational Pursuits: Hyper-Incentives from a Visceral Brain*, *in* THE PSYCHOLOGY OF ECONOMIC DECISIONS, VOL. I: RATIONALITY AND WELL-BEING 17 (Isabelle Brocas & Juan D. Carillo eds., Oxford University Press 2003).

Boyle, James, *The Second Enclosure Movement and the Construction of the Public Domain*, 66 LAW & CONTEMP. PROBS. 33 (2003).

Coase, R. H., *The Lighthouse in Economics*, 17 J. LAW & ECONOMICS 357 (1974).

Cole, Daniel H., POLLUTION AND PROPERTY: COMPARING OWNERSHIP SYSTEMS FOR ENVIRONMENTAL PROTECTION (Cambridge University Press 2002).

———, *The Varieties of Comparative Institutional Analysis*, 2013 WISCONSIN L. REV. 383.

Constantinidis, Panos, PERSPECTIVES AND IMPLICATIONS FOR THE DEVELOPMENT OF INFORMATION INFRASTRUCTURES 43 (IGI Global 2012).

Contreras, Jorge L., *Bermuda's Legacy: Policy, Patents, and the Design of the Genome Commons*, 12 MINNESOTA J.L. SCI. & TECH. 61 (2011).

Cox, Michael, Gwen Arnold, & Sergio Villamayor Tomás, *A Review and Reassessment of Design Principles for Community-based Natural Resource Management*, 15 ECOLOGY & SOCIETY 38 (2010).

David, Paul E., *The Economic Logic of "Open Science" and the Balance between Private Property Rights and the Public Domain in Scientific Data and Information: A Primer*, *in* THE ROLE OF THE PUBLIC DOMAIN IN SCIENTIFIC AND TECHNICAL DATA AND INFORMATION 19 (Julie M. Esanu & Paul F. Uhlir eds., National Academies Press 2003).

Decentralization: A Sampling of Definitions, Working Paper Prepared in Connection with the Joint UNDP—Government of Germany Evaluation of the UNDP Role in Decentralization and Local Governance (Oct. 1999), http://web.undp.org/evaluation/documents/decentralization_working_report.pdf.

Ellickson, Robert C., ORDER WITHOUT LAW: HOW NEIGHBORS SETTLE DISPUTES (Harvard University Press 1991).

Feldman, Yuval & Janice Nadler, *The Law and Norms of File Sharing*, 43 SAN DIEGO L. REV. 577 (2006).

Friedman, Lawrence M., THE LEGAL SYSTEM: A SOCIAL SCIENCE PERSPECTIVE (Russell Sage 1975).

Frischmann, Brett, INFRASTRUCTURE: THE SOCIAL VALUE OF SHARED RESOURCES (Oxford University Press 2012).

———, *Two Enduring Lessons from Elinor Ostrom*, 9 J. INSTITUTIONAL ECONOMICS 387 (2013).

Hardin, Garrett, *The Tragedy of the Commons*, 162 SCIENCE 1243 (1968).

Heise, Michael, *The Past, Present, and Future of Empirical Legal Scholarship: Judicial Decision Making and the New Empiricism*, 2002 U. ILLINOIS L. REV. 819 (2002).

Hess, Charlotte, *A Resource Guide for Authors: Open Access, Copyright, and the Digital Commons*, CPR DIGEST (March 2005), http://www.iasc-commons.org/sites/all/Digest/cpr72.pdf.

———, *Mapping the New Commons*, presented at "Governing Shared Resources: Connecting Local Experience to Global Challenges," the 12th Biennial Conference of the International Association for the Study of the Commons, University of Gloucestershire, Cheltenham, England (July 14–18, 2008), http://dlc.dlib.indiana.edu/dlc/handle/10535/304.

Hess, Charlotte & Elinor Ostrom, *Ideas, Artifacts, and Facilities: Information as a Common-Pool Resource*, 66 LAW & CONTEMP. PROBS. 111 (2003).

———, *A Framework for Analysing the Microbiological Commons*, 58 INT'L SOCIAL SCIENCE J. 335 (2006).

———, Eds., UNDERSTANDING KNOWLEDGE AS A COMMONS: FROM THEORY TO PRACTICE (MIT Press 2007).

Hettinger, Edward C., *Justifying Intellectual Property*, 18 PHILOSOPHY & PUBLIC AFFAIRS 31 (1989).

Honoré, Toni, *Ownership*, *in* OXFORD ESSAYS IN JURISPRUDENCE 107 (A. G. Guest ed., Oxford University Press 1961).

Hughes, Justin, *The Philosophy of Intellectual Property*, 77 GEORGETOWN L.J. 287 (1988).

Kinston, Christopher & Gonzalo Caballero, *Comparing Theories of Institutional Change*, 5 J. INSTITUTIONAL ECONOMICS 151 (2009).

Komesar, Neil K., IMPERFECT ALTERNATIVES: CHOOSING INSTITUTIONS IN LAW (University of Chicago Press 1994).

Kuznets, Simon, ECONOMIC GROWTH AND STRUCTURE: SELECTED ESSAYS (Norton 1965).

Landes, William M. & Richard A. Posner, THE POLITICAL ECONOMY OF INTELLECTUAL PROPERTY LAW (Harvard University Press 2004).

Lempert, Richard & Joseph Sanders, AN INVITATION TO LAW AND SOCIAL SCIENCE (Longman 1986).

Lewis, David, CONVENTION: A PHILOSOPHICAL STUDY (Harvard University Press 1969).

Llewellyn, Karl N., *Law and the Social Sciences—Especially Sociology*, 14 AMER. SOCIOLOGICAL REVIEW 41 (1949).

Madison, Michael J., Brett M. Frischmann, & Katherine J. Strandburg, *Constructing Commons in the Cultural Environment*, 95 CORNELL L. REV. 657 (2010).

Magliocca, Gerard, *Blackberries and Barnyards: Patent Trolls and the Perils of Innovation*, 82 NOTRE DAME L. REV. 1809 (2013).

McDonough, James F., III, *The Myth of the Patent Troll: An Alternative View of the Function of Patent Dealers in an Idea Economy*, 56 EMORY L.J. 189 (2006).

McGinnis, Michael D., *An Introduction to IAD and the Language of the Ostrom Workshop: A Simple Guild to a Complex Framework*, 39 POLICY STUDIES J. 169 (2011).

Monahan, John & W. Laurens Walker, SOCIAL SCIENCE IN LAW (7th ed., Foundation Press 2009).

North, Douglass C., INSTITUTIONS, INSTITUTIONAL CHANGE, AND ECONOMIC PERFORMANCE (Cambridge University Press 1990).

Ostrom, Elinor, GOVERNING THE COMMONS: THE EVOLUTION OF INSTITUTIONS FOR COLLECTIVE ACTION (Cambridge University Press 1990).

———, UNDERSTANDING INSTITUTIONAL DIVERSITY (Princeton University Press 2005).

———, *A Diagnostic Approach for Going Beyond Panaceas*, 104 PROCEEDINGS OF THE NATIONAL ACADEMY OF SCIENCES U.S. 15181 (2007).

———, *Polycentric Systems as One Approach to Solving Collective-Action Problems*, *in* CLIMATE CHANGE AND SUSTAINABLE DEVELOPMENT: NEW CHALLENGES FOR POVERTY REDUCTION 17 (M.A. Mohamed Salih ed., Edward Elgar Publishing 2009a).

———, *A Polycentric Approach for Coping with Climate Change*, World Bank Policy Research Paper 5095 (Oct. 2009b).

———, *A Long Polycentric Journey*, 13 ANN. REVIEW POLITICAL SCIENCE 1 (2010a).

———, *Polycentric Systems for Coping with Collective Action and Global Environmental Change*, 20 GLOBAL ENVTL. CHANGE 550 (2010b).

———, *Beyond Markets and States: Polycentric Governance of Complex Economic Systems*, 100 AMER. ECONOMIC REVIEW 641 (2010c).

———, *Institutional Analysis and Development: Elements of the Framework in Historical Perspective*, *in* HISTORICAL DEVELOPMENTS AND THEORETICAL APPROACHES IN SOCIOLOGY (C. Crothers ed.), vol. II, UNESCO ENCYCLOPEDIA OF LIFE SUPPORT SYSTEMS (UNESCO-ELOSS 2010d).

———, *Background on the Institutional Analysis and Development Framework*, 39 POLICY STUDIES J. 7 (2011).

———, *The Challenges of Achieving Conservation and Development*, THE ANNUAL PROCEEDINGS OF THE WEALTH AND WELL-BEING OF NATIONS, VOL. IV (Emily Chamlee-Wright ed., Beloit College 2011–2012).

———, *Nested Externalities and Polycentric Institutions: Must We Wait for Global Solutions to Climate Change before Taking Actions at Other Scales?*, 49 ECONOMIC THEORY 353 (2012).

Ostrom, Elinor & Sue Crawford, *Classifying Rules*, *in* ELINOR OSTROM, UNDERSTANDING INSTITUTIONAL DIVERSITY 186 (Princeton University Press 2005).

Ostrom, Elinor & Charlotte Hess, *A Framework for Analyzing the Knowledge Commons*, *in* UNDERSTANDING KNOWLEDGE AS A COMMONS: FROM THEORY TO PRACTICE 41 (Charlotte Hess & Elinor Ostrom eds., MIT Press 2007).

Ostrom, Elinor, Marco A. Janssen, & John M. Anderies, *Going Beyond Panaceas*, 104 PROCEEDINGS OF THE NATIONAL ACADEMY OF SCIENCES U.S. 15176 (2007).

Ostrom, Elinor, Roger Parks, & Gordon Whitaker, PATTERNS OF METROPOLITAN POLICING (Ballinger Pub. Co. 1978).

Ostrom, Vincent, *Polycentricity*, in POLYCENTRICITY AND LOCAL PUBLIC ECONOMIES: READINGS FROM THE WORKSHOP IN POLITICAL THEORY AND POLICY ANALYSIS (M. D. McGinnis, ed., University of Michigan Press 1999).

Ostrom, Vincent & Elinor Ostrom, *Public Goods and Public Choices*, *in* POLYCENTRICITY AND LOCAL PUBLIC ECONOMIES: READINGS FROM THE WORKSHOP IN POLITICAL THEORY AND POLICY ANALYSIS (M. D. McGinnis ed., University of Michigan Press 1999).

Ostrom, Vincent, Charles M. Tiebout, & Charles Warren, *The Organization of Government in Metropolitan Areas: A Theoretical Inquiry*, 55 AMER. POLITICAL SCIENCE REV. 831 (1961).

Posner, Richard A., *The Constitutionality of the Copyright Term Extension Act: Economics, Politics, Law and Judicial Technique*, *in* Eldred v. Ashcroft, 2003 THE SUPREME COURT REV. 143 (2003).

Pound, Roscoe, *Law in Books and Law in Action*, 44 AMER. L. REV. 12 (1910).

Ross, H. Laurence, SETTLED OUT OF COURT: THE SOCIAL PROCESS OF INSURANCE CLAIMS ADJUSTMENT 179 (Rev. 2d ed., De Gruyter 1980).

Sabatier, Paul, THEORIES OF THE POLICY PROCESS (2d ed., Westview Press 2007).

Schlager, Edella & Elinor Ostrom, *Property-Rights Regimes and Natural Resources: A Conceptual Analysis*, 68 LAND ECONOMICS 249 (1992).

Schweik, Charles M., *An Institutional Analysis Approach to Studying Libre Software "Commons,"* 6 UPGRADE 17 (2005).

Schweik, Charles M. & Robert English, *Tragedy of the FOSS Commons? Investigating the Institutional Designs of Free/Libre and Open Source Software Projects*, 12 FIRST MONDAY no. 2 (Feb. 5, 2007), http://firstmonday.org/htbin/cgiwrap/bin/ojs/index.php/fm/article/view/1619/1534.

Schweik, Charles M. & Meelis Kitsing, *Applying Elinor Ostrom's Rule Classification Framework to the Analysis of Open Source Software Commons*, 2 TRANSNAT'L CORPORATIONS REV. 13 (2010).

Simon, Herbert A., *Models of Bounded Rationality*, *in* DECISION AND ORGANIZATION (C. B. McGuire & Roy Radner eds., North-Holland 1972).

Swan, Alma, *Open Access and the Progress of Science*, 95 AMER. SCIENTIST 198 (2007).

Tenenberg, Josh, *An Institutional Analysis of Software Teams*, 66 J. HUMAN-COMPUTER STUDIES 484 (2008).

Van Zandt, David E., *The Lesson of the Lighthouse: "Government" or "Private" Provision of Goods*, 22 J. LEGAL STUDIES 47 (1993).

Wagner, R. Polk, *Information Wants to Be Free: Intellectual Property and the Mythologies of Control*, 103 COLUMBIA L. REV. 995 (2003).

Willinsky, John, THE ACCESS PRINCIPLE: THE CASE FOR OPEN ACCESS TO RESEARCH AND SCHOLARSHIP (MIT Press 2006).

9

The Governance of Infrastructures as Common-Pool Resources

Rolf Künneke and Matthias Finger

Introduction and Problem Statement

The notion of common-pool resources (CPRs) "refers to a natural or man-made resource system that is sufficiently large as to make it costly (but not impossible) to exclude potential beneficiaries from obtaining benefits from its use" (Ostrom 1990, 30). Traditionally, this notion is used in relation to natural resource systems, like forests, lakes, or river basins.[1] Common-pool resources are associated to very peculiar governance problems. There are significant problems associated to "crowding effects" and "overuse" of CPRs in conjunction with insufficient incentives to invest in the system in order to guarantee its sustainability.[2] Hence, one of the focal points of the governance of CPRs is the regulation of access and a fair distribution of costs and benefits between the users. The dominant focus of common-pool resource research is on the governance of socio-ecological systems.

Ostrom claims that similar common-pool resource problems can also be recognized in man-made resource systems like, for instance, irrigation canals, bridges, parking garages, or even mainframe computers (Ostrom 1990, 30). However, comparably little attention is paid to the governance of these kinds of socio-technical systems in CPR literature.[3] We aim to contribute to this field of research and especially with respect to infrastructures. Increasingly, there are problems related to "crowding effects" or "overuse" like, for instance, traffic congestion in public road systems, or physical bottlenecks in electricity and gas networks. These large-scale socio-technical systems seem to be confronted with similar problems as compared to socio-ecological systems, for instance, with respect to poor investment incentives in order to guarantee the system sustainability, and the regulation of access to prevent the excessive appropriation of goods or services.

This paper explores the significance of common-pool resource problems in infrastructures as socio-technical systems, and how they are resolved. The following issues are addressed: What are the features of infrastructures as common-pool resources? (second section); what are typical common-pool resource problems related to infrastructures? (third section); what are typical modes of organization to deal with CPR problems in infrastructures? (fourth section); what new insights can possibly be gained by interpreting infrastructures as common-pool resources? (fifth section).

Infrastructures as Common-Pool Resources

In this paper, infrastructures are perceived as complex socio-technical systems in which technological, economic, political, and social features strongly interact with each other (Perez 2002; Van de Poel 2003; Kroes et al. 2006; Geels and Schot 2007). The physical nature of infrastructures is determined by networks that connect various nodes and links. As a consequence, system complementarities create necessities for the coordination of activities. For instance, the delivery of electricity depends, among others, on the coordination between production units, the transport and distribution of power, and the transformation to a suitable voltage level. These coordination needs, which will be specified more in detail in the next section, highly determine the features of infrastructures as common-pool resources. Complementarities cause a strong mutual interrelation between the activities of different users of the network. Entering a public road system has direct implications for the other users if the road is close to its capacity limits, since travelling time increases. The transmission of electricity through the network cannot be technically controlled, but just follows the way of least electrical resistance imposing mutual restrictions to its users. This results in so-called loop flows of electric power through parts of the network that are economically not involved in a transaction.

Infrastructures can be perceived as non-excludable resources, for at least three reasons. First, infrastructures might be spread through a huge geographical area with difficult to monitor access points like, for instance, public road systems. Second, even if the access could be technically monitored, there might be politically motivated universal service obligations, since infrastructures provide essential services like drinking water, energy, or means of communication. Third, once the users have entered the network, it might be difficult or even impossible to precisely determine the services they appropriate from the network. Certain services cannot be individually monitored like, for instance, the use of many public roads, certain services that are necessary to technically balance the electricity network (i.e., load balancing, voltage control, and reactive power), or the quality control of drinking water. These are open access services from which each individual user takes benefit at the expense of others; that is, there is rivalry in the consumption. Because of the systemic nature of these services, it is difficult or even impossible to strictly assign them to individual users. By using the electricity network, there is an inherent need for load management, voltage control, and the provision of reactive power. However, different patterns of use and different technical characteristics of the user applications cause different needs for these services. Individual users extract these services from the system without reflecting on its technical or economic sustainability.

It has to be stressed that these appropriation problems do not occur for all services provided by infrastructures. Actually the appropriation of some services can be monitored very well and attributed to specific consumers. Examples include the consumption of cubic meters drinking water, kilowatt hours electric power or kilometers of transportation services in railway systems. But this is the exception rather the rule. The point is that significant infrastructure services fit the category of common-pool resource services and therefore its allocation is related to attribution problems.

Another typical feature of common-pool resources are the dubious and diffused property rights and decision rights with respect to the resource system and the appropriation of its services. Traditionally, infrastructures were vertically integrated firms that were able to control all relevant aspects of the resource system. This is the case of a "closed access CPR" (Ciriacy-Wantrup and Bishop 1975, cited in Ostrom 1990, 222n23). However, as a consequence of the institutional restructuring (i.e., liberalization), this vertical integration slowly eroded into an unbundled value chain with hybrid modes of organization and diffuse property rights structures.[4] Nonetheless, in a technical sense, the system remains a network with a strong degree of complementarity and consequently fundamental coordination needs. Under liberalized market conditions, the coordination needs are now to be performed by a multitude of actors with different interests and responsibilities. This development contributed to the emergence of CPR problems.

Infrastructures show a tendency towards an increasing size and complexity.[5] Many infrastructures started as local initiatives, but evolved into regional, national, and international operating utilities. At least some infrastructures (like energy, transport, and electronic communication) reached a scale and degree of complexity that is hardly to be monitored from one central authority or point, as it often was done in the past. The technical scope of these infrastructures generally crosses national boundaries and hence increasingly creates a need for international cooperation. Technical coordination is even more difficult under these circumstances because appropriate governance structures need to be defined under different legal systems and national systems of regulation. This contributes to the evolution of diffused property rights as mentioned in the previous paragraph.

Likewise in socio-ecological systems, infrastructures are typically used for multiple purposes. Drinking water might be used for cooking food or washing a car. Power is necessary for private consumption needs as well as facilitating industrial production processes. Rail tracks can be used for the transport of goods or persons. Depending on these purposes, different demands are made on infrastructure services, and there are different needs for long-term investments and system development. Related to this dynamic perspective, it also has to be taken into consideration that over time, the use of resource systems changes. New services are added or others are becoming less significant. The copper cables of the telephone network were initially designed to enable voice communication. Nowadays, they are mostly used for data communication with very different technical needs and system services.[6] In a common-pool resource system, these processes of change are accompanied by the need to redefine governance structures. New appropriation problems might arise, there are new investment needs, and new stakeholders can get involved in the exploitation of common-pool resources.

In conclusion, it can be stated that infrastructures can be perceived as common-pool resources since they fit major features of this notion: a non-excludable resource system, appropriation problems related to rivalry in consumption of essential services, coordination needs deriving from system complementarities, diffuse property rights and decision rights with respect to the resource system, and multiple-purpose services contributing to disperse and conflicting stakeholder interests. In the next section, we will further specify the nature of common-pool resource problems in infrastructures.

Common-Pool Resource Problems in Infrastructures

Common-pool resource problems are typically manifested by the "overuse" of certain goods or services beyond a sustainable consumption level, or "crowding effects" indicating that the individual acquisition of services takes more effort than expected. We relate CPR problems to four essential functions that have to be performed in all infrastructures in order to safeguard a satisfactory technical functioning (Finger et al. 2005, 240–41), that is, system management, capacity management, interconnection, and interoperability. These four functions define different categories of system services that are freely accessible but can be appropriated by individual users, and hence causing CPR problems.

System management pertains to the question of how the overall system (e.g., the flow between the various nodes and links) is being managed and how the quality of service is safeguarded. Typically, system management consists of short-term activities related to the actual coordination of activities within the network. This can be a very critical activity in liberalized infrastructures in which network activities are unbundled from commercial business. Indeed, actors pursue their own strategic objectives (e.g., conflictual objectives between the rail infrastructure operator and the rail transport operator), yet the system can only function if the operations of the involved actors are somewhat aligned. With growing fragmentation of the technical systems because of unbundling, outsourcing, and the like, there is therefore a growing need to coordinate all operations and actors involved. The most obvious example here is slot allocation, which is a new function that becomes necessary in both air and rail transport after the separation of infrastructure and transport. Obviously, slot allocation is an important mode of organization to avoid congestion and secure the safety of the system and thus resolves a common-pool resource problem.

Capacity management is another important system function. Networks are scarce resources because the capacity of nodes and links is limited. Capacity management deals with the allocation of this scarce network capacity to certain users or appliances. Different levels of capacity management can be distinguished (Ten Heuvelhof et al. 2003). On a strategic level, network access and scope are important issues. Which actors are, in general, allowed to use infrastructures and what is the desirable scope of service? On a tactical level, the actual access to networks needs to be facilitated by suitable regulations, for instance with respect to tariffs and technical quality standards. The operational level addresses real-time capacity management issues, which are related to the logistical aspects of directing the flows of services and goods through the various nodes and links. The physical limitations of networks pose high demands on the balancing of demand and supply of infrastructure services, which are often not storable. The electricity sector is a very illustrative example in this respect. Since electricity storage is only possible on a very limited scale and at very high costs, power production and consumption has to be balanced nearly instantaneously. There are very sophisticated models of load balancing developed for this sector in order to mitigate or avoid the overuse of the systems that results into major failures as blackouts.

Interconnection deals with the physical linkages of different networks that perform similar or complementary tasks (e.g., Economides 1996). As such, interconnection is closely related to the technical system's boundaries. Typical examples include the interconnection of different telecom networks, railroad tracks, or electricity systems. Interconnection occurs sometimes even beyond the limited boundaries of specific infrastructures. A similar development emerged in the transportation sector through the introduction of standardized containers. This technology allows for very fast and efficient intermodal traffic between roads, shipping, or air traffic. Containers allow for a much better interconnection between these different infrastructures. A failure to realize a sufficient degree of interconnection might cause congestion and an unsustainable use of the system. In addition, even severe economic problems arise as a consequence of an insufficient scale of operation and hence diseconomies of system. Typical symptoms include lower system reliability, less security of supply, and high transaction costs.

Interoperability is realized if mutual interactions between network elements are enabled in order to facilitate systems' complementarity. For example, in the railroad sector, the specification of the tracks needs to be aligned with the needs of the locomotives. In the aviation sector, airlines rely on specific navigation systems that guide planes to their destination without accidents. Interoperability ensures that the elements of the network are combinable. In other words, interoperability defines the technical and institutional conditions under which infrastructure networks can be utilized. Examples of modes of organization that resolve problems of interoperability are technical norms and standards, and regulatory conditions for access. In this sense, interoperability is also of strategic importance. It determines the conditions of use as well as the rules for entry and exit to this specific facility. In many public infrastructures, open access is required as a public service obligation. Sometimes, certain technical standards are defined in a way to establish barriers to entry for disturbing competitors.

It appears that in infrastructures, four essential functions can be identified that are closely related to common-pool resource problems. Since these functions are vital for the technical functioning of infrastructures, there need to be some modes of organization to support or enable them. The following section provides a brief overview of how these modes of organization evolved through the past decades.

The Governance of CPR Problems in Infrastructures

The four functions identified above are all essential, to various degrees, for the different infrastructures to properly operate. As said above, each of these essential functions requires proper institutional arrangements so that the infrastructure will ultimately function as a system. It is this systemic nature of the infrastructures that we have assimilated to a common-pool resource problem. The intellectual background of such considerations pertains to the coevolution between technology and institutions (Von Tunzelmann 2003; Nelson 1995; Tushman and Rosenkopf 1992). Indeed, infrastructures typically developed from integrated technologies, governed by a national monopoly, towards ever more distributed technologies, governed by a combination of market, government, and the third sector, something commonly called governance. One can distinguish between three stages (or three configurations) of this coevolution from integrated to distributed technologies and from government to governance. These three stages or configurations define different types of sectorial organization (or different degrees of market), namely monopolistic competition, access competition, and network competition. In each of these three configurations, the four essential functions play different roles and will be governed differently so as to ensure the technical system's integrity and the common-pool resource problems:

- In monopolistic competition (competition for the market), which is typical in water distribution and sewerage, all the four essential functions are still integrated into one single operator, but the responsibility for all these functions is transferred to a third party, generally a private actor.
- In access competition, which is typical in electricity, gas, and railways, the ultimate responsibilities for interconnection, interoperability, capacity management, and system management are transferred to the government, generally in the form of a sector-specific regulator.

- In network competition, which is typical for telecommunications, postal services, and air transport, interoperability, capacity management, and system management generally remain with the operators, while the responsibility for interconnection lies with the government, generally in the form of a competition regulator.

Figure 9.1 summarizes this evolution.

However, as these infrastructures evolve from integrated national monopolies to distributed technological networks, the role and responsibilities of government for ensuring the system's integrity and thus for addressing the common-pool resource problems is gradually reduced and replaced by new forms of governance, involving simultaneously the public, the private, and the third sector. This evolution parallels the evolution from national to simultaneously global *and* local infrastructure systems. Figure 9.2 presents this evolution.

It is here where the common-pool resource literature, and especially its focus on third sector/civil society involvement, is particularly relevant. Indeed, common-pool resource theories, especially Ostrom's, stress the fact that there are other solutions than bringing the common-pool resource under a central authority, namely by way of self-governance or "governance by network" (as opposed to governance by government ordering or by the market). However, Ostrom also admits that there must ultimately be some underlying governance rules, which points to the possibility that infrastructures—once simultaneously distributed and systemic beyond the national level—combine self-governance, government ordering, and markets.

Interestingly, we can observe what we call "infrastructure commons" in the third most advanced stage or configuration of infrastructure evolution, namely in telecommunications and postal services in the form of local FTTH (Fiber to the home) common networks, community Wi-Fi networks (Lemstra and Hayes 2009), or self-help city-couriers, for example. All over the world, local communities contribute to the development of these networks, often on a non-profit basis even in regions where "official" providers are absent because of an expected low profitability. While these local networks are still interconnected to the overall infrastructure system, they allow for a certain decoupling of these local systems from the overall systems. Similar evolutions can be found in distributed electricity and distributed public transport. Infrastructure commons therefore point to new and interesting ways to manage common-pool resource problems in large socio-technical systems, in particular ways where civil society self-governance can play a much more active role.

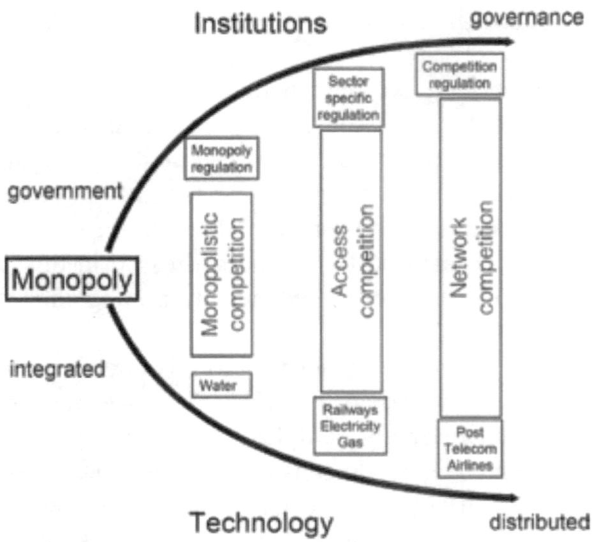

Figure 9.1. Different configurations between institutions and technology in infrastructures.

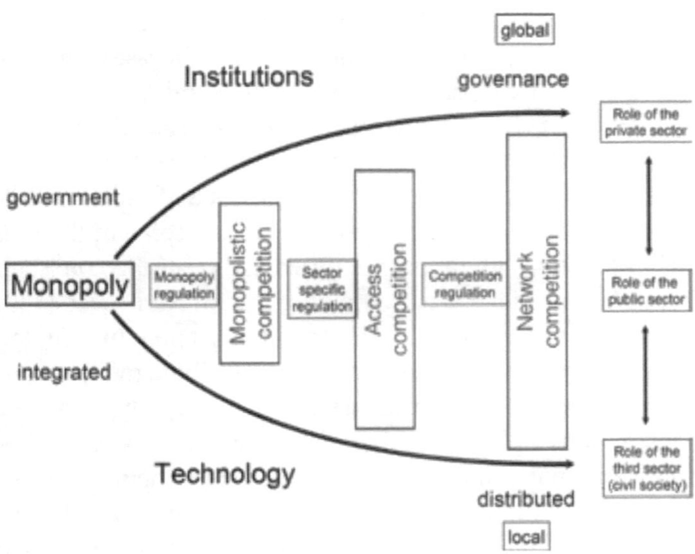

Figure 9.2. Changing roles and responsibilities in infrastructure regulation.

New Insights from the Interpretation of Infrastructures as CPRs?

In the previous sections, we demonstrated that infrastructures can be perceived as common-pool resources. There are distinctive CPR problems related to four essential functions. The modes of organization that are required to mitigate these problems are becoming increasingly complex as a consequence of institutional and technological developments. This brings us to the last question to be addressed in this paper: What new insights can possibly be gained by interpreting infrastructures as common-pool resources?

In this stage of research, the answers to this question are speculative and they certainly need further elaboration. The governance of infrastructures is becoming increasingly complex, both from an institutional and technological perspective, as demonstrated in the fourth section. Traditional approaches of strict governmental regulation, or even public ownership, are not anymore possible under the conditions of sector re-regulation and technological innovation resulting in an even stronger fragmentation of the system. But also the stronger reliance on competition and private sector involvement in liberalized infrastructures does not lead to the expected results. The common-pool characteristics of infrastructures are per definition related to fundamental market failures and market imperfections. Hence, we are confronted with a fundamental problem in which neither governmental intervention nor the markets are able to cope with the newly arising common-pool resource problems in these essential infrastructure sectors.

CPR literature might provide insights into a "third way" of regulating infrastructures next to (or even beyond) markets and governmental involvement. Interesting directions to be explored would be the involvement of local initiatives or communities in the governance of infrastructures. As a consequence of technological innovations, at least some of the four essential technical functions might be monitored and controlled on a subsystem level by locally embedded actors or authorities. What is needed is a much more detailed understanding of the conditions under which individual actors or local communities are prepared to contribute to the sustainability of essential functions of infrastructures. This is not only an issue of "getting the institutions right." Our short overview on the historical development of infrastructures in the fourth section clearly demonstrates that we have to account for the coevolution between institutions and technologies. Hence, certain CPR problems might be mitigated predominantly by technological means, others by regulation, private or third-sector governance, or a combination of both.

It appears that the resolution of CPR problems in infrastructures is an issue in which the coevolution between institutions and technology has to be taken into consideration. This is a novel facet that is not sufficiently recognized in the traditional CPR literature (refer, for instance, to Finger et al. 2005; Künneke 2008). When doing so, we observe that technological evolution—in particular, the growing role of the ICTs (Information and Communication Technologies)—allows for ever more decentralized and distributed technological solution in all infrastructures, which in turn leads to new forms of governance involving no longer exclusively government, but also the private and the third sectors.

Conclusion

In this paper, we explore the significance of common-pool resource problems in infrastructures. We investigate the features of infrastructures that can be interpreted as common-pool resources. Related to four essential functions (system management, capacity management, interconnection, and interoperability), we typify common-pool resource problems in infrastructures. We argue that the mitigation of these CPR problems is typically an issue of institutional and technological change. Since infrastructures are evolving into ever larger, more complex and global systems, the governance of CPR problems seems to shift from vertically integrated firms under strict governmental control towards a form of governance that increasingly involves the market, but that also has the potential to ever more involve the third sector. Indeed, the institutional and technological fragmentation of infrastructures on the one hand and the globalization of the infrastructure networks and business on the other hand, demand new approaches to govern these vital sectors. Interpreting infrastructures as common-pool resources provides insights into a "third way" of governance beyond government regulation based on local initiatives and private sector involvement, sometimes even without strong economic objectives. Further research is necessary into the decentralized governance of common-pool resources in infrastructures.

Notes

This paper was originally presented at the fourth Workshop on the Workshop (WOW4) Conference, Indiana University Bloomington, June 2–7, 2009.

1. Refer, for instance, to the Digital Library of the Commons, 2009 (http://dlc.dlib.indiana.edu/dlc/).

2. Hardin (1968) was a pioneer in this field of research based on his analysis of the tragedy of the commons.

3. Refer, for instance, to De Bruijne and Kars (2007) and Frischmann (2005a,b).

4. An illustrative example is provided by Künneke and Fens (2007).

5. With respect to information network, see, for instance, Noam (1992), who provides a very illustrative example of the different stages of network development.

6. The same holds for socio-ecological systems, which also need to adjust to changing societal needs. For example, some river basins might be traditionally used for fishing and the provision of drinking water, whereas nowadays recreation or marine transport have become more significant.

References

Ciriacy-Wantrup, S. V., and R. C. Bishop. 1975. "'Common Property' as a Concept in Natural Resource Policy." *Natural Resources Journal* 15: 713–23.

De Bruijne, M. L. C., and M. Kars. 2007. *CPR Theory as a Guideline for Capacity Management in Infrastructures? The Cases of Electricity and Mobile Telephony*. Eleventh International Research Symposium on Public Management (IRSPM XI), Potsdam University, Germany, April 2–4, 2007.

Economides, N. 1996. "The Economics of Networks." *International Journal of Industrial Organization* 14: 673–99.

Finger, M., J. P. M. Groenewegen, and R. W. Künneke. 2005. "The Quest for Coherence between Technology and Institutions in Infrastructures." *Journal of Network Industries* 6: 227–59.

Frischmann, B. M. 2005a. "An Economic Theory of Infrastructure and Commons Management." *Minnesota Law Review* 89, 917–1030.

———. 2005b. "Infrastructure Commons." *Michigan State Law Review* 89: 121–36.

Geels, F. W., and J. Schot. 2007. "Typology of Sociotechnical Transition Pathways." *Research Policy* 36: 399–417.

Hardin, G. 1968. "The Tragedy of the Commons." *Science* 162: 1243–48.

Kroes, P., M. Franssen, I. van de Poel, and M. Ottens. 2006. "Treating Socio-Technical Systems as Engineering Systems: Some Conceptual Problems." *Systems Research and Behavioral Science* 23: 803–14.

Künneke, R. W. 2008. "Institutional Reform and Technological Practice: The Case of Electricity." *Industrial and Corporate Change* 17: 233–65.

Künneke, R. W., and T. Fens. 2007. "Ownership Unbundling in Electricity Distribution: The Case of The Netherlands." *Energy Policy* 35: 1920–30.

Lemstra, W., and V. Hayes. 2009. "License-Exempt: Wi-Fi Complement to 3G." *Telematics and Informatics* 26: 227–39.

Nelson, R. R. 1995. "Co-Evolution of Industry Structure, Technology and Supporting Institutions, and the Making of Comparative Advantage." *International Journal of the Economics of Business* 2: 171–84.

Noam, E. M. 1992. "A Theory for the Instability of Public Telecommunication Systems." In *The Economics of Information Networks*, edited by C. Antonelli, 107–27. Amsterdam: North Holland.

Ostrom, E. 1990. *Governing the Commons: The Evolution of Institutions for Collective Action.* New York: Cambridge University Press.

Perez, C. 2002. *Technological Revolutions and Financial Capital: The Dynamics of Bubbles and Golden Ages.* Cheltenham, UK: Edward Elgar.

Ten Heuvelhof, E. F., M. Kuit, H. D. Stout, and J. Bauer. 2003. "Capacity Management in Infrastructure Sectors: Lessons from the Dutch Experience." In *Critical Infrastructures: State of the Art in Research and Application*, edited by Wil A. H. Thissen and Paulien M. Herder, 265–80. London: Kluwer Academics.

Tushman, M. L., and L. Rosenkopf. 1992. "Organizational Determinants of Technological Change: Towards a Sociology of Technological Evolution." *Research in Organizational Behavior* 14: 311–47.

Van de Poel, I. 2003. "The Transformation of Technological Regimes." *Research Policy* 32: 49–68.

Von Tunzelmann, N. 2003. "Historical Coevolution of Governance and Technology in the Industrial Revolutions." *Structural Change and Economic Dynamics* 14: 365–84.

10

The Science Commons in Health Research: Structure, Function, and Value

ROBERT COOK-DEEGAN

When Robert Merton wrote about the sociology of science in the 1970s, the central task at hand was explaining how a set of social norms and practices yielded knowledge—what was different about science compared to the humanities and the professions (Merton 1973). John Ziman and others addressed what makes the methods of science produce "reliable knowledge" (Ziman 1978). This paper addresses a related, but somewhat different aspect of science—how reliable knowledge can be turned into social benefit, using genomics as a case in point. The value of a science commons—a pool of knowledge that is widely available at little or no cost—is the central focus. The zone of intersection between reliable knowledge and useful knowledge falls squarely into what the late Donald Stokes described as "Pasteur's Quadrant" (1997), where research results both contribute insight into the workings of nature and at the same time find practical application.

The value of having knowledge widely and freely (or almost freely) available is particularly salient in Pasteur's Quadrant. Knowledge is more likely to advance, and to be applied, if it is available at little or no expense to a broad array of scientists and innovators. These features of network efficiency are well known in software and other fields characterized by widely distributed cumulative innovation under mantras such as "to many eyes, every bug is shallow," and theoretically described by Benckler (2002).

I shamelessly steal the term "science commons" from the new organization of that name that has spun out of the Creative Commons movement. Science Commons is dedicated to "making it easier for scientists, universities, and industries to use literature, data, and other scientific intellectual property and to share their knowledge with others. Science Commons works within current copyright and patent law to promote legal and technical mechanisms that remove barriers to sharing" (Science Commons 2005). (While I endorse their mission, they may not endorse my agenda or analysis. I have no direct connection to the organization, and do not speak for it.)

The main approach in what follows is historical, using background on how the science commons functioned in genomics to illustrate the role of a commons in general. Genomics will be the main topic, occasionally straying into collateral fields of biomedical research such as bioinformatics or molecular and cellular biology when they provide better examples.

There is some fuzziness around the edges of what constitutes a science commons, and how it relates to "the public domain." There can be variants of many terms marching under the banner of open science or public research. "Open access," for example, can mean free access to view information, but not necessarily freedom to use it in all ways without restriction. The information in patents, for example, is openly available, but users may need to get permission or pay fees to use a patented invention (including some basic methods used in science). To some, open science means no one can fence it in. Access to information, say through "viral" licensing or copyleft, may be conditioned on agreeing not to restrict subsequent users. Information may also simply be put into the public domain for any and all subsequent uses, by deposit at a freely available public database, for example. I focus on this last meaning, with information available to all at low or no cost. But again, this may not mean completely unfettered use, as sequence information in GenBank may be covered by patent claims. Jensen and Murray, for example, noted that more than 4,000 human DNA sequences are subject to claims in US patents (Jensen and Murray 2005). Sometimes there are restrictions on use of information and materials in the science commons, but those restrictions must also impose low or no costs to subsequent users, or else that information has left the science commons (e.g., through subsequent patenting, copyright, or database protection). There is no bright line dividing the science commons from proprietary R&D, and indeed in the case of some sequences, materials, and methods in molecular biology, the expense associated with use of genomic information may depend more on licensing terms and practices than what is or is not patented—and one person's "reasonable terms" may be out of reach for some users.

The world of genomics is not a simple world. Some of the data shown below, for example, are drawn from a free public database, the DNA Patent Database at Georgetown University (DNA Patent Database 2005).

That database is, in turn, drawn from the freely available US Patent and Trademark Database (USPTO Database 2005). But the search engine and database used to generate the DNA Patent Database are derived from an intermediate subscription database that is not widely or freely available, but available to subscribers at several thousand dollars a year, through the Delphion patent database (Delphion Database 2005). Duke pays a subscription to The Thomson Corporation for its use. This is a major tool for our research, and for us the subscription cost is balanced by ease of use and reliability. We pay for Delphion for its special features (such as corporate trees that track ownership of patents) and because its search results have proven more reliable than several alternatives, including the USPTO's own computers and software available in northern Virginia. We are happy to pay for a proprietary database because it helps us do our work and the price is reasonable, within reach of our nonprofit institution. Delphion does not restrict our use, and does not prevent our creating a free public database. I raise the example of a pay-for-use database sandwiched between two public resource databases to hint that the story will get complicated, and to signal early that this is not a diatribe against for-profit intrusions into research. This is important because many of the points that come out later will seem unfriendly to purveyors of databases. Those objections are not deep-seated rejections of capitalism in science, but rather pragmatic judgments about adverse effects of particular policies.

Innovation is exquisitely sensitive to policies of many kinds. Innovation depends on how much information is produced as well as how widely and easily it is shared. Funding of R&D is a major determinant of how much research is conducted, and thereby how much information is created. Policies governing the science commons—or alternative, more restricted informational spaces—determine how widely and quickly information and materials are distributed. My purpose here is to highlight why the science commons matters. Some reasons are obvious, but some are not so obvious, and some are even counterintuitive. One final conceptual point will be helpful to flag before proceeding into the narrative. There is extensive overlap between "academic health research" and the science commons in molecular biology. Academic science is important in many fields, not just the life sciences. In all lines of scientific and technical work, universities and nonprofit research institutions and government laboratories ("academic research institutions") play key roles. Everyone is trained in academe, not just academic scientists, but also those working in industry. And within industry, academic training is not just for those doing R&D, but also managers and professionals. Academe is also one place where the norms of Mertonian science have real traction, where the norms of openness, community, mutual criticism, and fair allocation of credit are supposed to be respected, at least as an ideal. In some circumstances, however, academic science is done under strictures of secrecy, or results are made available only at great cost or encumbered by restrictions on use. Such academic science is not part of a science commons. Great science goes on in industry, including or even particularly in the life sciences, but no one expects the norms of openness to prevail in industrial R&D, even if in some circumstances at some times scientists in companies publish in the open literature, present their findings at open scientific conferences, make materials freely available, and contribute data to public databases. When industrial R&D is widely shared openly, results flowing from industrial R&D can become part of the science commons, and there are several instances of this in the stories to follow. In sum, most academic research contributes to the science commons, and some industrial R&D also does so. Most industrial R&D is proprietary, as is some academic research.

The science commons thus does not reduce to academic research. It remains true nonetheless, that most of the science commons—at least in the life sciences—is based on academic research funded by government and nonprofit organizations, and most academic research probably enlarges the science commons, although to my knowledge no one has quantitatively assessed what fraction of the research funded by government and nonprofit organizations remains in the science commons. Policies put in place over the past three decades have raised concerns about how big the science commons will be, and in particular, whether and to what degree government and nonprofit funders and academic research institutions will maintain it. Richard Nelson of Columbia University, in particular, has expressed concerns about intrusions on open science, based on his decades of studying the innovation process as an economist (Nelson 2006).

Genomics: Public and Private Science in a Fishbowl

Genomics became the grounds for a vigorous, sometimes even vicious, fight over what should or should not be in the public domain, and under what conditions. Many of the fights were over preserving the science commons. How much genomic data should be in the science commons has been a matter of explicit policy-making in government, nonprofits, academic institutions, and private firms since 1992 or 1993, when the commercial promise of genomics became apparent, and private funding for genomics in for-profit companies began to accelerate.

Several features of genomics make it an interesting field to study as an instance of the science commons. It is clearly derived from a scientific project that was initially conceived as a public works project—to construct maps and derive a reference sequence of the human genome and other genomes. The original intent of the Human Genome Project was to produce information and tools to make that information useful and valuable. Some commercial uses were foreseen from the beginning, but the main focus was on producing public data of permanent scientific value.

The genome revolution began in the mid-1980s. It caught a wave of enthusiasm for "the new biotechnology" that had become both scientifically hot and also a darling on Wall Street. Cetus was founded in 1971 and turned to recombinant DNA techniques soon after they were discovered (Stanley Cohen, co-inventor of recombinant DNA, joined the Cetus Board in 1975). Genentech was founded in 1976. Those companies went public with high-profile stock offerings in 1980 and 1981, raising sums that startled the markets (Smith Hughes 2001).

The origins of the Human Genome Project were not in commercial biotechnology, however, but in publicly funded science. The ideas behind the Human Genome Project began to appear in 1985, while the embers of biotechnology were still warm but too distant from this particular part of molecular biology to catch fire. (And not for want of trying. Walter Gilbert tried to start Genome Corp. in 1987, for example, and had to resign from a National Research Council study as a consequence.) Scientists conceived a grand idea and focused on the scientific value of having a reference human genomic sequence (Cook-Deegan 1994).[1] Commercial interest lagged for several years, until in 1991 a conflict over patenting short sequence tags derived from human genes blew up into a major controversy, and created commercial interest in human genomic sequencing.

J. Craig Venter, a scientist in NIH's intramural (government laboratory) research program, started using automated DNA sequencing machines to rapidly identify sequences unique to human genes. A Genentech lawyer, Max Hensley, contacted the NIH technology licensing lawyer, Reid Adler, who in turn contacted Venter about filing a patent application on his method and the resulting DNA sequences. The method was eventually given over to the public domain through a statutory registration of invention, but the patent application for the sequences themselves continued through the patent examination process. That 1991 patent application generated tremendous controversy until 1994, when NIH Director Harold

Varmus decided to abandon the patents, following the advice of patent scholars Rebecca Eisenberg and Robert Merges (1995).

The controversy at NIH paradoxically induced interest in commercial biotechnology circles. In 1991 and 1992, noise over "Darth Venter's" turn to the dark side (by patenting DNA sequences from gene fragments) attracted the attention of scientist Randall Scott at Incyte in California, and Incyte began to focus on DNA sequencing of human genes. Through 1994, several other companies—including Human Genome Sciences, Mercator Genetics, Genset, Myriad Genetics, Millennium Pharmaceuticals, Genome Therapeutics (renamed from Collaborate Research), Hyseq, and Sequenom—were formed around the idea of mapping and/or the sequencing the human genome, or turned from other pursuits to those ends.

One company illustrates the public-science origins of private genomics in particular: Human Genome Sciences. Wallace Steinberg, a former Johnson & Johnson executive who had started several biotech companies after leaving J&J, decided to meet Venter, having read about him amidst the patenting controversy. He talked Venter into leaving NIH to form a non-profit research unit, eventually named The Institute for Genomic Research (TIGR), by promising Venter $70 million ($85 million by the time the deal was done) (Cook-Deegan 1994). That was enough to build a larger sequencing and sequence-analysis facility than existed anywhere else at the time. Human Genome Sciences Inc. (HGSI) was formed as a for-profit corporation that would own the patent rights to TIGR's results as well as pursuing its own research leads. There were also plans to form additional companies, Industrial Genome Sciences and Plant Genome Sciences, to exploit different opportunities deriving from high-throughput sequencing and other genomic technologies. Steinberg tapped William Haseltine to become chief executive at HGSI. Haseltine had been involved in several previous Steinberg startup firms. Haseltine also had his roots in academic science, most notably from his work on HIV/AIDS at Harvard.

Genomics startups were a subgroup of biotech startups. The first boomlet in genomics startups in the early 1990s paralleled a significant increase in pharmaceutical R&D among established pharma and biotech firms that started in the early 1980s. The 1980s marked an intensification of competition among pharma companies based on R&D. A pharmaceutical R&D arms race of sorts began in the early 1980s, and during that decade, firms delved ever more deeply into molecular and cellular biology to bolster their "absorptive capacity" for drug discovery (Cockburn and Henderson 1998; Fabrizio 2005, unpublished data), recognizing the importance of rapid and effective use of public domain science to their business plans. Not all companies did this with equal success. Indeed, their ability to tap public science was one of the indicators of firms' success in pharmaceuticals (Fabrizio 2004).

By historical happenstance, this birth of genomics out of publicly funded science took place as patent rights were being expanded and strengthened, by a combination of changes in legislation, in court decisions, and in patent offices. In academia, the major change was the Bayh-Dole Act of 1980, which gave grantees and contractors rights—and indeed a mandate—to seek patents on federally funded research results. Mowery and his coauthors review this history and some of its consequences in their book, *Ivory Tower and Industrial Innovation*, which combines economic empiricism, historical research, and policy analysis (Mowery et al. 2004).

Genomics, because of its timing as well as its commercial relevance—foreseeable to some immediately, to others a few years after its launch—took root as a field in American academe under the new Bayh-Dole regime. Academic institutions began to patent much more frequently after 1980, and genomics is one of the areas where this effect was pronounced. Moreover, patent rights were being expanded and strengthened in many areas of American law, including biotechnology. The Court of Appeals for the Federal Circuit (CAFC) was formed in 1982. It was designed to handle appeals of certain cases, including appeals of federal district court decisions about patent litigation. The CAFC quickly established itself as a generally pro-patent court. It and the patent office expanded the kinds of inventions that could be patented (including software and business methods, for example) and tended to strengthen the hand of patent-holders relative to those contesting patent rights (Jaffe and Lerner 2005). In the hands of the CAFC, more territory could be enclosed and patent fences generally got higher. These developments had a particularly strong impact on areas of rapid innovation, including both "wet lab" biotechnology and bioinformatics, fields directly relevant to genomics.

Three other factors are not related to changes in policy, but nonetheless make genomics a useful field to study for this policy history: (1) the story was compressed into a decade, so its narrative is shorter and crisper; (2) there was intense media coverage, producing an ample public record of events; and (3) the patentable inventions arising from genomics can be tracked because it is possible to identify relevant patents. Patents resulting from genomics R&D almost always make patent claims that use terms distinctive to DNA and RNA, which can be used to create a searchable patent database mapping to genomics research.[2]

Work Enabled by a Science Commons

A science commons can supply information needed to achieve social benefit that for-profit markets in goods and services may fail to achieve. Moreover, even in markets well served by the profit motive, a science commons can in some circumstances improve efficiency, when many disparate firms can draw on a common pool of knowledge and data, rather than having to construct the same information firm-by-firm at substantial cost because of duplication. One theoretical rationale for this effect has been set forth by Benkler (2002). The cases arising in genomics suggest that network theory may have some practical applications in the real world of science and its application. I will illustrate three social goals that can benefit from a robust scientific commons in genomics: advancing science, improving public health, and creating a shared foundation for productively diverse forms of industrial R&D and commercialization. But first, some historical background.

Public and Private Genomics in Mortal Combat

The beginning of the Human Genome Project was marked by conflict between scientists who thought it was a poor use of resources versus those who thought it was a useful and efficient way to spend public research dollars. By broadening the project to include maps, tools, and organisms in addition to the human, most scientists came around to support the Project. A 1988 report of the National Research Council reported that consensus (National Research Council 1988). That did not eliminate all conflict, however, because the question of which federal agency should play the larger role remained unresolved, and both the National Institutes of Health and the Department of Energy assumed active roles, in a roughly 2–1 ratio of funding. And even as the rival agencies in the United States settled into a generally amicable cooperative framework, other nations began to engage in genomics R&D.

The 1991 controversy over gene-tagging sequences erupted while the Genome Project was getting underway. As that controversy died down, an even more public conflict over sequencing the entire genome exploded in 1998, pitting a private company against the public sector genome project. The battleground for both these two conflicts was the science commons.

TIGR and HGSI were formed in 1992. The heads of the two private organizations, Venter (TIGR) and Haseltine (HGSI), never sang close harmony, despite their supposed corporate matrimony. As TIGR moved away from human gene sequencing and into microbial sequencing, including proof of principle that whole-genome shotgun sequencing could work, the noise from the TIGR-HGSI conflict got downright cacophonous. TIGR's scientific interests hardly coincided with what HGSI would want from its R&D partner, and two alpha-males confined in close corporate space found themselves in frequent conflict. In 1997, TIGR and HGSI severed their ties, with TIGR foregoing rights to future payments and HGSI foregoing rights to future TIGR discoveries (TIGR 1997). It was a divorce made in heaven.

Venter became a free agent, heading up a free-standing nonprofit research institute, until Michael Hunkapiller of Applied Biosystems approached him with another Big Idea (Shreeve 2004). In discussions with its parent company (then Perkin-Elmer Cetus, which became Applera), Applied Biosystems had begun to think seriously about sequencing the human genome with private funds. It would be a high-profile use of a promising new DNA sequencing instrument that was much faster and more scalable than existing sequencers. The question was whether the methods TIGR had used on smaller genomes, such as bacteria, could work on the human genome, and produce a final sequence faster than the public genome project. If so, a company could charge both for access to the data, and for access to informatic tools to mine the data. In order to charge users, the company would need a truly impressive bioinformatic capacity, and great tools for analyzing sequence data. If a private company decided to sequence the genome, it might even kick up a market for sequencing instruments, including Applied Biosystems machines, among the publicly funded laboratories doing DNA sequencing, who would buy the same machines to compete with the new genomic sequencing company.

In May 1998, Craig Venter became the head of a company, later named Celera Genomics, which would carry out the sequencing and pull together the computing infrastructure to assemble it into a reference sequence, and then begin to interpret the sequence information. Celera's 1998 establishment inaugurated another boom in genomics startups, this one entailing many more companies and much more money than the 1992–1994 boomlet.

The "private genome project" idea gathered steam and was announced through a sophisticated media roll-out strategy. The initial kernel of the media snowball was an exclusive to Nicholas Wade of the *New York Times* in May 1998 (Wade 1998). Thus began a privately financed scientific effort at Celera running into the hundreds of millions of dollars that competed head to head with the publicly financed Human Genome Project. The drama played out over three years and became the biggest story in science, and one of the most visible general interest stories of its period.

The story is often told as a race competition between Venter at Celera and the public Human Genome Project whose most conspicuous spokesmen were Francis Collins in the United States and Sir John Sulston in the United Kingdom. Collins was director of the National Human Genome Research Institute at NIH, and Sulston directed the Sanger Institute affiliated with the University of Cambridge and funded mainly by the Wellcome Trust of London (with additional funding from the UK Medical Research Council). The usual narrative strategy was to use the metaphor of a race, but in fact there were not just two human genome projects running in parallel, there were many.

A consortium of laboratories funded by government agencies and nonprofit organizations in North America, Europe, and Japan constituted the "public genome project." Sulston emerged as the champion of that faction, emphasizing open science, rapid sharing of data and materials, and a passionate appeal to refrain from patenting bits of the human genome except when they could foreseeably induce investment in developing end-products such as therapeutic proteins. Sulston was the leader and rhetorical warrior for Open Science.

Sulston's model for the Human Genome Project was the biology of the worm (Ankeny 2001)—a close-knit community of scientists who studied nematodes, and had made immense scientific progress in a hub-and-spoke model of biology. Two central laboratories—one at the University of Cambridge and another at Washington University in Saint Louis—did high-tech, whiz-bang, expensive mapping and sequencing projects on the worm genome. Those hubs shared data quickly and widely with the spokes—a vibrant network of smaller laboratories throughout the world. Sulston wrote *The Common Thread* with Georgina Ferry to tell the genome story from his point of view (Sulston and Ferry 2002). His was the public works model of genomics, with public funding producing a valuable scientific resource.

The Wellcome Trust was the crucial nonprofit funder that supported this open science model. Michael Morgan from Wellcome Trust believed fervently in open science, and wanted the "public" genome project to succeed. The Sanger Institute was the Trust's foremost research institution, and John Sulston its most visible scientist. NIH and Francis Collins, as a government organization and employee, respectively, had to be more cautious in their rhetoric—and were, most of the time.

The Wellcome Trust sponsored a Bermuda meeting of the major sequencing centers throughout the world in 1996 (despite the exotic sound of it, the weather was miserable, it was off-season, and the site was chosen deliberately to be neutral, not in the USA or Europe). One theme of the meeting was how to make sequence data widely available, modeled on the worm science world. A set of "Bermuda Rules" emerged from the meeting, mandating daily disclosure of DNA sequence data. The pledge to rapidly share data was linked to a plea not to patent DNA, unless a gene or DNA sequence had been studied further to show its function or practical utility. That kind of functional biology was not the business of the publicly funded DNA sequencing centers, so it was in effect a "no patents" policy for the sequencing centers. Venter was present at the beginning of the Bermuda meeting, in his pre-Celera days as head of TIGR, but fittingly he left early and was gone by the time the Bermuda Rules were agreed. This left him room to later repudiate them.

The Wellcome Trust played another important role in 1998, soon after Venter announced his intention to sequence the genome at a new startup company. Wellcome reacted to the announcement of the new company by proposing to do a faster, better public genome sequence by increasing its commitment to fund genomic sequencing through the public project. Wellcome's move, in turn, bolstered funding from the US government, UK government, and other government and nonprofit funders of the public genome project.

In addition to the upstart startup Celera and the public genome project, the private firms HGSI and Incyte were in effect conducting a different kind of genome project in parallel—call it a Human Genes Project. Their strategy centered on human *gene* sequences—DNA coding for protein products. Both companies had been sequencing genes for 5–6 years before Celera was even formed, and had been sending in patent applications the whole time. Incyte worked with a group of pharmaceutical company subscribers. HGSI had one main client—SmithKline Beecham (which later merged with Glaxo Wellcome to become Glaxo SmithKline).

The business strategies of Incyte and HGSI were both initially based on sequencing human genes. Their styles were quite different, however. Randall Scott at Incyte was part of a scientific network with many links to the public genome project. Indeed, at times Incyte was contemplated as a partner in the public project (Shreeve 2004). HGSI had some academic and industrial collaborations beyond SmithKline Beecham, but far fewer than Incyte. And Haseltine's relation to the public genome project was as an outsider. Scott of Incyte was in the public genome family, or at least ate some meals with them; Haseltine was never welcome at the table.

Haseltine reinforced his role as troublemaker for the public genome project when he wrote a 1998 editorial to the *New York Times* arguing Congress should pull the plug on the public project because it was already being done "without tax money" by his company and others (Haseltine 1998). Haseltine argued government funds for DNA sequencing would be better spent on smaller projects in individual laboratories to understand gene sequences. There were two problems with this argument. First, it assumed almost all the value of sequencing came from gene sequences, whereas molecular genetics has become focused on many regulatory processes that happen at the RNA and DNA level and are never translated into protein. It seems a safe bet that a lot of biology would never be approachable if we only got protein-coding sequences. Haseltine is an excellent scientist and knew this full well, although for commercial purposes, he could certainly make a good case that the most rapid returns were likely to come from coding sequences. This argument conflated commercial value with scientific value, but as an argument about public support for science, it is simply wrong, as the complexity of gene regulation is becoming obvious, and the importance of DNA sequences in addition to protein-coding regions is becoming apparent. Gene-based strategies made eminently good sense when hunting for drug targets, because drugs are designed to interact with proteins that are secreted outside of cells, that bind DNA, or that extend outward from the surface of cells. But as a tool to understand biology, the entire sequence was a much more powerful tool than just protein-coding regions.

The even deeper flaw in Haseltine's argument was about access to genomic information. Here he crossed the line from perhaps inadvertently disingenuous to deliberately misleading. The fact that genes were being sequenced by companies did no one but those companies any good if the sequences were not public. Academic scientists could, of course, approach HGSI or Incyte or other companies to collaborate, getting access to their data, but relatively few did so. The reason was that such collaboration came with strings—or ropes, or even cables. The constraints were patent rights—that is, exclusive property rights that were routinely being granted for full-length genes by the US Patent and Trademark Office. Collaboration with HGSI or Incyte meant nondisclosure agreements, publication review, and rights on resulting intellectual property. Sometimes this made sense, but it was not terribly attractive for those mainly interested in advancing science. A central condition of collaboration was control of information and constraints on open sharing of data. It made sense in a business context, but as a public works project in science, it made none. And to argue that proprietary gene sequencing was a substitute for public funding of genomic sequencing was ridiculous. Scientists could of course wait for patents to issue from privately sequenced genes, but that was not really a practical option because of the many-year delay. Perhaps scientists could hope HGSI and Incyte would publish the sequences voluntarily someday, but the companies would do that only when patents issued, or if it suited their business needs. The companies did publish, but only very selectively. To academic scientists in the field, waiting for companies to do the work would be surrendering to the competition in any event.

Pharmaceutical companies working with the Incyte and HGSI played from power—money and the ability to generate the data themselves if need be with their huge R&D war chests. Small academic laboratories were on the other end of the power curve, with relatively little leverage. Academic laboratories had a much better alternative, to scan the public GenBank for genes of interest, at no cost and with no strings attached. GenBank and other databases received sequences from thousands of laboratories throughout the world, as well as (eventually) the output of major DNA sequencing centers. Incyte and HGSI drew regularly on GenBank data, but company gene sequence data made their way back to public sequence databases only when a patent issued, or if the company chose to publish an article in the scientific literature.[3] In effect, company projects built on the foundation laid by the public genome project and drew regularly upon its data, but only occasionally contributed data back to public databases. This was sensible business practice, but it was misleading for Haseltine to imply that leaving the genome projects to companies and small laboratories would produce a genome project with the desired features of the concerted public project.

One forthright way to make Haseltine's case would have been to indeed allow the private gene sequencing firms to proceed, but for the government and nonprofit funders to pay to make the data public. There are two reasons Haseltine may have chosen not to take his arguments to this logical conclusion. First, the offer would likely have been refused by the companies, because their business plan was precisely to keep sequence data proprietary until they could be patented. Government procurement of the data would have vitiated this business plan, and turned the companies into contractors. The second reason was price. It would have been embarrassingly high, and certainly would have undercut the argument the work could be done "with no tax dollars." But pushed to its conclusion, Haseltine's line of argument could have made a clean case—it might have made sense for the government to buy this particular genomic real estate and dedicate it to the science commons, if the private sector could produce the data faster and cheaper. Haseltine started from the premise that human gene sequence data were valuable—and who could argue with that?

From 1998 until February 2001, when *Nature* and *Science* published rival articles containing draft reference sequences of the human genome prepared by the public genome project (Lander et al. 2001) and by Celera (Venter et al. 2001), there were in effect two competing projects focused on sequencing the entire human genome, and in parallel also several other "genome projects" focused on expressed sequences and bits and pieces of the genome of interest to research communities in both public and private sectors. In addition to the two companies sequencing human genes, many other companies were mapping and sequencing parts of the human genome. And thousands of laboratories were contributing sequencing and mapping information to databases and to scientific publications. By the time the initial genomic sequence publications came out, the ratio of private to public funding appeared to be roughly two private dollars for every one government or nonprofit dollar (see Figure 10.1).[4]

In 2001, the financial genome bubble burst. At the end of 2000, 74 publicly traded firms were valued at $94 billion, of which the largest 15 accounted for approximately $50 billion. By the end of 2002, those 15 firms' market value had dropped to $10 billion, but their reported R&D expenditures nonetheless climbed from $1 to $1.7 billion (Kaufman, Johnson, and Cook-Deegan 2004, unpublished data).

These data make three simple points: First, the private sector has invested heavily in genomics, but those investments are made in expectation of financial return. That is quite different from the public and nonprofit funding of genomics, which is mainly intended to produce public goods—knowledge and materials that are widely available to advance knowledge and combat disease. Second, private R&D investment is a powerful complement to the public and nonprofit funding. Private R&D follows public R&D in time, it draws on the science commons but does not necessarily contribute back to it. If successful, private R&D investment can create wealth and jobs as well as the social benefit from developing goods and services that would otherwise not be produced. This benefit is real, but it is distinct from the social value of the science commons.

Genomics also provides several examples of private funding to augment the science commons, such as the SNP Consortium, and the Merck funding to Washington University to fund gene sequencing (Cook-Deegan and McCormack 2001). And third, and most to the point for policy purposes, it would be foolhardy to generalize from the happy circumstances when private R&D expands the science commons—to expect private R&D to substitute for the science commons except in unusual circumstances, usually related to the grounds of competition among firms in a

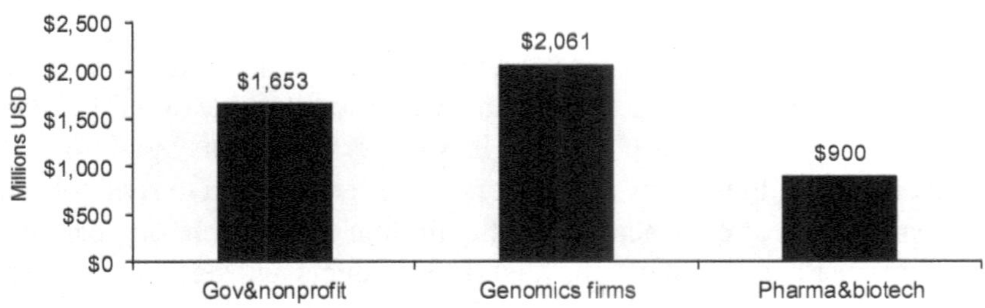

Figure 10.1. Genomics research funding, 2000.

Source: World Survey of Funding for Genomics Research, Stanford University, 2001 (unpublished data from Robert Cook-Deegan, Amber Johnson, and Carmie Chan, Stanford-in-Washington Program, based on a survey of over 200 funders).

particular industrial sector. Private industrial R&D will sometimes find it useful to contribute to the science commons, but expecting industry to do so always and consistently would be foolhardy.

Applications in Public Health: When Markets Fail

To see why having a healthy science commons matters, we move away from genomics to make a general point about health research. Murphy and Topel estimated that the gains in life expectancy from medical research 1970 to 1990 were staggering—in the range of $2.8 trillion per year ($1.5 trillion of this from cardiovascular disease reduction alone) (Murphy and Topel 1999). Many of the health benefits of discovering new information about health and disease come not from drugs or vaccines or medical services, but from individuals acting on information. Cutler and Kadiyala attributed 2/3 of the health gains in cardiovascular disease reduction to effects of "public information," such as stopping or reducing tobacco use, changing diet, getting more exercise, or monitoring one's blood pressure. The second largest determinant was technological change, such as introduction of new drugs and services, followed by increasing cigarette taxes to reduce tobacco use (Cutler and Kadiyala 2001). The estimated return on investment in medical treatment was 4–1, but on the "public information" it was 30–1.

Cutler and Kadiyala's result cannot be generalized, because smoking is a very large risk factor that is *sui generis*, and cardiovascular disease has proven far more malleable to many kinds of interventions than nonlung cancer and other chronic diseases. The path from scientific understanding of cause to prevention of cancer, diabetes, arthritis, and Alzheimer's disease, among others, appears far less linear, and so the value of public information about risk is correspondingly less powerful and has less impact on health outcomes. Few if any risk factors will ever be found to rival tobacco use as predictors of poor health. But the finding that information can have value irrespective of being translated into products and services in a paying market is nonetheless important. Even if public information will not be quite as powerful in reducing other chronic diseases as it has been for cardiovascular disease, the vector is likely to point in the same direction. We cannot say that public information will always prove more powerful than information channeled into new drugs, vaccines, biologics, devices, and medical services sold for profit in the health care system. Where there are public health benefits from public research results, however—and the probability there will be no such public health effects of genomics seems vanishingly small—the health science commons is essential, because it alone can supply the public information benefits. Both words in "public information" do a lot of work. We need new information that arises from science, but to capture social benefits based on that knowledge itself, we also need it to be public.

Genomics provides several other examples of how public information is valuable. The 2002 report from the World Health Organization, *Genomics and World Health* gave the example of fosmidomycin (Advisory Committee on Health Research 2002). This drug is currently being tested to treat malaria in Africa (Missinou et al. 2002). That use came to light as a consequence of sequencing the genome of the malaria parasite, and noticing a metabolic pathway not previously known to exist. The compound fosmidomycin was known to inhibit the pathway, and had been developed as a treatment for urinary tract infections. When the new possible use to treat malaria was revealed, fosmidomycin was pulled off the shelf and moved into clinical trials against malaria. This is a treatment that may never turn a profit for any company, but the social returns could be enormous if fosmidomycin works, because so many millions of people are infected with malaria. If not fosmidomycin, then perhaps other findings will lead to prevention or treatment of malaria, enabled by now having the full genomic sequence available for host, pathogen, and mosquito vector (Gardner et al. 2002; Holt et al. 2002). Making the information about these organisms available worldwide is essential to accruing the benefits of research. There is only a weak world market for drugs to treat malaria because it is largely an affliction in resource-poor populations. The usual profit motives of the intellectual property system cannot create incentives where there is no prospect of profit to pull products through an expensive discovery and testing process. But networks of nonprofit organizations, such as the Malaria Vaccine Initiative, the Global Fund, the WHO essential medicines program, and other sources of "public" capital might nonetheless be capable of discovering and developing new treatments despite the unlikely prospect of commercial profit.[5] In theory, public funds might induce a sufficient incentive to motivate profit-driven investments for diseases of poor people living in poor countries, but it is not true now, and betting that money will be found could prove wrong. Having a scientific commons with information relevant to vaccines and treatments at least offers an alternative pathway. Many of the scientists most motivated to study such diseases work in resource-poor countries; they do not have rich resources, but they do have strong motivation, as well as computers and access to public databases.

Another case example is SARS. Strains of the coronavirus that causes SARS were identified and sequenced within a month by at least three laboratories in Asia, Canada, and the United States. That sequence information was shared widely, and a "chip" to detect the virus was available for research and possible clinical use just a few months later. Making progress with such alacrity requires strong norms of open science, with obvious social benefit.[6]

Many of the infectious diseases that plague mankind have long eluded measures to combat them. In many cases, this is because they are difficult to grow in tissue culture, and therefore research progress is slow. With new technology, the genomes of hundreds of "nasty bugs" have been fully sequenced, giving scientists an entirely new tool to develop drugs, vaccines, and control measures. It is far from clear that this will tilt the battle decisively in favor of humans over schistosomes, trypanosomes, plasmodia, bacteria, viruses, and other organisms that maim and kill humans by the billions, but it is a new line of attack. In the case of organisms on the Select Agent list of "bioterror" bugs, there is now extensive research underway to develop preventive and treatment measures. For most infectious agents that afflict those in the poorest parts of the world, however, the prospect of profit will not create a demand-pull for innovation that could improve billions of human lives, unless indirect incentives such as prizes or guaranteed payments for effective remedies by third parties serve as surrogates for paying markets.

Unlike the "public information" case described above, however, here the market failure has a different cause. It is not due to the fact that the research results are "public goods," but because the potential users are deeply impoverished, and the economic incentives for drug development in advanced economies do not prevail. The failure here is one of profound inequality and distributive injustice. Nongovernment organizations around the globe, including major funders such as the Gates Foundation, the TB Alliance, the Global Fund, and others, are attempting to use philanthropy, government funding, and creative networking to address this form of market failure. Their efforts depend critically on access to scientific and technical information at low or no cost. Success on this front thus depends critically on the health of the scientific commons.

Another likely use of genomic information will be newborn screening, as more diseases are characterized, linked to possible intervention, and incorporated into routine testing. This must be done with care to avoid harms and false positives, but as knowledge accumulates, the list of conditions that can be treated will lengthen, and costs of testing should drop. Any benefits from newborn screening are unlikely to arise from strong profit motives, however, as most testing is done by state-funded laboratories in the United States and government public health programs in most other countries. The dollar amounts are small. [Two-thirds of US states spent between $20 and $40 per infant for all screening in 2002, and no state spent more than $61 (US General Accounting Office 2003)]. This is far less than most single genetic tests, or even routine medical laboratory tests. Newborn screening is now, and will likely continue to be, a public health service (Newborn Screening Steering Committee 2005). Any shift to DNA-based testing, or addition of tests beyond the current testing regimes, will face very serious cost constraints, and advances are unlikely to result from prospect of ample profits in this market.

Public Inputs to Private Science

Even if we were to stipulate that the "public information" impact of health research might be less important in the future than it has been in the past, does it diminish the role and importance of the science commons? In this section, the focus is not on social benefits foregone for lack of a robust commons. Instead, the argument shifts to efficiency gains to private R&D that follow from being able to draw upon the commons.

Several lines of research corroborate the intuition that a pool of public information and materials must surely "raise all ships" to the benefit of each. The case is likely to be stronger in health research than in other lines of research, just because of the well-known deep mutualism between public and private R&D in health research.

The late Edwin Mansfield's surveys of industrial leaders clearly showed that executives in firms believed their lines of business-related R&D depended on academic research, and pharmaceuticals to a greater degree than any other sector he characterized (Mansfield 1995). Narin and colleagues have repeatedly shown how industrial publications cite academic research, and patents related to pharmaceuticals and biotechnology cite academic research far more heavily than most other kinds of inventions (Narin and Olivastro 1992). When Steve McCormack and I read through the more than 1,000 DNA-based US patents issued 1980–1993, we found that 42% were assigned to universities (14% to private; 9% to public), nonprofit institutions (13%), or government (6%), compared to less than 3% academic ownership of patents overall (McCormack and Cook-Deegan 1996–1997, unpublished data). This is a tenfold enrichment of academic involvement in life sciences compared to most other kinds of invention.

The 1997 survey of the Association of University Technology Managers was the last year for which the questions made it possible to analyze life sciences separately from physical sciences. That year, life sciences accounted for 70% of licenses and 87% of income (Massing 1998).[7] Industries closest to health research depend on academe, and academic institutions are more heavily involved in technology transfer activities related to the life sciences. If we were looking for a place where public science matters to industry, life sciences would be a good place to start.

What is really going on? Beyond the special role of academic institutions as the training grounds for both technical and nontechnical workers in the knowledge economy, academic institutions also play a unique role in creating and sustaining the science commons. It is worth noting that the studies above generally focus on academic R&D, not specifically on the science commons, or only "open science." Recall that universities and nonprofit research centers do not always practice open science, and some elements in the commons come from private industry R&D. Academic research institutions are nonetheless the main stewards of the science commons. While we cannot be completely sure, it is quite likely that the main explanation for the importance of academic research is that it is open, producing data and materials available to all.

The most direct line of evidence for this comes from the Carnegie-Mellon Survey of industrial R&D managers. Cohen, Nelson, and Walsh conclude that "public research has a substantial impact on industrial R&D in a few industries, particularly pharmaceuticals," and

> The most important channels for accessing public research appear to be the public and personal channels (such as publications, conferences, and informal interactions), rather than, say, licenses or cooperative ventures. Finally, we find that large firms are more likely to use public research than small firms, with the exception that start-up firms also make particular use of public research, especially in pharmaceuticals. (Cohen, Nelson, and Walsh 2002)

This certainly corroborates the stories of genomics startup companies, including companies like Celera, depending heavily on their recent past in academic research, and their ongoing collaborations with (and sometimes customers and markets in) academic research. And it confirms the role of large firms in preferring to draw inputs from a science commons, rather than having to collect atomized, individually expensive fragments of proprietary technologies and data.

The history of genomics provides many examples of this, but two are particularly famous. One salient example is the decision in the period 1988–1991 by the National Institutes of Health not to sequence human genes (i.e., protein-coding regions), but instead to focus on systematically mapping and sequencing the entire genome (Cook-Deegan 2003). That decision opened the way for private firms Human Genome Sciences and Incyte to fill the void, attracting private capital to do what the public sector had chosen not to do. Because it fell victim to the law of unintended effects, NIH's decision not to pursue cDNA sequencing, however well-intended and understandable, was a mistake in retrospect.

The story behind that decision is mainly about the sociology of science, not a theory of the science commons, but it is instructive nonetheless. The decision not to sequence protein-coding regions was initially about fairness between big labs and small ones, not about commercial prospects. As the genome project took shape, the importance of maps of humans and various "model organisms" was apparent. What kinds of maps deserved substantial funding and concerted effort remained, however, a matter of ongoing dispute. One of the bones of contention was a "gene map" based on cDNA technology—that is, making DNA copies of the messenger RNA translated into protein within cells. Construction of cDNA libraries was standard fare, and remains a seminal technology in efforts to study expression of many genes through microarray technologies.

One question left open during the early debates about the Human Genome Project, 1987–1991, was whether the genome project would include "gene" sequencing—to start sequencing efforts with DNA known to code for protein, and therefore certain to provide codes for most of the important building blocks of cells, while also providing targets for drug development. A technical means to isolate the RNA that is translated into proteins was readily available. DNA could be made from such RNA molecules. This was called cDNA technology, "complementary" to the messenger RNA that is exported from the nucleus of the cell to its cytoplasm to be translated into protein. In fact, one could take it a step further and look for genes coding proteins likely to be of particular biological significance—and focus on just those cDNAs coding for secreted proteins and peptides (such as hormones or neurotransmitters), for receptor or transporter molecules extending outside the cell (with many trans-membrane domains), or proteins that bind DNA (with "zinc fingers), etc. These "functional motifs" could be predicted, if imperfectly, from DNA sequence data. One logical strategy to start the DNA sequencing program was to sequence cDNAs of particular interest first, then other cDNAs, and then turn to "genomic" DNA between genes. (DNA between genes would still be of interest because such sequences were likely to house regulatory signals for turning genes on and off, and affecting the timing of gene expression, as well as structures involved in cell division and the 3-dimensional shape of DNA in cells.)

At one of the first public discussions of the Human Genome Project, at Cold Spring Harbor in June 1986, Walter Gilbert responded to one attack on the idea of sequencing the genome by noting, "of course you would start by sequencing the cDNAs" (Gilbert 1986). When the congressional Office of Technology Assessment presented a plausible budget for funding the genome project, it included a cDNA sequencing component (US Congress, Office of Technology Assessment 1988). The Department of Energy did pursue some cDNA sequencing, but NIH's genome program did not. It was a matter of some discussion, but in the end it was largely James Watson's call, as director of the relevant NIH center. Several arguments were made against cDNA sequencing. First, it was already going to happen, since incentives to find genes were strong with funding from other NIH institutes, but incentives for individual labs to produce whole genomic sequence data were entirely dependent on "genome project" funding. Another, related, argument was about the sociology of science—if big sequencing centers did cDNA sequencing, they would inevitably also be at least tempted to pause to characterize particularly interesting genes, and turn to the fascinating biology sure to follow. There were two problems with this: (1) it would distract them from the major task at hand of deriving a complete reference sequence of the entire genome, and (2) it would give them an unfair advantage over the thousands of smaller laboratories lacking the DNA sequencing firepower.

It was the NIH decision not to fund cDNA sequencing that left the door open to Incyte and HGSI to follow human cDNA sequencing with private funding, because in the absence of a big public effort, the low-hanging fruit of the genome was there to be plucked, sequenced, and shipped off with claims to the patent office.

When Incyte and HGSI began to go down this path, those who saw genes as increasingly important inputs to their R&D efforts—particularly large pharmaceutical companies—got concerned, for two reasons. One was that the US Patent and Trademark Office was obviously patent-friendly, industry-oriented, and seemingly tone-deaf to the concerns of scientists about enclosing the public domain. Patents would issue. And if patents were granted, then any firm making, using, or selling a gene or gene fragment could be hit up for a piece of the action by the company that first sequenced it. Incyte and HGSI were clearly capable of filing patent applications on hundreds of thousands of gene tags, and thousands of full-length genes. Moreover, the small genomic startups had a running start on large pharmaceutical firms, the plodding Apatosaurus's of the biotech Jurassic.

Merck decided to take action (Williamson 1999).[8] It stepped forward to fund a public domain sequencing effort, starting with gene fragments and moving on to full-length cDNAs. The work was to be done at Washington University in Saint Louis, home of one of the largest public genome sequencing facilities, and the data were to be moved quickly into the public domain.

Merck funded the work through a nonprofit arm and had no privileged access to the data. Here was a large company funding data to flow into the science commons where it would be freely available to all. Why would it do this? Four reasons suggest themselves: (1) it poisoned the well for Incyte, HGSI, and other startup firms, creating an open, academic competitor (albeit funded by industry) to shut the window on securing exclusive property rights on genes, and thus limiting the number of genes that would have to be licensed; (2) it built goodwill with scientists, vital collaborators in Merck's drug discovery efforts; (3) it was great PR; and (4) it took advantage of nonprofit funding. If Merck paid for it as corporate R&D, it could deduct the R&D as an expense, but would also have to justify public domain science at stockholder expense. Through a nonprofit arm, Merck funded great science, burnished Merck's image, and enhanced Merck's future freedom to operate cleanly, without having to appropriate any returns on an "investment."

The SNP Consortium story started 5 years later, but followed the same general outline, with an added level of sophistication. During the late 1990s, it became apparent that there were many single-base-pair differences in DNA sequence among individuals. These were dubbed Single Nucleotide Polymorphisms, or SNPs, because of molecular biologists' penchant for impenetrable polysyllabic neologism (IPN) and three-letter acronyms (TLAs).

Single Nucleotide Polymorphisms could be used as DNA markers, to trace inheritance, to look for associations with diseases or traits, and to study population differences. They were valuable research tools. Many genomic firms, including Celera, began to signal they were finding SNPs and filing patent applications. Given the uncertainty about what the patent office would allow to be claimed in patents, it seemed possible patents on SNPs would be granted, meaning anyone using patented SNPs would need to get a license. This raised the prospect of needing to get licenses on hundreds or even thousands of SNP sequences from some unknown (but potentially large) number of patent owners. The Court of Appeals for the Federal Circuit had instructed the patent office that the "nonobvious" criterion for DNA sequence was met by any new DNA sequence, so "obvious" did not mean "obvious how to find it" but "sequence determined and in hand." The patent office was signaling it might permit patents for any plausible utility, demonstrated or not, and related to biological function or not (Doll 1998). SNPs might be patentable. This was just the kind of nightmare that Michael Heller and Rebecca Eisenberg had speculated might arise in their classic 1998 article on the "anticommons"—situations when too many exclusive rights upstream needed to be assembled, thus thwarting the development of final products, such as drugs, vaccines, biologics, or instruments (Heller and Eisenberg 1998).

This threat awakened some companies and scientific institutions to forge an alliance to defeat patent rights in SNPs (The SNP Consortium 2005; Holden 2002; Thorisson and Stein 2003). The SNP Consortium was founded in 1999 to first discover SNPs, file patent applications, map and characterize the SNPs, and then finally abandon the patent applications. The expense and paperwork of this elaborate dance were intended to ensure SNPs landed in the public domain unfettered by patent rights. It was deemed necessary as a defensive strategy to ensure that consortium members would have standing as inventors should disputes arise about priority for related inventions (in patent parlance, interference proceedings, the administrative procedure to determine the real first inventor). Here a group of private firms of various sizes found common cause in defeating patents on research tools. They valued their freedom to operate highly and the threat of patenting sufficiently to pay for a complicated, expensive procedure to enlarge the public domain.

Again, what in the world was going on? Private firms that dearly loved patents for their own products were working together with academic institutions to defeat patents? One interpretation might be that the public sector failed to support lines of research with a strong need for a science commons sufficiently. But members of the public genome project were well aware of the need for unfettered access to SNPs and were as worried about the problem as the private firms that wanted to use SNPs in their research. The issue here was the presence of many different kinds of genomics firms, some of which saw an opportunity to create and sell access to SNP research tools. It was no accident that this episode played out during the genomics bubble years, 1998–2001, when seemingly any startup with "omics" in its name could raise millions in private placements and months later (before any products hit the market) tens of millions through Initial Public Offerings of stock. It was conceivable that a company could raise private capital to find SNPs based on a possible paying market to use them in research. The public sector was simply not going to be able to mount a systematic SNP initiative fast enough and large enough to compete, and other companies wanted to avoid having to deal with the SNP upstart firms (yes, Celera was one of the firms with an interest in SNPs).

One interpretation of this story is that "the market," some market somewhere, solved the problem. The wonder of capitalism worked its magic by creating public domain resources at private expense to forestall the undue private appropriation of rents from research tools. OK, maybe so. The explanation is as complex as the sentence that contains it. And it is clearly true that private firms funded public domain science. Does it generalize? Can we learn to relax, and assume that excesses of the patent system will be compensated by enlightened capitalists guarding their long-term best interests and future freedom to operate? The Merck Gene Index and SNP Consortium show the answer is "sometimes yes." The nagging worry is that sometimes the answer may be no.

The Science Commons and Economic Efficiency: Costs of Data Access

A final historical pastiche before closing out the arguments. Consider again the prospect of an alternative universe in which free access to data about the medical literature and scientific data we take for granted in health research might instead be constrained by exclusive proprietary rights. If the history and geography had been different and database firms had turned their attention to genomics just a bit sooner, the story might have been quite different. As it was, the early algorithms for interpreting DNA sequence—such as the BLAST and Smith–Waterman algorithms—were developed by individuals committed to open science. In more recent years, patents have begun to issue on bioinformatic methods relevant to genomics. In some cases, these patents confer incentives to support "products" marketed by firms, with service teams and development teams to improve their quality.[9] How this story will play out remains to be seen, but the ideas of "open genomics" are being tested in the real world alongside more proprietary models.

Databases themselves could become a focus of concern. The early years of the Human Genome Project were marked by many decisions about the disposition of crucial databases. Human genetic disease and variation was lovingly cataloged by a team surrounding its founder, Victor McKusick of Johns Hopkins University, in Online Mendelian Inheritance in Man (OMIM). Many databases were established to retain data on human genetic maps of various types, and similar databases for other organisms. DNA sequence data were collected primarily by a trio of databases in the United States, Europe, and Japan, and these shared data among themselves. There was, in effect, just one major, central DNA sequence database beginning in the early 1980s. Creating and coordinating these databases, including the sequence databases, was its own titanic struggle (Smith 1990), but the battle was waged with only glancing concern for commercial potential. The databases contain many errors (Pennissi 1999), and creating financial incentives sufficient to encourage careful curation and maintenance is one reason to support proprietary rights in making databases. But that step should not be taken lightly, and now we have a decade-long experiment in the real world to inform such decisions, with strong protection in Europe and only copyright and contractual protections for databases in the United States.

How different it might have been had the genome project begun in Europe, just a decade later, when the European Community saw fit to create a new exclusive right in databases as an incentive for companies to create and maintain valuable data. The impacts of this new form of intellectual property have received particular attention from the scientific community. Scientists have become concerned that rights could hinder research. The landmark report on the topic was the *Bits of Power* report from the

National Research Council (1997), which has led to a line of further work. Much of the most advanced work has focused on weather, remote imaging, and other huge and complex data sets. There may be cause for worry, and not just for scientists, but for the innovation system as a whole. Exclusive property rights create friction and inefficiency. It may be that free access to data generated at government and nonprofit expense is far more efficient, and a more powerful prime for the economic engine, than allowing every incremental advance to form the basis for rent-seeking.

In the patent-happy United States that moves toward ever-longer copyright and protects creative works with the Digital Millennium Copyright Act, there is an anomaly. Data generated at government expense and published by the government cannot be copyrighted, and are thus freely available to anyone who wants to use them. American government agencies are generous suppliers of data to which others add value. It turns out that when it comes to data about the weather, it is the Europeans who are Scrooge, charging for access. And yet US businesses that provide weather information to various kinds of users have flourished, and the US market for such information is vastly larger than in Europe, despite the nearly equal size of the economies of the European Union and the United States. An analysis by Peter Weiss of the National Weather Service concludes, "The primary reason for the European weather risk management and commercial meteorology markets lag so far behind the US is the restrictive data policies of a number of European national meteorological services" (Weiss 2002).

Given that genomic databases and most health research databases are publicly administered and protect strong norms of open sharing, concern over database protections could prove a sideshow. Perhaps it is silly to think that DNA sequence might have been housed in a proprietary database owned by Reed Elsevier, Springer, or Thomson. But some databases do straddle nonprofit and for-profit worlds, and if a strong US database right were created, the rules of the game could change. SwissProt, a database with information about proteins of interest in molecular biology, has been the subject of dispute, both about how to fund it, and about its pricing and access policies driven by trying to ensure its long-term financial survival. The analogies between weather and DNA sequence data are not exact, but careful thinking about policies bearing on health research data, including genomic data, is crucial, because the creation of a US database right similar to the European counterpart remains a distinct possibility.

Conclusion: Deliberate Policies Preserved a Healthy Science Commons in Genomics

The various genome projects, both public and private, pursued quite disparate policies about sharing of data and materials. Proprietary technologies and data were created, mainly by private startup firms, and they contributed to the pace and success of the Human Genome Project. Deliberate policies of funding organizations, especially the Wellcome Trust and National Human Genome Research Institute and other funders of the "public genome project" created and preserved a large and important science commons of genomic data and technologies for analyzing DNA structure and function. Agreements such as the Bermuda Rules, privately funded initiatives such as the Merck Gene Index, and public-private hybrids such as the SNP Consortium were deliberately designed to promote broad access to data and materials.

Genome projects spanned a full range of openness, from rapid open access under the Bermuda Rules, to subscription-based access to genomic data and analytical tools at moderate cost (e.g., Celera), to highly proprietary gene-sequencing with public disclosure mainly limited to patents as they were granted and published (Human Genome Sciences and Incyte). The practical "public information" benefits from having information widely and inexpensively available, such as public health advances from new knowledge about health risk, reinforce the benefits for science, where a broad network of investigators can draw on masses of information. The value of the science commons is not an argument against the private R&D. It is, however, a powerful argument for the need to support open science and a healthy science commons upon which both public and private science can draw. Without explicit policies to foster the science commons, this valuable pool of knowledge would have been shallower, and a less productive fountain of social benefits.

Science is not just about creating knowledge, it is also about making it widely available and making it useful. Deliberate policies to promote open access and low-cost use enable some social benefits that profit-driven R&D cannot. Private genomics is a laudable complement to public genomics. Public genomics is, however, a creature of deliberate policies, not just to fund the science but also to ensure that the results are shared. It is not a system that can be left to mindless self-assembly or politics as usual. Without an expansive science commons, many benefits would be lost and private genomics would be vastly less productive and valuable.

Acknowledgments

Suparna Salil and Ilse Wiechers edited and helped format citations and references. Work was funded by The Duke Endowment, and by the National Human Genome Research Institute and the US Department Energy, through grant P50–HG003391.

Notes

This chapter was originally published in the *Journal of Technology Transfer* 32(3) (2007): 133–56.

1. Robert Sinsheimer, Renato Dulbecco, and Charles DeLisi each independently proposed the idea of sequencing the human genome.

2. This is not true of patent collections based on "gene patents," which flag patents containing sequence data (amino-acid or nucleic acid sequences from peptides and nucleic acid structures). The main reason is that many DNA-based patents claim methods, algorithms, or compositions other than DNA or RNA sequences. The algorithm for selecting patents into the DNA Patent Database is available at the site, http://dnapatents.georgetown.edu/SearchAlgorithm-Delphion-20030512.htm (accessed 2 April 2005). All patent studies have fuzzy edges, but the database is a tool that captures patents roughly corresponding to genetics and genomics.

3. After November 1999, a US patent application was published 18 months after being filed, if the applicant sought patent rights in any country with an 18-month publication rule. The companies did also publish occasionally in the scientific literature. HGSI, for example, listed 70 publications with one or more HGSI authors as of March 2005 on its website. These publications sometimes included sequence data, and if so, would make their way to GenBank, often before publication of the corresponding patent or patent application.

4. In a snapshot taken of year 2000 genomics research funding, ~70 nonprofit and government funders provided an estimated $1.6–1.7 billion; 74 publicly traded firms dedicated wholly to or including genomics research as a major function reported over $2 billion in R&D expenditures; and projecting 3–5% of R&D in major pharmaceutical firms was for genomics (based on survey responses and rough informal estimates of pharma R&D managers), established pharma firms were spending $800 million to $1 billion in genomics research. [World Survey of Funding for Genomics Research, Stanford-in-Washington program http://www.stanford.edu/class/siw198q/websites/genomics/entry.htm (accessed 2 April 2005)].

5. My colleagues Anthony So, Arti Rai, Jerry Reichman, Henry Grabowski, and others at Duke have joined many others from around the world to seek creative ways to ensure that essential drugs and vaccines are developed.

6. This story of sharing sequence information is commingled with a potential intellectual property story that could be complicated. At least three of the institutions that did the sequencing have applied for patents, and interference proceedings could be complex, as they are in different countries and on different strains that might need to be cross-licensed for many practical applications. A patent pool could emerge, or a monster interference proceeding to sort out the questions of inventorship. The legal costs could exceed the costs of deriving the sequence itself. See E. Richard Gold 2003. SARS Genome Patent: Symptom or Disease? *The Lancet* (361): 2002–2003.

7. The AUTM survey has continued in subsequent years, but the questions separating life sciences from physical sciences have been dropped. See Figs. 4 and 5, page 8 of the 1997 survey report (Massing 1998).

8. An excerpt from the press statement upon the first data release explained some details: "The Merck Gene Index is a broad collaborative effort, coordinated by Dr. Alan Williamson, Vice president, Research Strategy Worldwide, and Keith O. Elliston, Associate Director, Bioinformatics, of the Merck Research Laboratories. Dr. Greg Lennon's laboratory at the Lawrence Livermore National Laboratory (Livermore, California) has been supplying arrayed cDNA clones to Dr. Robert Waterston's laboratory (the Genome Sequencing Center) at the Washington University School of Medicine (St. Louis, Missouri) for sequencing. The sequence data are being submitted to the Expressed Sequence Tag (EST) division of GenBank on a regular basis for immediate distribution. [GenBank, built and distributed by the National Center for Biotechnology Information (NCBI) is a central repository of publicly-available gene sequence information, widely known and heavily used by researchers in government, academe, and industry]."

9. My Duke colleague Arti Rai is working on how ideas of "open source" in software might be applied (or not) to genomics. "Open source genomics" is the subject of her 5-year project.

References

Advisory Committee on Health Research, World Health Organization (2002). *Genomics and World Health*. Geneva, CH: World Health Organization.

Ankeny, R. (2001). The natural history of *Caenorhabditis elegans* research. *Nature Revies Genetetics*, *2*, 474–479.

Benkler, Y. (2002). Coase's penguin, or linux and the nature of the firm. *Yale Law Journal*, *112*, 369–446.

Cockburn, I., & Henderson, R.M. (1998). Absorptive capacity, coauthoring behavior, and the organization of research in drug discovery. *Journal of Industrial Economics*, *46*, 157–182.

Cohen, W.M., Nelson, R.R., et al. (2002). Links and impacts: The influence of public research on industrial R&D. *Management Science*, *48*, 1–23.

Cook-Deegan, R. (1994). *The Gene Wars: Science, Politics, and the Human Genome*. New York: W.W. Norton.

———. (2003). The colossus of codes. In J.R. Inglis, J. Sambrook, & J.A. Witkowski (Eds.), *Inspiring Science: Jim Watson and the Age of DNA* (pp. 387–395). Cold Spring Harbor, NY: Cold Spring Harbor Press.

Cook-Deegan, R.M., & McCormack, S. J. (2001). Patents, secrecy, and DNA. *Science*, *293*, 217. See especially accompanying online materials at http://www.sciencemag.org/cgi/content/full/293/5528/217/DC1. Accessed 30 October 2005.

Cutler, D.M., & Kadiyala, S. (2001). *The return to biomedical research: Treatment and behavioral effects.* Working paper. Retrieved from https://pdfs.semanticscholar.org/5dc5/2c4b500739878dd1b191d5480a8201b0ae1c.pdf. Accessed 3 April 2005.

Delphion Database (2005). *A division of the Thomson Corporation.* Retrieved from http://www.delphion.com. Accessed 3 April 2005.

DNA Patent Database (2005). *Georgetown University*. Retrieved from http://dnapatents.georgetown.edu. Accessed 2 April 2005.

Doll, J.J. (1998). The patenting of DNA. *Science*, *280*, 689–690.

Eisenberg, R.S., & Merges, R.P. (1995). Opinion letter as to the patentability of certain inventions associated with the identification of partial DNA sequences. *American Intellectual Property Law Association Quarterly Journal*, *23*, 3–51.

Gardner, M.J., et al. (2002). Genome sequence of the human malaria parasite *Plasmodium falciparum*. *Nature*, *41*, 498–511.

Gilbert, W. (1986). Response to questions at impromptu session on the human genome project at the molecular biology of homo sapiens symposium on quantitative biology. Cold Spring Harbor, NY: Cold Spring Harbor Laboratory. (Captured on tape by C. Thomas Caskey, transcribed and archived by Robert Cook-Deegan at the Human Genome Archive, National Reference Center on Bioethics Literature, Georgetown University.)

Haseltine, W.A. (1998). Life by design, gene mapping, without tax money. *New York Times*, A33.

Heller, M.A., & Eisenberg, R.S. (1998). Can patents deter innovation? The anticommons in biomedical research. *Science*, *280*, 698–701.

Holden, A.L. (2002). The SNP consortium: Summary of a private consortium effort to develop an applied map of the human genome. *Biotechniques* (June Supplement), *32*, S22–S26.

Holt, R.A., et al. (2002). The genome sequence of the malaria mosquito Anopheles gambiae. *Science*, *298*, 129–149.

Jaffe, A.B., & Lerner, J. (2005). *Innovation and Its Discontents*. Princeton: Princeton University Press. See especially Chapter IV, which lays out evidence for the "pro-patent" position of CAFC.

Jensen, K., & Murray, F. (2005). Intellectual property landscape of the human genome. *Science*, *310*, 239–240.

Lander, E.S., et al. (2001). Initial sequencing and analysis of the human genome. *Nature*, *409*, 860–921.

Mansfield, E. (1995). Academic research underlying industrial innovations: Sources, characteristics, and financing. *Rev Econ Stat*, *77*, 55–65.

Massing, D.E. (Ed.). (1998). *AUTM Licensing Survey: FY1997*. Norwalk, CT: Association of University Technology Managers.

Merton, R.K. (1973). *The Sociology of Science*. Chicago: University of Chicago Press.

Missinou, M.A., et al. (2002). Fosmidomycin for malaria. *Lancet*, *360*, 1941–1942.

Mowery, D.C., Nelson, R.R., et al. (2004). *Ivory Tower and Industrial Innovation, University-Industry Technology Transfer Before and After the Bayh-Dole Act*. Stanford: Stanford Business Press.

Murphy, K.M., & Topel, R. (1999). *The Economic Value of Medical Research*. Retrieved from https://pdfs.semanticscholar.org/99bb/8b3d4b9ce5dfbb6b91bea1457447d9241ecc.pdf. Accessed 3 April 2005.

Narin, F., & Olivastro, D. (1992). Status report: Linkage between technology and science. *Research Policy*, *21*, 237–249.

National Research Council (1997). *Bits of Power: Issues in Global Access to Scientific Data*. Washington, DC: National Academy Press.

———. (1988). *Mapping and Sequencing the Human Genome*. Washington, DC: National Academy Press.

Nelson, R.R. (2006). *The Market Economy, and the Scientific Commons*. Lecture to the University of Michigan Law School, 26 January 2006. Retrieved from https://www.law.umich.edu/centersandprograms/lawandeconomics/workshops/Documents/winter2006/nelson.pdf. Accessed 22 March 2006.

Newborn Screening Steering Committee, Maternal and Child Health Bureau, Resources and Services Administration, US Department of Health and Human Services (2005). *Newborn Screening: Toward a Uniform Panel and System*. Retrieved from https://www.hrsa.gov/advisorycommittees/mchbadvisory/heritabledisorders/uniformscreening.pdf. Accessed 3 April 2005.

Pennissi, E. (1999). Keeping genome databases clean and up to date. *Science*, *286*, 447–450.

Science Commons (2005). Executive director, John Wilbanks, with headquarters based at the Massachusetts Institute of Technology. Retrieved from www.sciencecommons.org. Accessed 2 April 2005.

Shreeve, J. (2004). *The Genome War: How Craig Venter Tried to Capture the Code of Life and Save the World*. New York: Knopf.

Smith, T.F. (1990). The history of the genetic sequence databases. *Genomics*, *6*, 701–707.

Smith Hughes, S. (2001). Making dollars out of DNA: The first major patent in biotechnology and the commercialization of molecular biology, 1974–1980. *Isis*, *92*, 541–575.

Stokes, D.E. (1997). *Pasteur's Quadrant: Basic Science and Technological Innovation*. Washington, DC: Brookings Institution Press.

Sulston, J., & Ferry, G. (2002). *The Common Thread: A Story of Science, Politics, Ethics, and the Human Genome*. Washington, DC: National Academy Press.

The Institute for Genomic Research (TIGR) (1997). *TIGR/HGS funding relationship reaches early conclusion*. Retrieved from http://jcvi.org/cms/press/press-releases/full-text/article/tigr-hgs-funding-relationship-reaches-early-conclusion/. Accessed 23 March 2006.

The SNP Consortium (2005). Retrieved from http://snp/cshl.org/about/. Accessed 3 April 2005.

Thorisson, G.A., & Stein, L.D. (2003). The SNP consortium website: Past, present and future. *Nucleic Acids Research, 31*, 124–127.

US Congress, Office of Technology Assessment (1988). *Mapping Our Genes: The Genome Projects—How Big? How Fast?* OTA–BA–373. Washington, DC: US Government Printing Office. 182–183 (Table B–1).

US General Accounting Office (2003). *Newborn Screening: Characteristics of State Programs*. Washington, DC: US General Accounting Office. GAO–03–449, 14ff, Appendix V.

US Patent and Trademark Patent Database (2005). Retrieved from http://www.uspto.gov. Accessed 2 April 2005.

Venter, J.C., et al. (2001). The sequence of the human genome. *Science*, *291*, 1304–1351.

Wade, N. (1998). Scientist's plan: Map all DNA within 3 years. *New York Times*, A1.

Weiss, P. (2002). *Borders in Cyberspace: Conflicting Public Sector Information Policies and Their Economic Impacts*. Washington, DC: National Weather Service, National Oceanic and Atmospheric Administration, US Department of Commerce.

Williamson, A.R. (1999). The Merck Gene Index project. *Drug Discovery Today, 4*, 115–122.

Ziman, J. (1978). *Reliable Knowledge: An Exploration of the Grounds for Belief in Science*. New York: Cambridge University Press.

11

Commons, Institutional Diversity, and Polycentric Governance in US Health Policy

Michael D. McGinnis

The US health system is deeply fragmented (Elhauge 2010). Each broad area of health policy—medical care, health insurance, and public health—consists of distinct types of organizations interacting within diverse institutional settings (Lammers et al. 2003). Private insurance and social programs provide uneven levels of insurance protection to different socioeconomic groups (Chapin 2015). The number of medical professions continues to expand, and the specialists who treat a single patient may or may not coordinate their treatments (Sultz and Young 2014). Government agencies at the national, state, and local levels regulate health insurance and the practice of medicine, implement public health measures, and deliver medical care for veterans and other patient groups (Field 2007). Ultimately, individual health outcomes vary systematically by age, race, class, gender, and urban/rural location (Wright and Perry 2010).

My argument rests on the audacious claim that this pervasive fragmentation can serve as a solid foundation upon which transformational change can be built. My optimism is grounded in the realization that all the components of medical care, health insurance, and public health that collectively comprise the US health system originated from the endless creativity of researchers, medical professionals, insurers, employers, government officials, patients and their advocates, and community leaders. In a never-ending process, individuals drawn from these groups devise new forms of medical treatment, implement programs to reduce medical errors and otherwise improve the quality of care, explore innovative payment mechanisms, and organize campaigns to promote healthier behavior.

Each program brings together individuals and organizations with access to different skills and resources in order to design, fund, implement, maintain, evaluate, and improve a plan of coordinated action intended to solve a particular problem. Participants collectively manage these joint ventures as a form of *common property*. That is, the resources developed for and used during these programs are made available to a specific group of individuals, each of whom has limited rights to certain uses of those resources, as well as carefully defined responsibilities on their part. Each program is jointly owned, operated, and managed by the individuals or provider organizations contributing to that program, and in some instances by beneficiaries as well.

The ubiquity of common property in the US health system suggests the potential relevance of research on the commons. My approach to health policy is grounded in the work of Elinor Ostrom, corecipient of the 2009 Nobel Memorial Prize in Economic Sciences, and more generally in the mode of institutional analysis known as the Bloomington School (Mitchell 1988; Aligica and Boettke 2009; Cole and McGinnis 2015). In her most influential book, *Governing the Commons*, Ostrom (1990) demonstrated that resource-dependent communities around the world have devised clever and sustainable methods of managing natural resources critical to their own survival. Of course, health care involves a far more complex array of actors and resources than the fisheries or irrigation systems upon which her empirical analysis was primarily based. Ostrom (2010a) recognized this broader perspective in her Nobel speech, where she emphasized that all complex economic systems require multiple layers of institutional oversight if that system is to be governed effectively. Gaps in governance at any level of aggregation can undermine the operation of the system as a whole, and the US health system exhibits many missed opportunities for improvements, especially the need for better coordination within and across all levels.

In this paper, I apply Ostrom's explanation of sustainable resource commons and related tools of institutional analysis to better understand the current health system and to suggest ways to evaluate potential improvements to that system. The first section summarizes Ostrom's research findings and provides a preliminary evaluation of their potential relevance to health policy. The second section integrates historical, conceptual, and strategic perspectives highlighting the critical roles played by institutional diversity, health commons, and regional stewardship. The third section shows why public, private, and non-profit organizations must work together to govern policy sectors, and articulates a vision of a multilayered or polycentric system of care. A brief concluding section connects this vision to broader concerns about the nature of democracy in our country.

Recognizing Health Commons

A *commons* is any resource to which members of a group share access. The relevant group could be well-defined, as in a restricted-access commons, or the commons could remain open to all comers. Examples include natural resource commons such as fisheries, lakes, forests, or common grazing land, and humanly constructed commons ranging from simple irrigation systems to highly complex technical infrastructures.

Commons pose vexing trade-offs between private interest and the collective good. Individuals may extract resource units from a common resource pool for their own private use, but if too many extract too much in too short a time, the commons may be degraded or destroyed. This "tragedy of the commons" (Hardin 1968) is especially likely if it remains an open access commons. To avoid such a tragedy, someone make take responsibility for ensuring the long-term replenishment of that resource and for maintaining the infrastructure needed to draw upon those resources in a sustainable way.

Hardin concluded there were only two viable policy solutions: a commons must either be managed by a central authority, or divided into separate parcels of private property. The latter option is based on the idea that the owner of valuable property will look after it with care, and the former option presumes that public servants want to do what is right for the community as a whole. In *Governing the Commons* (1990) and many other publications, Ostrom demonstrated the viability of a third alternative, by examining the ways in which resource-dependent communities have worked together to craft, monitor, enforce, and revise rules limiting their own behavior. These rules specify how many and what kinds of resources can be extracted, and by whom, and when, as well as requiring each resource user to contribute to collective efforts to maintain the common pool and its requisite infrastructure.

Principles of Design for Sustainable Resource Commons

By carefully comparing a large number of different types of natural resource commons from countries throughout the world, Ostrom identified eight *design principles* that were present, in one form or another, in successful cases of long-enduring community-based management regimes. To be clear, Ostrom did not claim that any of the individuals involved had consciously set out to satisfy these conditions, but rather that each group had ended up crafting a set of rules and procedures that either supported sustainability or left the resource vulnerable to degradation or destruction.

These design principles are briefly described below; for further details, consult Ostrom (1990) and Cox et al. (2010).

1. Clear boundaries define the resources to be protected and differentiate between individuals granted access to those resources and those excluded from participation.
2. Appropriators (resource users) have the capacity to self-organize, and their right to do so is either recognized by higher authorities or guaranteed by default.
3. The rules defining who can use the resource and who is responsible for providing for its maintenance are determined through participatory processes involving many of the same people who will be most directly affected by those rules.
4. There is at least a minimal level of congruence (consistency) between appropriation rules and provision responsibilities (for fairness considerations) as well as fitness to local biophysical conditions (for practicality).
5. Individual behavior and resource conditions are regularly monitored by someone accountable to appropriators (or by the appropriators themselves).
6. A series of graduated sanctions are available for application to rule violators (with stronger sanctions applied for more egregious violations).
7. Participants have access to multiple means of resolving disputes among themselves.
8. Nested enterprises exist or can be established for purposes of appropriation (resource extraction), infrastructure maintenance (provision), rule-making, monitoring, sanctioning, conflict resolution, financing, coordination, and evaluation.

The basic idea is that rules setting conditions on acceptable forms of resource extraction as well as the fulfillment of requisite duties are much more likely to be sustainable when most if not all of the resource users directly participate in the crafting, monitoring, enforcing, and revising of those rules. In effect, these conditions specify conditions under which the resource users themselves assert collective ownership over those resources and the rules in play.

These eight principles reinforce each other with subtle sophistication. As a whole, the rules limit the damage whenever individuals succumb to the temptation to exploit the common resource for personal benefit. Limits on acceptable forms of resource extraction must be clearly specified, and those limits must be both consistent with the physical reality of the resource itself and must result in outcomes that are deemed fair by most members of that community. Monitoring behavior is of little value unless those who violate rules are likely to be punished, but it rarely makes sense to expel a rule violator for a first offense, or for a few minor offenses. Groups need to fine-tune sanctions in a graduated manner, by imposing increasingly severe sanctions for more significant or repeated violations of the rules. Detection needs to be certain, but the rules must allow for forgiveness of those who made mistakes but wish to return to good standing within the group. Since group members will sometimes differ in their interpretations of the rules as applied to specific circumstances, all must have assurance that differences of opinion will be resolved in ways that reinforce the sense of community within that group. Finally, these principles ensure that mutually reinforcing forms of collective action will operate simultaneously at multiple levels of aggregation. Whenever smaller groups take responsibility for solving particular problems, those teams must not lose sight of the broader context within which they are acting.

It's worth emphasizing that these principles apply NOT to the characteristics of the resource system itself, but rather to the institutional arrangements through which that shared resource is managed. The design principles do not simply exist as such, but must be actively coproduced by participants.

Relevance to Health Policy

With regard to health policy, sustainability concerns become noticeable when health care costs absorb a significant proportion of the nation's total economy, and threaten to reduce expenditures on other public purposes. This is certainly the case in the United States, both nationally and within many states.

An especially powerful expression of this concern is Donald Berwick's 2009 plenary address to the annual meeting of the Institute for Healthcare Improvement (http://www.ihi.org), which by coincidence was delivered on the same day that Ostrom delivered her Nobel address in Stockholm. Berwick (2009) reflected on the irony that the United States has the most technologically advanced and expensive system of health care in the world, and yet the health outcomes of its citizens are, at best, mediocre. His primary concern was that the ever-increasing proportion of the US economy that is being devoted to health care would have strongly negative effects on overall economic growth and would restrict expenditures on other public services, especially education.

Berwick emphasized that research based on data from the *Dartmouth Atlas* (www.dartmouthatlas.org) documents substantial variation in the levels of utilization, quality, and cost of health care across approximately 300 community-centered regions (Gawande 2009; Wennberg 2010; Radley et al. 2012; IOM 2013; Tanenbaum 2013). Berwick suggested that leaders in those communities that experience higher than average quality of care for lower than average cost must be doing something right, and that Ostrom's design principles might help us understand the reasons for their success. He identified a few of these "positive deviants" and encouraged further study of the reasons for their success (IHI 2010). In sum, Berwick encouraged us to think about each community's health system as a kind of commons, and to recognize that regional health commons can be managed in different ways, and with substantially different results.

This research project summarized here began when Berwick and others approached Elinor Ostrom with a deceptively simple question: could these same design principles help explain regional differences in the costs and quality of medical care? Ostrom modestly responded that she didn't know, since it's not a good idea to take findings from one policy context and presume those same answers will work in other settings. But she also expressed her eagerness to investigate the matter further, and offered to host an informal working group on the subject. I was fortunate to be invited to participate.

Ostrom used the term "commons" informally, to encompass both public goods and common-pool resources. Technically speaking, she had limited her conclusions concerning design principles to the management of common-pool resources, in which individuals extract resources from a common pool for their own use. In parts of *Governing the Commons*, Ostrom extended coverage to local public goods, the benefits of which can be simultaneously enjoyed by a wide range of individuals without threat of exhaustion. Our first task was to determine whether or not anything related to medical care, health insurance, or public health fit the definition of a common-pool resource, or a public good, or a commons.

We managed to identify a few potential examples of common-pool resources, including public access to emergency services, limited time for consultations with physicians, fixed budgets for social insurance programs, the availability of hospital beds or testing facilities or healthy organs for transplantation. Overall, this was a disappointing list, since the examples did not add up to a significant portion of the health system as a whole.

We realized that many resources relevant to health are privately owned, including the professional skills of physicians, nurses, and other health care professions. Hospitals, clinics, and other corporate facilities may be owned by private corporations, by religious or secular-based non-profits, or by public agencies. Public health agencies typically focus on producing or overseeing the production of a wide range of public goods, including infectious disease control measures, suicide hotlines, information portals, and other ways to promote better community health.

We came to appreciate how difficult it was to fit any aspect of the health system into the standard definitions of private goods, public goods, toll goods, or common-pool resources (Ostrom and Ostrom 1977; Weimer and Vining 2010). Since health insurance pools the risk facing a defined group of individuals, it cannot be considered solely a private good. Fee-for-service payments are generally seen as instances of market exchange, but in practice these fees are affected by limits on copayments and other regulations, or have been set through negotiations between insurance companies and care providers. Health promotion campaigns may provide a public good, but in practice successful campaigns involve public regulation, social pressure, media framing, community-based activism, and individual choice. Finally, even though medical care primarily delivers private goods and services to individual patients, the facilities at which instances of care are provided can also be understood as common-pool resources (or as restricted-access commons).

Access to emergency room services seemed to be the most compelling example of a health-related common-pool resource, since there are a limited number of medical personnel who can treat patients at one time, and a limited number of examination areas. However, this analogy works well not because of the nature of the human or physical capital involved, but because of the broader institutional context within which ERs operate in the United States. Since so many Americans lack insurance coverage for primary care visits, a large number of the patients use the ER as a form of primary care (Hoffman 2006). Since hospitals are required to provide at least minimal care for anyone who comes to an ER, it is difficult to restrict coverage to those facing true emergencies. Congestion and long wait times for treatment can be frustrating to all, and overutilization of the resources of ERs to deliver what amounts to primary care adds significantly to the total expense of medical care in this country. This may sound like a potential case of a tragedy of the commons, but put the same emergency care facilities in a different institutional context and that storyline might lose all meaning.

In the US health system, private goods, public goods, toll goods, and common property are complexly interwoven. No matter how precisely one draws distinctions among types of goods and services in different parts of the health system, significant cross-connections and ambiguities will remain.

Lessons from a Regional Health Economy

Despite this conceptual ambiguity at the level of basic definitions, we continued to explore the broader idea of thinking of a regional health system as a kind of commons. My participation in the health commons working group evolved into a close relationship with ReThink Health, a group of health experts and leadership consultants who work directly with groups of reform-minded leaders in several communities. In this way, I began to explore connections between academic research on health systems and practical action at the community level.

As principal investigator of the Managing the Health Commons research project, funded by The Fannie E. Rippel Foundation, I oversaw a series of interviews with health care professionals, administrators, and community leaders in three communities. Two communities (Grand Junction, Colorado, and Cedar Rapids, Iowa) were selected because they had been nationally recognized as exemplars of high-quality health care delivered to the citizens of their communities at an unusually low cost, as determined by researchers in the *Dartmouth Atlas* project (IHI 2010).

We also conducted interviews locally. Bloomington, Indiana, had a long-standing tradition of community-wide cooperation on a wide range of public health issues, regarding recreational facilities, local food, and anti-smoking legislation. However, we soon learned that although community organizations were adept at obtaining funding from local, state, and national philanthropies, virtually all of these programs closed down shortly after the initial funding ran out. Missing was any sustained strategy to institutionalize these initiatives, or to make them sustainable.

Cedar Rapids turned out to be a difficult case for us to analyze, because two hospital systems in that area had just announced plans to construct cancer care facilities, despite an earlier agreement to avoid competition in that service area. The resulting mutual recriminations undermined their efforts to maintain levels of cooperation that had first emerged after a major flood a few years earlier.

So we focused our attention on Grand Junction, which had a much longer record of cooperation on health-related community matters. This section summarizes the key elements that lay behind the success of their efforts, as I understand the situation. I was fortunate to attend several of the regular monthly meetings of the Mesa County Health Leadership Consortium (MCHLC). Members included top-level executives from the largest private insurer, the leading physicians' association, the county public health office, and both of the major local hospitals, local clinics, hospice and mental health facilities, and the regional health information exchange, as well as other community leaders.

Our findings with respect to the potential relevance of Ostrom's design principles with regard to the health region centered on Grand Junction can be condensed as follows (McGinnis and Brink 2012):

1. *Clear Boundaries and Local Autonomy*. In the US health system, local stakeholders need to take direct action to assert even a minimal level of autonomy. For more than thirty years, the Mesa County Professional Independent Physicians Association (MCPIPA), which includes more than 85 percent of the physicians in this area, has ensured that doctors were empowered to make the best treatment decisions for their patients while improving the productivity of their practices. However, when needed, community leaders reached outside for assistance from a national professional association and state and national officials. For example, when the Federal Trade Commission and the Department of Justice were considering an unfair trade action against MCPIPA in the 1990s, a local physician asked the American Medical Association (AMA) to intervene, which helped convince the FTC to sign a consent decree that enabled MCPIPA to continue to operate as before.
2. *Wide Participation in Collective Choice*. A national professional association, the Institute for Health Improvement, helped establish the Mesa County Health Leadership Consortium (MCHLC) in 2010, in an effort to facilitate regular meetings among community leaders. As noted above, CEOs of key stakeholders meet monthly to discuss issues and opportunities that affect Mesa County. Each member organization is allotted one vote, and most decisions are made by consensus.

3. *Congruence with Local Conditions and Norms of Fairness*. In the 1980s, MCPIPA and the Rocky Mountain Health Plan (known locally as Rocky) built a financial pool from which equal reimbursements were paid to providers for health care services regardless of funding source. Allocations from this pool were implemented in a flexible way that took into account potentially inequitable effects. For example, when the Quality Health Network, a common system of electronic records, was established in the early 2000s, physicians near retirement were exempted from participation, since they would not have had enough time to recoup their investment. Eventually, all active physicians in the region used the same system.
4. *Monitoring and Graduated Sanctions*. As noted above, physicians in MCPIPA participate in a peer evaluation program with support from Rocky. Each physician receives a statement showing how their testing and treatment practices match up against other physicians in their practice area. MCPIPA also runs voluntary productivity improvement programs focused on patients with diabetes, heart disease, asthma, and other chronic illness. On a quarterly basis, MCPIPA sends a check to physicians who participated, and other doctors are informed of the percentage of their peers who are participating as well as the income they forfeited by not participating. Interview subjects mentioned examples of gentle mentoring of new physicians, followed by more substantial sanctions. After new physicians were "taken out to coffee" by old-timers and encouraged to adopt locally accepted forms of behavior, those who resisted these suggestions might later realize that they were no longer receiving many patient referrals.
5. *Nested Enterprises and Dispute Resolution*. In a commons overseen by administrators of large organizations, it is important to delegate responsibility for reaching specific targets to committees or stand-alone entities specializing in that task. MCHC members jointly support the Marillac Clinic (for uninsured patients), Hilltop Community Center (which runs the long-standing B4 Babies & Beyond prenatal program), and other enterprises. Plus, they use informal means to resolve disputes before they become big problems, by maintaining open communication among all parties.

All these programs and practices contribute to making the Grand Junction health care system an object of admiration. However, some have discounted their accomplishment by implying that this level of collaboration could only have occurred in a low population area that is geographically isolated from large urban areas, or that this region faced less difficult problems (Nichols et al. 2009; Bodenheimer and West 2010; Okie 2010; Thorton et al. 2010). For example, this region has an unusually low rate of infant mortality, but for decades a program has been in place to ensure that all babies receive regular prenatal care, no matter what the insurance status of their mother. Since healthier babies tend to require less expensive medical treatments later in life, it is widely acknowledged that this program helps lower the overall costs of medical care in that region. Interestingly, several interviewees chose to emphasize instead that this was simply the right thing to do.

In the meetings I observed, participants demonstrated a high level of political sophistication and social sensitivity in their deliberations. They openly shared concerns about potentially negative consequences of existing or proposed programs, and considered collective responses that might alleviate those concerns. They respected the boundaries set by their respective commercial interests and carefully avoided any actions that might be construed as price-fixing or collusion. They focused on meaningful tasks that could only be accomplished through joint action, and exhibited the good-natured banter of individuals genuinely comfortable with each other.

We concluded that the most critical key to the success of Grand Junction lies not in its geographic isolation or its reimbursement schemes or anything to do with the details of specific programs. Instead, the critical factor is that leaders of the regional health economy routinely communicate with each other, in ways that build and sustain mutual trust and respect.

Historical, Conceptual, and Strategic Perspectives on Institutional Diversity

I came to realize that to fully understand the US health system, we need to look beyond the design principles that dominated our attention in the health commons working group. There is much more to health and medical care than can be captured in the concept of a commons, especially one isolated from its broader institutional environment.

This section expands my line of argument in three directions. First, themes from broader literatures on policy and political economy set the historical context behind the incredibly diverse institutional landscape of health systems. Second, focus moves from the system as a whole to its component parts related to medical treatment, quality improvement, payment mechanisms, and health promotion. Third, a brief return to Grand Junction considers how similarly effective arrangements for regional leadership might be established in other settings. In brief, the critical requirement is for local leaders to find ways to knit together the full range of existing health-related goods, services, and programs, and use the resulting package to pursue a broader agenda of community governance.

Historical Overview of the Institutional Landscape

The US health system was constructed piecemeal, and its current complexity reflects the accumulated consequences of interrelated social, economic, political, and technological processes. This section briefly reviews the historical development of the organizational types that dominate different parts of this system. (Similar themes are developed in detail by Field 2007; Gordon 2005; Hillstrom 2012; Lammers et al. 2003; Shonick 1995; Starr 1982, 2013.)

Health policy was virtually nonexistent when the United States was established, except for public health measures like quarantines. Local authorities and churches established almshouses where people needing care were gathered, but this was not considered a major public responsibility. Given the rudimentary level of scientific knowledge, medical procedures were of limited efficacy, and what little market transactions that occurred in the delivery of medical care remained essentially unregulated. The Civil War revealed gross inadequacies in health infrastructure, which led state and national governments to build more hospitals and establish agencies such as the US Public Health Service. As appreciation of the germ theory of disease propagation spread, the public became more accepting of laws supporting compulsory vaccination and hospitals began to be seen as a good place to go for medical treatment.

By the Progressive Era, demand for medical services had dramatically increased, as had support for a much wider range of safety regulations. Professional organizations lobbied for licensing of physicians, and local and state health boards were established to oversee the approval process. Labor unions and other activists pressed for public support for sickness insurance to enable a wider class of people to afford the increasing costs of medical care. Similar movements in Germany and elsewhere in Europe led to universal health insurance, but the AMA effectively protected the economic and professional interests of private physicians against public regulation of their industry by railing against the imminent threat of socialized medicine. For this same reason, when old age pensions, unemployment insurance, and workman's compensation programs arose during the New Deal period, universal health insurance remained off the table. It was not until 1965 that the national Medicare program guaranteed health insurance for senior citizens. As Medicare and Medicaid became important sources of revenue for medical institutions, legislators and regulators used their market power to address other concerns, such as requiring all institutions receiving Medicare payments to provide basic emergency care to all comers. In this way, hospital emergency rooms (or departments) became an essential part of the health care safety net (Hoffman 2006).

As demand for medical care grew, new forms of health insurance plans were developed. Firms in the logging, mining, and railroad industries hired physicians to care for their employees, and labor unions offered members pension and health plans. Blue Cross and other non-profit insurers grew in importance, and were often exempted from state insurance regulations. During World War II, employers used health insurance benefits to attract and retain employees, since these benefits were not subject to the wage controls then in place. Fringe benefits were later ruled exempt from income taxes, which dramatically increased the domination of employer-based insurance. Meanwhile, commercial insurance agencies developed health insurance plans that proved financially lucrative, primarily by limiting coverage to healthy individuals with no costly preexisting conditions.

Throughout this period, most physicians remained independent professionals, who were granted privileges to practice in hospitals. In the 1970s, national agencies began to encourage the development of more integrated arrangements, combining hospitals, practicing physicians, and insurance companies in health maintenance organizations. HMOs served as the template for the Accountable Care Organizations (ACOs) that played a central role in the 2010 Affordable Care Act (McClellan et al. 2010). The ACA significantly decreased the number of uninsured Americans by offering states incentives to broaden access to Medicaid programs, requiring health insurers to offer packages of essential minimal benefits and to cover individuals with preexisting conditions, providing subsidies to individuals to purchase health insurance plans offered through new insurance marketplaces, and threatening new taxes on individuals who remained uninsured and on companies that did not provide health benefits to their employees. Though critics decried Obamacare as a massive government takeover of the health system, in reality it amounted to a series of opportunistic patches over gaps left uncovered by a still-evolving ecology of private insurance and social programs (Starr 2013).

As the costs of medical technology rose rapidly, and public expectations followed apace, non-profit hospitals had to adopt many of the cost-saving practices of for-profit hospitals, making the types of care provided by these originally very different kinds of organizations virtually indistinguishable in practice. Policy advocates and political entrepreneurs responded to the interests of particularly vocal interest groups, resulting in extension of disability benefits to those suffering from end-stage renal disease and support for the development of new drugs to treat HIV/AIDS. Cultural trends lowered social tolerance for drunk driving and smoking in public, and a coalition of state attorneys general successfully sued the tobacco industry and used their payments to fund smoking cessation programs. Interest groups active on abortion and other hot-button health-related issues have contributed mightily to overheated partisan debates and legislative gridlock in recent years.

In sum, markets in medical care and health insurance in the United States have always been deeply intertwined with social and cultural trends and with regulations established by public agencies and private professional associations. Since a high proportion of the population does have some kind of health insurance, movements to establish a comprehensive system always fall short of success (Gordon 2005; Starr 2013). At critical junctures, policy decisions made for reasons not directly related to the health system dramatically shaped the future evolution of that system, with the most consequential example being the rise of employer-funded health insurance plans. This fragmented approach was further solidified by the establishment of Medicaid, since requirements for eligibility vary by state.

Mini-Commons as Building Blocks for Regional Stewardship

The heat generated by clamorous partisan squabbling over the relative merits of markets and public interest regulation makes it nearly impossible for citizens to appreciate the true extent of institutional diversity in the US health system (Elhauge 2010; Field 2007; Lammers et al. 2003). This section highlights a particular kind of institutional arrangement that recurs, hidden in diverse manifestations, throughout this system.

I use the phrase *health-related mini-commons* to designate any program or project (including procedures and all associated resources) developed and operated jointly by different types of health care professionals and other stakeholders in the US health system. Each joint venture will have a unique combination of participants active in its conceptualization, design, implementation, funding, evaluation, and revision. Yet, at its core, each and every one is an instance of common property. As noted earlier, very few of the resources relevant to medical care, health insurance, or public health can be adequately described as either private property or pure public goods. Conversely, citizens and professionals in every community have extensive experience with a wide array of health promotion campaigns, different types of medical treatment, improvements in quality of care, and payment mechanisms based on different mixes of private insurance, copayment, and public support.

All forms of medical treatment require resources drawn from existing stocks of physical, financial, human, and social capital. Take the example of an operating room as a "clinical micro-system" (Nelson et al. 2007). Highly trained physicians, nurses, anesthesiologists, and technicians jointly make use of delicate and very expensive medical technology. They engage in mutual monitoring, because every member of a surgical team is encouraged to speak up immediately whenever they observe any potential breach of the sterile field. Also, someone will be assigned the responsibility of keeping count of sponges and other equipment used during the operation to ensure that nothing has been inadvertently left inside the patient to cause later complications. Despite their best efforts, mistakes will occur, and the reduction of medical errors is a high priority of all medical facilities. More generally, efficiency experts and consultants design, implement, and evaluate programs meant to make specific improvements to existing clinical processes (McKethan and Brammer 2010).

I use the term "mini-commons" to highlight the potential relevance of Ostrom's design principles to these programs. Each mini-commons was established for a specific purpose, and each has strict limits on the resources that the relevant stakeholders have made available for that purpose. Each program has rules to prevent overuse, and these rules were typically determined and implemented by the participating organizations themselves. Patients and care providers sometimes violate those rules, as demonstrated by the ongoing epidemic of prescription drug abuse. Finally, not all of these programs are going to remain in place for long periods of time, but those that do should fit the conditions identified by Ostrom.

A few caveats suggest caution when applying Ostrom's design principles to this very different policy setting. First, the health system also includes other kinds of property, including the examples of private property and public goods discussed above. Still, it's hard to deny that collective action lies at the heart of every aspect of health care. Second, the range of stakeholders involved in health-related mini-commons is wider and more diverse than was the case for the resource-dependent communities upon which the commons literature has been focused. Third, although long-term sustainability may require the active participation of the owner-operator-managers of these joint ventures, patients themselves are rarely consulted for advice on program details.

Health-related mini-commons play foundational roles in all parts of the health system, and the design principles can refer to different phenomena at the programmatic and systemic levels. The design principles referring to recognized autonomy and clear boundaries are not at issue in the setting of mini-commons, since each was built by a team working across professional boundaries for the purpose of designing a program to address the needs of some identified group of patients. When first constructed, its resources and the rules guiding their use will, by definition, reflect at least a minimal consensus among the relevant stakeholders concerning the nature of the problem they face, as well as their joint agreement to pursue a particular path toward its resolution. However, if that program is to be sustainable, the interests of all stakeholders must remain aligned, even as circumstances change. Interest alignment is not as easily assured as in the resource-dependent communities that Ostrom studied. In those resource-dependent communities, all shared a strong interest in the long-term viability of the resource; for health-related mini-commons, maintaining alignment of stakeholder interests is a constant struggle and requires concerted attention by program managers.

Individuals who participate in a health mini-commons need to be compensated in some way beyond the intrinsic benefits they experience from easing the pain of others. Similarly, sanctions against poor performance may combine material loss and social pressure. Since participants are drawn from organizations with diverse missions and specializations, disagreements will arise during implementation. Participants need opportunities to air their concerns, and access to procedures that help resolve disputes without damaging the underlying relationship among the parties.

The nesting principle connects conditions at both levels, since health-relevant mini-commons are the basic building blocks out of which the current US health system has been built. Each regional health system contains unique configurations of health service programs that are owned, operated, and managed as common property, along with other forms of capital. Few if any mini-commons will be naturally self-sustaining, and many would suffer from mission drift without regular supervision and evaluation. Even successful programs may act at cross-purposes, with one program undermining another program's prospects for success. When related programs are not well-integrated, dangerous gaps in coverage and care will remain.

In most communities, no one has taken on the challenge (or assigned the responsibility) of coordinating the design and support of critical health-related mini-commons, identifying gaps in coverage and filling those gaps with new programs, or of reconciling tensions between overlapping programs. In effect, this has been the strategy that leaders of the Grand Junction health system have been implementing for many years.

Strategically critical programmatic mini-commons in Grand Junction have included incentives for the recruitment of primary care providers, the B4 Babies & Beyond program providing pre- and post-natal care for all pregnant mothers and their babies, the community-funded Marillac Clinic for uninsured patients, a financial pool guaranteeing equal reimbursement for patients from all insurance groups, plus increments to reward exceptional performance, and the use of proceeds from a successful legal suit to build and maintain a system for sharing electronic medical records. None of these programs have been easy to sustain, but all major regional stakeholders worked together to find the necessary funds.

The term "regional stewardship" is a more uplifting description of what has happened in Grand Junction than positive deviance. The Merriam-Webster online dictionary defines stewardship as "the conducting, supervising, or managing of something; especially: the careful and responsible management of something entrusted to one's care." It also uses stewardship of natural resources as a clarifying example. When Hardin (1968) advocated privatization or collectivization as ways to avoid suffering a tragedy of the commons, he was presuming that individuals are naturally good stewards of their own private property and that public officials will (or should) fulfill their responsibility to serve as good stewards of publicly owned resources. When Berman and others identified Grand Junction as a positive deviant, based on the *Dartmouth Atlas* analysis, they were implicitly presuming that some degree of stewardship must have been occurring there that was sadly lacking in most other regions.

Regional stewardship did not arise fully formed in Grand Junction (McGinnis and Brink 2012). Habits of community collaboration were slowly built through projects to ensure sufficient irrigation water for agriculture and to restore habitats damaged by mining operations. When health system stakeholders met to discuss shared concerns, they selected a few critical targets for particular attention, constructed programs to address those targets, allocated resources to those programs, and gathered on a regular basis to evaluate these programs, and recalibrate as needed.

Over time, leaders knitted these programs into a broader regional health system. It's not a perfect system, as evidenced by continuing challenges regarding suicide rates and other aspects of public health. Nor is this the only path toward effective regional stewardship of health-related resources; formal regional councils and integrated-delivery systems have worked well in other regions. Still, too many regions have not taken even preliminary steps toward regional stewardship. Fortunately, ReThink Health and similar groups study and advise health leadership teams in communities throughout the country (Erickson et al. 2017), and important new perspectives on health reform are published every year (Emanuel 2017; Pearl 2017). The example of the Grand Junction leadership group remains important because they have demonstrated that it is possible to achieve transformational change by incremental steps, if those steps are guided by a strategy of resource stewardship focused on securing the long-term viability of critical component programs and on continued efforts to collectively address emerging challenges and explore new opportunities for improvement.

Polycentric Governance and Health Systems

Elinor Ostrom's research on community-based management of natural resource commons was firmly grounded in a realistic appreciation of the challenges involved in collective action and governance. By *governance*, I mean the processes through which the rules, norms, and social expectations that guide the behavior of individuals and corporate entities in a given area of policy are established and reinforced, whether by formal or informal mechanisms. In the United States, governance has always been a task jointly undertaken by public officials from the national, state, and local levels, and by important non-governmental actors from private corporations, professional associations, and voluntary organizations. Professional associations play important roles in setting and enforcing professional standards and norms, and non-profits organize volunteers' efforts to achieve socially desirable ends. Legislators and public agencies depend on different kinds of private actors for information or expertise, and for implementation of new laws or regulations. This interweaving of public and private is definitely the norm for the governance of health care—collaborations among stakeholder organizations constitute a dense network of programs, each constructed in response to the many subsidies, tax breaks, and regulations devised by policymakers to encourage new drugs and forms of surgery, quality improvements, new payment models, and other innovations.

Imagining a Polycentric System of Care

In systems of *polycentric governance* (Cole and McGinnis 2015), a diverse array of public and private authorities with overlapping domains of responsibility interact in complex and ever-changing ways, and out of these seemingly uncoordinated processes of mutual adjustment emerges a persistent system of social ordering that can support and sustain capacities for individual and group autonomy. This concept was introduced by Vincent Ostrom et al. (1961) as a vision of governance that recognized the potentially positive benefits of governmental fragmentation in US metropolitan areas (McGinnis 1999), and that presaged by several decades recent trends toward more explicit utilization of public-private partnerships for cross-sector governance (McGinnis and Ostrom 2012).

Polycentric systems provide groups seeking to resolve common problems or realize shared aspirations a range of choice among alternative institutional arrangements. The specific choices available in different communities will vary, as will outcomes. But to the extent that groups in that region and elsewhere can learn from each other's experiences, overall conditions should eventually improve.

In papers directed at practitioners, Ostrom (2009, 2010b) advocates a polycentric approach to climate change policy, and these papers could serve as an inspiration for aspiring stewards of health commons. Ostrom encourages climate policy advocates to rethink their preoccupation with global agreements, which by themselves do not guarantee actual changes in behavior. She draws upon the language of economics to demonstrate that climate change generates unintended negative and positive externalities for actors at all levels of aggregation from households to the global level. Since climate change is such a complexly multilayered policy problem, only a program of policies directed at each level can, in the end, be an effective response.

Ostrom (2010b, 551) confidently asserts that "To solve climate change in the long run, the day-to-day activities of individuals, families, firms, communities, and governments at multiple levels must change substantially." The lesson for health reform is clear: don't rely solely on changes in national policy. Ostrom articulates a vision of polycentric governance that could inspire aspiring stewards of health commons at the level of regional communities.

> What we have learned from extensive research is that when individuals are well informed about the problem they face and about who else is involved, and can build settings where trust and reciprocity can emerge, grow, and be sustained over time, costly and positive actions are frequently taken without waiting for an external authority to impose rules, monitor compliance, and assess penalties. . . . Local discussions and meetings generate information about the unrecognized costs of individual, family, and business activities as well as potentially lead to a change in the preferences of individuals involved and about the expected behavior of others. As a result of this communication, some actors adopt a sense of ethical responsibility for their own carbon footprint. . . . Building such a commitment, and trusting that others are also taking responsibility, can be more effectively undertaken in small- to medium-scale units that are linked together through diverse information networks. (Ostrom 2010b, 555–56)

My translation of Ostrom's vision into the context of health policy goes as follows. Individuals living within a polycentric system of care should be able to draw upon multiple options at all stages of the care continuum. When healthy, individuals should have easy access to reliable information about the symptoms of disease, and useful advice about how they might prevent themselves from becoming sick in the first place. When they fall victim to a specific disease, they should be able to choose among multiple entry points into the medical care system, including clinics specializing in mental and behavioral counseling. Primary care options should include regular visits to physicians, nurse practitioners, and clinics conveniently located in schools, at workplaces and shopping malls.

Whenever the need for urgent care arises, emergency assistance should be easily summoned by phone or by automatic devices. Wearable health technology can provide in-house monitoring of elderly individuals or patients suffering from chronic disease conditions, but such individuals should also be regularly visited by friends, family members, and neighbors, and perhaps by volunteers with a modicum of basic medical training. Hospice facilities should be greatly expanded, so fewer people need to die amid the clamor of intensive care units. All communities should provide generous support for web portals, public forums, and leadership meetings, and a primary concern of health policy should be to facilitate effective collective action among patient groups and care providers.

Missed Opportunities for Improved Coordination

This vision of polycentric care is far removed from present reality, but the seeds of its emergence are already in place. The commons perspective on the US health system helps us appreciate the many forms of collaboration already occurring in this system, and prompts us to identify missing links in the supporting mechanisms needed for us to move beyond these partial and potentially fragile successes. Today's health system is replete with missed opportunities for coordination—between patients and their care providers, among different types of health care professionals, between professional care providers and members of a patient's social support network, between insurers and care providers, among medical professionals, social workers, and public health officials, and among community leaders, administrators of medical institutions, and ordinary citizens.

Space does not allow a complete inventory of missed opportunities, but a few key ideas are worth consideration. First, in a patient-centered medical home, or PCMH, primary care providers and specialists, as well as social workers and patient advocates, are encouraged to operate together as a team. When the care a patient receives is coordinated, potential problems of drug interactions or inconsistent treatments might be avoided, reducing costs and improving the patient experience (Schwenk 2014). Second, coordinated care requires regular sharing of information regarding a patient's medical condition and treatment history, but efforts to build fully integrated health information technology systems routinely flounder on privacy concerns or commercial incentives to build software and equipment tailored for needs of particular organizations, rather than moving to a commonly shared standard (Burton et al. 2004). Third, shared decision-making protocols have been developed to help guide clinicians' discussions with patients, which, by eliciting the patient's underlying preferences among alternative scenarios, often result in less invasive treatments that do not require extended stays in hospitals or specialized clinics. In effect, better-informed patients can become directly engaged in directing their own treatment (Elwyn et al. 2013).

One crucial component missing in today's health system is a sense of collective responsibility. No public official has authority over strategic planning for the health system as a whole, or even for the full scope of any of the component sectors of medical care, health insurance, or public health. Nor is it widely agreed that such authority is needed, since many critics of the current system offer assurances that market forces, once unleashed, will push us in the right direction. Others insist that equal access to health care should be considered a basic human right. Lost in the heated rhetoric of partisan debates on health policy is any serious effort to agree upon the proper extent of public responsibility for the careful stewardship of local, state, or national resources related to health.

When I began this research project, I naturally presumed that improved discussion and coordination among all the major stakeholders in a local or regional health economy would be a good thing, since that idea resonated so well with the normative values and analytical perspectives I had absorbed during my long association with Elinor Ostrom and other institutional analysts. However, when I reviewed the history of previous efforts to establish formal institutions of health governance at the community or regional level, I was astonished to learn that the same thing has been proposed, in separate programs and in different ways, every ten or twenty years since the 1930s (Mehaldo 2014; Shonick 1995). Different reports used different terminology to describe why regional coordination was needed, and proposals differed in specifics. Ultimately, the record was dominated by false starts and hasty retreats.

In 1932, a national Committee on Costs of Medical Care proposed comprehensive reforms including a system of regional planning boards, but their support of group prepayment plans led the AMA to mobilize in opposition. The intensity of the AMA response convinced FDR to remove any mention of universal health insurance from the package of New Deal programs. The 1946 Hill-Burton Act (Hospital Survey and Construction Act) provided national assistance for the construction of new hospitals, especially in underserved rural areas. This program exhibited the classic symptoms of pork-barrel politics, and resulted in overconstruction of hospital capacity.

In urban areas, programs for neighborhood or community health centers failed to develop a powerful *national* constituency and fell victim to limits inherent in anti-poverty programs. The Comprehensive Health Planning Act (1966) and Health Planning and Resource Development Act (1974) mandated the establishment of regional health systems agencies, which were designed to require representatives from the broader community. However, metropolitan area-wide health facilities councils were strongly opposed by state-level officials, and neither act was fully implemented (Altman 1978; Koff 1988).

Most states passed CON (Certificate of Need) requirements under which state planning agencies could limit the construction of new medical facilities, but this program was unevenly implemented, and ended up becoming a means to protect the interests of the largest hospitals. This CON concept drew intense fire during the Reagan-era boom in deregulation, and it now continues in weaker forms in only a few states. Health Maintenance Organizations were pushed by national authorities beginning during the Nixon administration, but their proliferation led to public backlash because many HMOs restricted patient access to care in order to save money. The Accountable Care Organizations included in the Obama-era ACA were meant to be more community-friendly variants on the basic HMO model (Pasquale 2012; Burns and Pauly 2012), but the long-term future of this institutional form remains very uncertain in the current climate of hyperpartisanship.

This brief survey identifies an impressive litany of negative policy syndromes—aggressive use of negative and misleading rhetorical frames, excessive pork-barrel allocations, bureaucratic subversion, unfunded mandates, extreme partisanship, legislative gridlock, and regulatory capture by entrenched interests. Acting together or separately, these syndromes prevented full implementation of any effort to establish effective coordination among major stakeholders in regional health systems.

Direct efforts to mandate better health governance at the regional level seem doomed to fail. Voluntary coordinating agencies lacked sufficient authority to ensure compliance, and CON and other regulatory efforts were diverted to serve vested interests. Thus, we need something between, or fundamentally different from, fully voluntary or compulsory policy instruments.

A Polycentric Strategy for Health Reform

All of these ideas to improve coordination at different levels of aggregation have been tried before, with varying levels of success. The sheer number of policy syndromes that combined to undermine regional planning boards demonstrates that a more subtle and indirect approach is needed. It seems that any single reform idea, no matter how compelling, is likely to work effectively only when its implementation is supported by complementary changes in related institutions or practices.

To see how an indirect approach to systematic health reform might work in action, consider US environmental policy, which in recent decades has undergone a fundamental transformation, driven by mutually reinforcing changes in the behavior of public officials, private corporations, professional associations, advocacy groups, and individual consumers.

Look back a few decades and you'll see an economic system in which producers of all kinds routinely polluted the environment, with little or no consequences to themselves. This led to a race-to-the-bottom, in which poor states offered lower levels of environmental restrictions in hopes of attracting more industry to their local economies. Increasing concern on the part of the public (and environmental experts) led to the passage of laws assigning responsibility for pollution to corporate producers. In some states, these movements were effective in encouraging state and local officials to impose stricter environmental regulations, some of which were later implemented at the national level. These regulations established a floor below which environmental conditions were not allowed to fall.

But it wasn't just a question of interactions between private corporations and government regulators. Non-profit groups acted to enhance public knowledge and concern about the production methods of different corporations, and a process of naming and shaming began. Consumers took this information into account in their purchasing decisions. Companies began to compete over the relative greenness of their own corporate practices, and corporations most effective at capturing this market opportunity did so by deeply institutionalizing green concerns within their corporate cultures. Communities now routinely advertise themselves as environmentally friendly places to live.

How might we embark upon a mutually reinforcing path of movement toward a new equilibrium for the health care sector of the US public economy? We have to start from where we are today, a health system built on a multitude of health-related mini-commons that remain fragile as stand-alone programs. Although many hospitals have programs of community outreach, and encourage physicians and other employees to volunteer in various community programs, these remain mostly sideshows, well off the mainline of corporate activity. Regulatory efforts proliferate, but routinely generate unintended consequences because private responses to regulatory requirements focus on opportunities for increasing one's market share, rather than directly achieving the ends sought by the regulators. Also, regulations are too often implemented in a one-size-fits-all format, inappropriate for the local variation of community needs and preferences for health services.

Instead, medical care and health insurance regulators could focus on setting floors on acceptable policies, both in terms of quality control (such as not paying for unneeded surgeries or frequent readmissions) and setting minimal requirements for health insurance policies. Regulations should include incentive packages that encourage overcompliance, and could encourage provider organizations to publicize details on their own performance record. This will enable consumers to demand better value for their health care costs, in terms of quality and better fit to their own values.

Those providers who most effectively internalize quality control (reducing medical errors, improving care coordination, etc.) and active patient engagement in directing their own care will be best positioned to succeed in this competitive race to the top. As public satisfaction with their local health system improves, community leaders could highlight these improvements in hopes of attracting new jobs and residents.

This polycentric path to reform requires critical contributions from medical care providers, public officials, professional associations, community organizations, and individuals acting as patients, care providers, consumers, and citizens. Sustained progress on one front could serve to reinforce others, especially if health stakeholders and community leaders meet regularly to discuss mutual concerns and opportunities, and to learn from each other's experiences. But we can't force them to do so by regulatory fiat. Nor are the potential financial gains likely to be sufficiently large or short-term in realization to overcome the force of organizational inertia. Instead, local leaders need to want to learn from each other, and to take actions to do so on a regular basis. In sum, local health stakeholders and community leaders need to be willing to act as responsible stewards of a health system that they have, to a great extent, constructed themselves. Evoking that sense of responsibility lies at the core of the commons perspective on health reform.

Conclusion

This paper combines two conceptual lenses to offer a new perspective on potential reform of the US health system. First, the lens of commons research reveals the existing plentitude of mini-commons programs for medical treatment, quality improvement, innovative payment models, and health promotion. Since these programs are managed as common property, this widespread experience can serve as a foundation for extension of the commons perspective to the community level.

Second, the institutional literature on polycentric governance shines a bright light on the essentially local nature of health regions, thus greatly expanding the opportunities to experiment with innovative programs of medical care, insurance coverage, and public health. Working together, these perspectives should encourage health care professionals and the public at large to make more concerted efforts to understand the health care system as it is, to appreciate why it is so fragmented, and to experiment with changing it in a more consciously strategic fashion, in order to turn fragmentation, which may in the end be inevitable, to better purposes.

In the compound republic designed by the founders of the US Constitution, the primary role of the national government was to secure conditions that enabled effective self-governance at state and local levels (V. Ostrom 2008). Today, health policy serves as a political football in unrelenting and increasingly pointless confrontations between partisans on the left and right of our political spectrum. Broader appreciation of the positive aspects of a patchwork system, built primarily from the bottom up, should help direct our collective attention to identifying the strategic priorities that could guide future efforts to transcend the limits of the current system.

In a democracy, governance is not something that "the Government" does to us, but instead something we do to ourselves every day, as we reenact and reinforce expected patterns of interaction with each other. New laws and regulations and standards won't have any impact, ultimately, unless they are incorporated into our mutually negotiated expectations of each other. Implementing this vision of polycentric governance in health policy can succeed only if large portions of the citizenry become more actively engaged in their own care, and more generally engaged in their local communities. Following a polycentric path to health reform might end up being as good for our democracy as for our health.

Acknowledgments

This paper summarizes research presented in different forms at several venues, and it has not been previously presented in this form. During the seven years I have worked on this project, I have received much-needed advice, comments, and encouragement from many smart and generous colleagues. I am especially grateful to Paul Dragos Aligica, Linda Alis, Peter Boettke, Claudia Brink, Jane Brock, Connie Clark, Dan Cole, Ryan Conway, Glen Elwyn, Steve ErkenBrack, Elliott Fisher, Brett Frischmann, Bob Gibbons, Kathy Gilbert, Michael Hendryx, Kate Hilton, Evon Holladay, John Horowitz, Sherry Immediato, Jeff Kuhr, Laura Landy, Lois Lane, Carrie Ann Lawrence, Patty Lezotte, Joan Pong Linton, Lauren MacLean, Michael Madison, Gregg Meyer, Bobby Milstein, Al Mulley, Sheila

Nickle, Mark Norrell, Lin Ostrom, Kosali Simon, Larry Stevens, Rob Stone, Keith Taylor, Ted Townsend, Sue True, Jon Voight, Ruth Wageman, Jimmy Walker, Thom Walsh, and Greg Zoeller. For their generous financial support, I would like to thank The Fannie E. Rippel Foundation, ReThink Health, the Mercatus Center at George Mason University, the Center for Health Care Delivery Science and Institute for Health Policy and Clinical Practice at Dartmouth, and at Indiana University, the College of Arts and Sciences, Department of Political Science, and Ostrom Workshop. Of course, none of these individuals or institutions are responsible for any errors of fact or interpretation that remain.

References

Aligica, Paul Dragos, and Peter Boettke. 2009. *Challenging Institutional Analysis and Development: The Bloomington School*. New York: Routledge.

Altman, Drew. 1978. "The Politics of Health Care Regulation: The Case of the National Health Planning and Resources Development Act." *Journal of Health Politics, Policy and Law* 2(4): 560–80.

Berwick, Donald M. 2009. "Squirrel." Plenary Address, 21st Annual IHI National Forum on Quality Improvement in Health Care, Orlando, FL, December 8, 2009, included in Donald M. Berwick, *Promising Care: How We Can Rescue Health Care by Improving It*, San Francisco, CA: Jossey-Bass, 2014, pp. 180–94.

Bodenheimer, Thomas, and David West. 2010. "Low-Cost Lessons from Grand Junction, Colorado." *New England Journal of Medicine* 363 (Oct 7): 1391–93.

Burns, Lawton R., and Mark V. Pauly. 2012. "Accountable Care Organizations May Have Difficulty Avoiding the Failures of Integrated Delivery Networks of the 1990s." *Health Affairs* 31(11): 2407–16.

Burton, L. C., G. F. Anderson, and I. W. Kues. 2004. "Using Electronic Health Records to Help Coordinate Care." *Milbank Quarterly* 82: 457–81.

Chapin, Christy Ford. 2015. *Ensuring America's Health: The Public Creation of the Corporate Health Care System*. New York: Cambridge University Press.

Cole, Daniel H., and Michael D. McGinnis, eds. 2015. *Elinor Ostrom and the Bloomington School of Political Economy: Volume 1, Polycentricity in Public Administration and Political Science.* Lanham, MD: Lexington Books.

Cox, Michael, Gwen Arnold, and Sergio Villamayor Tomás. 2010. "A Review of Design Principles for Community-Based Natural Resource Management." *Ecology and Society* 15(4): 38, http://www.ecologyandsociety.org/vol15/iss4/art38/ES-2010-3704.pdf.

Elhauge, Einer, ed. 2010. *The Fragmentation of U.S. Health Care: Causes and Solutions*. New York: Oxford University Press.

Elwyn, Glyn, Jon Tilburt, and Victor Montori. 2013. "The Ethical Imperative for Shared Decision-Making." *European Journal for Person Centered Healthcare* 1(1): 129–31.

Emanuel, Ezekiel J. 2017. *Prescription for the Future: The Twelve Transformational Practices of Highly Effective Medical Organizations.* New York: Public Affairs.

Erickson, Jane, Bobby Milstein, Lisa Schafer, Katy Evans Pritchard, Carly Levitz, Creagh Miller, and Allen Cheadle. 2017. *Progress Along the Pathway for Transforming Regional Health: A Pulse Check on Multi-Sector Partnerships.* ReThink Health, in partnership with the Center for Community Health and Evaluation, March 2017, https://www.rethinkhealth.org/tools/pulse-check/.

Field, Robert I. 2007. *Health Care Regulation in America: Complexity, Confrontation, and Compromise*. New York: Oxford University Press.

Gawande, Atul. 2009. "The Cost Conundrum." *New Yorker*, June 1, 2009.

Gordon, Colin. 2005. *Dead on Arrival: The Politics of Health Care in Twentieth-Century America.* Princeton, NJ: Princeton University Press.

Hardin, Garrett. 1968. "The Tragedy of the Commons." *Science* 162(3859): 1243–48.

Hillstrom, Kevin. 2012. *U.S. Health Policy and Politics: A Documentary History.* Los Angeles, CA: Sage and CQ Press.

Hoffman, Beatrix. 2006. "Emergency Rooms: The Reluctant Safety Net." In *Putting the Past Back In: History and Health Policy in the United States*, edited by Rosemary A. Stevens et al., 250–72. New Brunswick, NJ: Rutgers University Press.

IHI (Institute for Healthcare Improvement). 2010. "How Will We Do That? Building Low-Cost, High-Quality Health Care Regions in America." May, www.IHI.org.

IOM (Institute of Medicine). 2013. *Variation in Health Care Spending: Target Decision Making, Not Geography*. July 24. Washington, DC: National Academies Press.

Koff, Sondra Z. 1988. *Health Systems Agencies: A Comprehensive Examination of Planning and Process*. New York: Human Sciences Press.

Lammers, John C., Joshua Barbour, and Ashley Duggan. 2003. "Organizational Forms of the Provision of Health Care: An Institutional Perspective." In *Handbook of Health Communication*, edited by T. Thompson, A. Dorsey, K. Miller, and R. Parrot, 319–46. Hillsdale, NJ: Lawrence Erlbaum Associates.

McClellan, Mark, Aaron N. McKethan, Julie L. Lewis, Joachim Roski, and Elliott S. Fisher. 2010. "A National Strategy to Put Accountable Care Into Practice." *Health Affairs* 29(5): 982–90.

McGinnis, Michael D., ed. 1999. *Polycentricity and Local Public Economies: Readings from the Workshop in Political Theory and Policy Analysis*. Ann Arbor: University of Michigan Press.

McGinnis, Michael D., and Claudia A. Brink. 2012. "Shared Stewardship of a Health Commons: Examples and Opportunities from Grand Junction, Colorado." White Paper prepared for the Alliance of Community Health Plans, Working Paper W12–14, Ostrom Workshop, Indiana University, Bloomington. http://php.indiana.edu/~mcginnis/healthcommons/HealthCommonsWhitePaper.pdf.

McGinnis, Michael D., and Elinor Ostrom. 2012. "Reflections on Vincent Ostrom, Public Administration, and Polycentricity." *Public Administration Review* 72(1) (Jan/Feb): 15–25.

McKethan, Aaron, and Craig Brammer. 2010. "Uniting the Tribes of Health System Improvement." Special issue, *The American Journal of Managed Care* 16(12): SP13–18.

Mehaldo, Evan M. 2014. "Evolution of Health Planning (1920s–1970s)" and "(1970s–Present)." In *Guide to U.S. Health and Health Care Policy*, edited by Thomas R. Oliver, 143–67. Washington, DC: CQ Press.

Mitchell, William C. 1988. "Virginia, Rochester, and Bloomington: Twenty-Five Years of Public Choice and Political Science." *Public Choice* 56: 101–19.

Nelson, Eugene C., Marjorie M. Godfrey, and Paul B. Batalden, eds. 2007. *Quality by Design: A Clinical Microsystems Approach*. Burlington, MA: Jossey-Bass.

Nichols, Len M., Micah Weinberg, and Julie Barnes. 2009. *Grand Junction, Colorado: A Health Community That Works*. Washington, DC: New America Foundation. https://www.rmhpcommunity.org/sites/default/files/resource/Grand_Junction_CO_A_Health_Community_That_Works_8.2009.pdf.

Okie, Susan. 2010. "How the Stars Aligned to Make Grand Junction a Success." *Health Affairs* 29(9): 1687–88.

Ostrom, Elinor. 1990. *Governing the Commons: The Evolution of Institutions for Collective Action*. New York: Cambridge University Press.

———. 2009. "A Polycentric Approach for Coping with Climate Change." Policy Research Working Paper No. 5095. Washington, DC: World Bank.

———. 2010a. "Beyond Markets and States: Polycentric Governance of Complex Economic Systems." *American Economic Review* 100(3) (Jun): 641–72.

———. 2010b. "Polycentric Systems for Coping with Collective Action and Global Environmental Change." *Global Environmental Change* 20(4) (Oct): 550–57.

Ostrom, Vincent. 2008. *The Political Theory of a Compound Republic: Designing the American Experiment*. 3rd ed. Lanham, MD: Lexington Books.

Ostrom, Vincent, and Elinor Ostrom. 1977. "Public Goods and Public Choices." In *Alternatives for Delivering Public Services. Toward Improved Performance*, edited by E. S. Savas, 7–49. Boulder, CO: Westview Press. Reprinted in McGinnis 1999.

Ostrom, Vincent, Charles M. Tiebout, and Robert Warren. 1961. "The Organization of Government in Metropolitan Areas: A Theoretical Inquiry." *American Political Science Review* 55 (4):831–42. Reprinted in McGinnis 1999 and Cole and McGinnis 2015.

Pasquale, Frank. 2012. "Accountable Care Organizations in the Affordable Care Act." *Seton Hall Law Review* 42(4): article 1.

Pearl, Robert. 2017. *Mistreated: Why We Think We're Getting Good Health Care—And Why We're Usually Wrong*. New York: Public Affairs.

Radley, D. C., S. K. H. How, A. K. Fryer, D. McCarthy, and C. Schoen. 2012. *Rising to the Challenge: Results from a Scorecard on Local Health Performance, 2012.* New York: The Commonwealth Fund.

Schwenk, Thomas L. 2014. "The Patient-Centered Medical Home: One Size Does Not Fit All." *JAMA* 311(8): 802–803.

Shonick, William. 1995. *Government and Health Services: Government's Role in the Development of U.S. Health Services 1930–1980.* New York: Oxford University Press.

Starr, Paul. 1982. *The Social Transformation of American Medicine.* New York: Basic Books.

———. 2013. *Remedy and Reaction: The Peculiar American Struggle over Health Care Reform.* Rev. ed. New Haven, CT: Yale University Press.

Sultz, Harry A., and Kristina M. Young. 2014. *Health Care USA: Understanding Its Organization and Delivery.* 8th ed. Burlington, MA: Jones & Bartlett.

Tanenbaum, Sandra J. 2013. "Reducing Variation in Health Care: The Rhetorical Politics of a Policy Idea." *Journal of Health Politics, Policy and Law* 38(1) (Feb): 5–26.

Thorton, Marsha, Jane Brock, Jason Mitchell, and Joanne Lynn. 2010. "Grand Junction, Colorado: How a Community Drew on Its Values to Shape a Superior Health System." *Health Affairs* 29(9): 1678–86.

Weimer, David L., and Aidan R. Vining. 2010. *Policy Analysis: Concepts and Practice.* 5th ed. Boston, MA: Longman.

Wennberg, John E. 2010. *Tracking Medicine: A Researcher's Quest to Understand Health Care.* New York: Oxford University Press.

Wright, Eric. R., and Brea L. Perry. 2010. "Medical Sociology and Health Services Research: Past Accomplishments and Future Policy Challenges." *Journal of Health and Social Behavior* 51: S107–19.

PART III

Continuing Projects

12

Digging Deeper into Hardin's Pasture: The Complex Institutional Structure of "The Tragedy of the Commons"

Daniel H. Cole, Graham Epstein, and Michael D. McGinnis

Hardin's (1968) "tragedy of the commons" remains a uniquely powerful and controversial contribution to both social and natural sciences. The classic allegory, which warns of the dangers associated with situations that generate private benefits and shared costs, is an integral part of the curricula in multiple disciplines. Its sustained influence is a product of both its ability to successfully predict resource collapse (Brook et al. 2003; Edmondson et al. 1956; Ludwig et al. 1993; Myers et al. 1997) and its myopic failure to consider the possibility that groups of resource users might recognize the dangers of overexploitation and successfully develop self-organized systems of common-property governance (Baland and Platteau 1996; Ostrom 1990; Wade 1994). The evidence concerning the viability of these small-scale common-property systems is by now irrefutable (Chhatre and Agrawal 2009; Cox et al. 2010; Gutiérrez et al. 2011), although their success ultimately depends upon the fit between common-property institutions and the complex social and ecological environment in which they operate (Acheson 2006; Feeny et al. 1990).

This paper expands on the issue of institutional fit in the context of Hardin's Herder Problem (as it is known among game theorists, e.g., Cole and Grossman 2010) to show that destruction of the open-access pasture is not a function of a lack of institutions but necessarily depends upon the interactions of various rules-in-use that together generate incentives to overuse.[1] Failure to recognize the role of these institutional interactions in the Herder Problem suggests that some institutions are so entrenched and taken for granted that even accomplished analysts fail to diagnose the problem accurately. Moreover, inaccurate diagnoses can lead to the deployment of ineffective policy responses that fail to grapple with the complex, often opaque matrix of rules, norms, customs, and conventions within which social and environmental problems arise.

To better illuminate that matrix, we employ the Social-Ecological System (SES) framework (Ostrom 2007, 2009; Ostrom and Cox 2010), an analytical tool that aims to systematize data collection and integrate knowledge to understand how a diverse assortment of social-ecological attributes and their interactions affects the sustainability of social-ecological systems. The framework has demonstrated its analytic utility through application to a wide range of environmental problems (Ban et al. 2013; Basurto and Ostrom 2009; Blanco 2011; Cinner et al. 2012; Fleischman et al. 2010; Gutiérrez et al. 2011).

Notwithstanding its contributions and general acceptance by diverse scholars, the SES framework is a complex tool that can confront an analyst with the seemingly endless task of identifying the entire range of relevant and potentially important social, ecological, and institutional attributes of a social-ecological system. Although a complete account of all these factors is generally unattainable, policy-relevant theoretical explanations must attend to all *categories* of the factors that substantially structure interactions and affect outcomes in these systems. Some of the institutions that give rise to particular patterns of behavior may not appear immediately obvious, and identifying these hidden but still effectual institutions requires careful attention to all the categories included in the SES framework.

In her paper introducing the SES framework, Ostrom (2007) argued for the importance of contextual understandings of social-ecological phenomena. Ironically, however, her application of the SES framework to Hardin's "tragedy of the commons" neglected important attributes of the institutional environment that play understated but significant roles in the demise of the open-access pasture. Like Hardin, Ostrom failed to consider certain institutional conditions that gave rise to the Herder Problem. She treated the *ex ante* situation in an overly abstract and non-contextual manner. By accepting Hardin's exclusive focus on the absence of private property rights to the pasture, Ostrom overlooked the contributions made by other aspects of the extant institutional context, factors that local groups would have to take into account when they select new institutions in pursuit of "alternative futures" (V. Ostrom 2008).[2]

This paper shows how a failure to account for preexisting institutional features of the environment can dramatically affect the outcome, leading to either an overexploited or an underexploited open-access pasture. Furthermore, the resulting diagnosis of what is needed to avoid destruction of the common resource may be incomplete and misleading unless the groups involved can understand how their proposed institutional innovations will interplay with the diverse assortment of historical, cultural, and macroinstitutional features of the surrounding environment (Clement 2010; Larson and Soto 2008; Pierson 2000; Ribot et al. 2006).

[The first] section introduces the SES framework and discusses its utility for diagnosing the attributes of a given system that jointly affect social and ecological outcomes. [The second] section then presents Ostrom's (2007) application of the SES framework to Hardin's (1968) Herder Problem, and discusses the problems with her application. [The third] section offers a revised application of the SES framework that draws attention to background institutional factors that include property rights in cattle, the "rule of capture" applied to the grass on the pasture, and institutions supporting market exchange that generate the individual incentives that drive collective destruction of the pasture. The paper concludes in [the fourth] section with a discussion on implications of the analysis for both institutional fitness and, more often overlooked, institutional interactions.

The SES Framework

The SES framework (Figure 12.1) conceptualizes social-ecological systems as partially decomposable systems (Simon 1962) consisting of six fundamental components. Four of these—resource systems (RS), resource units (RU), actors (A), and governance systems (GS)—are defined by sets of attributes (Table 12.1) that jointly shape interrelated processes of interaction (I), leading to observed and evaluated outcomes (O). Resource units, as an example, are defined by seven attributes, including: the rate at which harvested units are replaced (RU2), their economic value (RU4), and level of mobility (RU1). Each of these attributes has an impact on the information and incentives that actors face when making decisions in the social-ecological system. For instance, the likelihood that resource users will invest in activities to manage a resource is expected to form an inverted curvilinear relation with the replacement rate of that resource (Basurto and Ostrom 2009). At very slow replacement rates, gains in the distant future are likely to be heavily discounted, generating few positive incentives for collective action, while rapid replacement obviates the need for collective action over a given range of demand.[3] Thus, collec-

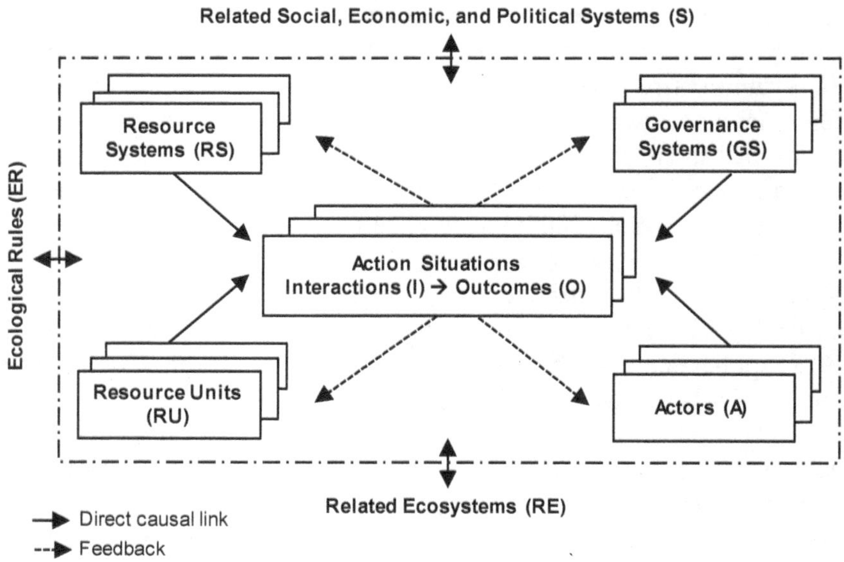

Figure 12.1. Basic structure of the SES framework.

Source: Adapted from Epstein et al. (2013).

tive action to manage a resource is most likely to occur in the context of resources with intermediate replacement rates.

A key feature of the framework is its explicit recognition that the effects of any attribute of a system may be mediated by other attributes of that system, most notably institutions that *jointly* influence the incentives of actors (Agrawal and Yadama 1997; Poteete and Ostrom 2004). In other words, although we expect intermediate rates of replacement to enhance prospects for collective action, a diverse assortment of relationships may be observed, as factors such as resource mobility (RU1), group size (A1), and property rights (GS4) vary across social-ecological systems. A thorough diagnosis depends upon an enumeration of the relevant attributes of a social-ecological system that are sufficient to account for behavior and outcomes in that system. Given the complexity involved, the SES framework is designed to allow scholars to leverage knowledge from prior research across relevant disciplines, specifically by focusing their attention on a smaller subset of discrete and easily coded attributes related to a particular question or method of inquiry. In this way, knowledge accumulates piecewise through iterative processes of hypothesis generation,

Table 12.1. Tier-one components of the SES framework

Resource systems	Resource units	Governance systems	Actors	Interactions	Outcomes	Related ecosystems
RS1 Sector	RU1 Mobility	GS1 Government organizations	A1 Group size	I1 Harvesting levels	O1 Social preference measures	RE1 Climate patterns
RS2 Boundary clarity	RU2 Replacement rate	GS2 Non-government organizations	A2 Socioeconomic attributes	I2 Information sharing	O2 Ecological performance measures	RE2 Pollution patterns
RS3 Size	RU3 Interactions	GS3 Network structure	A3 History of use	I3 Deliberation processes	O3 Externalities to other SESs	RE3 Flows into and out of focal SES
RS4 Infrastructure	RU4 Economic value	GS4 Property rights	A4 Location	I4 User conflicts		
RS5 Productivity	RU5 Size	GS5 Operational rules	A5 Leadership	I5 Investment activities		
RS6 Equilibrium properties	RU6 Distinctive markings	GS6 Collective-choice rules	A6 Norms/social capital	I6 Lobbying activities		
RS7 Predictability	RU7 Distribution	GS7 Constitutional rules	A7 Knowledge of SES			
RS8 Storage capacity		GS8 Monitoring and sanctioning processes	A8 Resource dependence			
RS9 Location			A9 Technology used			

Source: Based on Ostrom (2007).

testing, and refinement toward a more general theory of sustainability. The danger, however, is that in focusing only on a small subset of variables, scholars will neglect *interactions* among institutions that generate substantially different outcomes. Ironically, Ostrom's (2007) own analysis of Hardin's Herder Problem illustrates this very problem.

Ostrom's Application of the SES Framework to Hardin's Herder Problem

Ostrom (2007) sought to demonstrate the diagnostic utility of the SES framework by applying it to Hardin's (1968) "tragedy of the commons." In Hardin's description,[4] herders on an open-access pasture lacked incentives to conserve that pasture by controlling the number of cattle grazing upon it. Market incentives guided them (as if by an "invisible hand") to keep adding more and more cattle to their herds to maximize private profits, even though doing so reduced the social product, as the pasture deteriorated. Hardin (1968) believed the only way to avoid destruction of the open-access pasture was to either privatize the pasture or for governments to regulate access and use. Ostrom (1990) successfully rebutted Hardin's presumption that common-property solutions—self-regulation by the herders themselves—would be ineffective. But she did not question his presumption that property rights in the pasture were the focal institutions.

Ostrom (2007) depicted the situation, using the SES framework, as shown in Figure 12.2. This figure demonstrates the utility of the SES framework by showing how Hardin's (1968) entire textual analysis can be condensed to a few relatively simple variables and presented in an easy-to-understand graphical fashion. And it shows how individual case studies—stylized and real, thickly or thinly descriptive—might be diagnosed and compared using regularized variables. But, most importantly, it shows that incomplete attention to the set of institutions affecting social-ecological outcomes can lead to inappropriate diagnosis and analysis.

The most striking feature of Ostrom's (2007) treatment of Hardin's Herder Problem is the complete absence of Governance System variables, as if the entire situation is pre- or non-institutional. This might be an accurate reflection of Hardin's own understanding of the situation, but it is misleading. As a conceptual matter, what could it mean for any social system, as such, to be pre-institutional, that is, devoid of rules, norms, customs, or habits? Simply put, a social system without an institutional structure is not a *social* system.

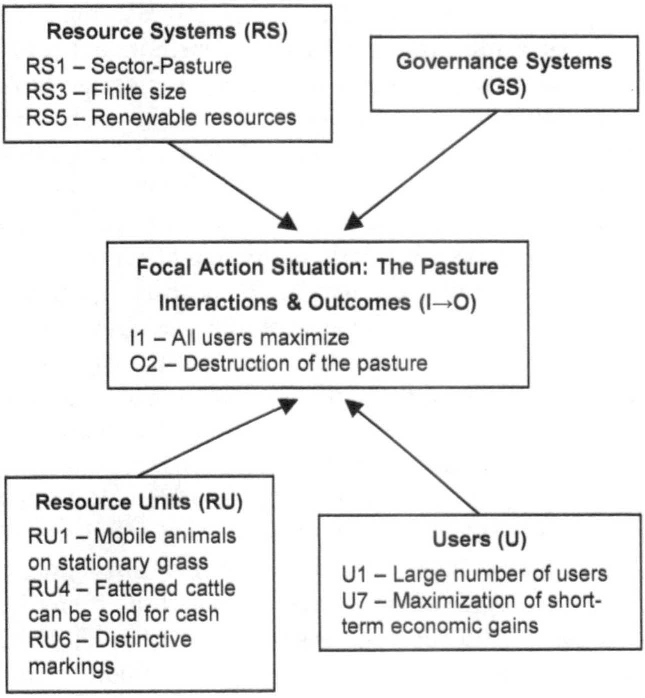

Figure 12.2. Ostrom's SES diagnosis of the Herder Problem.

It is doubtful that Ostrom actually believed such a null set of institutions was a practical possibility, although elsewhere (e.g., Ostrom 1990, 2–3, 140) she does invoke a Hobbesian state of nature (see Hobbes [1651] 1994) to describe the "tragedy of the commons" and the default conditions under which humans interact over common-pool resources.[5] Even if Ostrom (1990) did not intend the state of nature to be taken literally as a description of very early human society, the complete absence of Governance Systems variables reflects a Hobbesian interpretation in which no humanly devised institution has any relevance (i.e., would affect outcomes) in that setting.

Hardin (1968) did, of course, recommend the imposition of institutional arrangements associated with either markets and private property or governments and regulation to avoid the open-access tragedy. So it is not entirely fair to accuse Hardin of being unaware of the importance of institutions. A more reasonable criticism is that Hardin failed to realize just how institution-laden his allegoric setting already was, prior to the imposition of any institutional solution. Ostrom's (1990) research unequivocally demonstrated that Hardin overlooked viable institutional solutions, specifically common-property regimes that satisfy the design principles she identified.[6] We take Ostrom's primary point in this exercise to be a plausible explanation for why Hardin was unable to see other paths that might avert the tragedy by introducing other kinds of institutions.

The specific mode of argument used by Ostrom (2007) to make this point, however, may have a similarly narrowing effect on future analysts. By presuming that institutions were completely absent from Hardin's pasture (or, that it was pre-institutional), Ostrom was drawn to suggest the addition of new institutions, rather than investigating ways in which existing but unrecognized institutions contributed to that tragedy in the first place, or how the continued presence of existing institutions might undermine efforts to avert the tragedy by building new ones.

In fact, a null set of institutions is inconsistent with the "tragic" outcome that Hardin described and Ostrom indicates as Outcome (O2) in her SES analysis. In the absence of formal or informal institutions protecting ownership (or possession) of cattle, herders have little if any incentive to let loose their cattle on the open-access pasture, where others might claim them. Opportunities to profit from selling cattle would be limited by the absence of institutions that (1) recognize and protect ownership and (2) enforce impersonal contracts (see, e.g., Greif 2005; North 1990). Consequently, trade would be greatly restricted, and the pasture would not likely be overgrazed. The "tragedy of the commons" would not arise.[7]

Ostrom (2007, 15183) observed that "the animals . . . grazing on the pasture are the property of their owners," who receive "all the proceeds from the sale" of any cattle they have grazed on the open-access pasture. But, surprisingly, her application of the SES framework did not incorporate these social facts. Not only are they inconsistent with her empty Governance Systems box, they are central to Hardin's story. The overexploitation of the pasture results directly from the incentives created by the *combination* of the following institutional elements: (1) no property rights in the pasture land; (2) private ownership of cattle, including the right to alienate and the right to all proceeds from alienation; (3) an implicit rule that grass is, in effect, privatized to the herder as it is consumed and metabolized by that herder's cattle;[8] and (4) incentives stemming from the structure of market institutions. Each of these institutional variables is a matter of collective choice, which is to say, they could be otherwise. If one or more of these were altered, Hardin's tragedy might not have resulted in the first place.

A Revised Application of the SES Framework to Hardin's Herder Problem

Figure 12.3 revises Ostrom's (2007) depiction of the tragedy to incorporate institutional attributes of the social-ecological system that are needed to specify conditions for the deterioration of an open-access pasture. Some of these changes, most notably the explicit division between grass and cattle, are simply a matter of reorganization to clarify their role as discrete components of the social-ecological system. Others are novel. For example, the existence of an exogenous supply of cattle is not mentioned in either account, but presumably the cattle have some external origin, given that herders seem to collectively possess a large enough supply of cattle to deplete the pasture. Herders presumably also have access to alternative sources of feed upon which the cattle could be fattened for sale. The most important changes, in the Governance Systems component, signify that the tragedy of the open-access pasture is the product of interactions among institutions that assign individual rights over the cattle that convert unowned grass from the open-access pasture into privately owned beef.

Using the Roman law distinctions that continue to dominate modern theories of property (Birks and McLeod 1987; Cole 2002, 8–14; Cole and Ostrom 2012, 44–45),[9] the pasture (i.e., the land itself) is *res communes omnium* (the common property of all),[10] which means that no one can exclude anyone else from entry and use, but neither does entry and use (e.g., acts of occupation or possession) create rights of ownership (which would signify *res nullius* or non-property) in the pasture lands. The grass growing on the pasture is not *res communes* but *res nullius*, an unowned resource available for appropriation as private property (*res privatæ*) by acts of extraction or consumption. Conversion from non-property to property occurs via the "rule of capture," which applies to many "wild" natural resources, including not only wild animals and fish but also groundwater, oil, and gas, and in this case, unowned grass on the open-access pasture (see, e.g., Johnston 2005). The cattle that graze on the grass are *res privatæ*, owned by the herders who release them onto the pasture to feed. Because the cattle are domesticated animals, they remain private property even after they leave the land of their owners; they do not become open for recapture by others following their release onto the commons (see, e.g., Ingham 1900). While on the pasture, the cattle serve, in effect, as *agents* of the herders, converting the grass from open-access to private property simply by consuming it. We know this by virtue of the fact that the value of the added weight of each cow, attributable to grass

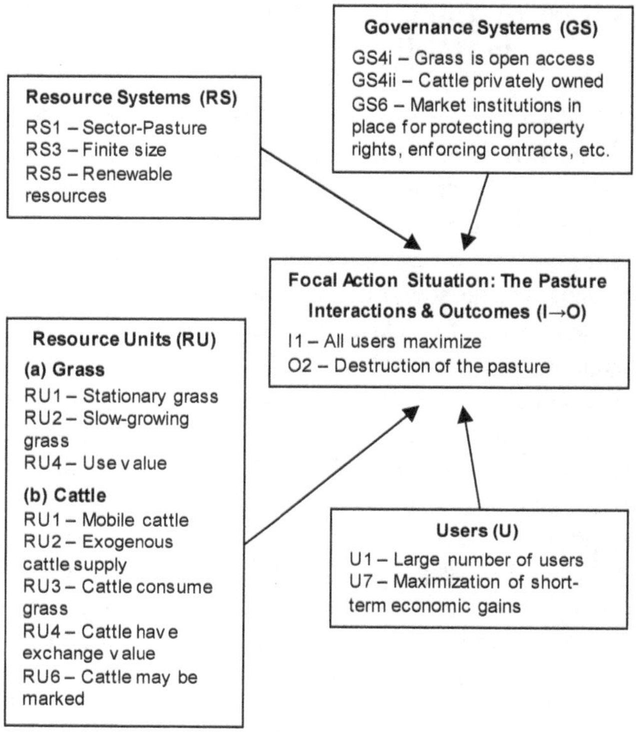

Figure 12.3. Revised application of the SES framework to the Herder Problem.

consumed from the pasture, belongs entirely to that cow's owner when the cow is sold in market.

These various property rules, as applied to the pasture, the grass, the cattle, and their owners, are *a fortiori* institutions. They are not socially immutable "brute facts" about the world but inherently alterable "institutional facts" (see Searle 1995). They belong to the Governance Systems box because they all play a significant role in driving behavior in and outcomes of Hardin's Herder Problem. Changing one or more of these property rules could easily alter the outcome because the ecological components of a system are inextricably linked via a variety of natural processes (Araral 2013; Holling and Meffe 1996). Imagine, for example, if the law treated domesticated animals just as it does wild animals so that any cow released (or escaping) onto the open-access pasture would become *res nullius* (just like the grass) and liable to recapture by anyone (see Arnold 1921; Ingham 1990). How likely would a herder be to release the first, let alone the next (or the *n*th), cow onto the pasture? The pasture would more likely be underutilized than overexploited. Or, what if the grass were not *res nullius* but *res communes* so that even after consumption by a herder's cow, all members of the community would have a right to share in the increased market value of that cow attributable to the amount of grass it consumed from the common pasture? Measurement problems would arise, but such a rule would also alter the incentives for overgrazing, as much as if the pasture itself was privatized.[11]

This is not to argue that any of the several property rules at work on Hardin's pasture *should* be different than it is—the analysis here is positive, not normative. There may be excellent socioeconomic reasons supporting the existing set of institutions, even if those choices in the aggregate contribute to potential commons tragedies.

Other background institutions play an integral role in Hardin's allegory. For one, private property rights (and correlative duties) in the cattle require enforcement mechanisms. In addition, Hardin presumes the existence of functional markets for cattle-based products, and such markets require money (or barter) and contracts plus contract-enforcement mechanisms. In the absence of institutions supporting market exchange, herders would graze cattle only for their use value, thereby reducing pressure on the pasture.[12]

Some resource systems and institutions left out of Hardin's allegory entirely, as well as Ostrom's application to it of the SES framework, can play a major role in determining social and ecological outcomes. To take only one example, cattle do not live by grass alone but also require water (Ensminger and Rutten 1991, 688). Where is the water on or near Hardin's pasture? And what rules or norms govern its use? Without answers to these questions, any SES analysis of Hardin's "tragedy of the commons" must remain incomplete. It is, however, a virtual certainty that without some reliable water source for the cattle, the pasture would not be overgrazed.

Institutional Interactions and Institutional Fit

This paper has shown that a myopic preoccupation with a single institutional variable applied to a single resource system (property rights in the pasture) while neglecting related and interacting resources (the grass and the cattle), and the institutions that condition human interactions with those resources, can result in impoverished analyses and misdiagnoses. If the Governance System in Hardin's Herder Problem were truly a null set, as both Ostrom (2007) and Hardin (1968) treated it, the "tragedy of the commons" would not have arisen. In an institutional vacuum, atomistic herders would lack incentives to graze more cows than they could physically protect from misappropriation.

Conceptually, the notion of a pre- or non-institutional social system is a contradiction in terms. Empirically, the world we inhabit is replete with institutions that prescribe what actions must, must not, or may be taken given certain conditions (Coleman 1987; Crawford and Ostrom 1995; Elster 2007). While some institutions, notably reciprocity norms, enable groups to solve a diverse assortment of social dilemmas (Axelrod 1984; Fehr et al. 2002; Ostrom 1998, 2009), others constrain, limit, or undermine cooperation, equality, and collective well-being (North 1990). Any system of institutional arrangements is, as a consequence, deeply complex.

Our analysis also has implications for the notion of "institutional fit," which suggests that institutions ought to fit or match the defining features of the problems they are meant to address (Folke et al. 2007; Young 2002, 2008). This paper demonstrates that institutional fitness is not just a matter of relations between discrete institutions and ecological circumstances but also concerns how various institutions (and sets of institutions) affecting resources interact with each other. Simply put, institutional fit is about both (1) how the rules fit the biophysical conditions and (2) how the rules fit with other rules. In fact, some have argued that Ostrom's (1990) successful common-property regimes are better understood as a special case of collective private property that depend upon interactions between shared appropriation and management rights within a group, and the ability to apply those rights to exclude other groups (Araral 2014).[13] Moreover, viewed in isolation, the absence of a property regime governing access to and use of a pasture cannot lead to any predictions about the level of use. Indeed, as Libecap (1989, 13–14) has explained, open-access may be economically optimal in conditions where supply is high and demand is low so that the costs of introducing and enforcing property rights and duties (among other institutions) would outweigh the benefits. Open-access is, in fact, the default condition in the absence of institutions (including social norms) created through collective action.

Institutional studies of commons and social-ecological systems often support an optimistic view regarding the potential for institutional change to lead to sustainable and equitable use of natural resources across diverse human societies. But sustainability is not merely a question of finding the best institution for a given environmental problem. Rather, multiple, interacting institutions in complex social-ecological systems generate incentives that can either support or degrade resource sustainability, among other social goals.

No single analysis can detail all the institutional arrangements that might conceivably affect outcomes in a complex social-ecological system, but analysts must work hard to avoid overlooking especially important institutional factors. Ostrom (2007, 15181) intended the SES framework to be "a step toward building a strong interdisciplinary science of complex, multilevel systems that will enable future diagnosticians to match governance arrangements to specific problems embedded in a social-ecological context." Ironically, she stopped short in her own SES-based analysis of Hardin's allegory of the "tragedy of the commons," but this paper demonstrates the power of the SES framework to point out such mistakes and suggest further improvements in our collective understanding.

The "tragedy of the commons" is not a consequence of the *absence* of institutions but instead a set of maladapted institutions that support incentives for overexploitation. The appropriate response is *not* necessarily to *create* new institutions; an alteration in existing institutional arrangements may sometimes be sufficient. Even when new institutions seem desirable, they must be analyzed within the context of the existing set of institutions with which they must interact.

The open-access pasture does not exist in splendid isolation but operates within a larger universe of interacting resources and institutions. Hardin's "tragedy of the commons" is not just about the pasture; it is equally about the grass, the cows, the herders, and the human society.

Acknowledgments

We thank Marty Anderies, Marco Janssen, Patty Lezotte, Arden Rowell, and presentation audiences at the Ostrom Workshop at Indiana University Bloomington, the Center for the Study of Institutional Diversity at Arizona State University, and the Midwest Law & Economics Association annual meeting at the University of Illinois College of Law. Financial support for Professor Cole's participation in this project was provided by a FORMAS grant from the Swedish Research Council for the joint research program, COMMONS.

Notes

This chapter was originally published in the *Journal of Institutional Economics* 10(3) (2014): 353–69.

1. Cole and Grossman (2010) argue that the Herder Problem is more in the nature of an Assurance Game than a Prisoners' Dilemma, but the outcome of the game may still resemble that of a Prisoners' Dilemma depending on levels of trust, communication, and so forth.

2. Ostrom might have been attempting merely to describe what she took to be Hardin's misunderstanding of the range of institutional solutions to the Herder Problem, but she does not explicitly specify which institutions, if any, were already present in that specific situation.

3. If resource replacement rates are slow enough, and returns from current exploitation are high enough, even private owners of resources can be expected to unsustainably overexploit those resources (see Clark 1973a, 1973b).

4. Earlier versions had been told by Aristotle (1941, §1262b34–35) in the fourth century BCE, and fisheries economists writing in the twentieth century CE, including Andersen (1983), Gordon (1954), and Scott (1955).

5. The phrase "common-pool resource" refers to a particular set of goods that are rivalrous in consumption but from which exclusion is very costly. These are distinguished from private goods (easy excludability and rivalrous in consumption), public goods (very costly to exclude but non-rivalrous in consumption), and toll goods (low-cost excludability and rivalrous in consumption) (V. Ostrom and E. Ostrom 1977, 12, fig. 1). These types of goods, with their varying characteristics, must not be confused with the various property systems (private, common, public, or hybrid) that might be deployed to manage them. Unfortunately, scholars still sometimes confuse or conflate common-pool resources with property systems used to manage them. For a recent example, see Araral (2014, 19), observing a "fundamental difference between CPR (the acronym he uses to denote common-pool resources) and private property." A common-pool resource system can be managed either via private property, common property, or public property, or admixtures of the three (see, e.g., Cole 2002; Cole and Ostrom 2012).

6. Ostrom's (1990, 90, table 3.1) eight design principles are: (1) clearly defined boundaries, (2) congruence between appropriation and provision rules and local conditions, (3) most affected individuals participate in rule-making, (4) reliable monitoring, (5) graduated sanctions, (6) rapid and low-cost conflict-resolution mechanisms, (7) minimal recognition and acceptance of local rules by external authorities, and (8) local rules nested in larger governance systems (for common-property regimes that are part of larger systems).

7. A tragedy of the commons could arise from mere subsistence use if the number of users is large enough relative to the size of the pasture, and their demand outstrips the replacement rate of the grass. But such a scenario is far less likely, and it is not the scenario that Hardin portrayed in his seminal paper.

8. The "tragedy of the commons" story is not restricted to this combination of privately owned cattle and open-access pastureland. What is critical is that part of a publicly available resource can be captured and used, either directly or indirectly, for private gain. An analogous tragedy might occur in the absence of

clearly defined property rights, but analysis of that case would have to incorporate transaction costs of capturing and protecting private gains.

9. We do not mean to suggest that the set of institutions conditioning access to and use of Hardin's pasture is determined by Roman law or, indeed, any formal legal system. However, Roman law property categories provide a convenient set of concepts for understanding the institutional structure of both formal and informal legal systems.

10. The Roman property category of *res communes* implied an unchangeable non-property status that is very different from modern conceptions of the phrase "common property," which imply group, communal, or collective ownership. Today, as Araral (2014, 19) observes, "common property" can denote a special form of private property; that is, property owned by more than a single individual. However, other modern forms of common property, such as tribal property or communes, appear more like public than private property (see, e.g., Cole and Ostrom 2012, 44, fig. 2.1).

11. Such a sharing rule is not fanciful. Rechlin et al. (2002), for example, discuss community forest systems in China and Nepal that require sharing of monetary and material benefits from forest harvests with all stakeholders. Somewhat closer to the present context, the great French novelist Victor Hugo, in his masterpiece *Les Misérables* ([1862] 1887, 75–76), discusses mid-mountain peasants who share the proceeds of the cattle they graze to produce cheese. In other cultures, a number of herders may own various shares of cows grazed on a common pasture (see Mors 1954). This is not to argue normatively for such a solution to a potential commons tragedy. We are merely making an analytical point about variability of property institutions.

12. On the distinction between "use value" and "exchange value," see, for example, Smith ([1776] 1994, 31). Note the implication that whether a commodity possesses exchange value or only use value depends substantially on the institutional setting and not simply on its scarcity (available supply relative to demand).

13. But see note 10, observing that common-property regimes may closely resemble either group private ownership or certain forms of public ownership.

References

Acheson, J. M. 2006. "Institutional Failure in Resource Management." *Annual Review of Anthropology* 35(1): 117–34.

Agrawal, A., and G. Yadama. 1997. "How Do Local Institutions Mediate Market and Population Pressures on Resources? Forest Panchayats in Kumaon, India." *Development and Change* 28(3): 435–65.

Andersen, P. (trans.) 1983. "On Rent of Fishing Grounds: A Translation of Jens Warming's 1911 Article, with an Introduction." *History of Political Economy* 15(3): 391–96.

Araral, E. 2013. "What Makes Socio-Ecological Systems Robust? An Institutional Analysis of the 2,000 Year-Old Ifugao Society." *Human Ecology* 41(6): 859–70.

———. 2014. "Ostrom, Hardin and the Commons: A Critical Appreciation and a Revisionist View." *Environmental Science & Policy* 36: 11–23.

Aristotle. 1941. *The Basic Works of Aristotle.* Translated and edited by R. McKeon, pp. 1127–324. New York: Random House.

Arnold, E. C. 1921. "The Law of Possession Governing the Acquisition of Animals *Ferae Naturae.*" *American Law Review* 55(3): 393–404.

Axelrod, R. 1984. *The Evolution of Cooperation.* New York: Basic Books.

Baland, J.-M., and J.-P. Platteau. 1996. *Halting Degradation of Natural Resources.* Oxford, UK: Oxford University Press.

Ban, N. C., M. Mills, J. Tam, C. C. Hicks, S. Klain, N. Stoeckl, M. C. Bottrill, J. Levine, R. L. Pressey, T. Satterfield, and K. M. A. Chan. 2013. "A Social-Ecological Approach to Conservation Planning: Embedding Social Considerations." *Frontiers in Ecology and the Environment* 11(4): 194–202.

Basurto, X., and E. Ostrom. 2009. "Beyond the Tragedy of the Commons." *Economia delle fonti di energia e dell'ambiente* 52(1): 35–60.

Birks, P., and G. McLeod (trans.). 1987. *Justinian's Institutes.* Ithaca, NY: Cornell University Press.

Blanco, E. 2011. "A Social-Ecological Approach to Voluntary Environmental Initiatives: The Case of Nature-Based Tourism." *Policy Sciences* 44(1): 35–52.

Brook, B. W., N. S. Sodhi, and P. K. L. Ng. 2003. "Catastrophic Extinctions Follow Deforestation in Singapore." *Nature* 424(6947): 420–26.

Chhatre, A., and A. Agrawal. 2009. "Trade-Offs and Synergies between Carbon Storage and Livelihood Benefits from Forest Commons." *Proceedings of the National Academy of Sciences USA* 106(42): 17667–70.

Cinner, J. E., T. R. McClanahan, M. A. MacNeil, N. A. J. Graham, T. M. Daw, Ahmad Mukminin, D. A. Feary, et al. 2012. "Comanagement of Coral Reef Social-Ecological Systems." *Proceedings of the National Academy of Sciences USA* 109(14): 5219–22.

Clark, C. W. 1973a. "The Economics of Overexploitation." *Science* 181: 630–34.

———. 1973b. "Profit Maximization and the Extinction of Animal Species." *Journal of Political Economy* 81(4): 950–61.

Clement, F. 2010. "Analysing Decentralised Natural Resource Governance: Proposition for a 'Politicised' Institutional Analysis and Development Framework." *Policy Sciences* 43(2): 129–56.

Cole, D. H. 2002. *Pollution and Property: Comparing Ownership Institutions for Environmental Protection.* Cambridge, MA: Cambridge University Press.

Cole, D. H., and P. Z. Grossman. 2010. "Institutions Matter! Why the Herder Problem is not a Prisoner's Dilemma." *Theory and Decision* 69(2): 219–31.

Cole, D. H., and E. Ostrom. 2012. "The Variety of Property Systems and Rights in Natural Resources." In *Property in Land and Other Resources*, edited by D. H. Cole and E. Ostrom, 37–64. Cambridge, MA: Lincoln Institute of Land Policy.

Coleman, J. S. 1987. "Norms as Social Capital." In *Economic Imperialism: The Economic Approach Applied Outside the Field of Economics*, edited by G. Radnitzky and P. Bernholz, 133–155. New York: Paragon House.

Cox, M., G. Arnold, and S. Villamayor Tomas. 2010. "A Review of Design Principles for Community-Based Natural Resource Management." *Ecology and Society* 15(4): 38.

Crawford, S. E. S., and E. Ostrom. 1995. "A Grammar of Institutions." *American Political Science Review* 89(3): 582–600.

Edmondson, W. T., G. C. Anderson, and D. R. Peterson. 1956. "Artificial Eutrophication of Lake Washington." *Limnology and Oceanography* 1(1): 47–53.

Elster, J. 2007. *Explaining Social Behavior: More Nuts and Bolts for the Social Sciences.* Cambridge, UK: Cambridge University Press.

Ensminger, J., and A. Rutten. 1991. "The Political Economy of Changing Property Rights: Dismantling a Pastoral Commons." *American Ethnologist* 18(4): 683–99.

Epstein, G., J. M. Vogt, S. K. Mincey, M. Cox, and B. Fischer. 2013. "Missing Ecology: Integrating Ecological Perspectives with the Social-Ecological System Framework." *International Journal of the Commons* 7(2): 432–53.

Feeny, D., F. Berkes, B. J. McCay, and J. M. Acheson. 1990. "The Tragedy of the Commons: Twenty-Two Years Later." *Human Ecology* 18(1): 1–19.

Fehr, E., U. Fischbacher, and S. Gächter. 2002. "Strong Reciprocity, Human Cooperation, and the Enforcement of Social Norms." *Human Nature* 13(1): 1–25.

Fleischman, F., K. Boenning, G. Garcia-Lopez, S. Mincey, M. Schmitt-Harsh, K. Daedlow, M. C. Lopez, X. Basurto, B. Fischer, and E. Ostrom. 2010. "Disturbance, Response, and Persistence in Self-Organized Forested Communities: Analysis of Robustness and Resilience in Five Communities in Southern Indiana." *Ecology and Society* 15(4): 9.

Folke, C., L. Pritchard, F. Berkes, J. Colding, and U. Svedin. 2007. "The Problem of Fit between Ecosystems and Institutions: Ten Years Later." *Ecology and Society* 12(1): 30.

Gordon, H. S. 1954. "The Economic Theory of a Common-Property Resource: The Fishery." *Journal of Political Economy* 62(2): 124.

Greif, A. 2005. "Commitment, Coercion, and Markets: The Nature and Dynamics of Institutions Supporting Exchange." In *Handbook of New Institutional Economics*, edited by C. Menard and M. Shirley, 727–86. Amsterdam, Netherlands: Springer.

Gutiérrez, N. L., R. Hilborn, and O. Defeo. 2011. "Leadership, Social Capital and Incentives Promote Successful Fisheries." *Nature* 470(7334): 386–89.

Hardin, G. 1968. "The Tragedy of the Commons." *Science* 162(3859): 1243–48.

Hobbes, T. [1651] 1994. *Leviathan.* Cambridge, MA: Hackett.

Holling, C. S., and G. K. Meffe. 1996. "Command and Control and the Pathology of Natural Resource Management." *Conservation Biology* 10(2): 328–37.

Hugo, V. [1862] 1887. *The Works of Victor Hugo.* Trans. I. F. Hapgood. New York: Thomas Y. Crowell.

Ingham, J. H. 1900. *Law of Animals: A Treatise on Property in Animals: Wild and Domestic and the Rights and Responsibilities Arising Therefrom.* Philadelphia, PA: T & J Johnson.

Johnston, J. S. 2005. "The Rule of Capture and the Economic Dynamics of Natural Resource Use and Survival under Open Access Management Regimes." *Environmental Law* 35(4): 855–98.

Larson, A. M., and F. Soto. 2008. "Decentralization of Natural Resource Governance Regimes." *Annual Review of Environment and Resources* 33(1): 213–39.

Libecap, G. D. 1989. *Contracting for Property Rights.* Cambridge, UK: Cambridge University Press.

Ludwig, D., R. Hilborn, and C. Waters. 1993. "Uncertainty, Resource Exploitation and Conservation: Lessons from History." *Science* 260(5104): 17–36.

Mors, P. O. 1954. "Cattle in Buhaya." *Anthropology Quarterly* 27(1): 23–29.

Myers, R. A., J. A. Hutchings, and N. J. Barrowman. 1997. "Why Do Fish Stocks Collapse? The Example of Cod in Atlantic Canada." *Ecological Applications* 7(1): 91–106.

North, D. C. 1990. *Institutions, Institutional Change and Economic Performance.* Cambridge, UK: Cambridge University Press.

Ostrom, E. 1990. *Governing the Commons: The Evolution of Institutions for Collective Action.* New York: Cambridge University Press.

———. 1998. "A Behavioral Approach to the Rational Choice Theory of Collective Action." *American Political Science Review* 92(1): 1–22.

———. 2007. "A Diagnostic Approach for Going beyond Panaceas." *Proceedings of the National Academy of Sciences USA* 104(39): 15181–87.

———. 2009. "A General Framework for Analyzing Sustainability of Social-Ecological Systems." *Science* 325(5939): 419–22.

Ostrom, E., and M. Cox. 2010. "Moving Beyond Panaceas: A Multi-Tiered Diagnostic Approach for Social-Ecological Analysis." *Environmental Conservation* 37(4): 451–63.

Ostrom, V. 2008. *The Intellectual Crisis in American Public Administration.* 3rd ed. Tuscaloosa: University of Alabama Press.

Ostrom, V., and E. Ostrom. 1997. "Public Goods and Public Choices." In *Alternatives for Delivering Public Services: Toward Improved Performance*, edited by E. S. Savas, 7–49. Boulder, CO: Westview Press.

Pierson, P. 2000. "Increasing Returns, Path Dependence, and the Study of Politics." *American Political Science Review* 94(2): 251–67.

Poteete, A. R., and E. Ostrom. 2004. "Heterogeneity, Group Size and Collective Action: The Role of Institutions in Forest Management." *Development and Change* 35(3): 435–61.

Rechlin, M. A., A. L. Hammett, W. R. Burch, and Y. Song. 2002. "Sharing the Wealth: A Comparative Study of the Distribution of Benefits from Community Forestry Management in Southern China and Nepal." *Journal of Sustainable Forestry* 15(2): 1–23.

Ribot, J. C., A. Agrawal, and A. M. Larson. 2006. "Recentralizing While Decentralizing: How National Governments Reappropriate Forest Resources." *World Development* 34(11): 1864–86.

Scott, A. D. 1955. "The Fishery: The Objectives of Sole Ownership." *Journal of Political Economy* 63(2): 116–24.

Searle, J. R. 1995. *The Construction of Social Reality.* London: Penguin.

Simon, H. A. 1962. "The Architecture of Complexity." *Proceedings of the American Philosophical Society* 106(6): 467–82.

Smith, A. [1776] 1994. *An Inquiry into the Nature and Causes of the Wealth of Nations.* New York: Modern Library.

Wade, R. 1994. *Village Republics.* San Francisco, CA: ICS Press.

Young, O. R. 2002. *The Institutional Dimensions of Environmental Change: Fit, Interplay, and Scale.* Cambridge, MA: MIT Press.

———. 2008. "The Architecture of Global Environmental Governance: Bringing Science to Bear on Policy." *Global Environmental Politics* 8(1): 14–32.

13

Building a Diagnostic Ontology of Social-Ecological Systems

ULRICH J. FREY AND MICHAEL COX

Humanity currently faces large environmental challenges, including declining resources such as fish, soil, forests and fossil fuels, and pollution problems such as acid rain and climate change. The difficulties of analyzing these problems result in large part from their complexity. Environmental and natural resource problems occur in highly complex social-ecological systems (SESs), where variables do not contribute linearly to an outcome. Instead, variables interact in webs of causation, and the effects of each variable are highly contingent on the scale of analysis and the presence of many other factors. As a result, producing theories relating causes to effects in these systems is extremely difficult, as outcomes emerge from unpredictable interactions. The effects of a variable may appear clear in one system, but contribute to widely divergent effects in others. We call the challenge of constructing theories of such complex systems the *complexity problem* (see Folke 2006 for a more complete treatment of the dimensions of complexity in social and ecological systems). One typical example of complexity in SESs are heterogeneous actors with divergent interests interacting with other stakeholders within an ecosystem that itself behaves in a non-linear and dynamic way.

Due to this complexity, it may be unclear where problems are located within a system. To some (Rittel and Webber 1973), it seems that the problems involved are "wicked," which means that concepts will never lose their ambiguity or fuzziness, that answers necessarily remain unclear or uncertain and that each case is unique. Therefore, there is little learning from past cases, thus little trial-and-error process.

In our view, this is too pessimistic. *Ontologies* are one attempt to clarify concepts. Even if this is not always successful, less ambiguity can definitely be reached as hundreds of working and productive ontologies in "fuzzy" domains demonstrate convincingly (see below). Moreover, SESs are comparable, as shown by large databases of similar systems (Gibson et al. 2005), meta-analyses (Gutiérrez et al. 2011) and the fact that a few frameworks are advantageously used by thousands of different researchers. However, it is indeed difficult to construct meaningful classes in an ontology that do not overlap substantially and which help to cut the domain at its joints.

In addressing this problem, the study of environmental management and policy faces several other challenges. One of these has been an historic overreliance on simplistic policy prescriptions and management strategies that do not adequately account for this complexity. This reliance has led to disappointing results in many areas around the world (Ostrom and Cox 2010). We refer to this overreliance as the *panacea problem*. Much work has been done in turn to address the panacea problem, including research programs in common-pool resource (CPR) management (Ostrom et al. 1994; Ostrom et al. 2002), and social and ecological resilience (Folke 2006; Gallopin 2006). These programs have now examined a multitude of variables that affect outcomes where natural resources are managed. As such, they do represent progress in addressing the complexity and panacea problems by distinguishing between more general patterns across systems and specific patterns to a particular system.

However, this progress has led to another challenge, which we refer to as the *scatter problem*. This is a lack of integration of many research findings into a cohesive set of theoretical statements that explain how relevant conditions interact to produce success or failure over time. The few theories that exist to explain the many findings and concepts are not enough. Unless we assume linearly additive and non-contingent causality, the current state of knowledge falls short of the kind needed to provide useful governance advice across a range of social-ecological settings. Overcoming this scatter problem is complicated by several others. First, data sets of different research groups tend not to be shared or constructed in ways that facilitate integration. For the most part they are not designed to be shared due to investment in time, money or other resources by the research teams. Related to this, the specification and measurement of variables is frequently idiosyncratic to a particular study area, and too informal to facilitate comparisons of findings across studies. Conceptual validity is often unclear and external validity low. This situation mirrors a dilemma found in the ecological sciences (Madin et al. 2008).

The argument set forth in this paper is that a diagnostic approach, when implemented with an ontology, could potentially address all three problems. In this paper we will first discuss the benefits of a diagnostic and ontological approach, and then introduce components of an ontology we have constructed to begin the implementation of these approaches.

Diagnosis, Complexity, and Panaceas

The process of diagnosis involves asking a series of questions of a system, where subsequent questions are based on the answers to previous questions and are increasingly specific to the system being analyzed. This can be facilitated by a multilevel *framework* that orders a set of variables based on how likely they are to be relevant to a broad range of systems. A framework is a classificatory structure designed to "identify relevant variables" (Ostrom 2009, 420), in this case for studying complex SESs. It is multilevel, shows subsystems, relationships and a "common set of potentially relevant variables" (Ostrom 2009, 420) embedded within different contexts (e.g., S or ECO in Figure 13.1). More broadly relevant variables occur at higher, more primary levels in the framework. Each question addresses a variable and its potential values at a particular level in the framework. An analyst begins at the first level, and then asks increasingly specific questions at lower levels of the framework.

Diagnostic thinking in environmental management was popularized by Young (2002) and then Ostrom (2007, 2008, 2009). Ostrom (2007), whose work is the basis for our ontology, initially proposed a multilevel SES framework, arranging the relevant variables within four primary components at the first level, as shown in Figure 13.1.

These components are: (1) the governance system; (2) the actors; (3) the resource system; and (4) the resource units. Each of these components contained multiple variables at the framework's second level. Subsequent levels have also been proposed, but have not so far been formalized.

Multiple levels of analysis, arranged in accordance to how specific the variables at each level are to a subset of systems, help analysts think diagnostically and address the complexity problem. Each time an analyst asks a question of a particular variable, this potentially eliminates many other variables from consideration. For example, if an urban groundwater system is analyzed, questions pertaining to ecological and biophysical attributes of a forest ecosystem are generally not relevant. A diagnostic approach supported by an ontology would formalize this branching pro-

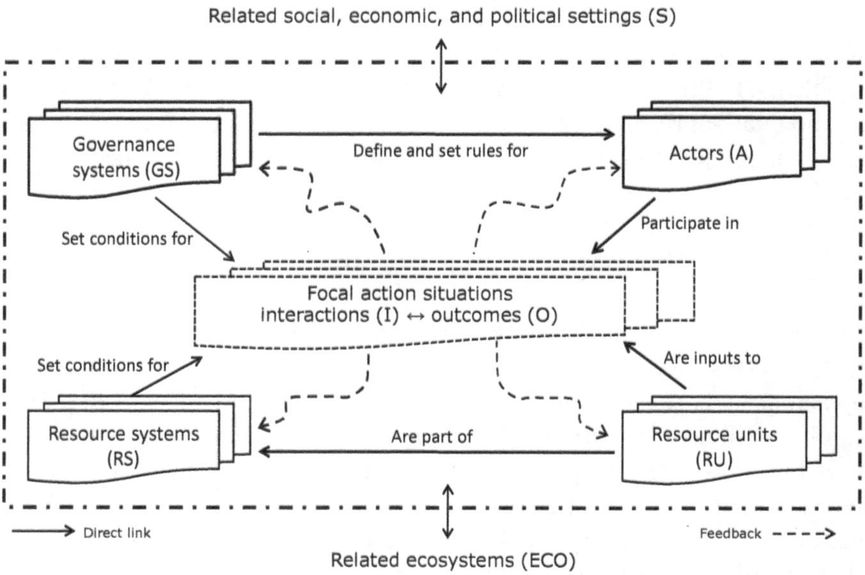

Figure 13.1. Tier 1 of the SES framework.
Source: Adapted from McGinnis and Ostrom (2014).

cess for any particular analysis, and would also emphasize the production of the type of information needed to decide whether the value that one variable takes on determines the potential relevance of another, more specific variable. Since ontologies are a conceptualization of a domain (e.g., of social-ecological systems), they are a kind of *operationalized framework*. As such, they are a tool for the diagnostic process, helping the analyst to choose the right questions at the right level and not miss important ones.

Diagnostics can also help with the *panacea problem*. The panacea problem occurs when an analyst constructs a theory that is either too specific or too general to be useful for a system to which it is applied. A theory may be defined as one or more general propositions used as explanation for a class of phenomena. Good theories may be falsified, are not circular, are internally and externally consistent, have a high explanatory power and are testable (Lakatos and Musgrave 1970; Popper 2002). States and markets, and the regimes of public and private property with which they are assumed to correspond, are frequently proposed solutions to environmental problems. However, these two solutions are much too general to be of much use in any particular system. The variability in the practical effects on outcomes *within* these categories is much too great in comparison with the variability *between* them (see Agrawal et al. 2008 for an application to forestry). Therefore, by themselves they are not very useful ways of categorizing complex institutional arrangements. They would require substantial taxonomic decomposition in order to be of more practical use to those who might implement them. The other extreme is when a highly specific theory is applied to a range of cases for which it is not accurate. Each of these is an example of a theory that is too simple to capture important variation across the systems to which it might be applied (see also Cox 2008).

With a multilevel framework, theories can be constructed at multiple levels of specificity as warranted by the similarities and differences among and between systems across levels. More specific theories will be accurate for a smaller subset of cases, but more useful for that subset. The reverse is true for more general theories. For example, some type of monitoring is likely to be beneficial for almost all systems where natural resources are managed. A theory positing this would be accurate for the great majority of systems, but would not provide much information regarding what type of monitoring should be implemented, or how it should be done in a particular system. Different types of monitoring, based on various configurations of rules and the types of actors carrying them out, will be better suited to different types of natural resource systems and social, economic, and political contexts. Theories of more specific factors complement the more general theories and are more useful for a smaller subset of systems. By constructing theories at the level of generality or specificity that is warranted by the data and information available, analysts can use a multilevel framework and diagnostic thinking to avoid the panacea problem.

Determining which level of specificity is warranted depends on the research question. If we are interested in a comparison of success of different SES like forests or irrigation systems, the first tier is probably the most relevant. If, on the other hand, a researcher is interested in differences in monitoring in irrigation systems, third- and fourth-tier variables are more of interest (Governance system (1) → Compliance (2) → Monitoring (3) → implementations of monitoring (4)). One particular way in which the diagnostic approach might be implemented is to embed it in a domain-specific ontology. Besides being able to address all three of the main problems discussed here, ontologies are well suited to implement the diagnostic approach. We now discuss the ways an ontology can improve upon the SES framework.

Ontologies

Ontologies and Diagnostics

Ontologies are a kind of representation. One of the earlier and more famous representations is the taxonomy of Carolus Linnaeus. He presented the available knowledge of animals and plants at that time in a unified and structured way in one place. The scientific advantages of such an effort are obvious: scattered information is collected in one place and may serve as a common starting point for domain experts by providing them with a unified and consistent vocabulary. Assumptions of other researchers working with it can be checked easily and double efforts can be avoided. However, this system is *not* an ontology but a *classification*. Ontologies have richer relationships between entities than taxonomies, where usually only one relationship is defined (Gruber 1995). One example for this is the relationship of "tree" and "branch." A tree "has" branches. Trees themselves are "a kind of" plants. This relationship is different and could be "is" or "is a kind of," but not "has."

Recently, ontologies have been most widely used in the field of bioinformatics as a means of *structuring* the vast new quantities of genetic data that have become available (Baclawski and Niu 2006). Ontologies have also been developed by various governmental organizations, including the U.S. National Library of Medicine (https://lhncbc.nlm.nih.gov/project/medical-ontology-research or http://www.openclinical.org/ontologies.html), the World Health Organization in the construction of its most recent International Classification of Diseases (ICD 11) and the Food and Agriculture Organization (FAO) (http://aims.fao.org/website/Fisheries-ontologies-/sub2). In addition, there are a few so-called "upper ontologies" (e.g., Cyc, Wordnet, SUMO) which are domain-independent and represent upper and more abstract concepts. Domain-specific ontologies may be latched onto these top-level ontologies, but usually are used as stand-alone products. There is less research on ontologies and SESs, but see Khazai et al. (2014) and Kumazawa et al. (2014).

Ontologies in general are at the very core of any knowledge-based system, since inferences of any kind of artificial intelligence have to be based on some information about the world.[1] The concept of ontology has been historically used in two completely different and separate ways and domains. The first use is in philosophy where the term was originally taken from. In philosophy it has a distinct history as the study of the nature of existence and reality. In this article, we do not use it in this first philosophical sense, but in a second sense, that of computer science. A common definition of an ontology in computer science is "an explicit specification of a conceptualization," while a conceptualization is "an abstract, simplified view of the world that we wish to represent for some purpose" (Gruber 1993, 1). So, a conceptualization is for example a certain domain like a forest. All concepts (terms) are specified by assigning an unambiguous meaning to them and define their relationships precisely (e.g., forest "has" trees). In the end, this process allows computers to automatically derive new relationships by using logic. For example, if a forest has trees and some trees have leaves, then computers can deduce that there must be leaves in every forest. Therefore, creating an ontology means taking a conceptualization of a domain of knowledge, or a simplified view of what is relevant in the world, and operationalizing it by formalizing it. In the remaining sections of this article we use some technical terms of ontology design. These terms, a short definition and an example are summarized in Table 13.1 and Figure 13.2.

Ontologies formalize in a very particular way. In order to construct an ontology of SESs, we would first construct the world (SESs) as *classes* of objects (e.g., resource units), the members of which are called *instances* (e.g., fish species A, tree species B) and share a common set of *attributes* via their common membership (e.g., shape, mobility).

Classes can have several relationships with each other. The most common is the "is a" relationship, where one class is a subclass of another, which is then called the superclass (e.g., fish and trees are subclasses of the superclass resource units). Therefore, any class can be a subclass to other classes (tree to resource unit) and be a superclass to others at the same time (tree to conifers).

If class A (tree species) is a subclass of superclass B (resource units), this means that any instance that is a member of A is also a member of B. This is most often a one-to-many relationship, with one superclass having many subclasses. Subclasses with a common superclass are called sibling classes. Subclasses can have their own subclasses.

Each class has a set of attributes associated with it. The term attribute is sometimes used to mean two things (Baclawski and Niu 2006): a variable, or placeholder for several different values (such as having a color), and the values themselves (such as being the color blue). Here we are referring to the placeholder concept. Subclasses inherit the attributes of their superclasses. For example, if we assign the attribute *biodiversity* to a class we call *ecosystems*, then every subclass of ecosystem (e.g., terrestrial or aquatic) would also have this attribute. It is also possible for a class to derive attributes from more than one superclass, which is called multiple inheritance.

Table 13.1. Definitions of key terms in ontologies

Term	Definition	Example
Ontology	A formal framework for representing knowledge; an explicit specification of a conceptualization, while a conceptualization is "an abstract, simplified view of the world that we wish to represent for some purpose" (Gruber 1993, 1).	http://www.openclinical.org/ontologies.html
Class	Concepts, types of objects, or kinds of things	cars; resource units
Subclass	A set of individuals in a class that are a subset of the set of individuals in another class. A class is by definition a subclass of itself.	electric cars; fish
Instance	Individuals or objects that are members of a class	Tesla S; herring
Relationship	Way in which classes and individuals relate to each other	"is a"
Attribute	Property, characteristic or parameter that classes and objects possess	red; length of 20–50 cm
Component	Part of a class	rear bumper; fin
Restriction	Description of what is or is not true (i.e., a class of all individuals for which all values of the property under consideration are either members of the class or are data values within the specified data range)	A car cannot be an animal.
Logical rule	Statement describing logical inferences that can be drawn from assertions (usually by automatic reasoning)	All fish can swim. A herring is a fish. Therefore, herrings can swim.
Disjoint class	If class A and B are disjoint, then no members of class A can be members of class B.	An animal either flies or cannot fly.

Source: Adapted partly from the OWL Web Ontology Language Reference 2004, http://www.w3.org/TR/owl-ref/#Class-def.

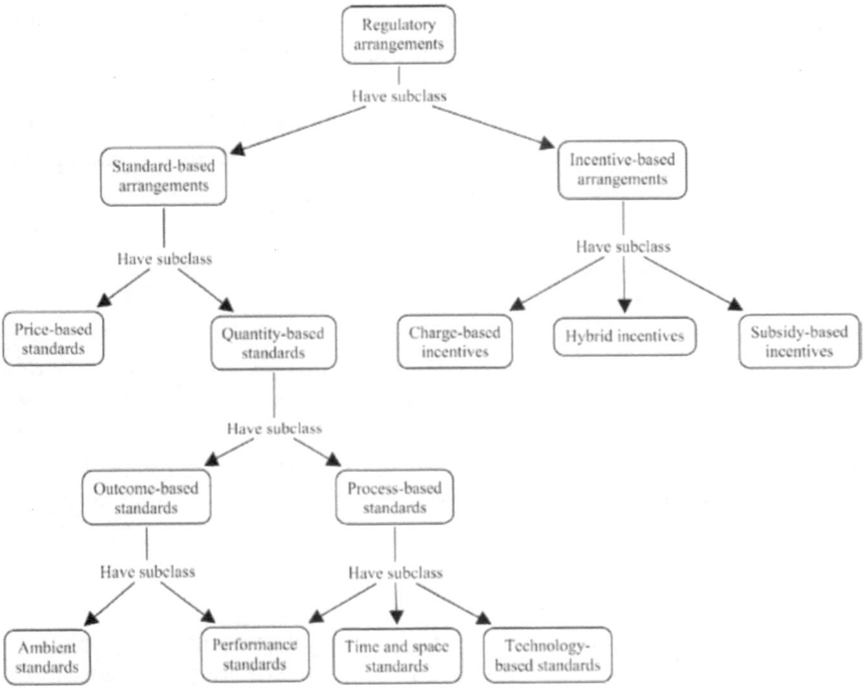

Figure 13.2. Example for key ontology concepts used in the text.

Another very common relationship is the "has a" relationship mentioned earlier, where one class is a component of another class. Trees *have* leaves, for example. Subcomponents do not inherit attributes of their supercomponents, although subclasses would inherit the subcomponents of their superclass, just as they inherit their attributes. So, while the component "branch" would not have genus or species as its superclass "tree species" has, any genus or species of tree would have branches and leaves as subcomponents, because these are components of the more general class of trees. Ultimately, an ontology can have as many types of relationships as a modeler cares to define as relevant to the system of interest.

One important question about ontologies concerns their flexibility. In creating classes, the conceptualization of the domain seems to be very rigid at first. What happens if new cases add variables that do not fit into the ontology? If they cannot be accommodated within the existing concepts (classes), the ontology loses its value. However, constructing an ontology is an ongoing process—new cases are valuable test instances for the ontology. If a new concept is missing, it is added by adding a new subclass, thus making the ontology richer.

Ontologies have additional advantages in being able to address the complexity, the scatter and panacea problems. We will turn to each problem in the following three sections.

Addressing the Scatter Problem

Today, the wealth of information available within a given scientific field has become problematic in itself. No researcher is able to be aware of all of the relevant information in his or her lifetime, let alone structure, organize and use it in regard for his or her research focus. Ontologies facilitate many tasks that would be impossible without them, and which may help address the scatter problem and panacea problems. Specifically, ontologies are able to:

1. *Decrease terminological confusion.* Ontologies are a suitable tool to provide a common ground for definitions of concepts. In order to develop an ontology, concepts used in it have to be stripped of their inherent semantic heterogeneity; this helps avoid inaccuracies, and pinpoints one meaning to fuzzy concepts (or forces the developer to abandon the term or to split it up in more precise subconcepts).
2. *Help unify knowledge.* Constructing ontologies forces the ontology engineer to not only disambiguate semantic heterogeneity, but to provide formal specifications for the terms used. The relationships between concepts have to be logically correct, or internally consistent (e.g., X implies Y or A is a part of B must be true for all concepts for which these relationships are defined—or a computer-based reasoner applied to the ontology will not be able to deduce new relationships correctly). This formalization process in turn helps the research community to work together on a set of specified and formalized concepts.
3. *Reduce incomparability.* Data incomparability is a common problem, because research data usually comes from many different sources. Different research goals and data formats prevent large-scale integration of research. It is important to point out that this is not a minor technical inconvenience, but is a real impediment in many disciplines (e.g., proteomics and genomics). Often, data

in separate databases simply cannot be compared or integrated, because there is no common ground in terms of common data fields and metadata, although the content may be very closely related. The huge amount of data being produced prohibits any "manual" or human-based solution. Ontologies have been put forward to solve this problem, since they provide an underlying structure to the data that would allow the automatic filtering and sorting of different data sources into identical records, since their content is related even if their format is not.

4. *Reduce redundancy of efforts and increase reusability.* As soon as one concept has been described formally (and satisfactorily to the research community) it can be used over and over again. It is then easy to integrate into other ontologies. Reusability is a major issue in software engineering, and many structural features of programming languages themselves are designed in a way to help this (e.g., object-oriented programming with capsuled classes and functions; modularity at the project level, etc.). Ontologies would in fact provide that important advantage to research as well. However, reaching consensus between experts about key concepts is difficult.

Our approach suggests to use a generally accepted and broadly useable framework—the SES framework—as starting point and use the process of ontology building to reach broader consensus, however imperfect.

Addressing the Panacea Problem

We now discuss the ways in which ontologies can help address the panacea problem:

1. *Ontologies allow automated reasoning.* Sometimes even structured queries do not suffice to extract important information because the amount of data is just too large. This is where another advantage of ontologies comes in: they allow automated reasoning. On the basis of ontologies and with the help of formal logic, new knowledge can be inferred from existing data. For example, if a particular kind of monitoring—say monitoring by hired guards from the state government—is effective in helping produce the sustainable management of a tropical forest ecosystem, this produces several findings at once. It supports a very specific relationship between

a certain type of monitoring in a certain type of resource system. But in the context of an ontology, where each of these classes are defined as subclasses of more general superclasses, this observation supports more general findings as well, which computers can automatically infer. A more general relationship that is supported is simply that monitoring helps produce sustainable outcomes in forest ecosystems—or more general yet, in any type of resource system. It is precisely this mix of general and specific theories that we need to move beyond the panacea problem, and ontologies can help us automate this important task.

2. *Ontologies are designed in a goal-oriented way*. For well-designed ontologies this implies that the concepts are at the right level for the problems at hand. In addition, the class hierarchies within ontologies reaching from the most general concepts to very specific instances enabled researchers to choose the right level of specificity.
3. *Ontologies formalize and operationalize existing guiding structures like frameworks*. By formalizing diagnostic frameworks which are in turn especially suited to address the panacea problem (as discussed above), ontologies extend these particular strengths of frameworks.

Addressing the Complexity Problem

The very structure of ontologies—a rigid hierarchy of classes that are clearly defined—helps to address complex issues in SESs: The parent-child relationship of a superclass and its subclasses is the primary way in which an ontology can implement a diagnostic approach and thus address the complexity problem. When analyzing a particular system, each class, for example a class A, represents a set of diagnostic questions. First, there is a potential question about the value of each attribute of class A—for example, does a high mobility of resource units influence manageability? Second, if class A has subclasses (say classes B and C), the analyst can ask to which of these subclasses, B or C, the instance they are studying belongs (e.g., listing all fish species that are harvested under subclass fish species). The answer to this last question leads to further questions based on the attributes and subclasses of classes B and C. If classes B and C are disjoint, meaning that an instance cannot be a member of more than one of them (e.g., coastal marine system vs. open-ocean system), then we only need to ask questions associated with one or the other, but not both. If a subclass of the class of resource systems is the class of coastal marine systems, then for those systems we do not need to ask about attributes that are only relevant for open-ocean systems, assuming these two subclasses are disjoint.

Additionally, the subcomponent relationship can play an important role in the diagnostic process. If a class has a subcomponent, this leads to an additional set of questions that need to be asked, based on the attributes, subclasses, and subsequent subcomponents of that subcomponent class. Subcomponent relationships affect the diagnostic process differently than do subclass relationships. This is because subcomponents of a class are not disjoint from each other, since, for example, a branch is a component (part) of several different trees: unlike subclasses, where a user may select a single subclass and ignore other disjoint subclasses, a user must examine each subcomponent of a class.

In an ontology there are many hierarchies along different types of classes and their subclasses and subcomponents. Instead of unpacking one single hierarchy then, as may have been implied in the original SES framework, the analyst would proceed along several scales in order to explore the relationships between different types and subtypes of important factors.

Practical Use of Ontologies

Apart from these advantages, much of the potential of ontologies lies in the fact that the knowledge coded in them can be used by and with computers. This allows them to accomplish the following useful tasks:

1. *Improve communication* between humans and between humans and computers. Information can be linked or grouped together that had been separated into different groups for various reasons (e.g., sections in a library, information on different websites, similar articles in a journal). Ontologies provide a common understanding of concepts and are in a fundamental way language independent. Content (e.g., in scientific databases, on websites in different languages) can be extracted, analyzed and used in more general ways, if the same ontology is used.
2. *Enable and facilitates searches and queries*. The enhanced interoperability of content is one fundamental prerequisite for searches and queries across data. Structuring data according to search terms is perhaps one of the most important tasks in modern science.

> Ontologies facilitate this, because the representation of knowledge is structured, uniform, reusable and formalized.

However, there are some tasks that ontologies are not suited for. They are not sophisticated enough to be stand-alone products without human intervention. In practice, this means that the construction, text-mining and merging of ontologies and the generation of new knowledge have to be constantly supervised and checked. Furthermore, to be of use they have to be updated and treated as dynamic learning systems with new content continuously added. Although reasoners in ontologies do have inferential capabilities, no ontology solves logical puzzles on its own. For them—and all other computer systems—the quality of human input is decisive in determining their usefulness. Last, but not least, ontologies are never goal free. They are always built towards a specific function; this in turn limits other uses any one of them may have.

Methods—Constructing a SES Ontology

Two Approaches and Their Limitations

Roughly speaking, constructing an ontology consists of first choosing the domain and the purpose of the ontology, then selecting the classes, their attributes and relationships (subclasses and subcomponents primarily) and the instances (for a more detailed description, see Gomez-Perez et al. 2004). The logical formalisms for drawing correct inferences were worked out in the first half of the 20th century and are available today as part of software packages like Protege (http://protege.stanford.edu/).

There are two basic ways of constructing ontologies. First, researchers may enter information manually. Second, automated text mining and information extraction can be used to build knowledge into an ontology. Both have their problems. The first method is work-intensive, slow and in most cases leads to incomplete projects, due to restrictions in resources and time. The second method often leads to poor quality, because text sources are unstructured, messy, vague and inconsistent. In addition, much uncertainty remains concerning the quality in regard to the unchecked parts of the ontology (which are the majority, since vast amounts of data are usually concerned).

There have been many attempts to overcome the limitations of both approaches. One example is the use of text sources structured by humans which follow a certain format like scientific articles or Wikipedia. Another idea is to "crowdsource" to many human reasoners the validation of inferences of the ontology reasoner, like Cyc does. Often both are used in combination, where automated text-mining is checked by human domain experts. Since the ontology used here begins with several key concepts of SESs which are well known from the literature, its first tiers are manually entered into the ontology. Its extensions, however, particularly at lower levels, might in the future be produced in part by text-mining, community-based extensions, and the integration of other ontologies.

Making the SES Ontology Work

In order to take full advantage of an ontology's promise for implementing the diagnostic approach, there are several rules that should be followed. To best understand these rules, it helps to imagine having a set of objects of interest in a particular domain of knowledge. Each of these has a set of attributes associated with it (e.g., forests have the attributes of average tree basal area and a level of biodiversity). In creating an ontology we are mainly interested in three things: (1) taking these objects and placing them into hierarchies of classes and subclasses; (2) specifying the important attributes that each class has; and (3) specifying other important relationships between classes, primarily the subcomponent-relationship. Here, we use a top-down approach, because the SES framework is already in place and can be used as a structure for the ontology.

None of these processes are automatic or unambiguous. Identifying key classes and attributes depends heavily on the goal of the ontology. For example, two groups of researchers focusing on a forest may have quite different questions that are best answered by the measurement of different variables. To allow for potentially different uses of an ontology, it is helped if it follows the principles of *minimal encoding bias* and *minimal ontological commitment* (Gruber 1995). This essentially means that it should not formalize and specify more than necessary, or in ways that are overly specific to the needs of a particular research group.

Gruber (1995) also emphasizes the importance of clarity, coherence, and extensibility for ontologies. Clarity is important for human users, while coherence supports valid inferences by both people and computers. Extensibility means that additional material can be added to an ontology without fundamentally altering existing material. We have taken each of these principles into account in the construction of our ontology.

One of the most fundamental decisions to make in constructing an ontology is when to create a subclass (or subcomponent) for an existing class. If a new subclass is not created, then the defining attribute to be associated with that subclass remains as an attribute of the original class. For example, we could use the resource system *sector* variable (e.g., pastures, forests, fisheries) from the original SES framework as either an attribute of the resource system class or as a means of creating a set of subclasses defined by the different values of that attribute. The class resource system would then become a superclass, that is, the parent class. Here we list the guidelines that we used for making this decision as we constructed our ontology with one example for each (see also Noy et al. 2001).

1. *Do not create single classes*: We avoid creating just one subclass of a superclass.
2. *Do not create too many subclasses*: If there are many subclasses of a superclass, we create intermediary classes between the two levels.
3. *Create disjoint classes*: We preferably create subclasses that are disjoint from each other (e.g., open-ocean vs. coastal systems).
4. *Create meaningful subclasses*: We preferably create a new subclass if its own attributes or subcomponents are not shared with the superclass or sibling subclasses.
5. *Create meaningful superclasses*: If a superclass of a set of subclasses has no unique attributes or subcomponents that the subclasses share through inheritance, we drop it from the ontology.
6. *Create similar classes*: We preferably create subclasses whose instances share common sets of values for their attributes.
7. *Create meaningful components*: We preferably create a subcomponent of a class if part of the definition of the class is that it is composed of multiple instances of the subcomponent.
8. *Create classes with a key property*: We preferably create subclasses or subcomponents of a class if these classes will take part in a relationship (e.g., be a subcomponent of) another class.
9. *Use the expertise of domain experts*: We are aware that the overall structure should reflect common usage of the terms by experts in the domain (here: we used the SES framework by Nobel Prize winner Elinor Ostrom as the starting point).

None of these rules are absolute. The first guideline is fairly intuitive. It is usually not very meaningful to create only one subclass of a class. There would be no other subclass in which to locate those instances that are a member of the superclass but not the subclass. The second guideline responds to the opposite situation, where there are too many subclasses, which is not usually very helpful either. The most useful hierarchy is generally neither too tall or too flat.

Next, if two classes are disjoint (rule 3), then a particular instance cannot be a member of both classes. This helps address complexity. If subclasses are disjoint, then an analyst knows that he or she is only dealing with one subclass, and does not have to worry about the attributes of its sibling classes. If two subclasses are not disjoint, which is often the case, then an analyst has to take both into account and deal with the ensuing complexity.

The fourth guideline is critical. If a class has, say, 10 attributes associated with it and we are considering if any of them should be used to create subclasses, we should use the one that leads to subclasses with their own, non-overlapping, sets of attributes (which would be subsets of the original 10). If we create subclasses that don't do this, we have not helped the analyst exclude from an analysis those variables that are not essential for his or her case. The most useful subclasses have attributes that are not shared with sibling classes or the superclass. Applying guidelines three and four to the resource sector example, we could use the sector variable (e.g., fishery, forestry, irrigation) as a means of breaking down resource systems into subclasses, which in this case would be disjoint from each other and have their own sets of attributes, along with some they have in common and inherit from their shared superclass.

The fifth guideline is directly related to the fourth. Just as we want subclasses with their own attributes, a useful superclass retains some attributes that are, through inheritance, shared by each one of the subclasses. If there are no such attributes, there is less need for the superclass, and the subclasses do not in fact have any attributes in common. For example, each resource system has a spatial or geographic extent, even if the sector subclasses are disjoint like in the examples shown above.

The sixth guideline reflects a different type of classification. In this situation, subclasses are not created because they have their own sets of variables or attributes associated with them. Instead, they may have the same set of attributes, but are still identifiable as different classes because they exhibit patterns in the values those attributes take on. This is the standard, well-known exercise of classifying objects based on their similarities across a standard set of variables, and it is commonly done in many disciplines.

The seventh rule regards subcomponents exclusively. As noted earlier, these play a different diagnostic role than do subclasses. If a class has a subcomponent class, this means that in order to understand the class we *must* look at the relevant attributes of at least one, but quite possibly several, instances of the subcomponent. In order to understand a particular tree, for example, we may need to examine many of its branches, roots, and leaves. If this is the case, then we should create these classes as subcomponents of the tree class.

The eighth rule amounts to saying that if a particular attribute value ends up being important in helping to define classes other than its own class, then it is probably important enough of a distinction to warrant its own subclass.

The final rule simply states that we should organize the ontology to be recognizable by, and therefore useful for, domain experts. One way we have done this in our ontology is to use superclasses that, while not necessarily having their own attributes (breaking rule 5) are commonly used to organize their subclasses in the relevant literature. While these are useful guidelines, it has to be kept in mind that although there are many best practices in designing an ontology, there is no single "right" way to do it. The structure, scope and level of detail of an ontology are heavily dependent on its goal.

Results—Converting the SES Framework into an Ontology

So far, we have demonstrated that ontologies may help with the complexity, panacea and the scatter problems by describing their potential. In order to make the usefulness of ontologies more concrete, we will now show how formalizing the SES framework into an ontology improves diagnostic thinking and the analysis of SESs. As already stated above, the design of an ontology depends heavily on its purpose (goal). In our case, the purpose is to facilitate the analysis of SESs regarding social, economic and ecological outcomes. In order to do so, the ontology should be able to accommodate all concepts of potential interest holding all variables that have been mentioned as potentially relevant in the literature.

In order to achieve this, the overall structure of the SES ontology is identical to the SES framework, that is, all first-level concepts including interactions, related ecosystems and social, economic and political settings are converted to superclasses (Figure 13.3).

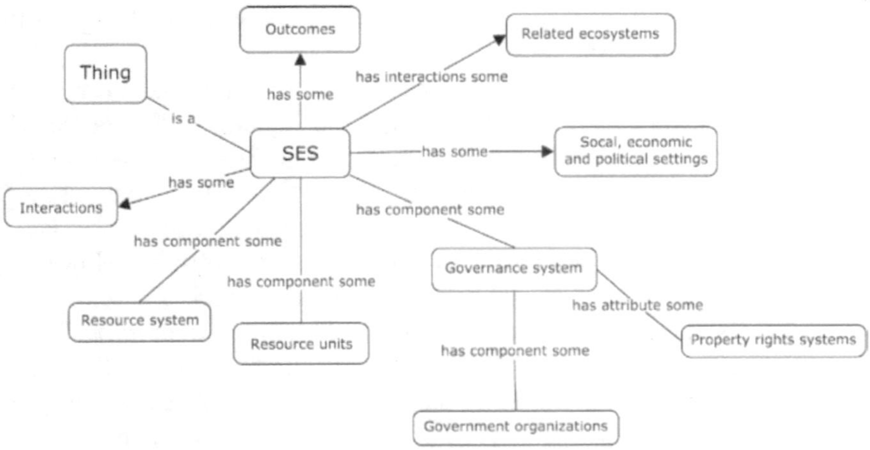

Figure 13.3. Top tiers of the SES ontology with relationships.

Starting with the top entity "thing," the superclass is "SES," with the second-tier variables becoming subclasses. A first difference to the SES framework consists in different relationships as can be seen in Figure 13.3: they are more precisely defined as, for example, "has attribute" or "has component," which is a distinction not made in the original framework. A further differentiation is made between "some," which stands for the logical equivalent of "there is at least one" and other logical types like "all." For visualization purposes, the class actors have been left out.

Below, we subdivide two concepts in order to present a more detailed analysis on lower tiers of the framework (which have been spelled out, for example, by Basurto et al. 2013).

If we want to analyze the sustainability of a SES, the superclass of resource units is particularly relevant. A more detailed diagnosis would also need to look beyond its seven subclasses. At this point, the rules for designing good ontologies described above (section ["Addressing the scatter problem"]) lead to the insight that "RU6 Distinctive Markings" is not at the right place in the framework, because there are no further possible subclasses. Resource units either have distinctive markings or not. Therefore, this would suggest to move this attribute further down.

Next, "RU5 Number of units" is very important for any analysis interested in the sustainability of an ecosystem, but it is definitely not a broad superclass. Instead, it is a very specific attribute to many species that are harvested in a particular system and thus should be associated with individual resource units at this level. Therefore, again, we would suggest to move this attribute further down.

Clearly, interactions between actors are important for outcomes. Here, the SES framework conveniently provides the superclass "Interactions." Designing an ontology means to carefully define relationships between classes. So, for example, the interaction "I4 Conflicts among users," relates to different sources of conflicts, like distribution of appropriated units, distribution of duties, rules treating groups differently, etc. However, these linkages have not been spelled out in the framework. Therefore, the ontology design process suggests that it would be important *to add links between top-level interactions*. While not complete for all lower tiers, this is done for the top tiers in our SES ontology with some classes (see Figures 13.4 and 13.5) developed in detail. The OWL-file is available on request.

One of the strengths of ontologies is the use of automatic reasoning. Here is an example: if the ontology contains two disjoint classes, say broad-leaved trees and conifers, with thousands of instances (tree species) that may, for example, have been imported from existing taxonomy files, two inconsistencies may be found easily. First, if one tree species has the property of having needles, but is sorted into the class of broad-leaved trees, this will pop up as an error. Second, if one tree species appears in both classes, this again will trigger an error, since the classes are disjoint (either–or). The more complex the relationships, the more useful this feature becomes, going beyond the above-mentioned examples of finding category mistakes.

Ontologies need lower, fine-grained levels to be of use. Therefore, we show two examples (Figures 13.4 and 13.5) on how this could be done in order to expand the SES framework. For this, we choose to decompose concept GS4 under the first tier "Governance systems."

As shown in Figure 13.4, we have two subclasses of property rights arrangements: the property regime, or type of actor to which the rights are assigned, and the actual rights that are assigned (see also Starrett 2003). We also specify that property rights are a subcomponent of property regimes. The literature on property regimes has traditionally subdivided them based on whether or not goods are privately owned, owned in common by groups (common property), owned by state governments (public property), or open-access without ownership (Hanna and Munasinghe 1995). There is also a more recently popular category, particularly in fisheries governance. These are co-management property regimes, which are a combination of public property and either common or private property regimes (Jentoft 1989). For illustrative purposes we include some subclasses of these regimes as well.

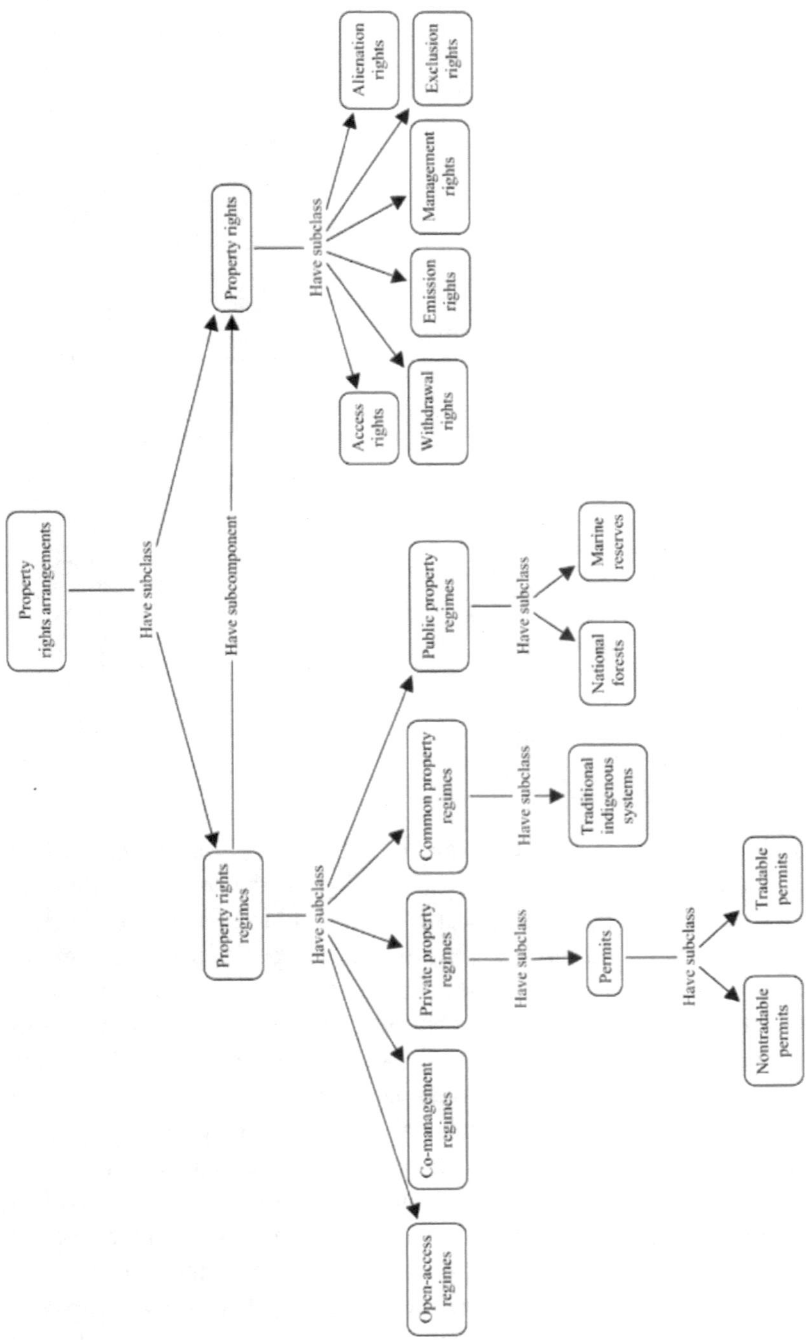

Figure 13.4. Possible property rights arrangements.

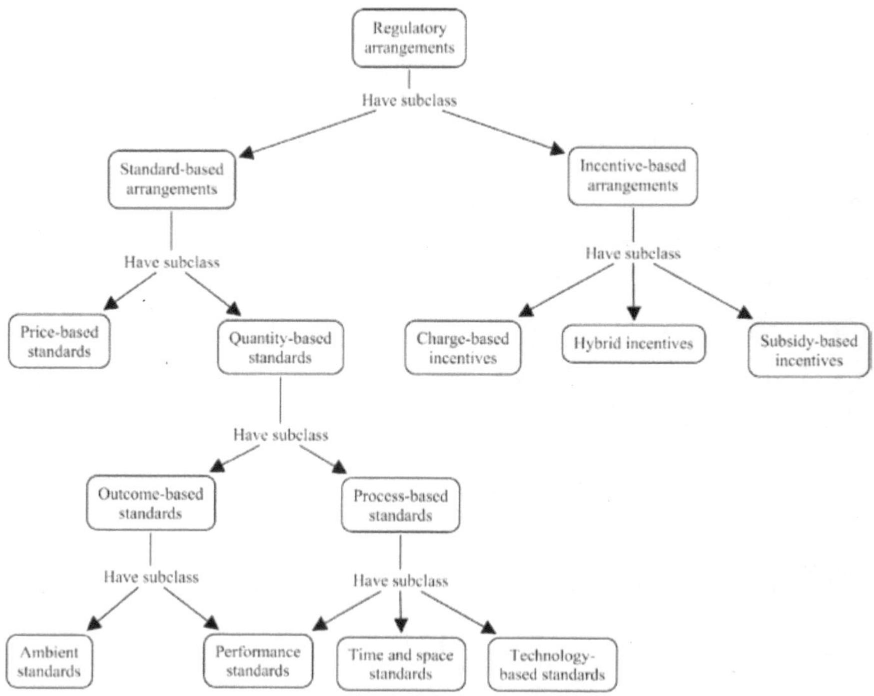

Figure 13.5. Regulatory arrangements.

Much of the policy literature makes rather simple arguments using these general property regimes, but this ontology makes clear that they are just one type of property rights arrangement, and have as subcomponents the specific property rights that give the actors specified in the regimes the rights to take a particular action with respect to a particular resource system or unit. This points to their complex nature. At the same time, this shows that no ontology can be without some design purpose which may differ according to goal and theoretical background.

The second example is regulatory arrangements (Figure 13.5), many of which are commonly referred to as command and control policies, the implication being that they involve greater impositions on those who must abide by them. In contrast, market-based instruments are assumed to exert less control. We resist this distinction and terminology here, because (1) we believe that the image of governance arrangements always propagating from a state government to a society that is otherwise entirely free of either constraints or self-governance is an unfortunate myth, and (2) markets ultimately require many rules to function, many of which can exert much control over those who participate in them.

All regulatory arrangements have an attribute *regulatory object*, which describes the unit (not the actor) that is being regulated (e.g., fish, pollutants).

We first divide regulatory arrangements into incentive-based and standard-based arrangements (Figure 13.5). Incentive-based arrangements do not forbid or require a particular behavior or outcome, but change the incentives involved in doing so. Thus, they are distinguished from the standard-based arrangements in that they make less use of certain rules that prescribe a particular action or outcome on the part of the targets of the policy. There are many words to describe the two most basic types of incentive-based arrangements, which we group into the subclasses of charge-based incentives and subsidy-based incentives.

All of the incentive-based arrangements share a common attribute *incentive amount*, describing the amount of the financial incentive (e.g., $-50 for a charge and $50 for a subsidy). The distinction between charges and subsidies is not based on them having different attributes, but by the value of this financial incentive and whether it is positive or negative (hybrids have both positive and negative incentive amount values). Each incentive also has an attribute *incentive event* that describes the event to which it is attached. For example, *tariffs*, as a kind of charge-based arrangement, are mostly attached to the transport of a good across political boundaries. Many taxes are attached to specific transactions, while many subsidies are attached to the production of a particular good. The third subclass is a hybrid between the other two, with the most common example being deposit-refund schemes.

The second main subclass of regulatory arrangements is standard-based arrangements, which are the most directly prescriptive subclass of the governance arrangements. We initially divide these into price-based and quantity-based standards, the second of which we unpack further here. Quantity-based standards regulate the amount of a particular physical quantity within a unit of time and/or space. We subdivide these into outcome-based and process-based standards. Outcome-based standards define a particular outcome and require that it be obtained without regard to any particular course of action, whereas process-based standards prescribe a particular course of action but not which outcome should result.

These few examples of designing an SES ontology hopefully make clear what could be gained by following this more formalized approach to analysis.

Conclusion

As just discussed, ontologies serve as a helpful diagnostic guide, explicitly guiding an analyst towards the questions that need to be asked, based on the components of interest. At the same time, good ontologies address the *panacea problem* by their hierarchical design, different levels of specificity and goal-orientedness. The *scatter problem* is addressed by strict definitions and relationships which may provide a common starting point like the framework does. Then, the formalized class structure with subclasses is well-suited for diagnostic thinking and thus addresses the *complexity problem*.

However, it is important to note that the ontology does not provide the actual diagnostic expertise that is required in order to use it effectively. For example, knowledge about causal relationships is not currently contained in the ontology, and yet causal relationships are central in guiding an analyst to ask certain questions and not others. Indeed, these are probably the most important relationships in determining what is and what is not important for a particular analysis. That an ontology could contain causal relationships is not out of the question, but this has certainly not traditionally been done. However, ontologies do help in discovering logical errors and inconsistencies in a framework. This, and the fact that missing relationships can be automatically added, greatly helps in designing consistent and unambiguous representations of SESs.

We also note that a downside of ontology formalization is the loss of nuances, since ontology design is mostly about standardization. This would not only mean that at least a part of the SES-community would have to agree and be prepared to work with to a certain set of definitions. On the other hand, technical requirements for the use of ontologies are rather low, since numerous tools are already available that allow ontology design for non-experts and provide worldwide availability via the Internet (http://webprotege.stanford.edu/). Researchers working with such ontologies could interact via well-established tools like wikis, comments on the website or mailing lists.

Our representation here is far from exhaustive. In the future, we plan to further refine and test the governance system component, as well as begin to unpack the other three main components of the SES framework. Additionally, we need to add at least one class for the large variety of important outcomes that occur in SESs (see Agrawal and Chhatre 2011). As this effort has likely indicated, this will be an inherently interdisciplinary and collaborative undertaking. The ontology introduced here could serve as a starting point—it is in a format that allows users to easily explore it (via

Protégé, a tool for building ontologies), and to make their own amendments and potentially new versions. In the future, the ontology discussed may be made available online (via the ontology development environment designed for the web called Webprotégé). This means that the technical implementation to work online with an ontology worldwide should be a minor issue with any university IT-department able to set it up in a matter of days. Given that the SES framework it is based on is very well known, this could also help to bring a wider community together to work with it. However, its usefulness ultimately depends on the input of the community with many successful examples leading the way.

An instructive example for collaborative research with interactive ontologies is http://www.ontologyonline.org. This site combines a browseable ontology with scholarly references and links to sites of other research groups. A good example of the potential for online ontology visualization can be found at the Bioportal site managed by the National Center for Biomedical Ontology (http://www.bioontology.org/bioportal). Other successful examples of the approach we might take include "OBI," which is an ontology for the description of biological and clinical investigations (http://obi-ontology.org/page/Main_Page), and the Gene ontology (http://www.geneontology.org/). This project aims to standardize the representation of genes across species and databases and provides a controlled vocabulary of terms.

Ultimately, how well the ontology is made is determined by how much it helps explore individual cases and, over time, to facilitate theory building across the multiple levels and scales that it contains. Undoubtedly, formalizing the key concepts of the research of SESs and linking them together via logically correct inferences—as the ontology does—is a first and important step in unifying the available knowledge, which has been done in other fields, with proven benefits.

Notes

This chapter was originally published in the *International Journal of the Commons* 9(2) (September 2015): 595–618.

1. For an introduction into knowledge-based systems, see Akerkar and Sajja (2010); for an account of the development of knowledge representing ontologies and software tools, see Gennari et al. (2003); and for the most recent spectacular success of a knowledge-based system able to beat humans in a knowledge retrieval task, Watson by IBM, see https://www.ibm.com/watson/.

References

Agrawal, A. and A. Chhatre. 2011. Against Mono-Consequentialism: Multiple Outcomes and Their Drivers in Social-Ecological Systems. *Global Environmental Change* 21(1):1–3.

Agrawal, A., A. Chhatre, and R. Hardin. 2008. Changing Governance of the World's Forests. *Science* 320(5882):1460–1462.

Akerkar, R. and P. Sajja. 2010. *Knowledge-Based Systems*. Sudbury, Mass.: Jones and Bartlett.

Baclawski, K. and T. Niu. 2006. *Ontologies for Bioinformatics. Computational Molecular Biology*. Cambridge, Mass.: MIT Press.

Basurto, X., S. Gelcich, and E. Ostrom. 2013. The Social-Ecological System Framework as a Knowledge Classificatory System for Benthic Small-Scale Fisheries. *Global Environmental Change* 23(6):1366–1380.

Cox, M. 2008. Balancing Accuracy and Meaning in Common-Pool Resource Theory. *Ecology and Society* 13(2):44.

Folke, C. 2006. Resilience: The Emergence of a Perspective for Social-Ecological Systems Analyses. *Global Environmental Change* 16(3):253–267.

Gallopin, G. C. 2006. Linkages between Vulnerability, Resilience, and Adaptive Capacity. *Global Environmental Change* 16(3):293–303.

Gennari, J., M. Musen, R. Fergerson, W. Grosso, M. Crubézy, H. Eriksson, N. Noy, and S. Tu. 2003. The Evolution of Protégé: An Environment for Knowledge-Based Systems Development. *International Journal of Human-Computer Studies* 58(1):89–123.

Gibson, C. C., J. Williams, and E. Ostrom. 2005. Local Enforcement and Better Forests. *World Development* 33(2):273–284.

Gomez-Perez, A., M. Fernandez-Lopez, and O. Corcho. 2004. *Ontological Engineering with Examples from the Areas of Knowledge Management, e-Commerce and the Semantic Web*. Heidelberg: Springer.

Gruber, T. R. 1993. A Translation Approach to Ontology Specifications. http://www.ksl.stanford.edu/KSL_Abstracts/KSL-92-71.html (accessed March 17, 2014).

———. 1995. Toward Principles for the Design of Ontologies Used for Knowledge Sharing. *International Journal of Human Computer Studies* 43:907–928.

Gutiérrez, N. L., R. Hilborn, and O. Defeo. 2011. Leadership, Social Capital and Incentives Promote Successful Fisheries. *Nature* 470(7334):386–389.

Hanna, S. and M. Munasinghe. 1995. *Property Rights and the Environment: Social and Ecological Issues*. Washington, D.C.: Beijer International Institute of Ecological Economics, World Bank.

Jentoft, S. 1989. Fisheries Co-management: Delegating Government Responsibility to Fishermen's Organizations. *Marine Policy* 13(2):137–154.

Khazai, B., T. Kunz-Plapp, C. Büscher, and A. Wegner. 2014. VuWiki: An Ontology-Based Semantic Wiki for Vulnerability Assessments. *International Journal of Disaster Risk Science* 5(1):55–73.

Kumazawa, T., K. Kozaki, T. Matsui, O. Saito, M. Ohta, K. Hara, M. Uwasu, M. Kimura, and R. Mizoguchi. 2014. Initial Design Process of the Sustainability Science Ontology for Knowledge-Sharing to Support Co-Deliberation. *Sustainability Science* 9(2):173–192.

Lakatos, I. and A. Musgrave. 1970. *Criticism and the Growth of Knowledge.* Cambridge: Cambridge University Press.

Madin, J. S., S. Bowers, M. P. Schildhauer, and M. B. Jones. 2008. Advancing Ecological Research with Ontologies. *Trends in Ecology & Evolution* 23(3):159–168.

McGinnis, M. and E. Ostrom. 2014. Social-Ecological System Framework: Initial Changes and Continuing Challenges. *Ecology and Society* 19(2): 30.

Noy, N. F. and D. L. McGuinness. 2001. Ontology Development 101: A Guide to Creating Your First Ontology. http://www.ksl.stanford.edu/people/dlm/papers/ontology-tutorial-noy-mcguinness-abstract.html (accessed March 17, 2014).

Ostrom, E. 2007. A Diagnostic Approach for Going beyond Panaceas. *Proceedings of the National Academy of Sciences* 104(39):15181–15187.

———. 2008. Frameworks and Theories of Environmental Change. *Global Environmental Change* 18(2):249–252.

———. 2009. A General Framework for Analyzing Sustainability of Social-Ecological Systems. *Science* 325:419–422.

Ostrom, E. and M. Cox. 2010. Moving Beyond Panaceas: A Multi-Tiered Diagnostic Approach for Social-Ecological Analysis. *Environmental Conservation* 37(04):451–463.

Ostrom, E., T. Dietz, N. Dolšak, P. C. Stern, S. Stonich, and E. U. Weber, eds. 2002. *The Drama of the Commons*. Washington, D.C.: National Academy Press.

Ostrom, E., R. Gardner, and J. M. Walker. 1994. *Rules, Games, and Common-Pool Resources*. Ann Arbor: University of Michigan Press.

Popper, K. 2002. *The Logic of Scientific Discovery*. New York: Routledge.

Rittel, H. W. and M. M. Webber. 1973. Dilemmas in a General Theory of Planning. *Policy Sciences* 4:155–169.

Starrett, D. A. 2003. Property Rights, Public Goods and the Environment. In *Handbook of Environmental Economics*, vol. 1. eds. K. G. Mäler and J. R. Vincent. Amsterdam: Elsevier.

Young, O. R. 2002. *The Institutional Dimensions of Environmental Change: Fit, Interplay, and Scale*. Cambridge, Mass.: MIT Press.

14

Polycentric Transformation in Kenyan Water Governance: A Dynamic Analysis of Institutional and Social-Ecological Change

Paul McCord, Jampel Dell'Angelo, Elizabeth Baldwin, and Tom Evans

In 2002, Kenya began to transition from a highly centralized system of water governance to one demonstrating a polycentric order. The country's current regime includes several features that scholars associate with polycentricity and have proposed should lead to effective water management in terms of equitable water distribution and coordination between multiple decision makers. Independent groups of local users are allowed to devise their own water allocation rules in response to changing ecological conditions. Local users also participate in regional, watershed-delineated users' associations that coordinate use throughout a watershed's catchment and impose regionally appropriate restrictions on water use during times of scarcity. Throughout Kenya, user groups are part of an overarching system of national laws that coordinates water governance between local, regional, and national actors.

The Kenya case allows us to examine two areas of research on polycentricity that are rarely addressed. First, we inspect a deliberate national government effort in transitioning toward polycentric resource governance, which few have investigated (exceptions include Andersson & Ostrom, 2008; Baldwin, Washington-Ottombre, Dell'Angelo, Cole, & Evans, 2016). Second, while many polycentricity scholars have developed propositions about why polycentric structures result in improved natural resource governance, few of these propositions have been empirically tested. Therefore, we move beyond a descriptive analysis of the governance structure to investigate whether Kenya's reforms have produced the beneficial outcomes predicted by theory.

In this paper, we combine data from fieldwork and archival research to ask: In a particular social-ecological system (SES), how have actor roles and local-level rules adjusted following the 2002 top-down reform? More specifically, to what extent do Kenya's postreform governance outcomes reflect the benefits predicted by polycentricity theorists? With respect to this research question, we test two hypotheses:

> *Hypothesis 1: In the postreform period, user groups will experiment with new approaches to governance by adjusting their rules.*
> *Hypothesis 2: Some of this experimentation will correlate with improved local conditions.*

In addition to directly testing the above hypotheses, we also draw on survey evidence to examine the way that communication and coordination within Kenya's polycentric system has affected governance within user groups. This inspection provides an opportunity to empirically examine the alignment of formal and informal outcomes with the theorized traits of a polycentric system.

Our investigation will focus on a SES within Kenya's Upper Ewaso Ng'iro basin on the northern and northwestern slopes of Mount Kenya.

To document regional- and national-level drivers leading to water reform, as well as changes to key subsystem variables (i.e., resource system, resource units, governance system, and actors) following reform, we use a new framework: the "combined IAD-SES framework," which was recently developed by scholars affiliated with the Ostrom Workshop of Indiana University (see Cole, Epstein, & McGinnis, 2014). This framework allows us to capture complex social, biophysical, and institutional arrangements and interactions at the regional and national level and explain the Government of Kenya's transition from top-down water governance to an approach in which responsibilities are distributed across multiple levels.

The structure of the remainder of the paper is as follows. First, we review the literature on polycentricity, identifying the key features of polycentric systems and the theoretical mechanisms by which these features might be expected to lead to improved natural resource governance. Next, the combined IAD-SES framework is described and used to briefly explain the Government of Kenya's transition from centralized to multilevel water governance. The study site is then described, followed by an explanation of the data and methods used in our empirical analysis. We then inspect postreform governance outcomes, including rules-in-use, at the community and catchment-level within the Upper Ewaso Ng'iro basin as of the summer of 2013. Finally, we discuss our empirical findings and their conformance with polycentricity theory.

Polycentricity

Polycentricity was first proposed as a possible approach to governance in the early 1960s. At the time, many metropolitan areas included city, county, and suburban jurisdictions, as well as the presence of state and federal agencies with specialized but limited authority in particular policy areas. Scholars of government tended to presume that such overlapping jurisdictions were chaotic at best and pathological at worst, and called for consolidation of service provision to improve efficiency (Aligica & Tarko, 2012; Cottrell, 1949). Vincent Ostrom, Tiebout, and Warren (1961) countered this argument by proposing that consolidated approaches to service provision were likely to be inefficient, because such "one size fits all" approaches could not account for divergent preferences among different groups of citizens, or differing economies of scale among different public services. In contrast, polycentric systems—with "many centers of decision making which are formally independent of each other"—might actually improve efficiency (V. Ostrom et al., 1961, p. 831).

In the decades since, a growing number of scholars have further developed the concept of polycentric governance, both theoretically and empirically. Much of this literature focuses on polycentric approaches to natural resource governance and development. Not unlike government scholars of the 1960s, many development scholars in the immediate postcolonial period tended to presume that centralized government control was necessary to ensure efficient use of natural resources (e.g., Scott, 1998; Shivakoti & Ostrom, 2001). Numerous scholars—including, most famously, Elinor Ostrom—countered this presumption through empirical documentation of cases in which local resource users were able to manage resources effectively (Agrawal & Gibson, 1999; E. Ostrom, 1990, 1999). As these cases have accumulated, the concept of polycentricity has developed beyond the original conception proposed by V. Ostrom, Tiebout, and Warren.

Polycentricity has been defined in numerous ways, and not all scholars agree about what makes a particular governance system "polycentric," although studies have tended to converge around a few key characteristics.

First, polycentric systems always involve multiple, independent centers of decision making (Andersson & Ostrom, 2008). Polycentricity is distinct from decentralization, however, in that mechanisms for coordination and cooperation between decision centers are crucial features of polycentric regimes (Pahl-Wostl & Knieper, 2014). Polycentric systems also feature overlapping jurisdictions that create partially redundant institutions (da Silveira & Richards, 2013; McGinnis, 1999). Overlap can be geographic, perhaps in the form of nested decision centers (Andersson & Ostrom, 2008), or may be functional, where multiple decision centers have authority in a given policy area (Galaz, Crona, Österblom, Olsson, & Folke, 2012).

Moreover, many scholars of polycentricity have asserted, either implicitly or explicitly, that these structural features give rise to good governance outcomes. For example, the presence of multiple, independent decision centers is thought to allow local decision centers to experiment with informal rules governing resource use, suggesting the possibility of innovation and learning (Andersson & Ostrom, 2008). It also allows local groups to devise rules that respond and adapt to local conditions, theoretically making polycentric systems more resilient to ecological shocks (Galaz et al., 2012). Because local actors best understand local needs and conditions, they may be better positioned to craft informal rules that meet localized needs more efficiently and equitably than government administrators' formal rules (Folke, Hahn, Olsson, & Norberg, 2005; Ribot, Agrawal, & Larson, 2006).

Perhaps more important, however, coordination and overlapping authority among these independent decision centers can enable mutual adjustment among decision centers (V. Ostrom, 1999). Indeed, mechanisms for communication and coordination distinguish between polycentric systems and those that are decentralized (Andersson & Ostrom, 2008; Pahl-Wostl & Knieper, 2014). Such coordination might, for example, allow local user groups to communicate with regional or national policymakers, giving them a "voice" in policy matters that can help improve outcomes (Andersson & Ostrom, 2008). Coordination can also be crucial where multiple local user groups are nested within a shared water basin, forest system, or fishery. Coordination and overlapping authority allows user groups to communicate and adjust their use in ways that benefit the system as a whole, essentially enabling collective action at multiple levels of governance (Cole & McGinnis, 2015).

It is not a foregone conclusion, however, that polycentric governance structures will always give rise to the beneficial governance outcomes predicted by theory. Indeed, V. Ostrom et al. (1961) were cautious to note that independent centers of decision making may not inevitably give rise to "orderly outcomes"; instead, this is an empirical question (p. 831). Recently, a number of studies have provided empirical evidence that polycentric governance regimes tend to have high performance (Basurto & Ostrom 2009; E. Ostrom, 1999; Pahl-Wostl, Lebel, Knieper, and Nikitina, 2012), particularly when compared with non-polycentric or less-polycentric systems (da Silveira & Richards, 2013; Pahl-Wostl & Knieper, 2014). There has been limited empirical testing, however, of the theoretical propositions that scholars have developed to explain the apparent success of polycentric systems, including experimentation with informal rules and adaptation to local conditions.

In this article, we undertake such empirical testing. We examine a system—water and irrigation governance in Kenya—that has recently adopted reforms instating the three basic features of polycentricity: multiple decision centers at the local, water basin, and national levels; overlapping authority among these decision centers; and formal and informal mechanisms of coordination and communication between these decision centers. Within that system, we examine processes and behaviors adopted by water users, focusing in particular on whether Kenya's polycentric structure gives rise to processes and behaviors predicted by polycentricity theory, such as local groups experimenting with new rules and adoption of rules in response to local conditions.

The Kenyan case is particularly interesting because whereas most previous studies have focused on polycentric governance systems that evolved over time, some of the structural elements that create a polycentric system in Kenya are the result of national policy changes due to reforms in 2002. Kenya has always had local and national centers of decision making, but the 2002 reforms formalized the creation of regional (water basin level) decision centers; created several formal mechanisms for coordination among local-, regional-, and national-level decision units; and prescribed overlapping authority over water allocation between these decision units. As a result, the Kenyan case provides the researcher with a rare opportunity to examine whether polycentric structures, imposed by national actors, give rise to the local-level behaviors and processes predicted by polycentricity theorists.

We turn now to a description of the Government of Kenya's transition from monocentric to polycentric water governance, which is aided by use of the combined IAD-SES framework.

Transformation from Monocentric to Polycentric Governance

The water governance structure that presently exists in Kenya was largely put in place following the 2002 Water Act (Liniger, Gikonyo, Kiteme, & Wiesmann, 2005). A number of drivers led to water reform, and since reform, significant changes have occurred with respect to the governance system, actor roles, and efforts to match governance responsibilities with hydrological borders. We briefly document these drivers and postreform changes at the national level using the combined IAD-SES framework.

The Combined IAD-SES Framework

The institutional analysis and development (IAD) framework, first described in publication in 1982 (Kiser & Ostrom, 1982), places action situation(s) at its center and uses exogenous biophysical conditions, community attributes, rules used by participants, and interactions among actors and their environments to explain decision making within action situations (Figure 14.1a). Further, decision making is influenced by the positions held by participants, the allowable actions, information availability, and the costs and benefits of decisions within the action situation. The framework has been described by some as one of the most important institutional analytical frameworks in policy sciences (Sabatier, 2007), and since its development, has been extended to a large and diverse number of empirical settings, including international development (e.g., Gordillo & Andersson, 2004), industrial regulation (e.g., Schaaf, 1989), banking reforms (e.g., Polski, 2003), land tenure (e.g., Mwangi, 2003), problems related to the water–energy–food nexus (e.g., Villamayor-Tomas, Grundmann, Epstein, Evans, & Kimmich, 2015), environmental conflicts (e.g., Dell'Angelo, 2012), and participation analysis (e.g., Bixler, Dell'Angelo, Mfune, & Roba, 2015).

Like the IAD framework, the more recently developed SES framework is structured around a central action situation (Figure 14.1b). First elaborated in E. Ostrom (2007), the SES framework seeks to identify components of and interactions between resource systems, resource units, actors, and governance systems in producing social-ecological outcomes (McGinnis & Ostrom, 2014). The SES framework operates as a diagnostic tool as it proposes a set of second- and third-tier variables for analysis of SESs (Table 14.1), and used in this way further elaborates upon elements originally appearing in the IAD framework. Since its inception, the SES framework has been applied to a variety of social-ecological settings, such

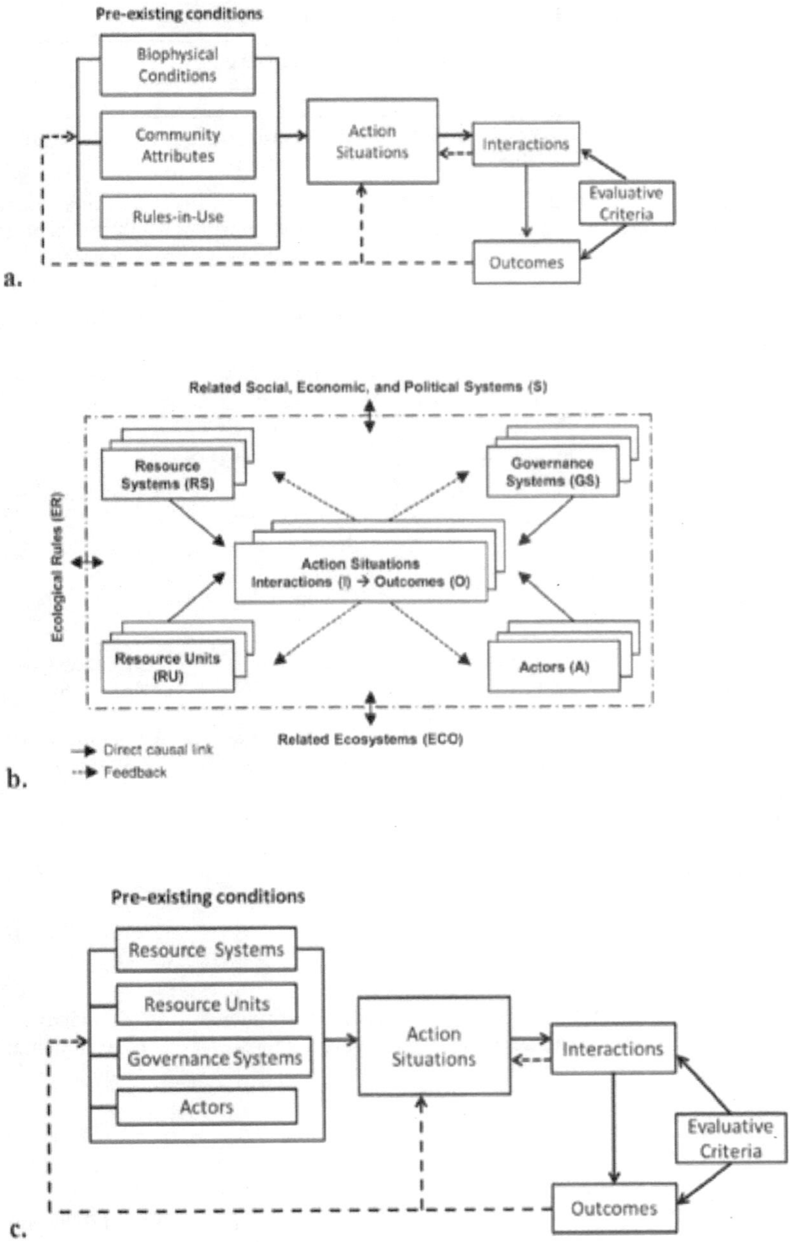

Figure 14.1. (a) The IAD framework, (b) the SES framework, and (c) the combined IAD-SES framework.

Source: Adapted from Cole et al. (2014).

Table 14.1. Second- and third-tier variables for diagnosing SESs

Resource Systems	Resource Units	Governance Systems	Actors
RS1 Sector	**RU1** Resource unit mobility	**GS1** Government organizations	**A1** Number of users
RS2 Clarity of system boundaries	**RU2** Growth or replacement rate	**GS2** Nongovernment organizations	**A2** Socioeconomic attributes of users a. Economic b. Cultural
RS3 Size of resource system a. Area b. Volume	**RU3** Interaction among resource units a. Strong to weak b. Predatory or symbiotic	**GS3** Network structure a. Centrality b. Modularity c. Connectivity d. Number of levels	**A3** History of use
RS4 Human-constructed facilities	**RU4** Economic value	**GS4** Property-rights systems a. Private b. Public c. Common d. Mixed	**A4** Location
RS5 Productivity of system	**RU5** Number of units	**GS5** Operational rules	**A5** Leadership/entrepreneurship
RS6 Equilibrium properties a. Recharge dynamics b. Recharge rate c. Number of equilibria d. Feedbacks i. Positive ii. Negative	**RU6** Distinctive markings	**GS6** Collective-choice rules	**A6** Norms/social capital
RS7 Predictability of system dynamics	**RU7** Spatial and temporal distribution a. Spatial heterogeneity b. Temporal heterogeneity	**GS7** Constitutional rules	**A7** Knowledge of SES/mental models
RS8 Storage characteristics		**GS8** Monitoring and sanctioning processes	**A8** Importance of resource
RS9 Location			**A9** Technology used

Source: Adapted from E. Ostrom (2009) and E. Ostrom and Cox (2010).

as fisheries (e.g., Basurto, Gelcich, & Ostrom, 2013; Cinner et al., 2012; Gutiérrez, Hilborn, & Defeo, 2011), forests (e.g., Fleischman et al., 2010), and water and irrigation (Cox, 2014; Madrigal, Alpízar, & Schlüter, 2011; E. Ostrom, 2011).

Despite the utility of the IAD and SES frameworks in studying, among other things, the sustainability of SESs, each has been criticized for perceived shortcomings: the IAD for insufficient attention to natural systems, and the SES for its inability to provide more than a static list of system components. Recognizing these shortcomings, Cole et al. (2014) devised the "combined IAD-SES framework," which integrates the SES variables entirely into the IAD framework (Figure 14.1c). The combined IAD-SES framework, therefore, allows the user to employ a multilevel analysis tool that recognizes the major subsystems of an SES (i.e., the SES framework) in a dynamic manner where temporal institutional variations are accounted for (i.e., the IAD framework). Given these strengths, this framework appears well-suited for detailing the drivers of institutional reform and the outcomes produced through such a reform.

We have chosen to employ the combined IAD-SES framework to detail Kenya's water reform for several reasons. First, separately the IAD and SES frameworks are both meant to incorporate feedback mechanisms; however, in the case of the SES, these mechanisms are not readily identifiable. Using the newly developed framework, we are able to identify not only the existing conditions from the social and ecological realms at the first time step, but also those produced following treatment at a second interval. Second, the interaction of adjacent action situations in producing outcomes has been well developed within the IAD framework (McGinnis, 2011), but by employing the combined IAD-SES framework, the user's attention is readdressed from looking primarily at outcomes produced from actor preferences and institutional arrangements to the role of broader subsystems in achieving social-ecological outcomes. Finally, as we will highlight, the institutional arrangements within the Kenya context are particularly complex, and to understand the transformation from one governance regime to another, a framework characterizing not only the breadth of interactions across time points but also the depth of interactions at a single time point, such as multilevel dynamics, is particularly useful. We believe the combined IAD-SES framework has been well developed for this purpose.

In describing Kenya's water management reform, we primarily employ information retrieved during the summer of 2013 from the Kenyan National Archives, the University of Nairobi, and the Ministry of Water and Irrigation. We focus on the period beginning just before the 2002 reform and ending at the time of data collection (i.e., 2013). Explanations for variable selection before and after the 2002 reform, as well as action situation dynamics, are detailed in the Appendix.

Application of the Combined IAD-SES Framework: Explaining Reform

In the early and mid-1960s as Kenya emerged from colonial rule, the government retained many of the water governance strategies that were put in place by the British. The centralized approach established during colonial rule was poorly suited for the conditions in Kenya and was eventually superseded by reforms at the turn of the twenty-first century (Baldwin et al., 2016). Among other features, these reforms represent a shift from top-down water governance to a polycentric approach by creating decision centers at multiple levels and providing for coordination between regional and local actors. In the paragraphs that follow, we describe the resource system, actors, and governance system in place prior to the 2002 reform. We go on to analyze the way these variables affected appropriation, rulemaking, monitoring, and conflict resolution. We conclude with a discussion of resource and governance outcomes as of 2013. Table 14.2 summarizes each of the SES subsystems at two time points, while Figure 14.2 uses the combined IAD-SES framework to dynamically capture forces motivating change, as well as the outcomes produced.

Pre-Existing Conditions before Water Reform

By the late 1990s, the groundwork for water reform was already being laid as, in response to a largely failing national system, NGOs, government representatives, community water projects (CWPs), and individual smallholders created an informal Water Users' Association (WUA) within Kenya's Likii River catchment (A5 in Figure 14.2—left-hand-side variables) to coordinate upstream–downstream water uses, share information, and resolve disputes (Liniger et al., 2005). This WUA would later be the model for catchment-level user groups following reform (described below). The immediate impetus for these actors in establishing the Likii WUA was a rash of upstream–downstream water conflicts fueled by excessive upstream river water withdrawals. However, the less apparent

Table 14.2. Key SES variables at two time points

Variable (Code)	Time Point 1—Late 1990s	Time Point 2—2013	Summary of Subsystem
Resource System (RS)			
Clarity of hydrological boundaries (RS2)	Clearly defined	Clearly defined	From 1964 to the late 1990s, despite the clarity of hydrological boundaries, water administration took place along political boundaries, which did not compel resource users to consider downstream individuals (A6). Following the 2002 water reform, water management matches hydrological boundaries, which has contributed to improved downstream water access in some locations
Streamflow trend (RS5)	Decreasing	Decreasing, but reports of improved downstream river water access in some locations	
Actors (A)			
Leadership (A5)	Leadership poorly aligned with biophysical units and limited in its consideration of local conditions. Informal user groups providing model for reform in late 1990s	Leadership recognized at multiple biophysical units	Smallholder farmers throughout Kenya are highly reliant on surface water for irrigation purposes. Before the 2002 reform, downstream users were severely disadvantaged due to the poor fit between hydrological scales and governance units, which did not compel upstream users to be overly aware of the catchment-wide consequences of their actions. After reform, leadership became better aligned with hydrological scales and has improved water access in some downstream locations
Norms (A6)	Minimal consideration of downstream users	Increased awareness of downstream users	
Resource dependence (A8)	High resource dependence	High resource dependence	

Continued on next page

Table 14.2. ***Continued***

Variable (Code)	Time Point 1—Late 1990s	Time Point 2—2013	Summary of Subsystem
Governance System (GS)			Kenya shifted from a top-down, monocentric style of water management to one with multiple levels corresponding with various hydrological scales after the 2002 reform. This put in place WRMA and the WRUAs as regional- and catchment-level managers of water and replaced the WAB and the Water Bailiffs. With the creation of WRUAs, connectivity between governing units improved, since local water users serve on each WRUA's management committee, and WRUAs work closely with their corresponding WRMA office. In turn, this has improved the presence of monitoring personnel and led to rules-in-use aimed at equitably appropriating water between upstream and downstream users
Government organizations (GS1a)	Water Apportionment Board, Water Bailiffs	Water Resources Management Authority, Water Resource Users Association	
Network structure (GS3a)	Formal structure: Top-down	Formal structure: Multilevel	
Connectivity between governing units (GS3b)	Minimal connectivity	Improved connectivity	
Water appropriation operational rules (GS5a)	Nairobi and region-based permit system. Ineffective operational rules for water appropriation between upstream and downstream users	Regional WRMA offices responsible for issuing water use permits. Operational rules for water appropriation between upstream and downstream users put in place by WRMA and WRUA	
Monitoring (GS8)	Water Apportionment Board personnel and Water Bailiffs significantly underfunded leading to poor monitoring	Local monitoring personnel in the form of WRUA representatives and, in some cases, WRMA staff	

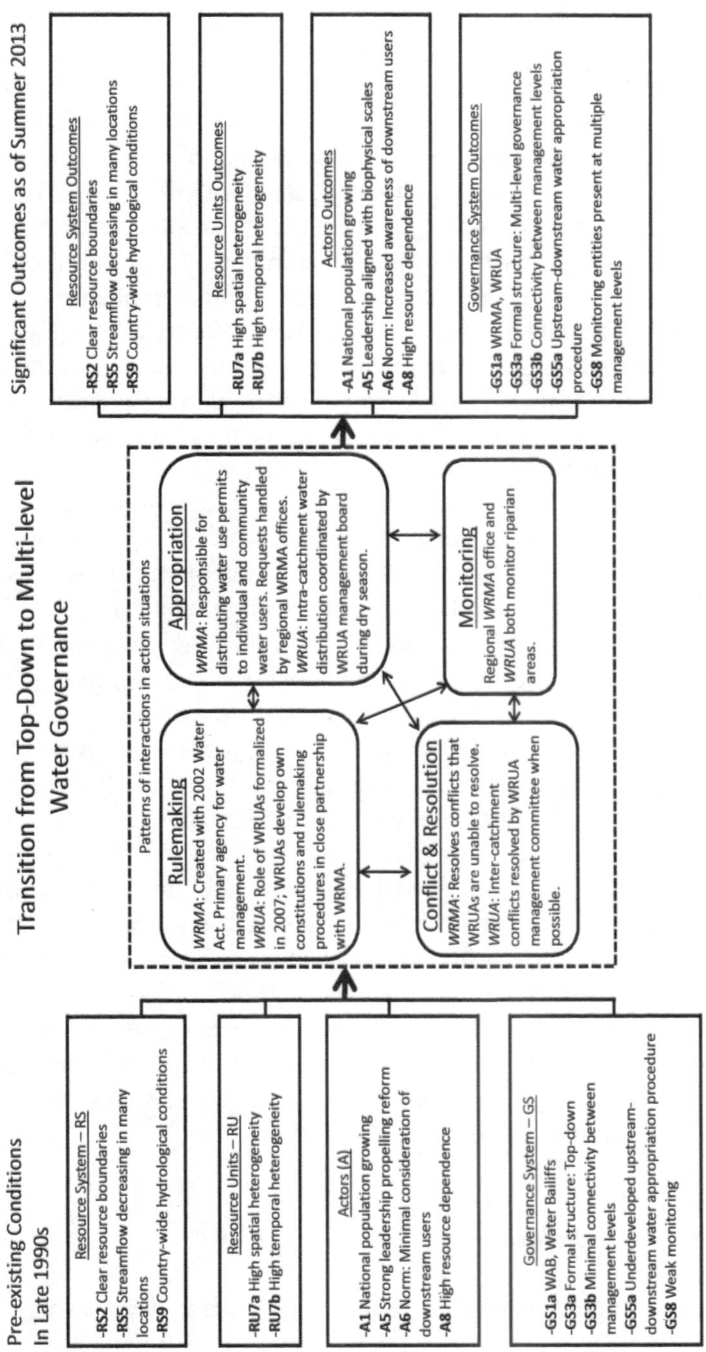

Figure 14.2. Application of the combined IAD-SES framework: Kenya's transition from monocentric to multilevel water governance.

drivers—although more universal throughout the country—had existed since the colonial era. We now explain these drivers.

The Nairobi-based Water Apportionment Board (WAB; GS1a) had several critical responsibilities during British rule and in the years following independence, including permit issuance, sanctioning of water misuse, and placing restrictions on use during periods of scarcity. While the WAB was a national agency based in Nairobi, reforms in the 1970s increased participation by local officials, primarily by opening numerous Water Bailiff offices throughout Kenya to issue permits and monitor permit compliance (GS1a) (Kenya Water Apportionment Board, 1972). These efforts were largely ineffective, however, as final authority remained with the central government. In fact, these adjustments led to a less-efficient permitting process: water users now needed to obtain permits from both local and national officials, and this process could take years to complete (Kenya Ministry of Water Development, 1983). The regional Water Bailiff offices were also significantly underfunded and often lacked the financial means to patrol riparian locations for non-permitted water users (GS8). If water users chose to avoid the permitting process, they ran little risk of detection. Thus, despite efforts to bolster local water governance, Kenya retained a largely ineffective top-down system of management (GS3a) with poor coordination across governance levels (GS3b) up to the turn of the twenty-first century.

Compounding these inefficiencies were incongruities between the hydrological system itself and the individuals charged with officiating the resource system. In their efforts to monitor water use and issue abstraction permits, Water Bailiffs were assigned to jurisdictions based on political (district) boundaries. This complicated management efforts as these water officials had no reason to consider the effects of upstream water use on downstream users so long as the downstream users were within another district (GS5a). Therefore, despite the clear natural borders (RS2) of the hydrological system (i.e., catchment areas), the management of water use led to opaque understandings of downstream water needs (A6); the result of which were frequent downstream water shortages, particularly during dry periods (A8 and RS5) (Liniger et al., 2005).

Kenya's 2002 Water Reform

As these water shortages intensified, efforts took place at both the regional and national levels to reform water management. An informal WUA was established in the Likii River catchment to coordinate use among water users. Following the initial success of this WUA, the Government of Kenya incorporated the WUA concept in its reforms by encouraging the creation of formal Water Resource Users Associations (WRUAs), which would become independent decision units at the catchment-level. National reforms also created a Water Resources Management Authority (WRMA), responsible for developing overall policy strategies for Kenya, as well as for certain appropriation, conflict resolution, and monitoring activities. The reforms also delineated overlapping and shared responsibilities for rulemaking, appropriation, monitoring, and conflict resolution at the community, WRUA, and national levels. Thus, a multilevel system took hold in which individual or community water users were nested within WRUAs, which were further nested within a WRMA region.

With the opening of regional offices within each of Kenya's water basins, WRMA officials were able to better enforce policy changes enacted after the water reform. From a water appropriation perspective, WRMA now requires users to obtain permits from one of these regional offices, or if the individual belongs to a community user group, the user group needs to collectively possess a WRMA permit. Further, an overlap between the responsibilities of WRMA and WRUA exists since WRMA must consult with the WRUAs on permit issuance. These permits formally limit the timing and quantity of water abstracted, and, in times of water scarcity, require a percentage of water to pass through the catchment to downstream users. Monitoring compliance with the terms of these permits is shared between WRMA personnel and members of the WRUA. Additionally, if the permit terms are violated or disputes arise between upstream–downstream users within the same catchment, WRUA and WRMA may share conflict resolution responsibilities. In cases where upstream–downstream conflicts occur across catchments, WRMA becomes the primary entity responsible for conflict resolution, creating an overlap of authority between WRUAs and WRMA.

The WRUAs did not become formally recognized as catchment-level user associations until 2007; nonetheless, informal WUAs were present in multiple catchments before 2007 and these informal groups provided a blueprint upon which the WRUAs that existed as of 2013 were crafted (Baldwin et al., 2016). A WRUA encompasses all members of a particular catchment that possess a WRMA water use permit, and they operate as truly representative entities, as the management committee for each WRUA is made up of members from the catchment: representatives from community user groups, CEOs of large-scale farms, and individual riparian households, among others.

The primary role of a WRUA is to prevent and resolve conflicts between water users within a catchment area (WRMA & WSTF, 2009), and to this end, they share many responsibilities with the regional WRMA office. In terms of rulemaking, WRUAs are allowed to devise their own constitutions; yet, this is done in partnership with WRMA, often using a template approved by WRMA. Their closest partnership with WRMA, however, arguably occurs with respect to water appropriation during the dry season. As river water becomes scarce, WRUAs are expected to devise a schedule of appropriation among the catchment members. This requires members to keep their river intakes shut on all days that they are not scheduled to receive water. In theory, this program allows a percentage of water to reach downstream users, even during the dry season. Crafting the schedule of appropriation is often done in close consultation with WRMA officials and requires WRMA's approval before implementation. Likewise, monitoring compliance with the dry season regulations and resolving conflicts as they arise is also typically shared between WRUA and WRMA personnel; yet, WRUAs may entirely defer conflict resolution duties to WRMA if the offense or grievance is deemed best handled at a higher level of governance.

Conditions as of the Summer of 2013

Following this national-level effort to reorient water governance institutions and actor roles, SES conditions as of 2013 indicate that certain features of polycentric governance and adaptive co-management of water resources now exist in Kenya (GS3a in Figure 14.2—right-hand-side variables). Adaptive co-management suggests that governance responsibilities are most effective when the scope of influence aligns with hydrological borders (Huitema et al., 2009). With the creation of WRUAs, water use activities within and across catchments became better coordinated, particularly during the dry season (GS3b and GS5a), and individual water users became increasingly aware of the consequences of their activities on other actors within and outside their catchment (A6). Our own interviews suggest that, despite these coordination efforts within catchments, the effectiveness of WRUAs in alleviating water disparities has been mixed: some downstream users continue to object to excessive upstream water use, while others feel that postreform water availability has improved (RS5).

In terms of monitoring (GS8), the 2002 reform has created redundancies in some catchments, a trait of polycentric governance. Regional

WRMA personnel will patrol riparian zones in search of unauthorized pumping, an effort that is also performed by members of the WRUA particularly when the dry season appropriation schedule has been imposed. This duplication of duties creates a safety net where a failure on the part of one institution is alleviated by the presence of another. While WRMA personnel may not be as prominent in some catchments compared to others, the very presence of a catchment-level governance entity (i.e., the WRUA) suggests leadership will be familiar with local conditions (A5), another important element of adaptive co-management (Huitema et al., 2009).

With the formal transition from monocentric to multilevel management described, we now analyze the outcomes of this nationally imposed polycentric shift on a SES within Kenya's Upper Ewaso Ng'iro basin. We begin by describing the SES of interest and then move on to a description of the data used before inspecting the outcomes of reform.

Study Area

The Upper Ewaso Ng'iro Basin

Both a climatic and social gradient exists in the Upper Ewaso Ng'iro basin (McCord, Cox, Schmitt-Harsh, & Evans, 2015). Nested within the basin are 25 CWPs where fieldwork was conducted. These CWPs span an area of approximately 1,800 km^2 and are located predominately on Mount Kenya's leeward side within five WRUAs (Figure 14.3). The CWPs nearest Mount Kenya, on average, receive greater precipitation totals; however, rainfall events across the region are variable. Throughout much of the study area, either a bimodal or trimodal rainfall pattern exists, with rainy seasons taking place from April to June, October to December, and a more unpredictable rainy season occurring from July to August under the trimodal pattern (Ericksen et al., 2011). This seasonality results in significant variability of surface water availability.

In addition to the study area's environmental gradient, a "social gradient" is also present. Until the early 1900s, much of the study area was occupied by Maasai and Samburu pastoralists (Wiesmann, Gichuki, Kiteme, & Liniger, 2000). Large ranches and farms owned by white settlers that were established during the colonial era (i.e., starting at the turn of the twentieth century) have today largely transitioned to Kikuyu- or Meru-owned small-scale farms, although some large landholdings remain. Many of these large landholdings have been transformed into highly technical

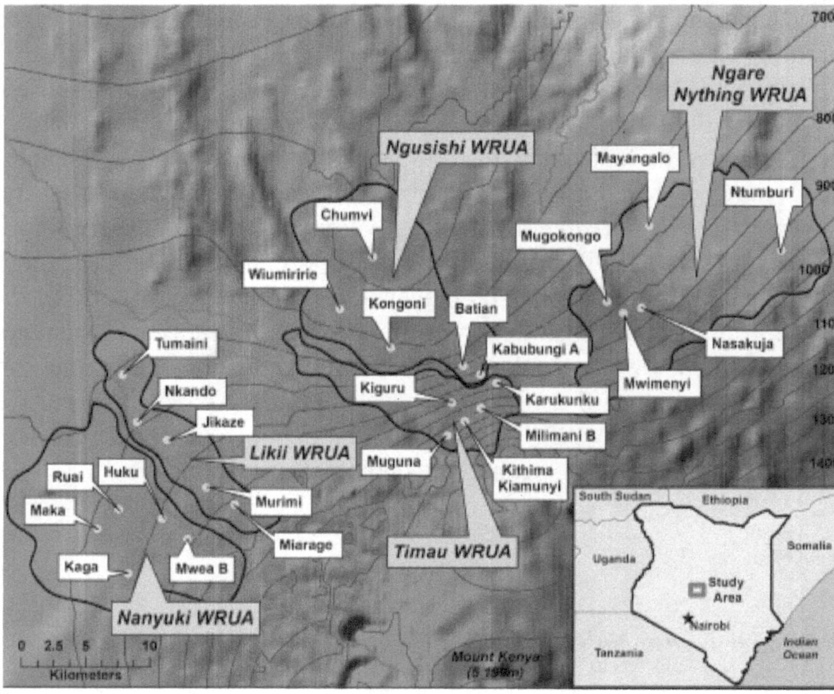

Figure 14.3. Study area.

Notes: Isohyets represent average annual precipitation (mm) to demonstrate the region's environmental gradient. Boundaries of WRUAs are approximations. Locations of water projects are represented by the centroid of the water project.

horticultural operations producing for international markets (Wiesmann et al., 2000). The Maasai and Samburu pastoralists, who once dominated the area, have largely been pushed north to the marginal arid and semiarid rangelands (Kiteme, Wiesmann, Künzi & Mathuva, 1998).

Population growth within the Upper Ewaso Ng'iro basin, which witnessed an increase from 50,000 in 1960 to approximately 500,000 in 2000 according to Ngigi, Savenije, and Gichuki (2007), as well as increases in the number of smallholder farmers, typify the trend throughout much of Kenya during the postcolonial era. These growth processes were encouraged by the Government of Kenya's subdivision of former British ranches to be used for smallholder farms, as well as immigration from nearby densely populated areas in search of locations with high agricultural potential. In the process, population growth has added new pressures to land and water resources. As evidence, multiple rivers within the Upper Ewaso Ng'iro basin have experienced decreasing flows since the early 1960s (Liniger et al., 2005). In some areas, the decrease in river water availability has shifted livelihood practices from smallholder sedentary agriculture to pastoralism.

The Community Water Projects

CWPs are small, member-based irrigation infrastructure projects that allow smallholders to access irrigation water (although the primary goal of CWPs is to provide water for domestic use). Many CWPs were initially funded by government programs or donors, with subsequent management and infrastructure improvements undertaken by the CWP's membership. Some CWPs date back to the colonial era, although the number of CWPs increased rapidly in the postcolonial period supported by government programs aimed at increasing small-scale agriculture.

We focus our attention on 25 CWPs within the Upper Ewaso Ng'iro basin. Each of the 25 CWPs has an intake from either one of the study area's major rivers or from a natural spring as is the case with the CWPs in the Ngusishi WRUA (refer to Figure 14.3). Intakes can be closed during periods of rationing between CWPs in the same WRUA. After flowing through the intake, water is then gravity-fed to households through a series of buried pipes. CWPs vary in their water use restrictions, as some only allow for irrigation of small plots of land, while others are more flexible. Typically, this is influenced by the number of members within a CWP, which is highly variable and can be related to population growth within an area, as well as decisions made by the CWP's management committee to either restrict membership or allow membership growth.

CWPs have long exhibited autonomy in crafting their own institutions, a tradition dating to the colonial era. Important differences, therefore, exist in management strategies, including water appropriation strategies during the wet and dry seasons. CWP management committees make decisions as to whether or not a CWP will institute a rotation schedule (i.e., alternating water delivery between separate CWP distribution lines on a day-to-day basis) during the wet season and how dry season water shortages will be managed. These decisions are typically influenced by the number of members within a CWP. It is not uncommon for larger CWPs to enforce a wet season rotation in which households receive water three or fewer times in a week, while CWPs with smaller memberships may be able to forgo a rotation program during periods of high river levels. When river levels decrease in the dry season, household-level water availability is typically restricted in both large and small CWPs.

Data and Methods

Data

We use three types of data for this study: survey responses, household-level water-flow measurements, and archival research. Surveys were administered to members of the CWP management committee, which included a set of chairperson surveys (i.e., the manager of the water project; $N = 25$); a set of caretaker surveys ($N = 19$); and a collective survey of the CWP's chairperson, vice-chairperson, secretary, vice-secretary, and treasurer ($N = 19$). Responses from the chairperson surveys revealed the historical context, rules and monitoring policies, and water rotation and rationing strategies within each CWP. Caretaker surveys offered insight into the infrastructural design and repairs made to each CWP's pipe network. And, the collective survey with the CWP management committee was used to better understand group decision making.

Household-level water flow was measured on a weekly basis from July 2013 to January 2014. In smaller CWPs, 10 households were measured on a weekly basis, while in larger CWPs, 20 households were measured weekly. Using a stopwatch, measurements were taken by timing the duration to fill an 18-L bucket; measurements were then converted to liters per minute. In so doing, we have obtained a temporal record of weekly flow measurements in each CWP. The large amount of sediment in the CWP pipes prohibited the use of flow sensors to measure household-level water flow.

Archival research provided an understanding of Kenya's legal water institutions. This research was conducted in Nairobi during June 2013 in the Kenyan National Archives, the University of Nairobi, and Kenya's Ministry of Water and Irrigation, and includes statutes, regulations, and historic documents from Ministry of Water and Irrigation field offices. These three sets of data (i.e., the survey responses, the household-level water-flow measurements, and the archival research) will be used in the next section to inspect postreform experimentation with rule changes and how these rule changes correlate with location conditions.

Polycentric Transition Outcomes: Inspection of the Upper Ewaso Ng'iro Basin SES

Hypothesis Testing

In examining the outcomes of water reform, we focus particularly on the rules-in-use within each CWP. We attempt to link CWP governance strategies with propositions from the polycentricity literature and hypothesize the following: First, in the postreform period, user groups will experiment with new approaches to governance by adjusting their rules (hypothesis 1), and second, some of this experimentation will correlate with improved local conditions (hypothesis 2). We begin our examination of the outcomes following water reform by describing a case in which rule changes have clearly led to an outcome that polycentricity theorists would view as favorable. This is followed with additional evidence (or lack thereof) of outcomes predicted by polycentricity theory.

Monitoring and maintenance roles within CWPs are an element that appear to have been adjusted within at least one WRUA following the 2002 reform. CWPs typically employ a caretaker who is responsible for inspecting CWP pipelines for leaks, responding to complaints of poor water flow by members, monitoring to ensure that no members are taking water illegally, and disconnecting members if rules are violated. However, in the Ngusishi WRUA, CWP monitoring rules differ from the other four WRUAs. Rather than the CWPs of the Ngusishi WRUA employing caretakers, *scouts* are provided by the WRUA to monitor water-use activities along the CWPs' main lines. This stands in stark contrast to the other four WRUAs where WRUA officials only patrol the riparian zones, not the CWP's infrastructure. Scouts also make repairs to the main line(s). All sublines and some main lines within the Ngusishi CWPs are also maintained and monitored by representatives from the households along that particular line.

It is unclear if the scout system employed in the Ngusishi WRUA is preferable to the caretaker system within the other four WRUAs. The CWP may benefit by avoiding the cost of employing an individual within the monitor/maintenance position, as the WRUA pays for the scout; however, the scout may also be seen as an "outsider" and not trusted to the same degree as the caretakers within the other WRUAs. A natural experiment may well take place in which other WRUAs trial the approach taken by the Ngusishi WRUA. This experimentation with monitoring obligations in the Ngusishi WRUA confirms our first hypothesis. Additional examples of rule adjustments and experimentation are now explored, as well as the proficiency of experimentation efforts in adapting to local conditions (i.e., hypothesis 2).

To better understand other rule adjustments in response to the 2002 water reform, further background is necessary. The WRUAs and WRMA leverage considerable influence with respect to catchment-level water appropriation, particularly during the dry season. If a WRUA has directed a catchment's member groups to follow the agreed-upon appropriation schedule, a CWP's river intake is expected to only be open during the days in which that particular CWP is scheduled to receive water. Before the 2002 Water Act, rationing between CWPs was absent since formal catchment-level regulations did not exist. CWPs had little reason to consider the volume of water withdrawn from the river and upstream CWPs were the *de facto* beneficiaries. Some upstream CWP chairpersons have expressed their longing for the pre-WRUA period, claiming that water rationing has forced them to devise new rotation schedules (or alter existing schedules) within their CWPs, and that these changes have obstructed their abilities to meet the household consumption and irrigation needs of members.

In response, certain CWPs have adjusted their rules-in-use, particularly rules regarding new membership. As of the summer of 2013, 8 of the 25 CWPs had capped their membership (Table 14.3). In many cases, this was a recent decision made by management committees as they struggled to meet the needs of their members in the face of increasing population and water provisioning restrictions. Membership control represents a response to water scarcity and a divergence in the rules-in-use found among the 25 CWPs. It also suggests a divergence in water allocation outcomes. To explore this, we have calculated a single coefficient of variation (CV) value of pipe network water flow for each CWP using the household-level water-flow data from July 2013 to January 2014 (Table 14.3). To estimate the CV of water flow, the mean flow over time was calculated for each household within each CWP. The average of all household mean flows was calculated as well as the standard deviation of the household mean flows. The CWP-level CV of flow was then generated by dividing the standard deviation of CWP flow by average flow. We have grouped CWPs, as well as their CV of water flow, according to their decision to either cap membership or allow membership to grow. This allows us to compare the two groups based on summation of their CV of water flow ranks using a Mann–Whitney–Wilcoxon test.

This comparison of rank sums suggests that the difference between CV of water flow for CWPs that have capped membership compared to

Table 14.3. Community Water Project change in CWP membership and CV of water flow

CWP	WRUA	Membership Capped	CV of Water Flow[a]
Jikaze	Likii	Yes	0.1935
Miarage		No	0.2592
Murimi		No	0.1824
Nkando		No	0.2066
Tumaini		No	0.2568
Huku	Nanyuki	No	0.1223
Kaga		No	0.5470
Maka		No	0.1860
Mwea B		No	0.4953
Ruai		No	0.4492
Batian	Ngusishi	No	0.8262
Chumvi		No	0.5220
Kabubungi		Yes	0.1201
Kongoni		Yes	0.3022
Wiumiririe		No	0.3747
Mayangalo	Ngare Nything	No	0.8044
Mugokongo		Yes	0.1985
Mwimenyi A		No	0.2230
Nasakuja		No	0.3220
Ntumburi		No	0.3593
Karukunku	Timau	Yes	0.1145
Kiguru		No	0.0773
Kithima-Kiamunyi		Yes	0.1690
Milimani B		Yes	0.1695
Muguna		Yes	0.4641

[a]Calculated from weekly household-level measurements taken from July 2013 to January 2014. Household-level measurements started on a rolling basis where the first CWP visited (i.e., Nkando) had its first measurements taken on July 8, 2013, while the final CWP visited (i.e., Kiguru) had its first measurements taken on September 9, 2013. Thus, the overall total number of visits to each CWP are not equal.

those allowing membership to grow is statistically significant, and that variability is significantly higher in CWPs that allow new members to join compared to those that have limited their membership (Table 14.4). Thus, households within CWPs that have capped their memberships appear to receive more predictable water delivery. While other factors such as population and infrastructural components almost certainly affect this relationship, the statistical significance of this test suggests that institutions play a role in influencing water allocation outcomes as well. This tends to confirm our hypothesis that experimentation with rules-in-use can lead to successful adaptation to local conditions (i.e., hypothesis 2).

Table 14.4. Mann–Whitney–Wilcoxon Test Results

Change in CWP Membership in Past 5 Years	Number of CWPs	Rank Sum	Expected Rank Sum
No change (capped membership)	8	70	104
Increase	17	255	221
Total	25	325	325

Note: The test was significant at a critical value of 0.05. The group of CWPs that have capped their memberships (8 CWPs) have actual rank sums that are lower than their expected rank sum and lower than the actual rank sums of the group of CWPs that are allowing membership to increase (17 CWPs). Thus, the CWPs that have capped their memberships have a lower rank in variability of water flow.

Coordination among Local and Regional Actors

In addition to testing the above hypotheses, we also examine some ways that Kenya's reforms have created or encouraged coordination among multiple levels of management, and how these coordination mechanisms have affected CWP governance. The most notable postreform coordination mechanism exists between CWPs and their respective WRUA. At the local level, the CWP membership elects the individuals who serve on the management board, including the CWP's chairperson. Along with water use decision-making obligations within the CWP, the chairperson also serves on the WRUA's management committee, which makes catchment-wide decisions concerning water appropriation, monitoring, and sanctioning. Thus, coordination between the CWP and WRUA legislative bodies is directly linked by the representative procedure that elects each of the CWP's chairpersons. This process suggests more active and effective dialogue between WRUAs and CWPs, and that CWPs coordinate with WRUA officials when management concerns span community boundaries. For instance, 24 of the 25 CWP representatives stated that coordination with WRUA helps to prevent conflicts, and 15 of these individuals claimed that, of the higher levels of governance, WRUAs are most frequently relied upon to handle disputes between CWPs.

This increased level of coordination between CWPs and WRUAs—as well as between CWPs in the same catchment—has been accompanied by adjustments in institutional and physical infrastructure to ensure that WRUAs are achieving their goal of improving the quantity of water resources to all members of the catchment. For example, both the WRUA and WRMA now expect all CWPs to have a flow-measuring device near their river intake position, and will impose fines if devices are not installed. Similarly, to ensure that all CWPs withdraw an equal amount of water, WRUAs now tend to require that all CWPs install uniform (6-inch) intake pipes. In addition, WRMA (in partnership with the WRUA) has increased the frequency with which it assesses penalties to CWPs withdrawing water in excess of permits. These new requirements and fees improve efforts to guarantee catchment-wide water access, but they also burden communities with additional financial obligations and water use restrictions. Some CWP chairpersons expressed frustrations related to the increased fees following the 2002 Water Act. One chairperson described the reform as operating in a "commercial way" that has precluded the "normal person" from accessing water if they cannot afford it. Another claimed that the 2002 reform "has not been good" since it has increased costs within CWPs. These and other CWP leaders explained that they have been forced to raise fees in response to the increased financial burden, and in some cases CWPs have increased their memberships to help pay the increased fees.

Discussion

The preceding analysis of Kenya's water reform demonstrates that the government has deliberately created the basic features of a polycentric system: multiple, independent decision centers at the CWP, WRUA, and WRMA levels; overlapping authority over several aspects of water governance; and mechanisms for coordination between governance levels. Arguably, however, the more interesting question is how these changes have affected governance on-the-ground among and between local CWPs and WRUAs, particularly with respect to rule adjustment and experimentation, as well as the emergence of new forms of collective action.

The 2002 reform appears to have provided a stimulus for all CWPs within the Upper Ewaso Ng'iro SES to experiment with their rules-in-use in order to meet the needs of their members. While CWPs had the authority to make their own rules before 2002, the rule experimentation that is now taking place is fundamentally different given that CWPs now occupy rulemaking space with their WRUA, as well as WRMA. A CWP that is nested within a WRMA-approved WRUA—as is the case with all of the CWPs in this study—has representatives who participate in catchment-level decision making about permit issuance, regional-scale water allocation, and water conservation strategies. This representation gives CWP leaders a level of legitimacy that they lacked in the past. However, it also requires CWP chairpersons to balance the wants of their members with the requirements specified at higher levels of management. This is precisely where the decision of some CWPs to limit their memberships has originated, since WRUAs mandate a percentage of river water reach downstream users. While balancing the requirements of the WRUA with the wants of CWP members can be challenging, it is important to recognize that by taking on these challenges, CWPs are now provided with a path toward user-group legitimacy, an important trait of a polycentric system and a trait that was glaringly absent before the 2002 reform.

The literature on polycentricity also suggests that coordination among local, regional, and national actors should encourage mutual adjustments and the undertaking of collective action at multiple levels. Our examination of the Upper Ewaso Ng'iro basin shows that, postreform, CWPs are reducing their water use to ensure water availability for downstream users. However, they are doing so to comply with rules imposed upon CWPs in a top-down fashion, with some resistance from CWP managers. It thus may be premature to consider water allocation arrangements within WRUAs to be "collective action" in the classic sense; WRUA members communicate and coordinate their water use, but actual reductions in CWPs' water allocations have come about due to formal legal requirements rather than due to bottom-up strategies. Nonetheless, the coordination mechanisms created by the reforms—particularly the creation of the WRUAs—have helped to ensure that CWPs will comply with the requirements and that the mandates will achieve the intended result of increased water availability.

Key understandings with respect to the literature on polycentricity have been revealed from this study. We have found evidence that a deliberate push for polycentric resource management *can* encourage local decision making and rule experimentation, especially as local chairpersons respond to policy changes from decision makers at higher levels of management. While additional experimentation may occur over time, we conclude that Kenya's top-down reforms *allow*, rather than *encourage*, experimentation, adaptation, and learning.

Similarly, while CWPs have autonomy to craft their own rules, this is primarily limited to internal matters, and WRMA retains the right to impose rules in top-down fashion—for example, mandating certain infrastructure investments. However, it appears that local-level rule diversification would actually be quite minimal within the 25 CWPs without these top-down policy-induced changes. Additionally, it is possible that simply not enough time has elapsed since the 2002 Water Act, and that with the passage of time more experimentation will naturally occur. In this vein, we may be witnessing the less-than-optimal institutions established by local resource managers as they grapple with the complexity of their system (E. Ostrom, 2005).

Finally, our examination of the 25 CWPs, and their respective WRUAs, suggests that a polycentric system is developing not solely on paper, but on-the-ground as well. Yet, while some beneficial conditions have arisen following the 2002 reform, other governance outcomes predicted by theorists have been slow to emerge, and the actual benefits of these outcomes may fall somewhat short of those predicted by theory. It additionally remains to be seen whether the conditions in our study area are pervasive across Kenya and whether other CWPs have experienced a similar level of interaction with regional and national actors.

Conclusion

This study set out to identify how actor roles and local-level rules have changed following the 2002 water reform, and to determine the extent to which the postreform governance outcomes reflect benefits predicted by polycentricity theorists. With regards to this inquiry, we hypothesized the following: (i) In the postreform period, user groups will experiment with new approaches to governance by adjusting their rules, and (ii) some of this experimentation will correlate with improved local conditions.

We found evidence—albeit limited—in support of these hypotheses. Kenya's polycentric shift may have provided a "shock" which led to rule changes and a divergence in rules-in-use employed by CWP chairpersons, particularly those rules related to user-group membership and monitoring. These adjustments appear to be ongoing and indicate some amount of experimentation with management strategies. We also found evidence that the coordination mechanisms created by the reforms have prompted CWPs to curtail water use to the benefit of other CWPs; however, this has largely occurred by way of a top-down approach that may not fully match theorists' predictions about collective action.

By taking an empirical approach, this study has addressed critical questions concerning the institutional dynamics that are involved in a national water governance polycentric transition. In the process, it has raised topics that are ripe for future research, including the different and often contradictory features of polycentric reforms and the barriers to on-the-ground deployment of polycentric principles when, formally, multiple centers of governance exist. Further investigation into these topics will advance the governance community's understandings of polycentric resource governance.

Appendix

Selection of variables to be included in the combined IAD-SES framework at the pre-reform time step was guided by the following steps:

1. An understanding of the water management system as of 2013 was obtained through review of information gathered during archival research. From this understanding, we worked backwards to the time step just before the 2002 reform to identify SES framework variables where it was possible to make a causal connection to 2013 outcomes.
2. In identifying these pre-reform SES variables, we first focused on isolating second-tier variables for each subsystem that could either help characterize the pre-reform landscape, or function as a direct driver of reform, or both.
   a. Before selecting a variable, a "yes" response was required of the following question: "Is this variable critical to understanding the SES in the context of Kenyan water governance, or is this variable a driver of water policy reform?"
3. Where greater detail was needed, we unpacked the identified attributes into third-tier variables by repeating steps 2 and 2a for each variable previously identified.

To characterize the dynamics within the adjacent action situations that produced the postreform conditions, we adhered to the following steps:

1. An assessment was made of which broad action situation processes could be reasonably articulated using the pre-existing conditions from the pre-reform time step.
2. Given our understanding of the water management system as of 2013, a narrowing of potential action situations was performed by identifying decision-making processes that reasonably led to the 2013 conditions.
3. To demonstrate the connectivity within the adjacent action situations, the elements identified for each action situation needed to both influence and be influenced by the other decision-making strategies within the web of action situations.

Selection of the combined IAD-SES framework postreform conditions was guided by the following steps:

1. Tracking the steps of reform from pre-reform conditions to the adjacent action situations, an assessment was made of the SES framework variables that were directly altered during this course of development.
2. After acknowledging these second- and third-tier variables, we further detailed the postreform conditions by referring to information collected through 2013 archival research.

Acknowledgments

We gratefully acknowledge support from the U.S. National Science Foundation (grant SBE1115009). We also thank three anonymous reviewers for their valuable input.

Note

This chapter was originally published in *Policy Studies Journal*, online June 23, 2016, doi:10.1111/psj.12168. Reprinted with the permission of John Wiley & Sons.

References

Agrawal, Arun, and Clark C. Gibson. 1999. "Enchantment and Disenchantment: The Role of Community in Natural Resource Conservation." *World Development* 27: 629–49.

Aligica, Paul D., and Vlad Tarko. 2012. "Polycentricity: From Polanyi to Ostrom, and Beyond." *Governance* 25(2): 237–62.

Andersson, Krister P., and Elinor Ostrom. 2008. "Analyzing Decentralized Resource Regimes from a Polycentric Perspective." *Policy Sciences* 41(1): 71–93.

Baldwin, Elizabeth, Camille Washington-Ottombre, Jampel Dell'Angelo, Daniel H. Cole, and Tom P. Evans. 2016. "Polycentric Governance and Irrigation Reform in Kenya." *Governance* 29(2): 207–25.

Basurto, Xavier, Stefan Gelcich, and Elinor Ostrom. 2013. "The Social-Ecological System Framework as a Knowledge Classificatory System for Benthic Small-Scale Fisheries." *Global Environmental Change* 23(6): 1366–80.

Basurto, Xavier, and Elinor Ostrom. 2009. "Beyond the Tragedy of the Commons." *Economia delle fonti di energia e dell'ambiente* 52: 35–60.

Bixler R. Patrick, Jampel Dell'Angelo, Orleans Mfune, and Hassan Roba. 2015. "The Political Ecology of Participatory Conservation: Institutions and Discourse." *Journal of Political Ecology* 22: 164–82.

Cinner, Joshua E., Tim R. McClanahan, M. Aaron MacNeil, Nicholas A. J. Graham, Tim M. Daw, Ahmad Mukminin, David A. Feary, et al. 2012.

"Comanagement of Coral Reef Social-Ecological Systems." *Proceedings of the National Academy of Sciences* 109(14): 5219–22.

Cole, Daniel H., Graham Epstein, and Michael D. McGinnis. 2014. "Toward a New Institutional Analysis of Social-Ecological Systems (NIASES): Combining Elinor Ostrom's IAD and SES Frameworks." Indiana Legal Studies Research Paper, No. 299; Indiana University, Bloomington School of Public and Environmental Affairs Research Paper, No. 2490999. Available at SSRN: http://ssrn.com/abstract=2490999.

Cole, Daniel H., and Michael D. McGinnis, eds. 2015. "Introduction to Volume 1." *In Elinor Ostrom and the Bloomington School of Political Economy: Volume 1, Polycentricity in Public Administration and Political Science*. Lanham, MD: Lexington Books, xxxiii–xlvii.

Cottrell, Edwin A. 1949. "Problems of Local Governmental Reorganization." *The Western Political Quarterly* 2(4): 599–609.

Cox, Michael. 2014. "Applying a Social-Ecological System Framework to the Study of the Taos Valley Irrigation System." *Human Ecology* 42(2): 311–24.

da Silveira, Andre R., and Keith S. Richards. 2013. "The Link between Polycentrism and Adaptive Capacity in River Basin Governance Systems: Insights from the River Rhine and the Zhujiang (Pearl River) Basin." *Annals of the Association of American Geographers* 103(2): 319–29.

Dell'Angelo, Jampel. 2012. *Abusing the Commons? An Integrated Institutional Analysis of Common-Pool Resource Governance in Conflict Situations*. PhD diss., Sapienza University of Rome and Autonomous University of Barcelona.

Ericksen, Polly, Mohammed Said, Jan de Leeux, Silvia Silvestri, Lokman Zaibet, Shem Kifugo, Koert Sijmons, et al. 2011. *Mapping and Valuing Ecosystem Services in the Ewaso Ng'iro Watershed*. Nairobi, Kenya: International Livestock Research Institute.

Fleischman, Forrest D., Kinga Boenning, Gustavo A. Garcia-Lopez, Sarah K. Mincey, Mikaela Schmitt-Harsh, Katrin Daedlow, Maria Claudia Lopez, Xavier Basurto, Burney Fischer, and Elinor Ostrom. 2010. "Disturbance, Response, and Persistence in Self-Organized Forested Communities: Analysis of Robustness and Resilience in Five Communities in Southern Indiana." *Ecology and Society* 15(4): 9.

Folke, Carl, Thomas Hahn, Per Olsson, and Jon Norberg. 2005. "Adaptive Governance of Social-Ecological Systems." *Annual Review of Environment and Resources* 30: 441–73.

Galaz, Victor, Beatrice Crona, Henrik Österblom, Per Olsson, and Carl Folke. 2012. "Polycentric Systems and Interacting Planetary Boundaries—Emerging Governance of Climate Change–Ocean Acidification–Marine Biodiversity." *Ecological Economics* 81: 21–32.

Gordillo, Gustavo, and Krister Andersson. 2004. "From Policy Lessons to Policy Actions: Motivation to Take Evaluation Seriously." *Public Administration and Development* 24(4): 305–20.

Gutiérrez, Nicolas L., Ray Hilborn, and Omar Defeo. 2011. "Leadership, Social Capital and Incentives Promote Successful Fisheries." *Nature* 470(7334): 386–89.

Huitema, Dave, Erik Mostert, Wouter Egas, Sabine Moellenkamp, Claudia Pahl-Wostl, and Resul Yalcin. 2009. "Adaptive Water Governance: Assessing the Institutional Prescriptions of Adaptive (Co-)Management from a Governance Perspective and Defining a Research Agenda." *Ecology and Society* 14(1): 26.

Kenya Ministry of Water Development. 1983. *Annual Report, Meru District.* Kenya National Archives.

Kenya Water Apportionment Board. 1972. 1972 Water (General) Rules. http://faolex.fao.org/cgi-bin/faolex.exe?rec_id=016336&database=faolex&search_type=link&table=result&lang=eng&format_name=@ERALL. Accessed June 7, 2016.

Kiser, Larry L., and Elinor Ostrom. 1982. "The Three Worlds of Action: A Metatheoretical Synthesis of Institutional Approaches." In *Strategies of Political Inquiry*, ed. Elinor Ostrom. Beverly Hills, CA: Sage Publications, 179–222.

Kiteme, Boniface P., Urs Wiesmann, Erwin Künzi, and Joseph M. Mathuva. 1998. "A Highland-Lowland System under Transitional Pressure: A Spatio-Temporal Analysis." *Eastern and Southern Africa Geographical Journal* 8: 45–54.

Liniger, Hanspeter, John Gikonyo, Boniface Kiteme, and Urs Wiesmann. 2005. "Assessing and Managing Scarce Tropical Mountain Water Resources: The Case of Mount Kenya and the Semiarid Upper Ewaso Ng'iro Basin." *Mountain Research and Development* 25(2): 163–73.

Madrigal, Róger, Francisco Alpízar, and Achim Schlüter. 2011. "Determinants of Performance of Community-Based Drinking Water Organizations." *World Development* 39(9): 1663–75.

McCord, Paul F., Michael Cox, Mikaela Schmitt-Harsh, and Tom P. Evans. 2015. "Crop Diversification as a Smallholder Livelihood Strategy within Semi-Arid Agricultural Systems near Mount Kenya." *Land Use Policy* 42: 738–50.

McGinnis, Michael D. 1999. *Polycentricity and Local Public Economies: Readings from the Workshop in Political Theory and Policy Analysis.* Ann Arbor: University of Michigan Press.

———. 2011. "Networks of Adjacent Action Situations in Polycentric Governance." *Policy Studies Journal* 39(1): 51–78.

McGinnis, Michael D., and Elinor Ostrom. 2014. "Social-Ecological System Framework: Initial Changes and Continuing Challenges." *Ecology and Society* 19(2): 30.

Mwangi, E. N. 2003. *Institutional Change and Politics: The Transformation of Property Rights in Kenya's Maasailand.* PhD diss., Indiana University.

Ngigi, Stephen N., Hubert H. G. Savenije, and Francis N. Gichuki. 2007. "Land Use Changes and Hydrological Impacts Related to Up-Scaling of Rainwater

Harvesting and Management in Upper Ewaso Ng'iro River Basin, Kenya." *Land Use Policy* 24: 129–40.

Ostrom, Elinor. 1990. *Governing the Commons: The Evolution of Institutions for Collective Action*. New York: Cambridge University Press.

———. 1999. "Coping with Tragedies of the Commons." *Annual Review of Political Science* 2: 493–535.

———. 2005. *Understanding Institutional Diversity*. Princeton, NJ: Princeton University Press.

———. 2007. "A Diagnostic Approach for Going Beyond Panaceas." *Proceedings of the National Academy of Sciences* 104(39): 15181–87.

———. 2009. "A General Framework for Analyzing Sustainability of Social-Ecological Systems." *Science* 325(5939): 419–22.

———. 2011. "Reflections on 'Some Unsettled Problems of Irrigation.'" *The American Economic Review* 101: 49–63.

Ostrom, Elinor, and Michael Cox. 2010. "Moving Beyond Panaceas: A Multi-Tiered Diagnostic Approach for Social-Ecological Analysis." *Environmental Conservation* 37(4): 451–63.

Ostrom, Vincent. 1999. "Polycentricity." In *Polycentricity and Local Public Economies*, ed. Michael D. McGinnis. Ann Arbor: University of Michigan Press, 52–74.

Ostrom, Vincent, Charles M. Tiebout, and Robert Warren. 1961. "The Organization of Government in Metropolitan Areas: A Theoretical Inquiry." *American Political Science Review* 55(4): 831–42.

Pahl-Wostl, Claudia, and Christian Knieper. 2014. "The Capacity of Water Governance to Deal with the Climate Change Adaptation Challenge: Using Fuzzy Set Qualitative Comparative Analysis to Distinguish Between Polycentric, Fragmented and Centralized Regimes." *Global Environmental Change* 29: 139–54.

Pahl-Wostl, Claudia, Louis Lebel, Christian Knieper, and Elena Nikitina. 2012. "From Applying Panaceas to Mastering Complexity: Toward Adaptive Water Governance in River Basins." *Environmental Science & Policy* 23: 24–34.

Polski, Margaret M. 2003. *The Invisible Hands of US Commercial Banking Reform: Private Action and Public Guarantees*. Boston, MA: Kluwer.

Ribot, Jesse C., Arun Agrawal, and Anne M. Larson. 2006. "Recentralizing while Decentralizing: How National Governments Reappropriate Forest Resources." *World Development* 34(11): 1864–86.

Sabatier, Paul A. 2007. "The Need for Better Theories." In *Theories of the Policy Process, 2nd ed.*, ed. Paul A. Sabatier. Boulder, CO: Westview Press, 3–17.

Schaaf, Jeanne. 1989. *Governing a Monopoly Market under Siege: Using Institutional Analysis to Understand Competitive Entry into Telecommunications Markets, 1944–1982*. PhD diss., Indiana University.

Scott, James. 1998. *Seeing Like a State: How Certain Schemes to Improve the Human Condition Have Failed*. New Haven, CT: Yale University Press.

Shivakoti, Ganesh, and Elinor Ostrom. 2001. *Improving Irrigation Governance and Management in Nepal*. Oakland, CA: ICS Press.

Villamayor-Tomas, Sergio, Philipp Grundmann, Graham Epstein, Tom P. Evans, and Christian Kimmich. 2015. "The Water-Energy-Food Security Nexus through the Lenses of the Value Chain and the Institutional Analysis and Development Frameworks." *Water Alternatives* 8(1): 735–55.

Wiesmann, Urs, Francis N. Gichuki, Boniface P. Kiteme, and Hanspeter Liniger. 2000. "Mitigating Conflicts over Scarce Water Resources in the Highland-Lowland System of Mount Kenya." *Mountain Research and Development* 20(1): 10–15.

WRMA, and WSTF (Water Resources Management Authority and Water Services Trust Fund). 2009. *Water Resource Users Association Development Cycle (WDC)*. Nairobi, Kenya: Water Services Trust Fund.

PART IV

Persisting Challenges

15

Coevolving Relationships between Political Science and Economics

ELINOR OSTROM

Important developments in science frequently occur at the boundaries of disciplines when scholars from two or more fields discover each other and begin to address old questions in new ways. Since the 1950s, the border-zone of economics and political science has generated a rich endowment of pathbreaking work as well as creative controversies. Four developments have occurred at the boundaries of political science and economics that have affected the central questions that we ask, the empirical evidence amassed, and questions for future research. These include: (1) Public Choice, (2) the Tragedy of the Commons Debate, (3) New Institutional Economics, and (4) Behavioral Approaches to Explaining Human Actions. In this short essay, I will briefly review the challenges that these approaches have brought to scholars working at the borders of major disciplines and some of the general findings stimulated by these approaches before identifying some of the major issues on the contemporary agenda.

The Challenges of Interdisciplinary Approaches

The Public Choice Approach

The publication of Arrow's *Social Choice and Individual Values* in 1951, Downs's *An Economic Theory of Democracy* in 1957, Black's *The Theory of Committees and Elections* in 1958, Buchanan and Tullock's *The Calculus of Consent* in 1962, and Olson's *The Logic of Collective Action* in 1965 generated a new approach—called public choice. A group of economists, political scientists, and sociologists used methods originally developed in economics to examine public sector processes and outcomes. An organizing question underlying work in the public choice tradition has been: what incentives do actors face when making decisions in the public sector or outside a strict market setting? After identifying incentives in specific situations, public choice theorists predict how individuals will act and how behavior will aggregate into collective outcomes. Incentives result from the structure of a situation that is affected by the type of goods involved, combined with attributes of a community and the rules used for making decisions about provision, production, distribution, and consumption of those goods.

The early work challenged not only the implicit conceptual models that political scientists utilized but the notion that order stemmed primarily from central direction. Instead of presuming the existence of only two kinds of order—the market and the state—political economists have come to recognize *public economies* where large, medium, and small governmental and nongovernmental enterprises engage in both competitive and cooperative relationships. Without prejudging the performance of complex metropolitan areas, V. Ostrom, Tiebout, and Warren (1961) proposed, for example, that the multiplicity of local jurisdictions in a metropolitan area be conceived as a 'polycentric political system'. A large body of work has since relied on their distinction between the *provision* of a collective good by citizens, elected representatives, and NGOs, and the *production* of a collective good by a government or private agency. Given that the appropriate scale for organizing the provision side is frequently not the same as for organizing the production side of a collective good, one should expect to find messy polycentric systems of provision and production units operating at multiple scales in regard to almost any collective good.

The public choice or 'rational choice' approach was quickly adopted by many political scientists who rapidly developed and applied it to the study of many types of institutional arrangements (see Barry and Hardin 1982 for an early review). Empirical studies flourished, including those that focused on legislatures (Riker 1962; Shepsle 1989), voting systems (Tsebelis 1990), and bargaining (Miller 1992). The approach was strongly criticized by other political scientists, however, because it portrayed human behavior as narrowly self-interested, shortsighted, and constrained only by formal rules. Critics observed that people do vote, do contribute to philanthropic efforts, do follow norms, do engage informally, and do make long-term commitments contrary to predictions of some of the new theoretical models.

The Tragedy of the Commons Debate

Another important interdisciplinary development that started in the same era is the analysis by economists and ecologists of 'the tragedy of the commons' (Gordon 1954; Hardin 1968). This theory, like that of Olson, challenged the earlier work of political scientists who presumed that individuals were motivated to contribute efforts toward solving common problems when it was in their long-term interest to do so. Both Gordon and Hardin posited that individuals focused on maximizing immediate short-term benefits and were helpless to do anything but overharvest resources. The prediction that individuals would destroy the resources was consistent with noncooperative game theory models of one-shot or finitely repeated dilemma settings. In these settings, everyone is posited to maximize their own short-term benefits, but end up achieving less net benefits than feasible if they had found a way to cooperate with one another.

This work opened up an immense body of theoretical and empirical work as well as substantial policy debates. Many studies provided empirical data and theoretical arguments to challenge the presumption that individuals were forever trapped in a remorseless tragedy by documenting many common-property institutions around the world where individuals had overcome the tragedy (McCay and Acheson 1987; Ciriacy-Wantrup and Bishop 1975; National Research Council 1986). Still other in-depth analyses documented the accelerated overharvesting of forests that occurred after national governments declared themselves to be the formal owner of forested land (Arnold and Campbell 1986; Ascher 1995).

Commons scholars did not, however, find any 'sure cures' for the problem of overuse. They found that failure occurs in regard to private property, government property, and common property. Overharvesting did occur, of course, when a valuable resource was effectively an open-resource due to a lack of rule defining and limiting who had access and other rights to use and manage the resource. Gordon and Hardin, along with the myriad of scholars and policymakers from multiple disciplines who accepted the tragedy metaphor as a general theory, were correct in identifying a challenging problem—especially under open-access conditions. Their analysis was incomplete, however, because they failed to recognize the rich variety of complex institutional arrangements that had been used to solve these problems while their own solutions of government or private ownership often failed to solve the problem.

New Institutional Economics

The 'New Institutional Economics' (NIE) field has challenged both economists and political scientists. Coase started the first foray in 1937 with his pathbreaking article on 'The Nature of the Firm'. Asking 'why do firms exist' was an embarrassing question for economists. Why should one find firms existing in the midst of highly competitive markets? He challenged the presumed dichotomy of the world into Markets for production, allocation, and distribution of private goods and Hierarchy for the production, allocation, and distribution of public goods. Coase answered his own question by pointing to the diversity of costs (particularly transaction costs) that are associated with using the market, which were absent from neoclassical theory.

Influenced by Coase, North (1981) initiated studies of institutional change that challenged the static focus of both political science and economics. NIE scholars demonstrated that self-organized institutions had guaranteed property rights of merchants long before the creation of a State (Milgrom, North and Weingast 1990). Scholars in the NIE tradition are expanding the model of human behavior used to explain institutional behavior so as to be broadly consistent with developments in cognitive science (Denzau and North 1994; North 2005). Williamson (1975) examined a diversity of internal mechanisms within firms to keep agents accountable and to reduce transaction costs, and provides one of the clearest presentations in the literature of the dysfunctions of a strict hierarchy. Research in political science on principal-agent theory (Miller 1992) owes a great deal to the NIE initiatives.

Added to theoretical rigor is the development of an experimental tradition that enables scholars to test predictions under controlled settings that can be replicated by others and modified to examine the impact of specific rules or other variables that affect decisions and outcomes in complex settings. Experimental scholars have developed an extremely careful set of methods that have greatly improved the reliability and veracity of their results over time. By carefully inducing preferences, developing instructions that convey the meaning of the theoretical structure under investigation, freely sharing instructions with others, and making the data from the experiments available, experimental scholars have strongly validated many propositions derived from noncooperative, game-theoretical models related to behavior in markets (see, e.g., Smith and Walker 1993).

Behavioral Economics

Political scientists were relatively unaware of the early days of game theory. Over time, as the power of game theory grew due to its generality and precision, it has steadily become a tool that is used by more and more social scientists. That one can use the same set of tools to analyze a game of tennis, the decision of when to run for office, predator-prey relationships, how much to trust a stranger, and how much to contribute to a public good makes game theory one of the most important analytical tools available to all of the social sciences. On the other hand, game theory has frequently been dismissed by political scientists as just another abstract theory.

While experimental results gave strong support to predictions of institutional theorists related to market incentives, simple social dilemma games that generate crystal clear theoretical predictions have not been supported in a large number of experimental settings around the world. Experimental researchers have generated findings related to the extension of trust (see Fehr 2009; Walker and Ostrom 2009 for an overview), the division of benefits in settings that lack external enforcement, and the provision of public goods (Sefton, Shupp and Walker 2007). Findings from these types of games in multiple labs have been inconsistent with a theory that presumes individuals maximize short-term, objective payoffs to self alone. This evidence challenges the core assumptions of micro-economics, as well as those of public choice theorists. Given consistent findings across a large number of experiments conducted in multiple countries with varied amounts of payoffs, the findings have to be taken seriously.

Political Science and Political Economy Have Coevolved

The last half-century has been a time of challenge. Political scientists and political economists have reacted in multiple ways to these challenges. Some have continued in their own paths undaunted by the calls for change. Others have attempted to build on the core of the challenges as well as more classical political and economic theorists including Hobbes, Hume, Tocqueville, the authors of *The Federalist Papers*, Commons, Hayek, Smith, and Schumpeter, to craft an interdisciplinary approach to the study of the governance of public economies at multiple levels (Allen 2005; Shivakumar 2005). New frameworks, theories, and models have been developed (see Greif and Laitin 2004; Gibson et al. 2005; Boettke 2005; E. Ostrom 2005; 2007; 2009).

One of the healthiest aspects of the coevolution of political science and economics has been a strong commitment to the use of theory in the design of research and a resultant increase in the cumulation of theory. Slowly, a new foundation for the political and social sciences is emerging. It is not yet broadly accepted, but many scholars are independently drawing on, improving, and extending this work. In the remainder of this short overview, I will first discuss some of the general findings that have emerged from multiple studies and then turn to some of the major questions on the future agenda.

Diverse Forms of Order—None Always Good or Bad

A general finding relates to the recognition of multiple forms of order. One form of political order is created when a central power uses a monopoly of force to impose its central will on the subjects of an entire country (Hobbes 1960[1651]). The work of Levi (1988) and Sawyer (2005) demonstrate how costly and unstable it is to rely entirely on a central monopoly of force to govern effectively. Other forms of order at all levels of organization exist and need to be studied seriously. Putnam (2000) points to the importance of networks in the creation of essential social capital that enables complex governance systems to evolve without all links being planned from the top. Keohane (1984) provides us with new ways of viewing political order at the international level without depending on the hegemony of one state.

Organizations that are omitted from basic textbooks focusing on markets or the state are major actors for good or evil in contemporary political life. A host of organizations in addition to governments undertake the provision of collective goods (Bryce 2005). Some generate benefits for themselves and others, such as groups of resource users like the lobster fishermen of Maine (Acheson 2003) or organizations of recreational users in Sweden (Anttila and Stern 2005). Others are organized informally to provide benefits for themselves, but not always for others (Helmke and Levitsky 2004). The performance of a system depends on the match of the structure of the system to the scale and structure of problems individuals within that system face and the incentives participants face to generate broad or narrow benefit streams and not on whether a system looks neat on an organization chart.

Structure and Performance of Local Public Economies

In regard to the organization of governments serving a metropolitan area, however, scholars have now provided an analysis of why complex systems may perform better than simple and highly centralized systems may perform. The optimal scale of organization for the production and provision of goods and services differs radically for different types of goods and services usually considered to be in the public sector. This leads to the prediction that public economies in metropolitan areas with many governmental enterprises organized at diverse scales that have the authority to undertake joint activities will perform more effectively than either one large-scale (metropolitan-wide) government or a large number of governments organized entirely at a small scale. This prediction was counterintuitive for many scholars, who had long argued that the performance of metropolitan governments would be enhanced by streamlining and creating a single, consolidated government for a metropolitan area.

Considerable research on local public economies and multi-level systems more generally (see Houghe and Marks 2001; Bickers and Williams 2001) has demonstrated that social order can emerge from polycentric systems and need not be imposed by a centralized system. In our own extensive studies of police performance, ranging from carefully matched neighborhoods in one metropolitan area to a random sample of 80 metropolitan areas, we have consistently found:

- Small- to medium-sized police departments outperform large police departments serving similar communities—and at similar or lower costs.
- Services that are characterized by substantial economies of scale (e.g., crime lab, dispatching) are produced by large units, and services characterized by diseconomies of scale were produced by small units. Thus, polycentric systems facilitate the search for more efficient modes of production.
- Citizens living in the most fragmented metropolitan areas receive more police presence on the streets for their tax expenditures than do citizens living in the most consolidated areas (see articles reprinted in McGinnis 1999).

In addition to the research on police, scholars have conducted rigorous empirical research that has challenged the presumptions that larger public school districts achieve higher performance (Teske et al. 1993; Fischel 2001), that fragmentation of governments leads to higher costs (Schneider 1986), and have provided further insights to the way local governments are constituted (Oakerson and Parks 1989). In light of a meta-analysis of 20 empirical studies of the effect of local government structure in the United States, Boyne (1992, 352) concludes that: "In sum, the broad pattern of the evidence suggests that lower spending is a feature of fragmented and deconcentrated local government systems. By contrast, consolidated and concentrated structures tend to be associated with higher spending."

Governing Common-Pool Resources

The empirical research related to local public economies generated many studies whose results are broadly consistent with the theoretical analyses of early public choice theorists. Empirical research undertaken to study 'the tragedy of the commons' on the other hand, has contradicted the initial theoretical work. Studies have demonstrated that many of those facing multiple social dilemmas have crafted institutions to govern their own resources, and sustained these regimes for very long periods of time in many instances.[1] Design principles that characterize robust, long-lasting institutional arrangements for the governance of common-pool resources have been identified (E. Ostrom 1990) and supported by further testing (de Moor, Shaw-Taylor and Warde 2002; Weinstein 2000; Cox, Arnold and Villamayor Tomás 2010).

In addition to the earlier case studies, quantitative studies have shown that local-scale common-pool resources, such as irrigation systems, tend to be effectively self-organized by resource users themselves (Lansing and Kremer 1993). Lam (1998) examined the performance of more than 100 irrigation systems in Nepal that are either self-organized by the farmers or constructed and operated by the national government. Lam shows that the farmer-managed systems outperform the government-managed systems in terms of their productivity and more equitable water distribution, controlling for the size of the system and physical variables. The difference in performance is striking since most farmer-managed systems are constructed using primitive techniques, while government systems have been constructed with donor assistance using modern engineering designs. Joshi et al. (2000) conducted rigorous research related to 229 irrigation systems in Nepal. They found that farmer-managed irrigation systems were able to outperform government-owned and managed systems in regard to agricultural productivity, technical efficiency, and equity of service delivery.

A National Research Council (2002) report provides an overview of the substantial research showing that many common-pool resources are governed successfully both by nonstate provision units as well as by government and private property. No simple governance system has been shown to be successful in all implementations, but effective monitoring and sanctioning are essential factors affecting performance (Dietz, Ostrom and Stern 2003; Hayes and Ostrom 2005; Gibson, Williams and Ostrom 2005). Heikkila and Gerlak (2005) have applied the theoretical insights derived from the studies of the emergence and robustness of institutions related to smaller-scale common-pool resources along with findings from literature on policy entrepreneurs and social capital to a study of very large, multiactor, multiple-scale watershed-management institutions.

In a recent study, Chhatre and Agrawal (2009) focus on factors that affect trade-offs and synergies between the level of carbon storage in forests and the livelihood of those using the forest. When local communities have high levels of rule-making authority and monitor the activities in the forests, they find that larger forests are more effective in enhancing both carbon and livelihood outcomes. Coleman (2009) and Coleman and Steed (2009) also find that a major variable affecting forest conditions is the investment by local users in monitoring. Further, when local users are given harvesting rights, they are more likely to monitor illegal uses themselves. Other focused studies also stress the relationship between local monitoring and better forest conditions (Ghate and Nagendra 2005; E. Ostrom and Nagendra 2006; Banana and Gombya-Ssembajjwe 2000; Webb and Shivakoti 2008).

The structure of a finitely repeated common-pool resource game has also been examined in experimental laboratory studies. In this setting, it has been shown that when appropriators from a common-pool resource are in a minimal institutional setting without any knowledge of the others or any capacity to communicate, outcomes approach the predicted outcome of the conventional theory. On the other hand, as soon as subjects are allowed to communicate, they achieve far better outcomes than predicted by the conventional theory. In noncooperative game theory, communication is viewed as 'cheap talk' and makes no difference in predicted outcomes in social dilemmas.

Once communication is allowed, however, subjects spend time and effort assessing each other's trustworthiness and reaching agreements about the best strategies they should jointly take. Further, individuals in a laboratory setting are willing to monitor each other and invest in costly sanctions in order to punish those who overharvest, as well as in devising rules that they themselves enforce on each other (see E. Ostrom, Walker and Gardner 1992). In other words, in a controlled setting, individuals solve social dilemmas and achieve substantially greater payoffs than predicted once communication is allowed. Janssen et al. (2010) demonstrate the importance of communication in enabling users to effectively use the opportunity to punish others. Without communication, punishment can evolve into a retribution effort and reduce all participants' payoffs.

Revisiting the Model of Homo Economicus

Research growing out of the study of the commons, the work of new institutional economists, and that of behavioral game theorists has opened up serious reconsideration of the narrow model of the economic actor that was developed in neoclassical economics and initially applied to political settings without modification. The 'classical' model of individual choice used by many political economists—based on noncooperative game theory and neoclassical economic theory—uses extreme assumptions about individual capabilities and motivations. These include an unlimited computational capability and a focus on short-term, individual, net benefits. In other words, internal calculations are based on the increasing short-term material benefits and costs to the individual making the calculation and no one else.

In some field settings, the classical theory of individual behavior generates empirically confirmed results. In highly competitive environments, we can assume that the individuals who survive the selective pressure of the environment act as if they maximized their individual utility dependent on a key variable, such as profits, associated with survival in that environment (e.g., profits or fitness) (Satz and Ferejohn 1994). When individuals face a relatively simple decision situation where institutions generate accurate information about the variables relevant to a particular problem, that problem can be adequately represented as a straightforward, constrained maximization problem.

Many of the situations of interest in understanding how public economies govern and manage collective goods, however, are uncertain, complex, and lack the selective pressure and information-generating capabilities of a competitive market. Therefore, one strategy for dealing with this problem has been to assume bounded rationality—that persons are intendedly rational but only limitedly so—rather than the assumptions of perfect information and utility maximization used in the classical theory (Simon 1972). Information search is costly, and the information-processing capabilities of human beings are limited. Individuals, therefore, often must make choices based on incomplete knowledge of all possible alternatives and their likely outcomes. Punctuated changes in policy outputs are more likely to result than smooth transitions (Jones, Sulkin and Larsen 2003). With incomplete information and imperfect information-processing capabilities, all individuals may make mistakes in choosing strategies designed to realize a set of goals (V. Ostrom 1986). Over time, however, they can acquire a greater understanding of their situation and adopt strategies that result in higher returns. Bounded rationality is highly likely to be an effective tool for studies of field settings where the researchers may not be able to specify the specific structure of the situations participants face any more than the participants themselves. Bounded rationality, however, deals primarily with the information condition related to individual choice.

Consistent findings from behavioral game theory, as well as from neuroscientific studies of the brain of subjects in different settings (McDermott 2004), have shown that a richer theory of individual valuation is necessary. Scholars are now positing a family of models that change the basic assumptions of the classical model (see Levine 1998; Fehr and Gächter 2000; Bolton and Ockenfels 2000; Gintis 2000; Casari and Plott 2003; Cox 2004). Several assumptions are shared across these new theories of individual behavior: (1) individuals are assumed to have heterogeneous preferences in the same objective situations; (2) some individuals may include the payoffs obtained by others in their own utility calculation while others may not; and (3) payoffs to others may bring positive, negative, or no utility to an individual.

The classical model of noncooperative game theory now becomes a special case of the revised theories for when individuals attach no utility to the payoffs of others. Once scholars begin to assume that there are multiple 'types' of players interacting in a setting, attention can then be focused on how specific aspects of the structure of the situation affect behavior over time, such as sequential moves, type of feedback, forms of communication, and how individuals are assigned to positions. Camerer (2003, 117) has well-captured the broad understanding of many institutional theorists when he commented that: "Institutional arrangements can be understood as responding to a world in which there are some sociopaths and some saints, but mostly regular folks who are capable of both kinds of behavior."

The possibility that there are individuals who take into account the payoffs of other individuals changes theoretical foundations greatly. Now one needs to ask how individuals provide reliable signals to each other about their preferences and intentions and how they gain information about the actions and outcomes of others. Further, behavior that evolves over time in different structures is also of considerable importance where those who are inclined to seek jointly beneficial outcomes may achieve significantly higher payoffs over time if they are able to identify one another. Once successful 'contingent cooperators' are noticed by others, these successful strategies may be learned and adopted more widely in a population (Güth and Kliemt 1998). Some of the intriguing rules devised by users of common-pool resources through the ages can now be integrated into contemporary theory (see, e.g., Casari and Plott 2003) rather than relegated to an irrational and incomprehensible past.

The Potlatch between Economics and Political Science

Herbert Simon (1999) has likened the exchange between economics and political science to a 'potlatch' where each discipline has brought 'gifts' to the other. After years of suspicion regarding the 'gifts' brought by the 'other' discipline, Simon concludes that the extensive methodological and empirical development of the last 50 years has prepared all of the social sciences for a better interaction in the future. "Gift-giving between economics and the other social sciences can become a genuine exchange, going in both directions" (1999, 117). Leach and Sabatier (2005) strongly demonstrate that the exchange should also include psychological theory for the many policy processes that involve understanding the process of gaining trust among participants.

Empirical evidence has steadily mounted that demonstrates the capability of humans to design complex systems that are neither markets nor the state. Variance in performance has been measured in regard to efficiency, equity, accountability, and resilience of these nonmarket and nonstate institutions, but some achieve high levels of performance. Instead of presuming that all complex systems need to be replaced with a centralized order, growing evidence has mounted that the challenge is developing well-tested theories that enable us to harness complexity (Axelrod and Cohen 2000) rather than eliminate it.

In a special issue of *Public Choice* summarizing what has been learned in the last half-century, Shughart and Tollison (2005) also identify the issues that need to be addressed by political economists in the new century. Among the many important questions identified in this issue are: How can the independence of a judiciary be assured in a democratic polity? How can constitutions be protected from erosion by self-interested politicians seeking increased powers? How can democracy gain real roots in countries governed for more than a century by autocratic rulers? "Why are some government regimes, be they local, state or national, more corrupt than others?" (2005, 242). They then identify the "most important unanswered question on the public choice agenda" is also among the oldest: "Why do people vote?" (2005, 245). The latter question returns us to the challenge raised by behavioral economics as well as by NIE scholars—can we continue to use the narrow model of human motivation of immediate maximization of material benefits to self? Working out where this narrow engine of explanation continues to be a useful foundation for political economists and how to build a more complex model of human behavior that takes into account longer-term benefits to others, as well as to self, is one of the most important challenges facing political economists of the twenty-first century.

Acknowledgments

This is a revised version of a paper presented at the 2003 APSA meetings at a panel on "What Has Political Science Been: What Should It Become?" Support from the National Science Foundation and from FORMAS through the Human Cooperation to Manage Natural Resources (COMMONS) program is gratefully acknowledged as are the useful comments of Hartmut Kliemt and Patty Lezotte's careful and cheerful editing.

Notes

This chapter was originally published in *Rationality, Markets and Morals* (*RMM*) 3 (2012): 51–65.

1. See *The Comprehensive Bibliography of the Commons* at http://dlc.dlib.indiana.edu/dlc/.

References

Acheson, J. (2003), *Capturing the Commons: Devising Institutions to Manage the Maine Lobster Industry*, New Haven: University Press of New England.

Allen, B. (2005), *Tocqueville, Covenant, and the Democratic Revolution*, Lanham: Lexington Books.

Anttila, S. and C. Stern (2005), "The Voluntary Provision of Snowmobile Trails on Private Land in Sweden", *Rationality and Society* 17(4), 453–74.

Arnold, J. E. M. and J. G. Campbell (1986), "Collective Management of Hill Forests in Nepal: The Community Forestry Development Project", in: *Proceedings of the Conference on Common Property Resource Management*, National Research Council, Washington: National Academies Press, 425–54.

Arrow, K. (1951), *Social Choice and Individual Values*, 2nd ed., New York: Wiley.

Ascher, W. (1995), *Communities and Sustainable Forestry in Developing Countries*, San Francisco: ICS Press.

Axelrod, R. and M. Cohen (2000), *Harnessing Complexity*, New York: The Free Press.

Banana, A. Y. and W. Gombya-Ssembajjwe (2000), "Successful Forest Management: The Importance of Security of Tenure and Rule Enforcement in Ugandan Forests", in: Gibson, C., M. McKean and E. Ostrom (eds.), *People and Forests: Communities, Institutions, and Governance*, Cambridge/MA: MIT Press, 87–98.

Barry, B. and R. Hardin (1982), *Rational Man and Irrational Society? An Introduction and Source Book*, Beverly Hills: Sage.

Bickers, K. and J. T. Williams (2001), *Public Policy Analysis: A Political Economy Approach*, New York: Houghton Mifflin.

Black, D. (1958), *The Theory of Committees and Elections*, Cambridge: Cambridge University Press.

Boettke, P. J. (2005) (ed.), "Polycentric Political Economy", *Journal of Economic Behavior and Organization* 57(2) (special issue).

Bolton, G. E. and A. Ockenfels (2000), "ERC: A Theory of Equity, Reciprocity and Competition", *American Economic Review* 90(1), 166–93.

Boyne, G. A. (1992), "Local Government Structure and Performance: Lessons from America?", *Public Administration* 70, 333–57.

Bryce, H. J. (2005), *Players in the Public Policy Process: Nonprofits as Social Capital and Agents*, New York: Palgrave Macmillan.

Buchanan, J. M. and G. Tullock (1962), *The Calculus of Consent*, Ann Arbor: University of Michigan Press.

Camerer, C. F. (2003), *Behavioral Game Theory: Experiments in Strategic Interaction*, Princeton: Princeton University Press.

Casari, M. and C. R. Plott (2003), "Decentralized Management of Common Property Resources", *Journal of Economic Behavior and Organization* 51, 217–47.

Chhatre, A. and A. Agrawal (2009), "Trade-offs and Synergies between Carbon Storage and Livelihood Benefits from Forest Commons", *Proceedings of the National Academy of Sciences* 106(42), 17667–7670.

Ciriacy-Wantrup, S. V. and R. C. Bishop (1975), "'Common Property' as a Concept in Natural Resource Policy", *Natural Resources Journal* 15(4), 713–27.

Coase, R. (1937), "The Nature of the Firm", *Economica* 4(16), 386–405.

Coleman, E. (2009), "Institutional Factors Affecting Ecological Outcomes in Forest Management", *Journal of Policy Analysis and Management* 28(1), 122–46.

Coleman, E. and B. Steed (2009), "Monitoring and Sanctioning in the Commons: An Application to Forestry", *Ecological Economics* 68(7), 2106–113.

Cox, J. (2004), "How to Identify Trust and Reciprocity", *Games and Economic Behavior* 46, 260–81.

Cox, M., G. Arnold and S. Villamayor Tomás (2010), "A Review of Design Principles for Community-Based Natural Resource Management", *Ecology and Society* 15(4), 38.

de Moor, M., L. Shaw-Taylor and P. Warde (2002) (eds.), *The Management of Common Land in Northwest Europe, c. 1500–1850*, Belgium: BREPOLS Publishers.

Denzau, A. T., and D. C. North (1994), "Shared Mental Models: Ideologies and Institutions", *Kyklos* 47, 3–31.

Dietz, T., E. Ostrom and P. Stern (2003), "The Struggle to Govern the Commons", *Science* 302, 1907–12.

Downs, A. (1957), *An Economic Theory of Democracy*, New York: Harper and Row.

Fehr, E. (2009), "On the Economics and Biology of Trust", *Journal of the European Economic Association* 7(2–3), 235–266.

Fehr, E. and S. Gächter (2000), "Cooperation and Punishment in Public Goods Experiments", *American Economic Review* 90(4), 980–94.

Fischel, W. A. (2001), *The Homevoter Hypothesis*, Cambridge/MA: Harvard University Press.

Ghate, R. and H. Nagendra (2005), "Role of Monitoring in Institutional Performance: Forest Management in Maharashtra, India", *Conservation and Society* 3(2), 509–32.

Gibson, C., K. Andersson, E. Ostrom and S. Shivakumar (2005), *The Samaritan's Dilemma: The Political Economy of Development Aid*, New York: Oxford University Press.

Gibson, C., J. Williams and E. Ostrom (2005), "Local Enforcement and Better Forests", *World Development* 33(2), 273–84.

Gintis, H. (2000), "Beyond *Homo Economicus*: Evidence from Experimental Economics", *Ecological Economics* 35(3), 311–22.

Gordon, H. S. (1954), "The Economic Theory of a Common Property Resource: The Fishery", *Journal of Political Economy* 62, 124–42.

Greif, A. and D. D. Laitin (2004), "A Theory of Endogenous Institutional Change", *American Political Science Review* 98(4), 633–51.

Güth, W. and H. Kliemt (1998), "The Indirect Evolutionary Approach: Bridging the Gap between Rationality and Adaptation", *Rationality and Society* 10(3), 377–99.

Hardin, G. (1968), "The Tragedy of the Commons", *Science* 162, 1243–48.

Hayes, T. M. and E. Ostrom (2005), "Conserving the World's Forests: Are Protected Areas the Only Way?", *Indiana Law Review* 38(3), 595–617.

Heikkila, T. and A. K. Gerlak (2005), "The Formation of Large-Scale Collaborative Resource Management Institutions: Clarifying the Roles of Stakeholders, Science, and Institutions", *Policy Studies Journal* 33(4), 583–612.

Helmke, G. and S. Levitsky (2004), "Informal Institutions and Comparative Politics: A Research Agenda", *Perspective on Politics* 2(4), 725–40.

Hobbes, T. (1960[1651]), *Leviathan or the Matter, Forme and Power of a Commonwealth Ecclesiasticall and Civil*, ed. Michael Oakeshott, Oxford: Basil Blackwell.

Houghe, L. and G. Marks (2001), *Multi-Level Governance and European Integration*, Lanham: Rowman & Littlefield.

Janssen, M., R. Holahan, A. Lee, and E. Ostrom (2010), "Lab Experiments for the Study of Social-Ecological Systems", *Science* 328(5978), 613–17.

Jones, B. D., T. Sulkin and H. A. Larsen (2003), "Policy Punctuations in American Political Institutions", *American Political Science Review* 97(1), 151–69.

Joshi, N. N., E. Ostrom, G. P. Shivakoti and W. F. Lam (2000), "Institutional Opportunities and Constraints in the Performance of Farmer-Managed Irrigation Systems in Nepal", *Asia-Pacific Journal of Rural Development* 10(2), 67–92.

Keohane, R. O. (1984), *After Hegemony: Cooperation and Discord in the World Political Economy*, Princeton: Princeton University Press.

Lam, W. F. (1998), *Governing Irrigation Systems in Nepal: Institutions, Infrastructure, and Collective Action*, Oakland: ICS Press.

Lansing, J. S. and J. Kremer (1993), "Emergent Properties of Balinese Water Temple Networks", *American Anthropologist* 95(1), 97–114.

Leach, W. D. and P. Sabatier (2005), "To Trust an Adversary", *American Political Science Review* 99(4), 491–504.

Levi, M. (1988), *Of Rule and Revenue*, Berkeley: University of California Press.

Levine, D. K. (1998), "Modeling Altruism and Spitefulness in Experiments", *Review of Economic Dynamics* 1(3), 593–622.

McCay, B. J. and J. M. Acheson (1987), *The Question of the Commons: The Culture and Ecology of Communal Resources*, Tucson: University of Arizona Press.

McDermott, R. (2004), "The Feeling of Rationality: The Meaning of Neuroscientific Advances for Political Science", *Perspectives on Politics* 2(4), 691–706.

McGinnis, M. (1999) (ed.), *Polycentricity and Local Public Economies: Readings from the Workshop in Political Theory and Policy Analysis*, Ann Arbor: University of Michigan Press.

Milgrom, P. R., D. C. North and B. R. Weingast (1990), "The Role of Institutions in the Revival of Trade: The Law Merchant, Private Judges, and the Champagne Fairs", *Economics and Politics* 2(1), 1–23.

Miller, G. (1992), *Managerial Dilemmas: The Political Economy of Hierarchy*, New York: Cambridge University Press.

National Research Council (1986), *Proceedings of the Conference on Common Property Resource Management*, Washington: National Academies Press.

——— (2002), *The Drama of the Commons*, Washington: National Academies Press.

North, D. C. (1981), *Structure and Change in Economic History*, New York: Norton.

——— (2005), *Understanding the Process of Economic Change*, Princeton: Princeton University Press.

Oakerson, R. J. and R. B. Parks (1989), "Local Government Constitutions: A Different View of Metropolitan Governance", *American Review of Public Administration* 19(4), 279–94.

Olson, M. (1965), *The Logic of Collective Action: Public Goods and the Theory of Groups*, Cambridge/MA: Harvard University Press.

Ostrom, E. (1990), *Governing the Commons: The Evolution of Institutions for Collective Action*, New York: Cambridge University Press.

——— (2005), *Understanding Institutional Diversity*, Princeton: Princeton University Press.

——— (2007), "A Diagnostic Approach for Going beyond Panaceas", *Proceedings of the National Academy of Sciences* 104(39), 15181–5187.

——— (2009), "A General Framework for Analyzing Sustainability of Social-Ecological Systems", *Science* 325(5939), 419–22.

Ostrom, E. and H. Nagendra (2006), "Insights on Linking Forests, Trees, and People from the Air, on the Ground, and in the Laboratory", *Proceedings of the National Academy of Sciences* 103(51), 19224–9231.

Ostrom, E., J. Walker and R. Gardner (1992), "Covenants with and without a Sword: Self-Governance is Possible", *American Political Science Review* 86(2), 404–17.

Ostrom, V. (1986), "A Fallabilist's Approach to Norms and Criteria of Choice", in: *Guidance, Control, and Evaluation in the Public Sector*, Berlin–New York: Walter de Gruyter, 229–49.

Ostrom, V., C. Tiebout and R. Warren (1961), "The Organization of Government in Metropolitan Areas", *American Political Science Review* 55, 831–42.

Putnam, R. (2000), *Bowling Alone: The Collapse and Revival of American Community*, New York: Simon and Schuster.

Riker, W. H. (1962), *A Theory of Political Coalitions*, New Haven: Yale University Press.

Satz, D. and J. Ferejohn (1994), "Rational Choice and Social Theory", *Journal of Philosophy* 91(2), 71–87.

Sawyer, A. (2005), *Beyond Plunder: Toward Democratic Governance in Liberia*, Boulder: Lynne Rienner Publishers.

Schneider, M. (1986), "Fragmentation and the Growth of Government", *Public Choice* 48, 255–63.

Sefton, M., R. Shupp and J. M. Walker (2007), "The Effect of Rewards and Sanctions in Provision of Public Goods", *Economic Inquiry* 45(4), 671–90.

Shepsle, K. A. (1989), "Studying Institutions", *Journal of Theoretical Politics* 1(2), 131–49.

Shivakumar, S. (2005), *The Constitution of Development*, New York: Palgrave Macmillan.

Shughart, W. F. and R. Tollison (2005), "The Unfinished Business of Public Choice", *Public Choice* 124(1–2), 237–47.

Simon, H. A. (1972), "Theories of Bounded Rationality", in: McGuire, C. B. and R. Radner (eds.), *Decision and Organization*, Amsterdam: North Holland, 161–76.

——— (1999), "The Potlatch between Economics and Political Science", in: Alt, J., M. Levi, and E. Ostrom (eds.), *Competition and Cooperation*, New York: Russell Sage Foundation, 112–22.

Smith, V. and J. M. Walker (1993), "Rewards, Experience and Decision Costs in First Price Auctions", *Economic Inquiry* 31, 237–44.

Teske, P., M. Schneider, M. Mintrom and S. Best (1993), "Establishing the Micro Foundations of a Macro Theory: Information, Movers, and the Competitive Local Market for Public Goods", *American Political Science Review* 87(3), 702–13.

Tsebelis, G. (1990), *Nested Games: Political Context, Political Institutions and Rationality*, Berkeley: University of California Press.

Walker, J. and E. Ostrom (2009), "Trust and Reciprocity as Foundations for Cooperation", in: Cook, K., M. Levi and R. Hardin (eds.), *Whom Can We Trust? How Groups, Networks, and Institutions Make Trust Possible*, New York: Russell Sage Foundation, 91–124.

Webb, E. and G. P. Shivakoti (2008) (eds.), *Decentralization, Forests and Rural Communities: Policy Outcomes in South and Southeast Asia*, New Delhi: Sage India.

Weinstein, M. S. (2000), "Pieces of the Puzzle", *Georgetown International Environmental Law Review* 12(2), 375–412.

Williamson, O. E. (1975), *Markets and Hierarchies: Analysis and Antitrust Implications*, New York: Free Press.

16

Policy Analysis in the Future of Good Societies

ELINOR OSTROM

The study of public policy during the last century has been dominated by the paradigm that policy was what a government did, and particularly what a national government did. Thus, policy analysis was directed toward advising national governments. Endless articles have started or concluded with an analysis of what "the" policymaker should do whether the article was written by an economist, a political scientist, a policy analyst, or a journalist. The hypothetical "social planner" has been the recipient of considerable unasked-for advice in articles devoted primarily to a top-down analysis of a public policy problem.

In this new century, the concept of policy analysis should be substantially broadened. National governments will remain among the targets of advice, but greater attention should be devoted to regional and local governments. More importantly, one of the important targets for all policy analysis in the future should be citizens organized in diverse ways related to a multiplicity of issues. But isn't doing policy analysis what citizens ask their officials to do? Do they not select officials that they think will make good policy? Why should precious time be wasted in instructing citizens to do policy analysis when citizens select public officials to do this?

That is certainly the way that many policy textbooks have been written. How are citizens to know whether their officials are making intelligent decisions, however, if they themselves have no criteria and no insight into the benefits and costs of diverse policies? A citizenry devoid of skills in policy analysis is a set of *subjects* who can easily become the *objects* of an authoritarian regime.

In the development of policy analysis so that advice can be given to both officials and the citizens they serve, social scientists face several challenges. During the past century, policy analysts trying to solve diverse problems have been strongly influenced by a narrow, short-term economic view of human rationality combining an all-powerful computation capacity, on the one hand, with no capability to adapt and stick to moral norms of trustworthiness, reciprocity, and fairness, on the other. When models based on these assumptions are applied to a highly competitive market for homogenous, packageable goods, economic theory has produced one of our most powerful and useful forms of policy analysis. When applied to the problems of provision and production of public goods and the management of common-pool resources, however, these models have led scholars to conclude that citizens are unable to solve these problems (even though they are the engine of innovation and economic growth in the other theories), and that an external authority is needed to impose solutions on helplessly trapped individuals.

Thus, one of our great needs is overcoming disciplinary limits. Another is learning to overcome our addiction to overly simple solutions to complex problems. A third is the need to more self-consciously create arenas for experimentation and learning. I will briefly develop each of these themes below.

Disciplinary Limits and How We Need to Overcome Them

Developing a broader theory of rationality useful for policy analysis immediately requires input from multiple disciplines. Many economists are struggling with the lack of predictive and explanatory power of their theories outside of competitive market settings—particularly those who have seen the lack of empirical support for so many predictions (Camerer, 1997; Selten, 1990, 1991; Fehr and Schmidt, 1999; Frey, 1997). Social psychologists (Messick, 1999), evolutionary psychologists (Cosmides and Tooby, 1992), sociologists and anthropologists (Kollock, 1998; Boehm, 1999), and political scientists (Axelrod, 1984; Axelrod and Cohen, 2000; Simon, 1997) are all concerned about building a better foundation for understanding behavior as a necessary step before trying to improve public policy.

Scholars who have long been interested in diverse public policies have often found themselves somewhat limited by their own disciplinary boundaries within contemporary universities. Cynics sometimes state it this way: "The world has problems, but universities have departments" (see Brewer, 1999: 328). The incentives to stay within the confines of the way a discipline asks questions—particularly for younger scholars—are powerful and frequently counterproductive for the achievement of knowledge needed to analyze policy questions. Even the efforts of senior scholars can be criticized by those who worry about an escape from a tight disciplinary focus. As Brewer himself envisioned the nature of policy analysis, it involves asking the following types of questions:

- What goal values are sought and by whom?
- What trends affect the realization of these values? Or where did the problem originate?
- What factors are responsible for the trends? Or what are the driving or influencing conditions?
- What is the probable course of future events and developments especially if interventions are not made?
- What can be done to change that course to realize or achieve more of the desired goals, and for whom (Brewer, 1999: 328)?

These questions are not the primary domain of *any* single discipline. When honest scholars have tried to examine these types of questions from their own disciplinary lenses, they have acknowledged the limits of their own view and thus the importance of involving other disciplines in their explanation.

For example, Robert Ellickson first attempted as a lawyer to understand the structure of rules and norms that affected how farmers in Shasta County, California, related to one another in regard to a wide variety of everyday problems including who was responsible for fencing in (or out) the cattle that farmers were pasturing on their own land. The farmers had hardly used lawyers or the courts to establish local rules regarding constraining externalities. Ellickson found that the legal theories taught in law school, and even by many of the interdisciplinary approaches that combined law with one of the social sciences (e.g., law and economics, law and society), were insufficient. In light of his experience, Ellickson argued that to develop even a rudimentary theory of social order, theorists would need to understand the behavior of multiple "controllers" (e.g., individuals who watched over events of importance to a community, from neighbors through various organizational and governmental forms of regulation).

> In other words, a general theory of social control requires subtheories of human nature, of market transactions, of social interactions, of organizations, and of governments. For starters a theorist thus needs a command

> of psychology, economics, sociology, organization theory, and political science. (Ellickson, 1987: 80)

Progress in policy analysis can be enhanced by following Ellickson's advice.

The Limits (or Failure) of Simple Policy Solutions

Another recurrent theme in American academia is to criticize the number of governments that exist in the United States and the competition that exists among them. During the 1960s and 1970s, for example, the "Metropolitan Reform" movement was the dominant way of thinking about urban governance. The cause of many problems was posited to be the presence of many units of government that were seen as redundant and inefficient. In addition, multiple units of government were viewed as competitive and providing a means whereby the rich could escape without contributing to the provision of public services needed by the poor and disadvantaged members of central cities (see Hawley and Zimmer, 1970; Rusk, 1993; and literature summarized in Stephens and Wikstrom, 1999). Policy analysts repetitively recommended simple, top-down, command-and-control solutions in the belief that those doing analysis of policy problems for large territories would achieve close to optimal policy solutions for difficult problems.

In the field of education, beliefs that large numbers of schools were inefficient and that massive consolidation would lead to increased efficiency as well as equity led to the reduction of school districts in a long series of massive campaigns against considerable citizen opposition during the last three-quarters of this century. In 1932, almost 130,000 school districts existed in the United States. This number was halved by 1952 and quartered by 1962, and halved once again by the early 1970s. Today we have around 15,000 school districts in the United States for a population that has almost doubled since the campaign to consolidate schools was initiated (see V. Ostrom, Bish, and E. Ostrom, 1988). During the heat of this policy reform effort, research was almost nonexistent on the effect of school size, number of schools in a region, and related issues. It was such a simple solution to what was perceived by academics and public officials as an obvious problem that both were willing to push hard for this reform.

Since the 1970s, considerable research on the effects of these variables on school performance has provided contrary evidence to the implicit theory used by policymakers to support the school consolidation movement. A recent study for the National Bureau of Economic Research, for example, finds that having a larger number of schools in a metropolitan area is associated with higher average student performance (as measured by students' educational attainment, local wages, and test scores) while also being characterized by lower per-pupil spending (Hoxby, 1994; see also Pritchett and Filmer, 1999). After years of trying to increase size and reduce the number of schools, policymakers are reconsidering the consequences of past reforms and recommending charter schools, voucher systems, and other reforms to create more responsive schools (see Gardner, 2000, for a review of recent books on these reforms). Similarly, empirical studies of the effect of the size and number of urban public service providers also found that small size and multiplicity did not have the adverse consequences frequently attributed to them and that improvements (rather than reductions) in performance were frequently associated with the presence of a multiplicity of units of government (see McGinnis, 1999, for an overview). Hawkins and Ihrke (1999), for example, have conducted a recent survey of more than 70 empirical studies of fragmentation showing that more than two-thirds of the empirical articles do not support the policies recommended by the metropolitan reform movement.

A second set of simple policies gone amok relates to the presumed necessity of nationalizing ownership and management of common-pool resources such as forests, rivers and lakes, irrigation systems, grazing areas, and inshore fisheries, and imposing one set of policies for an entire nation. Common-pool resources are characterized by difficulties of excluding beneficiaries and subtractability of use (E. Ostrom, Gardner, and Walker, 1994). In other words, the benefits affect all who use the resource whether they restrain their use or not, and what one person withdraws, no one else can withdraw. In the conventional theory, appropriators are frequently assumed to be homogeneous in terms of their assets, skills, discount rates, and cultural views. They are also assumed to be short-term, profit-maximizing actors who possess complete information. In the conventional theory, *anyone* can enter the resource and take resource units. Appropriators only gain property rights to what they harvest, which they then sell in an open competitive market. The open-access condition is a theoretical given. With these assumptions, the logical conclusion is that common-pool resources will be overused and eventually destroyed.

Many textbooks on environmental policy present this conventional theory of an open-access common-pool resource as the *only* theory needed for making effective policies (but, see Baland and Platteau, 1996). Massive deforestation in tropical countries and the collapse of multiple ocean fisheries are cited by many policy analysts and public officials as sufficient evidence to confirm the general validity of the theory. Garrett Hardin's (1968) dramatic article in *Science* convinced others that the conventional theory captures the core of the problem. The metaphor of resource users helplessly trapped in a relentless tragedy has been used by scholars and policymakers to rationalize central government control of forests, inshore fisheries, and many other common-pool resources. Thus, analysts have tried to "see like a state" and generate reform proposals that are built on the essential role of the state as the source of all rules (Scott, 1998).

Recent research has found that many appropriators have organized themselves so as to regulate the use of common-pool resources, and some have sustained resources and their own organizations for very long periods of time (McCay and Acheson, 1987; Berkes, 1989; E. Ostrom, 1990; Blomquist, 1992; Bromley et al., 1992; Tang, 1992; among many others). Further, national governmental agencies are frequently found to be unsuccessful in their efforts to design effective and uniform sets of rules to regulate important common-pool resources across a broad domain. Many developing countries nationalized all land and water resources during the 1950s and 1960s. The institutional arrangements that local users had devised to limit entry and use lost their legal standing, but the national governments lacked funds and personnel to monitor these resources effectively. Thus, common-pool resources were converted to a *de jure* government property regime but reverted to a *de facto* open-access regime (Arnold, 1998).

The incentives of the collective-action problem that resource users faced were accentuated because now they were told that they would not receive the benefits of adopting a long-term view in their use of the resource. When resources that were previously controlled by local participants have been nationalized, state control has usually proved to be less effective and efficient than control by those directly affected, if not disastrous in its consequences (Curtis, 1991; Panayotou and Ashton, 1992; Ascher, 1995). The substantial increase in the rates of deforestation following adoption of policies to nationalize forests that had earlier been governed by local user-groups has been well documented for Thailand (Feeny, 1988), Africa (Shepherd, 1992; Thomson, 1977; Thomson, Feeny, and Oakerson, 1992), Nepal (Arnold and Campbell, 1986), and India (Gadgil and Iyer, 1989; Jodha, 1990, 1996). Similar increases in uncontrolled overharvesting have occurred in regard to inshore fisheries taken over by state or national agencies from local control by the inshore fishers themselves (Cordell and McKean, 1992; Cruz, 1986; Dasgupta, 1982;

Higgs, 1996; Pinkerton, 1989). These policies have confused resources that are genuinely large-scale in extent with resources that exist throughout a nation but are not highly interconnected and vary substantially in the structure of their ecological systems from place to place.

Both sets of policy reforms—centralizing urban governance and the governance of common-pool resources—have been based on an overly simplified view of the nature of social order. Policy analysts tend to distrust local citizens to create effective forms of governance. Consequently, they assume that multiplicities of self-organized regimes (some formal, some informal) are by their very nature disorderly and ineffective. Order is presumed to result from central direction. Unfortunately, this perspective is viewed as self-evident. It is hard to make progress against self-evident truths. These common-sense assumptions, however, lead to proposals to improve the operation of political systems that have had the opposite effect. By removing decisions about the ways to innovate, adapt, and coordinate efforts from those who are directly affected, these policy reforms have created institutions that are less able to respond to the problems for which they were created.

Creating Arenas for Experimentation and Learning

Thus, underlying much policy analysis of the last several decades has been a presumption that the responsibility for designing institutional rules to overcome various kinds of public problems should be assumed by large-scale and centralized governments (for different views, however, see Simon, 1997; Landau, 1969; V. Ostrom, 1987, 1997; Bendor and Mookherjee, 1987). Policy analysts have had great faith in their own capacity to analyze theoretical models of typical problems and come forward with a set of institutional fixes that will lead those involved in a collective-action problem to take actions generating higher, rather than lower, outcomes. In doing so, policy analysts tend to think of citizens or users as motivated by narrow, self-interested preferences and of themselves as motivated by a general public interest. Both assumptions are exaggerated. As discussed above, we need to be working with a broader theory of a boundedly rational, learning, and potentially norm-using individual (see E. Ostrom, 1998). The evidence gathered from studies of the behavior of policy analysts and government officials is consistent with a presumption that officials are similar to citizens in regard to their internal motivation. Officials may be placed in institutional settings, however, that bring substantial temptations for personal gain and even illegal payoffs without much chance for others to learn about behavior. Officials may also be isolated from the people and locations they are supposed to represent and not have much knowledge about time and place information. Officials in one jurisdiction (or one department within a larger jurisdiction) may put the interest of their own unit ahead of achieving objectives requiring full participation of all units. Thus, finding ways of solving collective-action problems exist within the public sector as well as in the private sector.

A better foundation for public policy is to assume that neither citizens nor their officials are able to analyze all situations fully, but given a conducive, macropolitical regime, they may make efforts to solve complex problems through trial-and-error testing out of different rules for solving various collective-action problems. Recent recognition of the need for demonstration projects and learning general guidelines or "best practices" from the more successful policies are consistent with this effort. To learn from policy experiments requires some long-term continuity of both leadership and citizenry. Our capacity to learn from policy experiments may thus be threatened by the increased mobility of public officials and citizens.

Because many analysts have become disillusioned with the performance of highly centralized systems in the management of natural resources, numerous proposals have been advanced to support radical decentralization of centralized regimes (see Agrawal, Britt, and Kanel, 1999 and Agrawal and Ribot, 1999, for an overview of the relevant literature). One form of decentralization is to radically move decision making down to a horizontal layer of governments that is composed entirely of local bodies each of which governs a smaller-scale resource system. From one simple solution—centralizing everything— policy analysts are flipping to another simple solution—radical decentralization. Neither full centralization nor full decentralization promises much in the way of learning, even though greater experimentation can occur in decentralized systems. The likelihood of successful solutions of many policy questions is not, however, increased by jumping from one pet solution to another. A serious study of complex, polycentric systems needs to be on the agenda for policy analysts as well as the citizens and officials they serve.

Teaching Policy Analysis

The issues raised in this essay lead one to return to the question of how we teach policy analysis at both an undergraduate and graduate level. In many of these courses, citizens are described as passive consumers of political life. We have robbed citizens of almost any kind of active political life in our textbook renditions of democracy other than going to the polls.

Thus when students take courses on policy analysis, they do so partly with an image that they themselves will become public officials whether elected or appointed. Few students actually taking policy analysis are trying to inform themselves on how to become better citizens. As we reformulate the intellectual foundations of policy analysis, we also need to pay serious attention to how we teach the future citizens of a democratic system. Given the complexity of contemporary life, we need to energize the innovative potential of future citizens who see themselves engaged in trying to improve their own societies and polities. Focusing on what citizens do rather than entirely on what government officials do is an essential step in developing better policy analysis for future generations.

Further, we need to think about how to overcome the disciplinary walls that have been erected in the contemporary university scene. If students are to understand a diversity of policy questions, they need to gain real knowledge of the substantive areas of interest and not be limited to studying only in a department of political science or even to a school of policy analysis. At the Center for the Study of Institutions, Population, and Environmental Change, we require students to "cross-train." Students with a strong background in anthropology, economics, or political science are introduced in their graduate program to a heavy dose of ecology, the analysis of spatial metrics, the use of geographic information systems, and the analysis of remotely sensed data. Similarly, students with strong backgrounds in the latter areas receive a strong introduction to skills learned in anthropology, economics, and political science. Throughout our training efforts, we stress the skills needed to analyze complex adaptive systems.

Acknowledgments

I am appreciative of the support provided by the Earhart Foundation to the Workshop in Political Theory and Policy Analysis, the useful comments of Noah Pickus and Brian Cook, and the outstanding editing by Patty Zielinski.

Note

This chapter was originally published in *The Good Society* 11(1) (2002): 42–48. Reprinted with the permission of The Pennsylvania State University Press.

References

Agrawal, Arun, with Charla Britt and Keshav Kanel. *Decentralization in Nepal: A Comparative Analysis*. A Report on the Participatory District Development Program. Oakland, Calif.: ICS Press, 1999.

Agrawal, Arun, and Jesse Ribot. "Accountability in Decentralization: A Framework with South Asian and West African Cases." *Journal of Developing Areas* 33 (1999): 473–502.

Arnold, J.E.M. "Devolution of Control of Common Pool Resources to Local Communities: Experiences in Forestry." Paper presented at the meeting of the UNU/WIDER Project on "Land Reform Revisited: Access to Land, Rural Poverty, and Public Action," Santiago, Chile, April 16–18, 1998.

Arnold, J.E.M., and J. Gabriel Campbell. "Collective Management of Hill Forests in Nepal: The Community Forestry Development Project." In *Proceedings of the Conference on Common Property Resource Management*, National Research Council, 425–54. Washington: National Academy Press, 1986.

Ascher, William. *Communities and Sustainable Forestry in Developing Countries*. San Francisco: ICS Press, 1995.

Axelrod, Robert. *The Evolution of Cooperation*. New York: Basic Books, 1984.

Axelrod, Robert, and Michael D. Cohen. *Harnessing Complexity: Organizational Implications of a Scientific Frontier*. New York: The Free Press, 2000.

Baland, Jean-Marie, and Jean-Philippe Platteau. *Halting Degradation of Natural Resources: Is There a Role for Rural Communities?* Oxford: Clarendon Press, 1996.

Bendor, Jonathan, and Dilip Mookherjee. "Institutional Structure and the Logic of Ongoing Collective Action." *American Political Science Review* 81 (1987): 129–54.

Berkes, Fikret, ed. *Common Property Resources: Ecology and Community-Based Sustainable Development*. London: Belhaven, 1989.

Blomquist, William. *Dividing the Waters: Governing Groundwater in Southern California*. San Francisco: ICS Press, 1992.

Boehm, Christopher. *Hierarchy in the Forest: The Evolution of Egalitarian Behavior*. Harvard, Mass.: Harvard University Press, 1999.

Brewer, Garry D. "The Challenges of Interdisciplinarity." *Policy Sciences* 32 (1999): 327–37.

Bromley, Daniel W., David Feeny, Margaret McKean, Pauline Peters, Jere Gilles, Ronald Oakerson, C. Ford Runge, and James Thomson, eds. *Making the Commons Work: Theory, Practice, and Policy*. San Francisco: ICS Press, 1992.

Camerer, Colin F. "Progress in Behavior Game Theory." *Journal of Economic Perspectives* 11 (1997): 167–88.

Cordell, John C., and Margaret A. McKean. "Sea Tenure in Bahia, Brazil." In *Making the Commons Work: Theory, Practice, and Policy*, ed. Daniel W. Bromley et al., 183–205. San Francisco: ICS Press, 1992.

Cosmides, Leda, and John Tooby. "Cognitive Adaptations for Social Exchange." In *The Adapted Mind: Evolutionary Psychology and the Generation of Culture*, ed. Jerome H. Barkow, Leda Cosmides, and John Tooby, 163–228. New York: Oxford University Press, 1992.

Cruz, Wilfrido D. "Overfishing and Conflict in a Traditional Fishery: San Miguel Bay, Philippines." In *Proceedings of the Conference on Common Property Resource Management*, National Research Council, 115–35. Washington: National Academy Press, 1986.

Curtis, Donald. *Beyond Government: Organizations for Common Benefit*. London: Macmillan, 1991.

Dasgupta, Partha. *The Control of Resources*. Cambridge, Mass.: Harvard University Press, 1982.

Ellickson, Robert C. "A Critique of Economic and Sociological Theories of Social Control." *Journal of Legal Studies* 26 (1987): 67–99.

Feeny, David H. "Agricultural Expansion and Forest Depletion in Thailand, 1900–1975." In *World Deforestation in the Twentieth Century*, ed. John F. Richards and Richard P. Tucker, 112–43. Durham: Duke University Press, 1988.

Fehr, Ernst, and Klaus M. Schmidt. "A Theory of Fairness, Competition, and Cooperation." *Quarterly Journal of Economics* 114 (1999): 817–68.

Frey, Bruno S. *Not Just for the Money: An Economic Theory of Personal Motivation*. Cheltenham, England: Edward Elgar, 1997.

Gadgil, Madhav, and Prema Iyer. "On the Diversification of Common-Property Resource Use by Indian Society." In *Common Property Resources: Ecology and Community-Based Sustainable Development*, ed. Fikret Berkes, 240–72. London: Belhaven Press, 1989.

Gardner, Howard. "Vouchers or Charters or What." *The New York Review of Books* 47 (2000): 44–49.

Hardin, Garrett. "The Tragedy of the Commons." *Science* 162 (1968): 1243–48.

Hawkins, Brett W., and Douglas M. Ihrke. "Reexamining the Suburban Exploitation Thesis in American Metropolitan Areas." *Publius* 29 (1999): 109–21.

Hawley, Amos, and Basil G. Zimmer. *The Metropolitan Community: Its People and Government*. Beverly Hills, Calif.: Sage, 1970.

Higgs, Robert. "Legally Induced Technical Regress in the Washington Salmon Fishery." In *Empirical Studies in Institutional Change*, ed. Lee J. Alston, Thráinn Eggertsson, and Douglass C. North, 247–79. New York: Cambridge University Press, 1996.

Hoxby, Caroline. "Does Competition among Public Schools Benefit Students and Taxpayers?" Working paper # 4979. Cambridge, Mass: National Bureau of Economic Research, 1994.

Jodha, Narpat S. "Depletion of Common Property Resources in India: Micro-level Evidence." In *Rural Development and Population: Institutions and Policy*, ed. G. McNicoll and M. Cain, 261–83. Oxford: Oxford University Press, 1990.

———. "Property Rights and Development." In *Rights to Nature*, ed. Susan S. Hanna, Carl Folke, and Karl-Göran Mäler, 205–22. Washington: Island Press, 1996.

Kollock, Peter. "Social Dilemmas: The Anatomy of Cooperation." *Annual Review of Sociology* 24 (1998): 183–214.

Landau, Martin. "Redundancy, Rationality, and the Problem of Duplication and Overlap." *Public Administration Review* 29 (1969): 346–58.

McCay, Bonnie J., and James M. Acheson. *The Question of the Commons: The Culture and Ecology of Communal Resources*. Tucson: University of Arizona Press, 1987.

McGinnis, Michael, ed. *Polycentricity and Local Public Economies: Readings from the Workshop in Political Theory and Policy Analysis*. Ann Arbor: University of Michigan Press, 1999.

Messick, David M. "Alternative Logics for Decision Making in Social Settings." *Journal of Economic Behavior and Organization* 39 (1999): 11–28.

Ostrom, Elinor. *Governing the Commons: The Evolution of Institutions for Collective Action*. New York: Cambridge University Press, 1990.

———. "A Behavioral Approach to the Rational Choice Theory of Collective Action." *American Political Science Review* 92 (1998): 1–22.

Ostrom, Elinor, Roy Gardner, and James Walker. *Rules, Games, and Common-Pool Resources*. Ann Arbor: University of Michigan Press, 1994.

Ostrom, Vincent. *The Political Theory of a Compound Republic: Designing the American Experiment*. 2d rev. ed. San Francisco: ICS Press, 1987.

———. *The Meaning of Democracy and the Vulnerability of Democracies: A Response to Tocqueville's Challenge*. Ann Arbor: University of Michigan Press, 1997.

Ostrom, Vincent, Robert Bish, and Elinor Ostrom. *Local Government in the United States*. San Francisco: ICS Press, 1988.

Panayotou, Theodore, and Peter S. Ashton. *Not by Timber Alone: Economics and Ecology for Sustaining Tropical Forests*. Washington: Island Press, 1992.

Pinkerton, Evelyn, ed. *Co-operative Management of Local Fisheries: New Directions for Improved Management and Community Development*. Vancouver: University of British Columbia Press, 1989.

Pritchett, Lant, and Deon Filmer. "What Education Production Functions *Really* Show: A Positive Theory of Education Expenditures." *Economics of Education Review* 18 (1999): 223–39.

Rusk, David. *Cities without Suburbs*. Washington: Woodrow Wilson Center Press, 1993.

Scott, James C. *Seeing Like a State: How Certain Schemes to Improve the Human Condition Have Failed.* New Haven, Conn.: Yale University Press, 1998.

Selten, Reinhard. "Bounded Rationality." *Journal of Institutional and Theoretical Economics* 146 (1990): 649–58.

———. "Evolution, Learning, and Economic Behavior." *Games and Economic Behavior* 3 (1991): 3–24.

Shepherd, Gill. *Managing Africa's Tropical Dry Forests: A Review of Indigenous Methods*. London: Overseas Development Institute, 1992.

Simon, Herbert A. *Models of Bounded Rationality: Empirically Grounded Economic Reason*. Cambridge, Mass.: MIT Press, 1997.

Stephens, G. Ross, and Nelson Wikstrom. *Metropolitan Government and Governance: Theoretical Perspectives, Empirical Analysis, and the Future*. Oxford: Oxford University Press, 1999.

Tang, Shui Yan. *Institutions and Collective Action: Self-Governance in Irrigation*. San Francisco: ICS Press, 1992.

Thomson, James T. "Ecological Deterioration: Local-Level Rule-Making and Enforcement Problems in Niger." In *Desertification: Environmental Degradation in and around Arid Lands*, ed. Michael H. Glantz, 57–79. Boulder: Westview Press, 1977.

Thomson, James T., David Feeny, and Ronald J. Oakerson. "Institutional Dynamics: The Evolution and Dissolution of Common-Property Resource Management." In *Making the Commons Work: Theory, Practice, and Policy*, ed. Daniel W. Bromley et al., 129–60. San Francisco: ICS Press, 1992.

Index

Contributors

Elizabeth Baldwin researches energy and environmental policy. Her work focuses on the role that non-state actors play in implementing energy and environmental policies, the way that laws and legal rules structure stakeholder involvement, and the degree to which such stakeholder involvement affects policy outcomes. Baldwin is an assistant professor at the University of Arizona's School of Government and Public Policy. She earned her PhD in 2015 from the School of Public and Environmental Affairs at Indiana University Bloomington. She also holds a JD from the Indiana University Maurer School of Law and a BS in Environmental Policy from Unity College.

Daniel H. Cole is professor of law and professor of public and environmental affairs at Indiana University Bloomington. He is author or editor of eight books, including *Property in Land and Other Resources* (Lincoln Institute, 2012), which he coedited with Elinor Ostrom, and more than fifty articles, book chapters, and essays, most of which cross the boundaries of law, economics, and political science.

Robert Cook-Deegan is professor, School for the Future of Innovation in Society, and Consortium for Science, Policy & Outcomes at Arizona State University. He founded and directed Duke's Center for Genome Ethics, Law & Policy 2002–2012, and Duke-in-Washington through June 2016. Before Duke: National Academies of Science, Engineering and Medicine 1991–2002; National Center for Human Genome Research (NIH) 1989–1990; and congressional Office of Technology Assessment 1982–1988. MD, University of Colorado, 1979; and BA in chemistry (magna cum laude), Harvard, 1975. Author of *The Gene Wars: Science, Politics, and the Human Genome* and more than 250 other publications.

Michael Cox is an environmental social scientist who studies community-based natural resource management as well as path dependence and technological transitions in agricultural systems. He has conducted empirical fieldwork-based analyses of irrigation systems in the southwest United States, Peru, and Kenya. His current empirical work is focused on community-based fisheries and rice farming systems in the Dominican Republic. For the past several years, he has led a synthetic project on social-ecological governance, the details of which can be found at http://sesmad.dartmouth.edu/. Before coming to Dartmouth, he worked under Elinor Ostrom at Indiana University's Ostrom Workshop.

Jampel Dell'Angelo is assistant professor of water governance in the Department of Environmental Policy Analysis at the Institute for Environmental Studies (IVM), Vrije Universiteit Amsterdam. He is an environmental social scientist interested in the political economy of natural resources, in particular, water. His research is on the multilevel dimensions of cooperation and conflict over freshwater resources. The focus of his research spans from socio-environmental dynamics of climate change adaptation in community irrigation schemes of rural Kenya to global patterns of virtual water appropriation. He employs mixed methods and builds on theoretical pluralism, combining perspectives from the Bloomington School of Political Economy and the Barcelona School of Political Ecology.

Graham Epstein is a postdoctoral researcher in the School of Environment, Resources and Sustainability at the University of Waterloo. His work on collective action and the sustainability of social-ecological systems has been published in journals such as *Ecological Economics*, *International Journal of the Commons*, and *Current Opinion in Environmental Sustainability*. He is currently working on several research projects seeking to better understand how policies might be designed to facilitate the management of trade-offs across different actors, activities, and objectives in fisheries.

Tom Evans is professor in the School of Geography and Development at the University of Arizona, professor in the Department of Geography at Indiana University, and senior research fellow with the Vincent and Elinor Ostrom Workshop at Indiana University. His work addresses the intersection of social and environmental systems with an emphasis on household-level decision making in the context of diverse governance arrangements.

Previous work focused on dynamics of deforestation/reforestation while more recently his work has investigated the impact of climate change on smallholder farming systems in Kenya/Zambia and the ability of multi-level governance regimes and farmer adaptive capacity to mitigate effects of drought.

Matthias Finger is known for his expertise in matters of governance of network industries. He holds a PhD in political science and a PhD in adult education from the University of Geneva, and has been an assistant professor at Syracuse University (New York), an associate professor at Columbia University (New York), and a full professor of Management of Public Enterprises at the Swiss Federal Institute of Public Administration. Since 2002, he holds the Swiss Post Chair in Management of Network Industries at Ecole Polytechnique Fédérale in Lausanne, Switzerland. Since 2010, he also directs the Florence School of Regulation's Transport Area at the European University Institute in Florence, Italy. Professor Finger is the editor in chief of the journal *Competition and Regulation in Network Industries* (Sage), an editor of special issues of *Utilities Policy*, and a member of the Swiss electricity regulatory authority (ElCom). He was a member and vice president of the Swiss railways regulatory authority (SKE) between 2004 and 2015.

Ulrich Frey, Dr. rer.nat Dr. phil., studied Philosophy and English at the Universities of Regensburg and Freiburg (Germany). He obtained his PhD in Philosophy from the University of Braunschweig in 2007 and his PhD in Biology in 2016. He is currently a postdoctoral research fellow at the German Aerospace Center in Stuttgart (Germany). He has published books, book contributions, and peer-reviewed articles on social-ecological systems, natural resource management, human cooperation, public goods, altruism, evolutionary psychology, and philosophy of science.

Brett M. Frischmann is the Charles Widger Endowed University Professor in Law, Business and Economics at Villanova University. Professor Frischmann's interdisciplinary work appears in leading publications, including *Columbia Law Review*, *Journal of Institutional Economics*, *Journal of Economic Perspectives*, *University of Chicago Law Review*, and *Review of Law and Economics*, among others. His forthcoming book coauthored with philosopher Evan Selinger, *Re-Engineering Humanity* (Cambridge University Press), will examine techno-social engineering of humans and modern techno-driven Taylorism. Professor Frischmann's books on the relationships between infrastructural resources, governance, commons, and spillovers include *Infrastructure: The Social Value of Shared Resources* (Oxford University Press, 2012); *Governing Knowledge Commons* (Oxford University Press, 2014, with Michael Madison and Katherine Strandburg); and *Governing Medical Knowledge Commons* (Cambridge University Press, 2017, with Michael Madison and Katherine Strandburg).

Charlotte Hess is emerita at Syracuse University where she was associate dean for Research, Collections and Scholarly Communication for the SU Libraries. For twenty years before that, she worked as head of Library and Information Services at the Workshop in Political Theory and Policy Analysis at Indiana University. Hess was the founder and director of the Digital Library of the Commons (1998–2008) and the information officer for the International Association for the Study of the Commons (1996–2009). She has written and lectured extensively on knowledge, cultural, and new commons. She collaborated with Elinor Ostrom on a number of publications and papers, including their 2007 coedited book *Understanding Knowledge as a Commons: From Theory to Practice* (MIT Press). Hess's papers are openly accessible at www.ssrn.com; http://dlc.dlib.indiana.edu/dlc/; and http://surface.syr.edu/.

Rolf Künneke is full Professor Economics of Infrastructures at the Faculty of Technology, Policy and Management (TPM) of Delft University of Technology. He applies an institutional economic perspective toward responsible innovation, institutional design, regulation, and modelling of energy systems. He analyzes the interrelatedness of technical and institutional features of sustainable energy infrastructures. He worked with Elinor Ostrom on the governance of social-ecological and socio-technical systems.

Michael Madison is professor of law and faculty director of the Innovation Practice Institute at the University of Pittsburgh School of Law. He writes and teaches about intellectual property law and policy, and about questions concerning the production and distribution of knowledge and innovation. He is the author of more than 45 journal articles and book chapters, the coauthor of *The Law of Intellectual Property* (Wolters Kluwer, 5th edition 2017), and the coeditor of *Governing Knowledge Commons* (Oxford University Press, 2014) and *Governing Medical Knowledge Commons* (Cambridge University Press, 2017).

Paul McCord is a postdoctoral research associate at Michigan State University working on telecoupling and sustainability questions as well as geospatial modeling. He received his PhD from Indiana University in 2017. While completing his dissertation, he received support from the Ostrom Workshop to study and assess the sustainability of water governance regimes in the Mount Kenya region.

Michael D. McGinnis is associate dean for social & historical sciences and graduate education in the College of Arts and Sciences, and professor of political science, at Indiana University Bloomington. He is a senior research fellow (and former director) of the Vincent and Elinor Ostrom Workshop. He has a PhD in political science from the University of Minnesota and a BS in mathematics from The Ohio State University. He has published articles and book chapters on topics in public policy, institutional analysis, humanitarian aid, arms control, game theory, faith-based organizations, and US health policy.

Elinor Ostrom was founding director and senior research director of the Vincent and Elinor Ostrom Workshop in Political Theory and Policy Analysis, Distinguished Professor and Arthur F. Bentley Professor of political science, and professor in the School of Public and Environmental Affairs at Indiana University Bloomington. She was the cowinner of the 2009 Sveriges Riksbank Prize in Economic Sciences in Memory of Alfred Nobel.

Vincent Ostrom was founding director of the Vincent and Elinor Ostrom Workshop in Political Theory and Policy Analysis and Arthur F. Bentley Professor Emeritus of political science at Indiana University Bloomington.

Walter Reid is director of the Conservation and Science Program at the David and Lucile Packard Foundation. Previously, from 2005 to 2006, he was a professor with the Woods Institute at Stanford University. From 1998 to 2005, Dr. Reid created and then was the director of the Millennium Ecosystem Assessment. From 1992 to 1998, Dr. Reid was vice president of the World Resources Institute in Washington, DC. Dr. Reid earned his PhD in Zoology (Ecology and Evolutionary Biology) from the University of Washington in 1987 and his BA in Zoology from the University of California at Berkeley in 1978.

Katherine J. Strandburg is the Albert B. Engelberg Professor of Law at the New York University School of law. Her research considers the implications of user and collaborative innovation for innovation law and policy and the legal and policy ramifications of "big data." Her work includes the books *Governing Medical Knowledge Commons* (2017) and *Governing Knowledge Commons* (2014) (coedited with Brett Frischmann and Michael Madison), which report and analyze case studies of commons-based innovation, as well as numerous articles and book chapters analyzing whether and how the law should change in light of the importance of user and open innovation. She is a faculty director of NYU's Engelberg Center on Innovation Law and Policy and Information Law Institute.

www.ingramcontent.com/pod-product-compliance
Lightning Source LLC
LaVergne TN
LVHW091334280926
848997LV00053B/10
* 9 7 8 0 7 3 9 1 9 1 1 3 2 *